P9-CPV-430

LANGUAGE ARTS Survival Guide

PRENTICE HALL CANADA INC.

The English language is spoken by people throughout the world. Each group has made a unique contribution to the language. The *Survival Guide* contains rules for using the traditional forms of English spoken and written in Canada. But the test of a language is in how well it works and how well it communicates thoughts and feelings—not whether it follows certain rules. We hope that the *Survival Guide* will help you learn to communicate capably and expressively.

SERIES EDITORS
Margaret Iveson
Samuel Robinson

EDITORIAL CONSULTANT
Alan Simpson

TEACHER CONSULTANTS
Stephen Bailey
Donna Carpenter
Joan Czapalay
Dirk Verhulst

ISBN 0–13–624354–1

A Ligature Book

Canadian Cataloguing in Publication Data
Main entry under title:

Language arts survival guide

(MultiSource)
Includes index.
ISBN 0–13–624354–1

1. Language arts (Secondary). 2. English language–Study and teaching (Secondary). I. Iveson, Margaret L., 1948– . II. Robinson, Sam, 1937– . III. Series.

LB1576.L36 1993 428 C93–094060–1

2 3 4 5 BP 97 96 95 94
Printed and bound in Canada.

The Language Arts Survival Guide *is part of the MultiSource program, which includes student magazines, literature anthologies, non-print media components, and unit guides. For further information about MultiSource, write to Prentice Hall Canada Inc., 1870 Birchmount Road, Scarborough, Ontario, M1P 2J7, or call 1–800–567–3800.*

MultiSource
TM

I know I could get higher marks if I could edit and proofread my work better.

Have you ever had moments like these?

My report has to have visuals, but I'm no good at drawing.

if so,

the Language Arts Survival Guide is the book for you.

I can't think of anything to write about.

I always get stage fright when I have to give a speech.

Find What You Need

When you need help with communication, turn to this *Survival Guide*. It's filled with suggestions for creating ideas and expressing them clearly in written, spoken, or visual form.

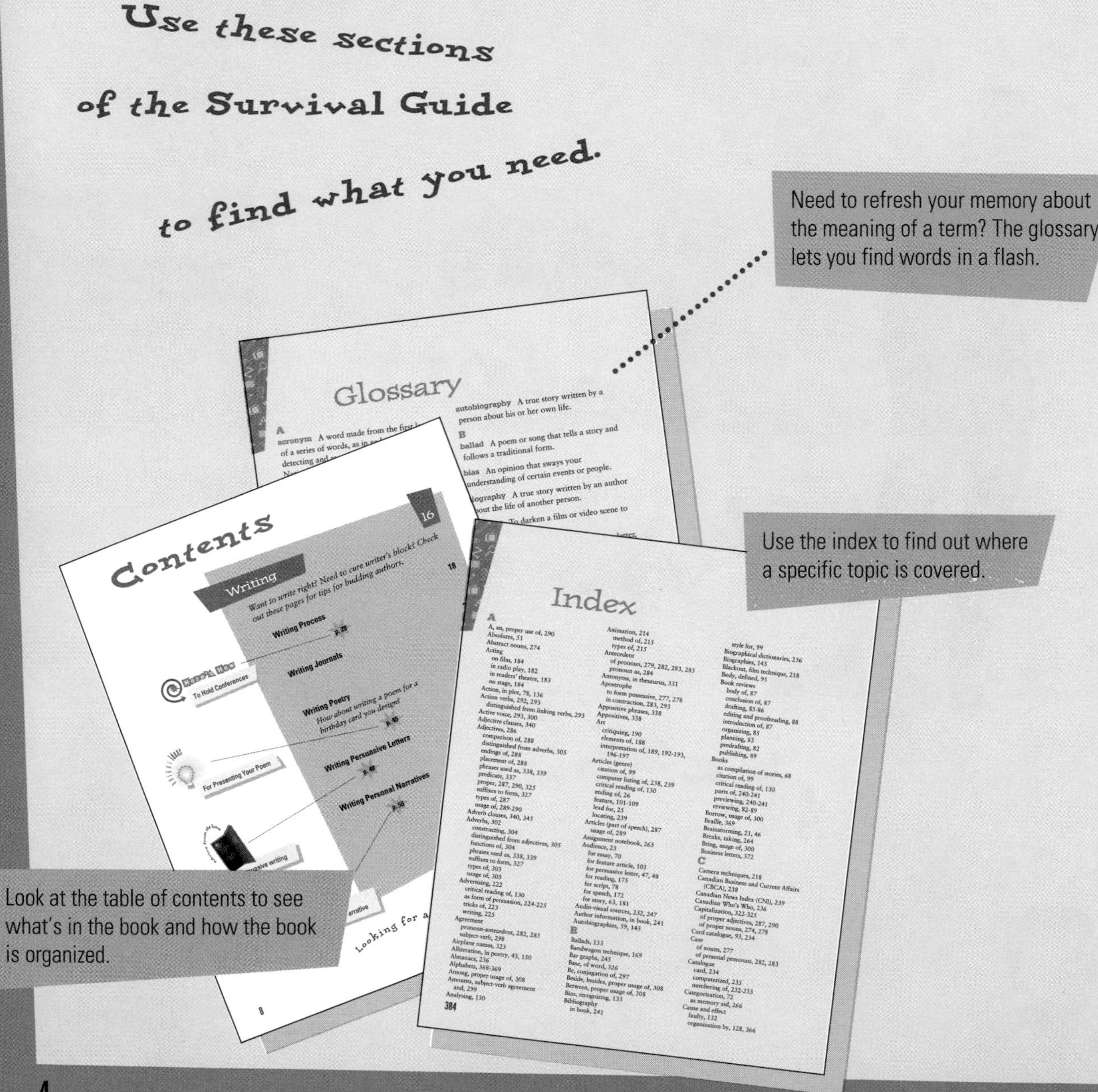

Use these sections of the Survival Guide to find what you need.

Need to refresh your memory about the meaning of a term? The glossary lets you find words in a flash.

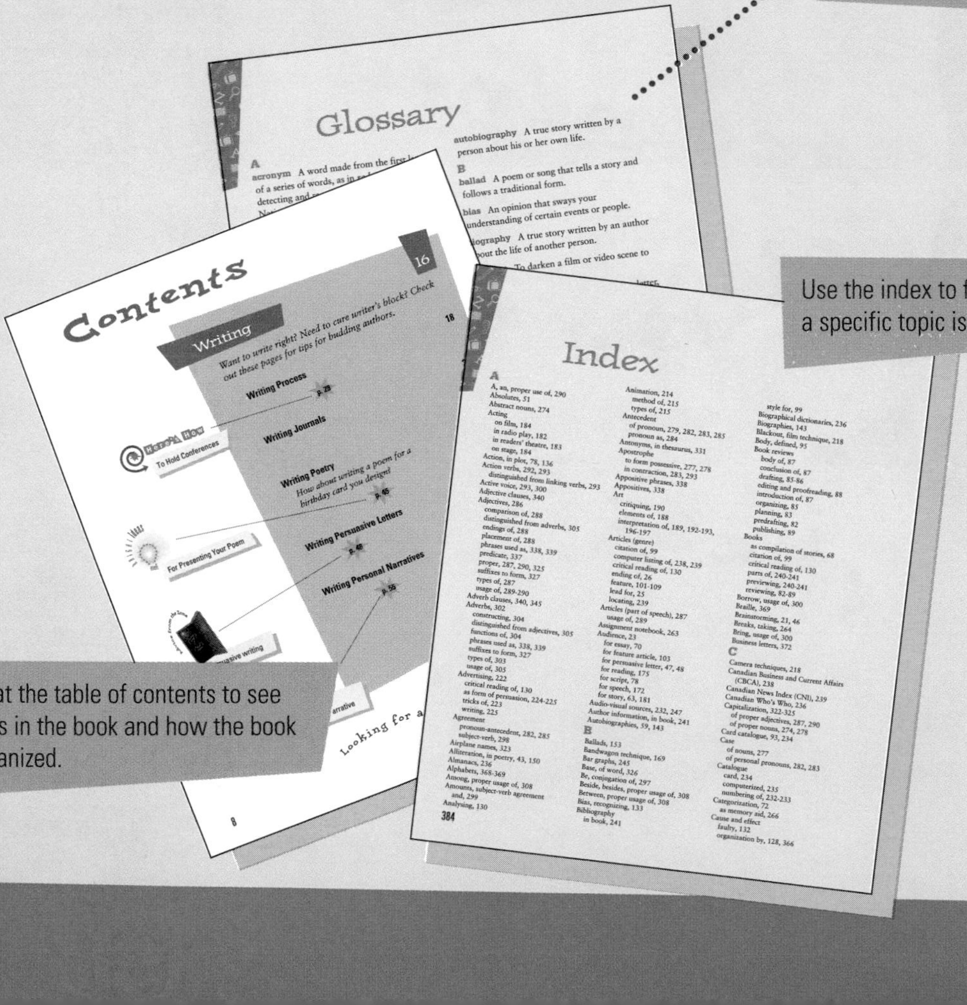
Glossary
Contents
Writing
Writing Process
Writing Journals
Writing Poetry
Writing Persuasive Letters
Writing Personal Narratives
Index

Use the index to find out where a specific topic is covered.

Look at the table of contents to see what's in the book and how the book is organized.

Short Stories

These colour-coded tabs show what section you're reading.

Cross-references help you find related information right away.

Has speech writing got you stumped? See the chart on the next page. Also, review persuasive writing. **See page 46.**

PREDRAFT

DRAFT

REVISE

EDIT AND PROOFREAD

PUBLISH

Notice how colours and symbols make the book easy to read.

In the chapter on writing, these five stamps show which writing stage is being described.

RELATED WRITING

This symbol identifies more writing ideas.

How to Use this *Survival Guide* . . .

1500 Tips for Communicating Successfully

You'll find helpful information on reading, writing, listening, speaking, viewing, and creating—plus an easy-to-use handbook on grammar, punctuation, and spelling. Also, a variety of special features gives you extra help and information.

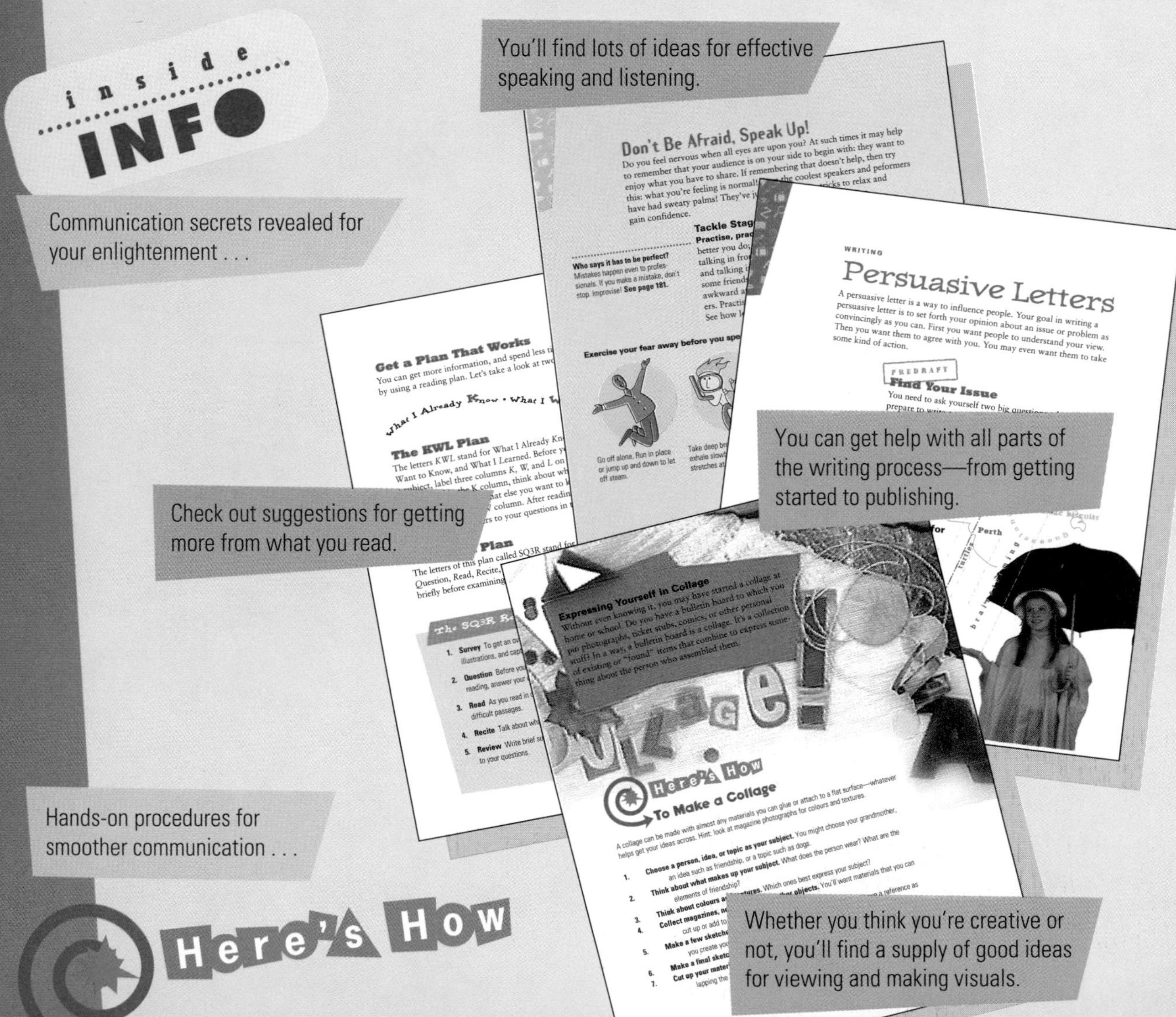

inside INFO
Communication secrets revealed for your enlightenment . . .
You'll find lots of ideas for effective speaking and listening.
Don't Be Afraid, Speak Up!
Persuasive Letters
Get a Plan That Works
You can get help with all parts of the writing process—from getting started to publishing.
Check out suggestions for getting more from what you read.
Expressing Yourself in Collage
Here's How To Make a Collage
Hands-on procedures for smoother communication . . .
Here's How
Whether you think you're creative or not, you'll find a supply of good ideas for viewing and making visuals.

TRy it!

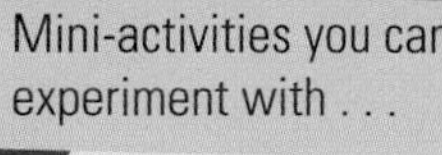

Mini-activities you can experiment with . . .

Make your studying easier and more successful by finding out which methods work best for you.

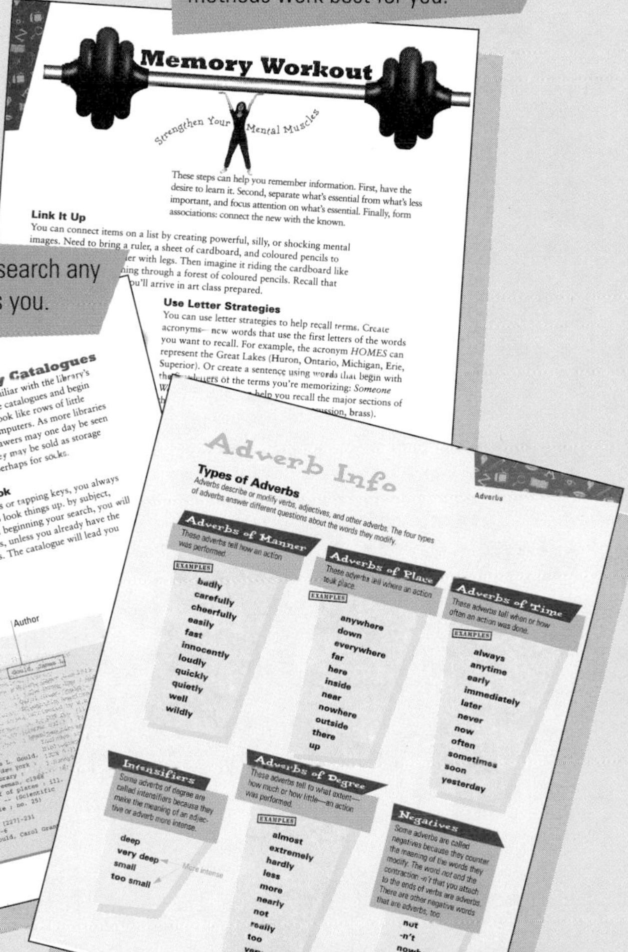

Memory Workout

Strengthen Your Mental Muscles

These steps can help you remember information. First, have the desire to learn it. Second, separate what's essential from what's less important, and focus attention on what's essential. Finally, form associations: connect the new with the known.

Link It Up

You can connect items on a list by creating powerful, silly, or shocking mental images. Need to bring a ruler, a sheet of cardboard, and coloured pencils to ... with legs. Then imagine it riding the cardboard like ... through a forest of coloured pencils. Recall that ... you'll arrive in art class prepared.

Use Letter Strategies

You can use letter strategies to help recall terms. Create acronyms—new words that use the first letters of the words you want to recall. For example, the acronym *HOMES* can represent the Great Lakes (Huron, Ontario, Michigan, Erie, Superior). Or create a sentence using words that begin with the ... of the terms you're memorizing: *Someone* ... help you recall the major sections of ... (... percussion, brass).

Adverb Info

Types of Adverbs

Adverbs describe or modify verbs, adjectives, and other adverbs. The four types of adverbs answer different questions about the words they modify.

Adverbs of Manner

These adverbs tell how an action was performed.

EXAMPLES: badly, carefully, cheerfully, easily, fast, innocently, loudly, quickly, quietly, well, wildly

Adverbs of Place

These adverbs tell where an action took place.

EXAMPLES: anywhere, down, everywhere, far, here, inside, near, nowhere, outside, there, up

Adverbs of Time

These adverbs tell when or how often an action was done.

EXAMPLES: always, anytime, early, immediately, later, never, now, often, sometimes, soon, yesterday

Intensifiers

Some adverbs of degree are called intensifiers because they make the meaning of an adjective or adverb more intense.

deep, very deep — more intense; small, too small

Adverbs of Degree

These adverbs tell to what extent—how much or how little—an action was performed.

EXAMPLES: almost, extremely, hardly, less, more, nearly, not, really, too, very

Negatives

Some adverbs are called negatives because they counter the meaning of the words they modify. The word *not* and the contraction *-n't* that you attach to the ends of verbs are adverbs. There are other negative words that are adverbs, too.

not, -n't, nowhere

Find out how to research any topic that interests you.

Search with Library Catalogues

Now that you've made yourself familiar with the library's offerings, it's time to slide up to the catalogues and begin your search. The catalogues will look like rows of little drawers, or they will look like computers. As more libraries computerize their listings, the drawers may one day be seen only in antique stores, where they may be sold as storage containers for floppy disks or perhaps for socks.

Three Paths to Your Book

Whether you're flipping cards or tapping keys, you always have three choices of how to look things up: by subject, by author, or by title. When beginning your search, you will probably start with subjects, unless you already have the names of authors or books. The catalogue will lead you to books.

The Card Catalogue — Title, Author, Subject

234

Get quick answers on grammar, word use, spelling, and much, much more.

BRIGHT Ideas

Menus of choices bring variety to your work. . . .

Problem-solving strategies to overcome difficulties . . .

Advice from the Zone
Z

Contents

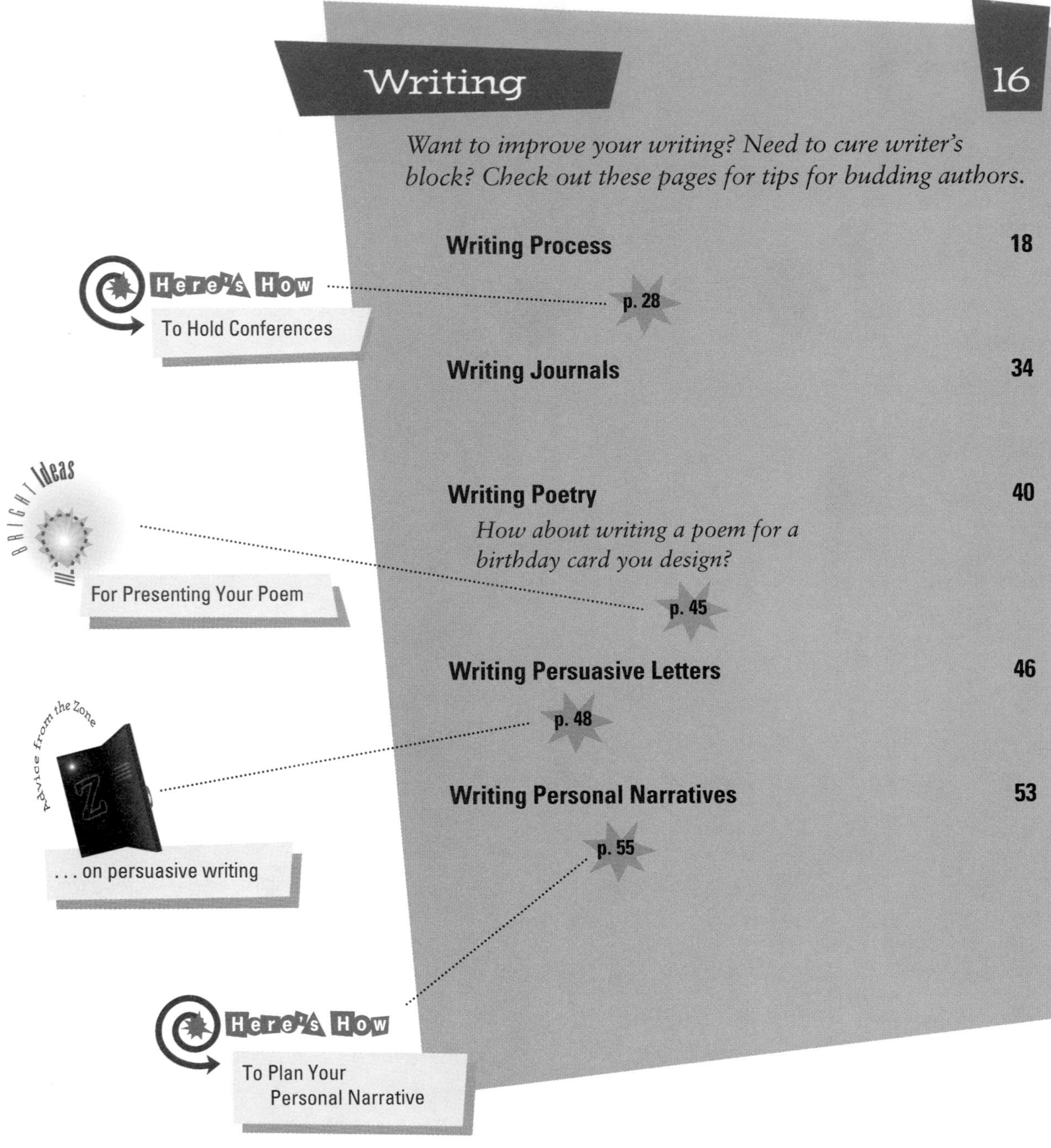

Looking for advice on communication?

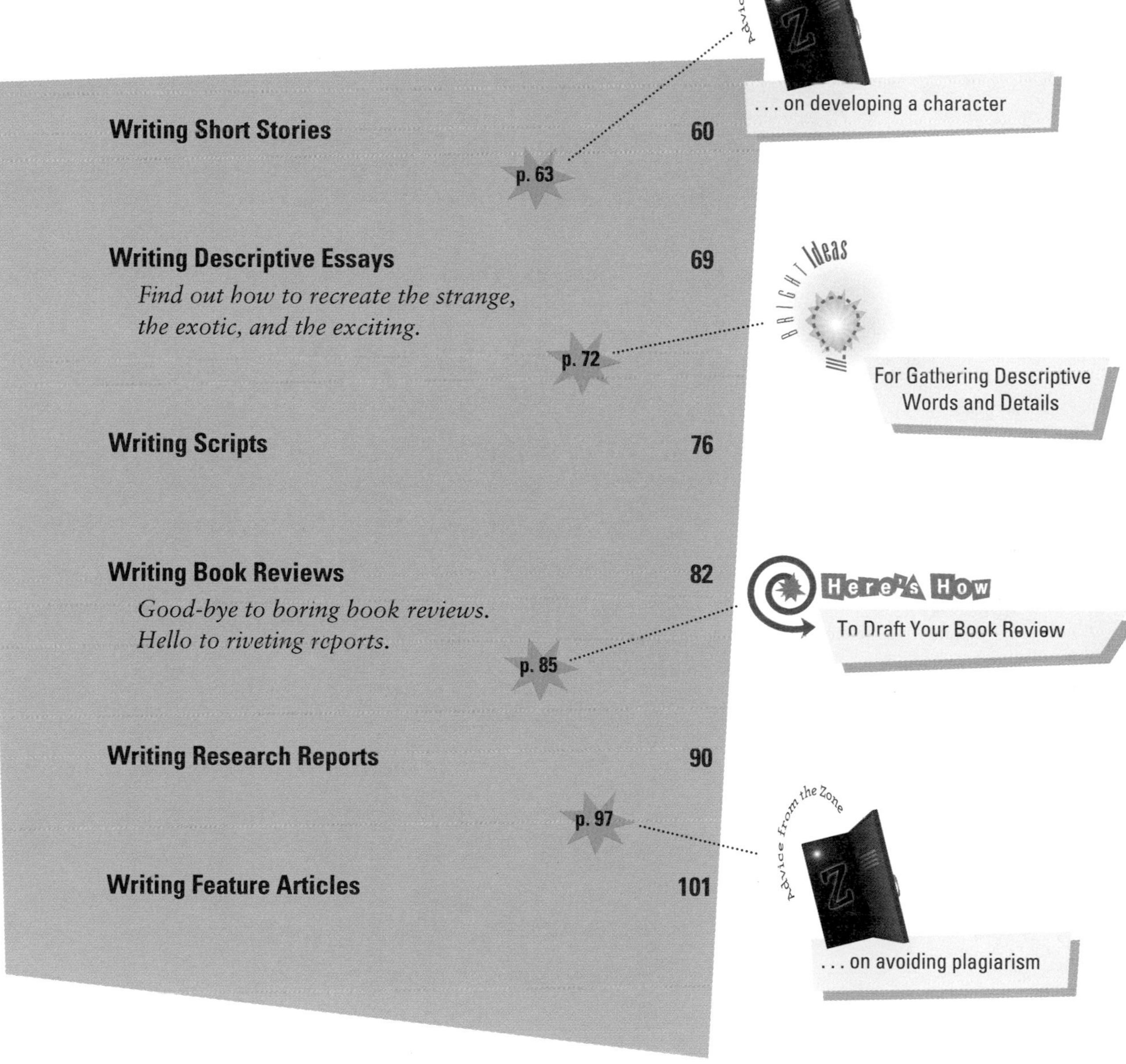
Advice from the Zone
. . . on developing a character
Bright Ideas
For Gathering Descriptive Words and Details
Here's How
To Draft Your Book Review
Advice from the Zone
. . . on avoiding plagiarism

Write to the mysterious being in the Zone!

Reading 110

Skim or scrutinize—either way you can read countless magazines, books, and other sources. Browse through this section for tips on effective reading.

Here's How

Here's How

Need step-by-step advice?

How about a Here's How?

Interested in sampling some useful suggestions?

Turn on some Bright Ideas.

rite
write
?
right
writ

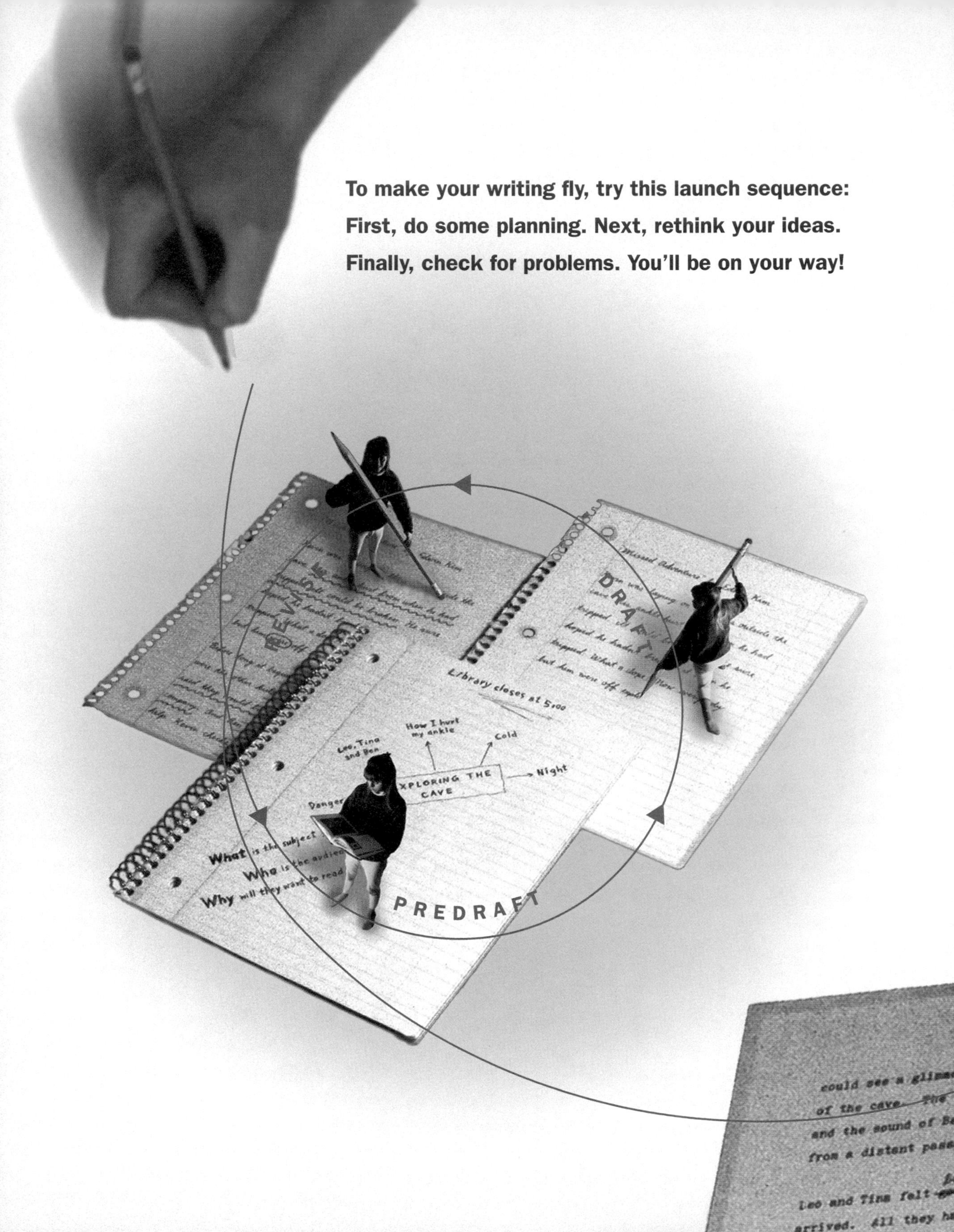

To make your writing fly, try this launch sequence:
First, do some planning. Next, rethink your ideas.
Finally, check for problems. You'll be on your way!
PREDRAFT
DRAFT
Library closes at 5:00
How I hurt my ankle
Cold
Night
Leo, Tina and Ben
XPLORING THE CAVE
Danger
What is the subject
Why will they want to read

Writing

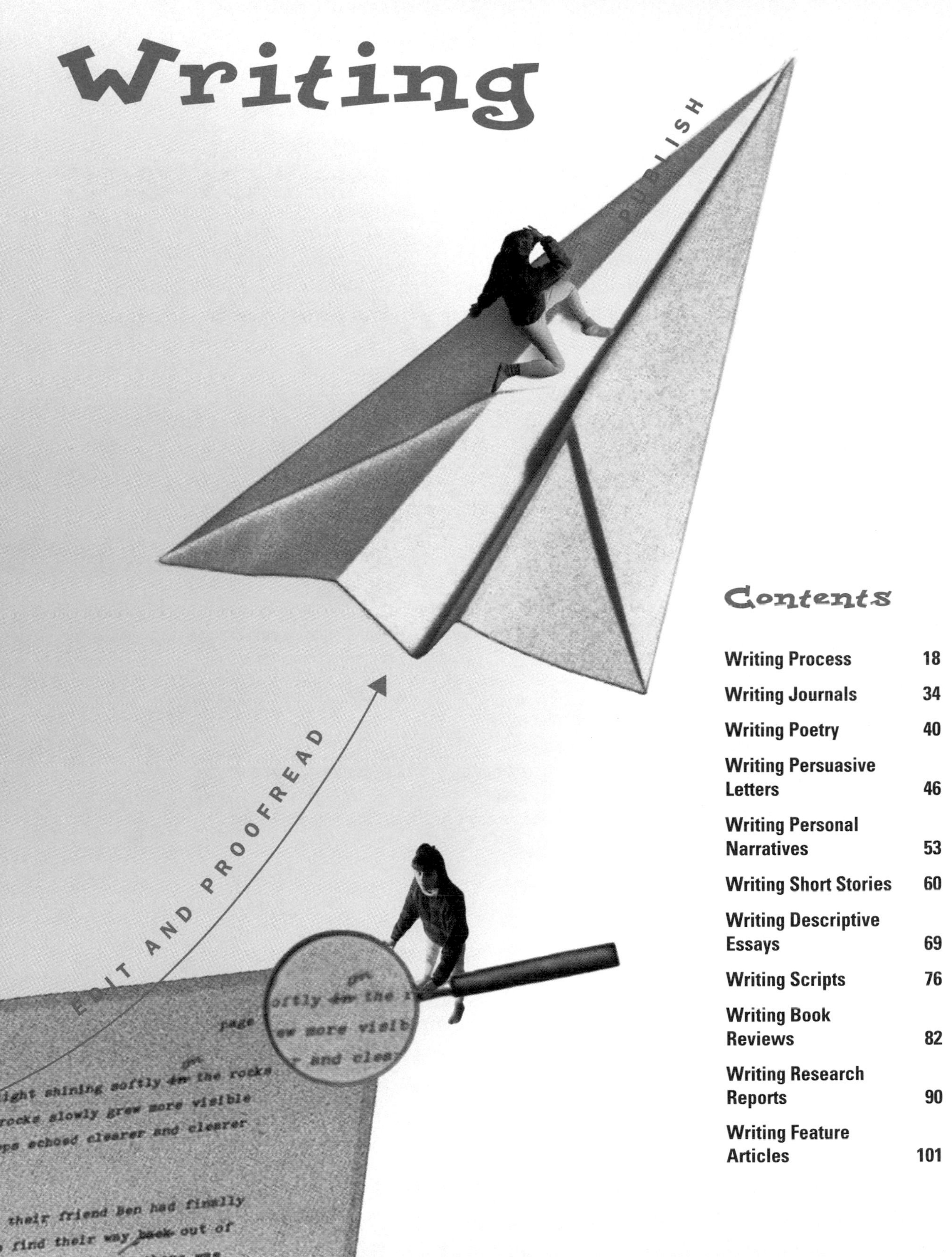
PUBLISH
EDIT AND PROOFREAD

Contents

WRITING

The Writing Process

When you face a blank paper or an empty computer screen, do you wonder how you will ever fill it with a finished work? Don't let writing frighten you! It is a process of discovery that is different for everyone. Most writers work through a series of stages. You can learn to get the most out of each stage—and to put them together in the way that works for you.

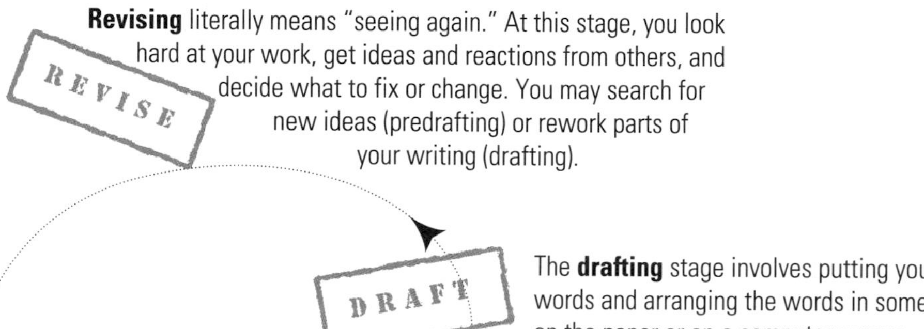
REVISE
DRAFT

Revising literally means "seeing again." At this stage, you look hard at your work, get ideas and reactions from others, and decide what to fix or change. You may search for new ideas (predrafting) or rework parts of your writing (drafting).

The **drafting** stage involves putting your thoughts into words and arranging the words in some reasonable order on the paper or on a computer screen.

PREDRAFT

The **predrafting** stage includes everything that goes on in your head and on paper as you try to pin down a good writing idea, explore it, and create a plan for writing.

EDIT AND PROOFREAD

At the **editing and proofreading** stage, you polish your style and correct errors in grammar, usage, mechanics, and spelling. You complete these steps after you have a revised draft that suits you.

PUBLISH

Publishing includes any way you share or present your writing. You might submit a piece for publication in a magazine, present it orally, or give it to a friend to read.

Get Organized

You might get an idea for a story from a news report or a song lyric. You might find a great word in a book you are reading that you want to use later in your writing. Or you might start a poem and decide that it would make a better story. The best writing often comes from those kinds of discoveries. But how can you keep track of them? Many writers use writing folders and journals. **To learn more about journals, see page 34.** Journals are great for jotting down ideas and for exploring them through writing and drawing.

Keep a Writing Folder

Writing folders let you keep your writing in one place to see your progress as a writer and to store ideas for easy reference. You can use computer files or a loose-leaf notebook with dividers. This chart shows you one way to set up a writing folder.

inside INFO

"Reading, though, is the way to learn to write. Someone interested in writing should just read . . . Writers can show you directions."
—Carol Shields

Here's How To Set Up a Writing Folder

1. **Create a section for writing ideas and writer's helps.** Save anything that may spark ideas for writing: cartoons, quotations, maps, ads, photographs, postcards. Writer's helps might include a revising checklist, proofreader's marks, transition words, interesting words, hard words, and your most frequent errors. **See pages 28 and 373.**
2. **Create a section for works in progress.** You may want to set up separate sections for short stories, essays, poems, and other genres or forms. Include works that could be polished or perhaps adapted to another form.
3. **Create a section for published works.** You may want to set up separate sections for the different forms of writing. Save pieces that you might use as a model for writing in a particular genre and pieces that you might want to discuss with a friend or teacher. Date each work.

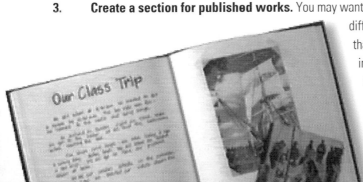

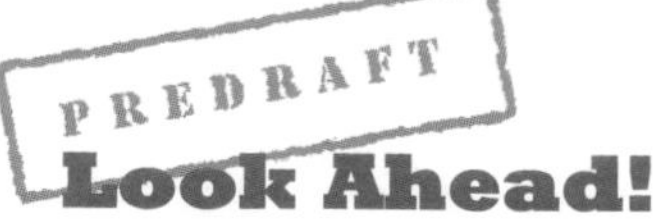
PREDRAFT

Look Ahead!

Much of the writing process occurs before you start putting words together. This thinking and planning process is predrafting. It may involve any or all of the following activities, in any order:

- finding ideas
- planning and organizing what you want to say
- choosing the best idea
- gathering facts, making observations
- exploring an idea and narrowing it down
- deciding on form (short story? poem? letter?), purpose, audience, and tone

inside INFO

"There is an outline or a plan in my head. . . . I have to have a plan because there has to be something that can be changed. You can't start out with nothing, and have nothing changed into something."
—Madeleine L'Engle

No two writing projects are the same. Sometimes you may start narrowing a subject you've chosen and then decide to scrap it and choose another. At other times you will find a topic easily and then struggle over many revisions. There will also be times when you find a good topic immediately and write a piece that requires almost no changes.

PREDRAFT

Search for Ideas

Ideas for writing are all around you—in this room, out the window, in your family, on the news. When you're stuck for an idea, try to think of one in each of those categories. If you keep a writing folder, journals, or learning logs, look them over, too. Drawing and doodling can also trigger ideas. The following page shows you some other ways to find ideas.

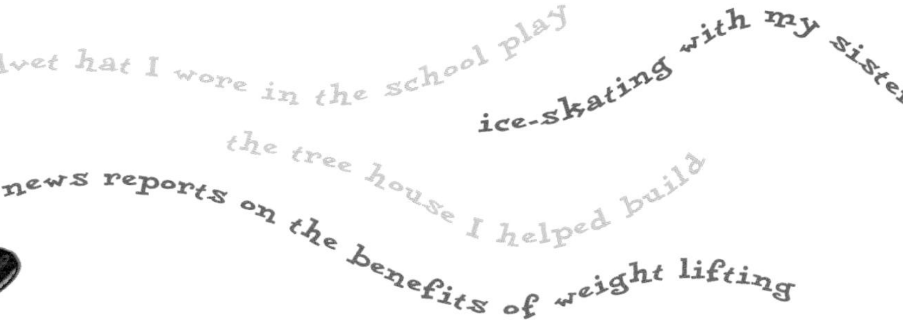
the velvet hat I wore in the school play
ice-skating with my sister
the tree house I helped build
news reports on the benefits of weight lifting

Freewrite

When you freewrite, the goal is to produce ideas, not to polish them. Write fast and freely with a pencil or at a computer. Don't worry about complete sentences or stop to evaluate your ideas. Let one idea lead you to the next.

Try it!

Freewriting at the computer can be even more productive if you write without seeing the words. Darken the screen while you write. Then turn up the brightness, and read what you've written. You may be surprised by your own creativity.

Brainstorm

You can brainstorm by yourself or with several others. When you brainstorm, choose a topic and list every related idea that occurs to you—even those that seem a little wild. A word or phrase will do for each idea.

provincial parks
family trips
fantasy of being alone
running into wild animals
camping out
my life as a bear
beautiful cranes

Make a Cluster or Web

Whether you call it a cluster or a web, you can use it to discover ideas, develop details, or narrow a topic. Start by writing an idea—a word or phrase—and drawing a circle around it. Surround this idea with related ideas and draw a line connecting each new idea to the original one. Then branch out to ideas suggested by the new ones. Keep going!

quiet
solitude
wilderness
Provincial Parks
migrating birds
wildlife
bears
endangered species
snowy owls
activities
hiking
backpacking
canoeing

inside INFO

"I launch a book usually through an emotion. . . . something happens to me and I become emotionally involved, and then I create a character and put the character into a situation that's current, and on my mind. I have themes—things that I'm interested in—and they're almost a thread through my writing."

—Robert Cormier

PREDRAFT

Choose Your Subject

A good subject for writing is something you really want to express or explore. Test your best ideas by asking questions such as these:

Which idea

. . . excites my imagination?

. . . touches my feelings or involves important concerns?

. . . makes me curious?

. . . is something I know a great deal about?

PREDRAFT

Go Exploring

Once you've chosen an idea, take time to think about it. Talk with other people about it. Read about your idea, or draw pictures of it. Brainstorm, freewrite, make clusters. Begin to zero in on details.

Try Looping

Another strategy for exploring an idea is looping. It can help you find a new way to look at your idea. Follow these steps:

1. On an index card, freewrite several sentences about your idea. Circle the most interesting phrase.
2. On another index card, freewrite from the circled phrase. Circle the most interesting phrase, and freewrite again.
3. Repeat this process as many times as you want.
4. Then spread out your cards and reread all your sentences. Linking the circles may give you a new angle.

Freewrite about your idea...

Provincial parks are special places. Many people love to visit them.

People go to parks to camp out and hike, to see the wildlife, and to enjoy the peace and quiet of the wilderness.

Unfortunately, too many people go, and noise and crowds are a problem.

New angle: We could lose the peace and the quiet that make provincial parks such special places.

Narrow Your Subject

You can't write effectively about a huge idea. Run a big topic such as space exploration or endangered species through an imaginary funnel. Choose the aspect, the one species, the one personality you most want to write about.

Fill In Missing Information

Do you know enough about your topic from freewriting, brainstorming, and clustering? Sometimes you might need to explore it further or do some research. You can collect information you need from interviews, books, magazines, and related videos. **To learn about taking notes, see page 252.**

PREDRAFT

Make Plans

Once you have an idea that inspires you, you need to make some plans. Before you sit down to write about your idea, you face key decisions about form, purpose, audience, and tone. These decisions will help you chart a course through the rest of your writing process.

Thinking about writing a narrative or a poem? Learn about different types of narratives and poems on **pages 40 and 53.**

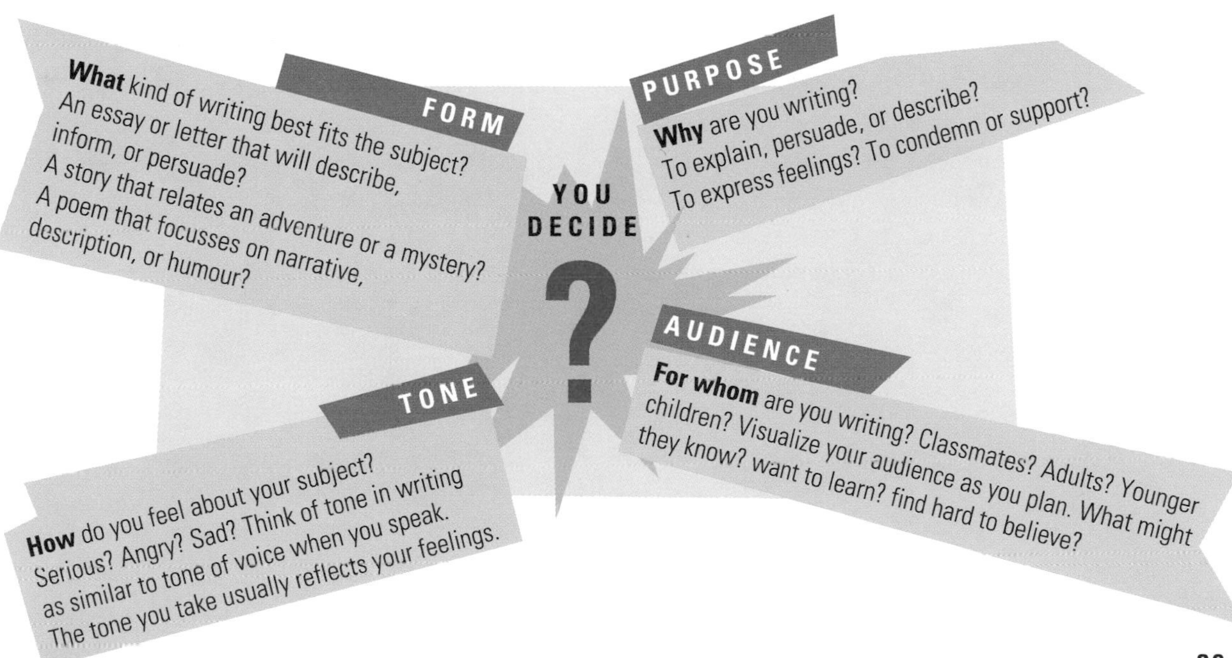
FORM
What kind of writing best fits the subject?
An essay or letter that will describe, inform, or persuade?
A story that relates an adventure or a mystery?
A poem that focusses on narrative, description, or humour?
PURPOSE
Why are you writing?
To explain, persuade, or describe?
To express feelings? To condemn or support?
YOU DECIDE
?
TONE
How do you feel about your subject?
Serious? Angry? Sad? Think of tone in writing as similar to tone of voice when you speak.
The tone you take usually reflects your feelings.
AUDIENCE
For whom are you writing? Classmates? Adults? Younger children? Visualize your audience as you plan. What might they know? want to learn? find hard to believe?

Organize Your Ideas

Gather all your clusters, drawings, lists, and any notes you've made on index cards. Keep them close at hand and look at them often. Before you write, you need to select your main points and the details that support each idea. You also need to try different arrangements of both ideas and details.

inside INFO

"If I want to capture a scene or an emotion or a character, I go like the wind and don't worry too much about how well it's written. If I have a problem with something, I leave it and go on, and fill the gap later."

—Robert Cormier

DRAFT

Let Your Words Flow

Now you're ready to write your first draft. As you put words together on paper, follow your plan, but don't be afraid to change course if you find a better idea along the way. Write quickly and get caught up in the excitement of discovery. Since you'll want to make changes later, use the guidelines on the next page to create a draft that is easy to revise.

BRIGHT Ideas

FOR PLANNING YOUR WRITING

Here are two ways to plan. You may be able to develop another way to plan, one that works for you.

Informal Plan Put your ideas on index cards and rearrange them until you have a workable order. Or try looping to make your plan. Informal planning works well for poems, short stories, and other creative writing. **For tips on looping, see page 22.**

Formal Plan Write main ideas and supporting details on separate index cards. Organize the cards and then use them to create an outline showing each main idea with the details that support it. Formal planning usually works best for research reports and persuasive letters or essays. **For more on outlining, see page 255.**

Here's How To Set Up a Draft

On Paper

Write on every other line.
Leave wide margins.
Write on one side of the paper only.
Keep writing! You can check spelling, grammar, usage, and mechanics later.

On a Computer Screen

Double-space for easy reading.
Don't worry too much about order. Word blocks are easy to move.
Keep typing! You can check for mistakes later.

Start with a Strong Lead

If your lead—the first sentence or sentences—grabs your readers, they'll likely want to read on. One good strategy for finding a lead is to freewrite as many possible leads as you can and then pick the best one. Another option is to write your lead last when you know what you're leading up to.

You might start with a dramatic moment, a description of a scene, a surprising statement, or some lively dialogue. This chart shows a variety of leads for different forms of writing.

Leads

Article or essay, serious tone
Provincial parks face a growing danger—if we are not careful, we may love them to death.

Personal narrative, informal tone
My parents and I had spent an entire month packing for the canoe trip, and we still weren't ready.

Short story, suspenseful tone
"Leave that bear cub alone! There's a mother bear around here somewhere!"

Poem, lyric tone
Cranes rise from misty marshes.

TRy
it!

Try "chunking"—writing whole thoughts or actions in chunks, or paragraphs. Don't worry too much about the order of your chunks. You can rearrange them later, when you revise.

Show—Don't Tell

If someone tells you that his upstairs neighbour is noisy, it doesn't mean much. You need to see and feel how noisy "noisy" is. In the same way, the best writing allows a reader to see or experience a subject through the use of vivid words and specific details.

Telling:

My upstairs neighbour is noisy.

✔ Showing:

The thumping bass of my neighbour's stereo made the windows rattle and the vases dance across my coffee table.

Overcome Writer's Block

Has this happened to you? You're staring at the sheet of paper and can't think of anything to write. Every writer complains about "writer's block" once in a while. You might try this strategy to get yourself going again: Just start writing—even if it's nonsense. Or pretend you've finished your draft and are writing your ending. Use the ending like a destination on a map to remind you of where you're going.

Finish with a Good Ending

Your conclusion can be as important as your lead. It's the last thing your readers see and may be what they remember best. A good ending can summarize what you've been saying, add a final bit of information, or even pack a surprise. Here are examples of endings for different kinds of writing.

Endings

Article or essay
Too many people and too much noise can make the forest feel like a busy city street.

Personal narrative, informal tone
As we dragged the canoe back on shore, I knew I'd never been more tired—or dirtier!

Short story, suspenseful tone
"We'll tell you all about our adventure," said Ed. "Just bear with us!"

Poem, lyric tone
Hoarse bird-voices crying free.

Catch Your Reader's Interest

Like the aroma of a delicious meal, a good title gives the reader a hint of what the piece is about, arouses curiosity and interest, but doesn't tell all. Some writers think of a good title first. Others wait until they've finished a piece. Here are some possible titles for different types of writing.

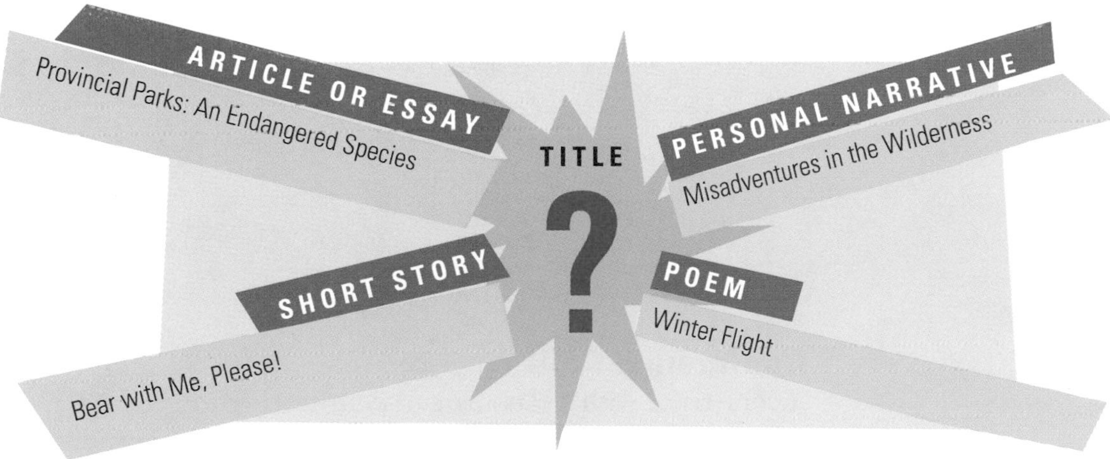
ARTICLE OR ESSAY
Provincial Parks: An Endangered Species
TITLE
?
PERSONAL NARRATIVE
Misadventures in the Wilderness
SHORT STORY
Bear with Me, Please!
POEM
Winter Flight

REVISE

Take Another Look

As you reread and revise any draft of your writing, remember that you can always return to the predrafting and drafting stages! You might make minor adjustments in content, or you might want to create an entirely new draft.

Big Changes

Changing a main idea
Changing the form or tone
Changing the purpose or audience
Major reordering or **adding** of information

Small Changes

Substituting words
Rewriting lead or ending
Adding or **deleting** information
Reordering details or paragraphs

The new work that results from these changes will be a second draft or perhaps a new piece of writing. Keep your drafts in your writing folder. **To find out how you can learn from drafts, see page 31.**

inside INFO

Don't despair! Professional writers often find they need a third draft or even further stages of revision before they're happy with their work. The results are worth the effort.

inside INFO

Put a little space between you and your draft. If you can, tuck it away for a few days and work on something else. When you look at your draft again, imagine that you are seeing it for the first time.

Use a Revising Checklist

A handy tool to keep in your writing folder is a revising checklist like the one below. Include questions aimed at your own specific writing problems.

Revising Checklist

1. Are my purpose and main idea clear?
2. Do my language and content suit the audience?
3. Have I kept the same tone throughout?
4. Are the title and lead interesting? Is the ending strong?
5. Is every idea supported with details?
6. Are the ideas in a logical order?
7. Does each sentence fit?
8. Is there any unnecessary repetition?

Conference Call!

A conference with a classmate or your teacher can be a great help when you're revising because you get to see your writing through another person's eyes. In peer conferences, you get to look at another student's writing process as you discuss that person's draft. In teacher conferences, you benefit from your teacher's knowledge and writing experience.

Here's How

To Hold Conferences

Peer or Teacher Conferences

When your draft is discussed:

1. Bring any questions you want to ask.
2. Don't be defensive.
3. Listen carefully. Take notes.
4. Ask questions if you don't understand a comment.
5. Show your appreciation for help.

Peer Conferences

When you discuss a classmate's draft:

1. Listen carefully as your classmate reads his or her draft.
2. Start by pointing out what you like.
3. Make your comments as specific as possible.
4. Make criticism constructive: "How do you think you might . . . ?"
5. Never tell the writer what to do.

REVISE

Make Improvements

Now it's time to look over your notes from conferencing and from using your revising checklist. You may find some contradictions. Remember, only you can decide which changes will improve your writing. This chart shows you three kinds of revisions and how to make them on paper.

Have you left anything out? If you think you missed important ideas or have made some new discoveries about your subject, do more research. **See page 228.** If you need to add more details, try clustering or brainstorming. **See page 21.**

Add

- **descriptive details**
- **information, examples**
- **dialogue**

Use a caret (^) to add short inserts. Write longer sentences in the margins. Draw arrows or use numbers or letters to show where the inserts go. Cut and paste to add paragraphs.

Subtract

- **unnecessary repetition**
- **parts that don't belong or are incorrect**

Cross out or use a delete symbol. If appropriate, replace.

Rearrange

- **ideas and details**

Use arrows and circles to move sections, or use numbers or letters to indicate the new order.

Check Out a Revision

Here is the beginning of one student's first draft. She has noted areas she will change or rework. On the next page, you can see her revised draft.

BEGINNING OF FIRST DRAFT

I thought I knew all about rowing because I had taken a boat out on our pond many times. Last summer I went rowing in salt water and discovered what I didn't know.

We ~~My cousin Lisa and I~~ had forgotten lunch. My cousin Lisa and ~~We~~ were fishing on a small island. I volunteered to row back to shore.

My lead is boring. Start with dialogue?

Fix the order this way? Or redo?

BEGINNING OF SECOND DRAFT

"Of course, I'm an experienced rower!" I bragged. "I'll row back to shore, get our lunch, and be back on this island in no time. Keep on fishing!" I wasn't really lying to my cousin Lisa. I'd just never rowed in salt water before.

Everything went fine for about five metres. Suddenly I wasn't getting anywhere. I began rowing harder. Then I realized that I was drifting out to sea. I began to panic.

The student has totally rewritten the beginning, making it much more lively. She uses dialogue to set up the situation, then moves quickly to the action.

EDIT AND PROOFREAD

Fine-Tune Your Writing

When you wrote and revised your draft, you paid most attention to content. Now is the time to focus on making your writing smoother. Let it communicate your ideas as successfully as possible. You can correct any errors in grammar, usage, mechanics, and spelling.

Need some tips on accuracy, completeness, and style? Learn how to identify problems at the word, sentence, and paragraph levels—and how to fix them. **See Handbook, page 270.**

Be Systematic

Since you must focus on so many aspects of your writing when you edit and proofread, it helps to work with a peer editor. It also helps to have a system. Try following this plan.

First Check Identify places for improvement.

Careful Check Decide how to make each improvement, and carry it out.

Last Check Proofread all your changes.

Look for Rough Spots

Read your revised draft silently and then aloud. If you stumble over places in your writing, there's probably a reason. Look for weak nouns and verbs, sentences that are too long or too short, paragraphs that are scrawny or overblown. Check for clarity of organization and for good transitions.

Look for Errors

When you check for errors, you'll find it easier to look for only one kind of error at a time. Try following this plan.

Here's How

To Look for Errors

1. Read through your writing carefully, checking for problems in grammar and in usage.
2. Check your capitalization and punctuation.
3. Look for spelling errors.

Here is how the student ended the story you've been reading. She has marked errors and corrected them.

Need to mark your draft? See page 373 for proofreader's marks.

EDITED ENDING

"The curent has you! yelled Lisa, who hadnt taken her eyes off me. She ~~tells~~ told me exacly what to do.

My sisters were watching from the shore, and I could feel my face turning red. That day I learned about the danger of being too confident, and I discoverd the power of the sea.

Make Your Own Watch List

Make a "watch list" of your most frequent errors. Then, the next time you write, you'll know what errors to watch out for. Your watch list should include (1) your most frequent grammar and usage errors, (2) capitalization and punctuation errors you tend to make, and (3) the words you most often misspell. Keep the list in your writing folder.

PUBLISH

Go Public!

You're finally satisfied with your writing. Now that you've invested so much time, effort, and creativity, your work deserves some form of presentation. Here are some publishing ideas you might try.

- Make an audiotape of your work to send to a local radio station.
- Record your work on videotape, and show the film to friends or family.
- Perform your work as a play.
- Submit your finished work to a contest, magazine, or newspaper.
- Illustrate your work with drawings or photos and then display it.
- Read your work aloud to friends, family, or another class.

inside
INFO

You learn how to write by writing, by thinking of yourself as a writer, by studying your past work, and by reading as a writer—to discover how other writers write.

PUBLISH

Save Your Writing

Your previous work can be your best teacher, but only if you save it. Make an extra copy or printout of each finished work and put it in your writing folder along with your drafts.

Here's How

To Reflect on Your Writing

1. **Ask yourself questions such as these to help you think about the work you just completed and published:**

   What do I like best about this piece?

   What could be improved?

   Which stage of writing went most smoothly?

   Which ideas might I develop into new writing?

2. **Ask yourself questions such as these to help you think about what you learned from writing this piece:**

   Did I find a new way to generate ideas?

   Did I make a new discovery about myself or an experience?

   Did writing this piece help me to better understand a type of literature?

   Did I experiment with a new form of writing?

NOW...

The world of writing is open to you. In the pages ahead, you will find many useful tips and strategies for writing stories, poems, letters, scripts, research reports, and more. Take what you have learned about the writing process and get to know your own process.

But first, read about journals—perhaps the most important resource writers have.

WRITING Journals

Personal writing is a great way to get to know yourself. You can think about what you already know, wonder about what you don't know, and express opinions and feelings. Personal writing can take many forms. Keeping a writer's response journal will help you to explore your experiences, ideas, and feelings. Similarly, you can use dialogue journals and learning logs to respond to what you are reading and learning. When you write personal letters and personal papers, you can share your thoughts with someone else!

Writing to Discover

How can you make discoveries about yourself and your world? Some people use artwork to free up their minds and to begin focussing. They begin by sketching or doodling, and then they add words and sentences. You can use journals as another way to think on paper.

Here's How To Think on Paper

Let your reading, observations, and imagination be an open door to adventure and exploration.

1. **Write questions to yourself. Log answers as they come to you.**

   What is it like to live a day in my life? *It's really hectic, and I'm always running late.*

   What is most important to me? *Friends, family, music, my cat.*

2. **Let your answers lead you to new questions.**

   Why is music so important to me? *I share it with my friends. I write songs to express my feelings and ideas. It makes me feel more connected to the world.*

   Why didn't I like the story that I just read? *The ending was disappointing. I could write a better ending.*

3. **Dream. Let your imagination fly.**

   What things do I daydream about? *Meeting space aliens, saving rain forests, exploring the Northwest Territories.*

   What do I want my future to be like? *Good question! Many directions are possible.*

Writer's Journals

What should I write?

Your journal is a place where you can let go. Try writing non-stop for several minutes at a time. Don't revise what you've written. You'll find it interesting to go back later and see what you wrote "off the top of your head." Thoughts and dreams, experiences and memories, reactions to stories, odds and ends of information—all these can make a writer's journal a valuable source of writing ideas.

Get Started

Even with the best intentions, it's hard to fit another activity into your busy life! Like many other writers, you may want to set aside a special place and time for writing each day. Try to find a spot where you can be alone and undisturbed. You'll want to keep your journal and writing tools ready: a personal supply of pens, pencils, and coloured markers, or maybe just one special fountain pen.

Pen won't move? Don't worry; you too can write journal responses. **See page 114.**

BRIGHT Ideas

FOR SETTING UP A JOURNAL

Like everything else about a journal, the tools you use are a personal choice. Here are some possibilities:

Keep your journal on lined paper in a notebook or loose-leaf binder. You may want to add blank paper or graph paper if you like to include drawings and other artwork.

Use a computer if you have one.

Use index cards or a small pocket-size notebook. These work well when ideas come to you on the run.

Create your own book. You might sew a cover on blank or lined pages, or decorate the cover of a notebook with stickers and illustrations.

Write About Things That Interest You

Marishana transferred to our school in the middle of the year. She was confident and naturally graceful, wore gold saris, and had a crisp British accent. She'd been everywhere, and she'd done everything—except rope a calf.

Write about interesting or quirky people. A student wrote this journal entry to develop a character for a short story.

I didn't want to look too eager, so I rocked back in my chair as if I really had to think about his offer. The next thing I knew, me, my chair, and my lunch were on the floor.

Write about that really embarrassing thing you did yesterday. After you stop blushing, experiences like this can be a big help in writing a personal narrative or a humorous story.

Under a street sign that said "Caution: Falling Rocks," a couple kissed, unaware of their surroundings.

Describe the funny sight you saw on the way home. Use this opportunity to develop descriptive writing skills.

Include quotations, poems, newspaper clippings, photos, and sketches, and make notes around them. These items might spark ideas for stories or feature articles.

Some Special Journals

The word *journal* comes from the French word *jour,* which means "day." A journal is anything you write in daily—or regularly. Here is a sample of different kinds of journals you might like to try.

Diaries

Diaries are not the same as writer's response journals. A diary is usually used for briefly noting personal feelings and day-by-day events. For example, "I wore my red jacket today, and everyone liked it." The ideas in a diary are seldom revisited and less likely to grow into another piece of writing that is shared with an audience.

Dialogue Journals

Wouldn't it be great to have a record of a really good conversation you had with a friend? You can use a dialogue journal to have a two-way discussion with someone else. You might exchange ideas with someone reading the same book that you are reading. Or you might ask your teacher why a certain writer creates stereotyped characters. The two of you will write alternately in the journal to create a running conversation. Try using a computer, if one is available, to enter and store your conversations.

Learning Logs

A learning log is a place to record new facts and concepts, and it is usually devoted to one subject. A learning log for a subject like music or science might contain your growing understanding of new facts and ideas.

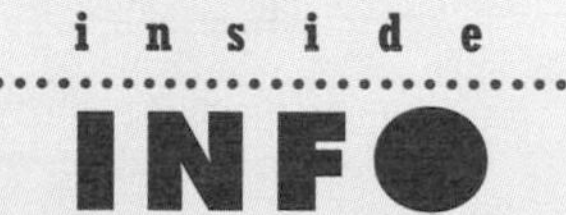
inside
INFO

"Writing is easy. All you do is stare at a blank sheet of paper until drops of blood form on your forehead."

—Gene Fowler

RELATED WRITING

Personal Papers

As you look over your journals, you may find an idea that you want to share with someone else. A good way to explore an idea is to write a personal paper.

Find Your Focus

Begin by freewriting about your subject until you can describe it in a clear sentence. Then try completing a chart like the one below to help you plan your paper.

Need to brush up on freewriting? See page 21.

Subject:	The Joys of Learning to Skate
Opinion:	Anything worth doing is worth a few falls.
Tone:	Humorous
Purpose:	To describe how I feel when I finally succeed
Audience:	Family and friends

Draft a Personal Paper

Your paper might be free-form, or it might follow a traditional essay format.

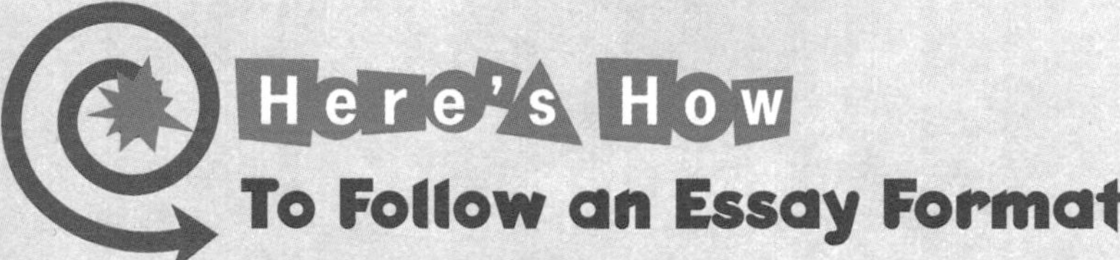
Here's How

To Follow an Essay Format

1. **Introduce your subject with a "hook" to catch your reader's interest.** Then give the purpose of your essay, your *thesis.*
   "This had better be worth the bandages!" my dad said, as he helped me patch up the bruises from my first skating attempt.
   "It will be!" I replied. I wanted to be a figure skater.
2. **Develop your subject in one to three good paragraphs.**
   Day after day, I struggled on, falling to rise again . . .
   It's funny how much stubbornness it takes to keep trying . . .
   They are right, the skaters. It's a bit like being a bird . . .
3. **End your essay with an unexpected event, a new thought, or a statement that summarizes your feelings.**
   As I glided along triumphantly, little did I dream that in two short years I would be competing in a local championship!

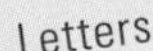

Personal Letters

Personal letters are conversations in writing. They are a way to stay in touch and share thoughts and experiences with faraway friends.

RELATED WRITING
Nora Blake
535 White Castle Road
Reading
Berks 3F1 5GB
England

Write for Your Reader

What kind of letter would you like to find in your mail today? When you write a letter, remember to write the kind of letter that you'd like to receive. Make your letter lively and interesting. Think about including funny or serious news, your thoughts and feelings, and questions for your friend to answer. When you answer a letter, be sure to answer any questions that the writer asked you.

Jazz Up Your Letter

One great way to jazz up a letter is to write it on a greeting card made by you. Another is to start in an interesting way. "There's nothing much to tell about" weakens the letter before it even begins. Remember to write freely and naturally, as if you were talking, and to end your letter on an upbeat note. Include a photograph, a funny cartoon, or one of your own sketches!

Revise and edit your letter so that your readers will not lose their way or their interest. **See pages 27–31.**

WRITING

Poetry

Grab an idea and turn it over; take hold of a moment. Try writing a poem. When you write a poem, you have many new tools to use. You can even create some of your own rules. Writing a poem is finding just the right words to capture a moment, an idea, a feeling, an observation.

PREDRAFT

Capture an Idea

Your world is full of ideas for poems. Look around you. You can find ideas hidden in objects as different as a fine painting and a bin of trash. You can write about a tiny moment or a huge event, a close friend or a stranger you passed on the street. Brainstorm for ideas. Make a list of everything that pops into your head.

Visualize Your Subject

How do you recognize a good idea for a poem? Start with your list of ideas. Which one evokes a powerful feeling? Why do you feel that way? Which subject brings a vivid picture to your mind?

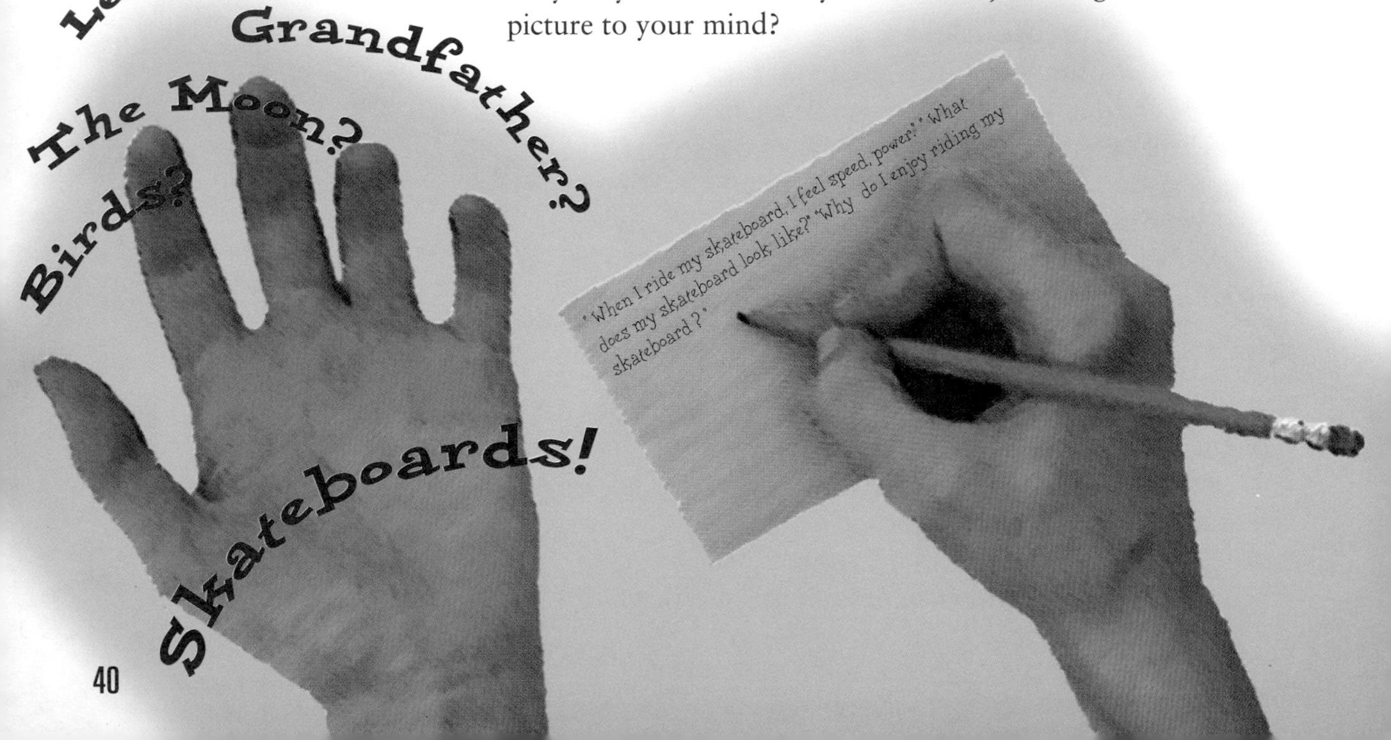

Rain?
Sharks?
Sunrise?
My Cat?
Leaves?
Grandfather?
The Moon?
Birds?
Skateboards!
"When I ride my skateboard, I feel speed, power!" "What does my skateboard look like?" "Why do I enjoy riding my skateboard?"

Advice from the Zone

Dear Z:
I have trouble writing even a simple story. So I'm totally panicked at the thought of writing a poem. Either I freeze up, or zillions of ideas spin through my head. What should I do?
—Breathless

Dear Breathless:
Relax, take a deep breath. Here are some ways to tune in to poetry. Listen to your favourite piece of music and see what picture comes to mind. Or sketch a special person, object, or design and add words suggested by your drawing. Look through a family photo album of people, places, and events in your past. Or just close your eyes and catch the first image that floats into your mind. Then freewrite. Loosen up and enjoy yourself!

Z.

Focus on Your Subject

Think about your subject. Quickly list words and phrases to describe it. Or use a web. Does your subject have a particular size, shape, weight, or colour? How does it affect your senses? Can you smell, touch, taste, or hear it? Can you compare what you see or feel to something else? Look at George Swede's poem, for example. What does he compare the wrinkles on the fisherman's face to?

Around the eyes
of the old fisherman
permanent ripples
—George Swede

PREDRAFT

Plan Your Poem

You have spent some time living with your idea—finding details to express it and discovering more about how it affects you. Now it's time to think about the poem you will write.

Tune In to a Tone

How do you feel about your subject? That feeling often sets the tone of your poem. Do you feel sad? mischievous? nostalgic? angry? joyful? List the first emotions that come to your mind. Or talk aloud about your subject, and listen for your tone of voice. The words on your list may also suggest the tone you're after.

Poetry . . . an image in your mind, the rhythm of your voice

DRAFT

Let It Roll

Get ready! Just let the words and ideas flow freely in the first draft of your poem.

Freewrite Your Poem

Glance through your list of key images and details about your subject. Now freewrite your draft as if you were writing a paragraph. Describe your subject in words, short phrases, or sentences. Unless you have a definite sense of words breaking themselves into lines, write your poem in your natural voice—just the way you would tell it to a friend.

Find the Line Breaks

Read the words of your draft aloud. Where do the natural breaks come—the ones made as you speak, or the ones made by your changing thoughts? Rewrite your poem. Use these natural breaks to shape your poem into lines.

Choose a Matching Form

Does your poem seem to fit a certain poetic form? Often your words and your content will help you decide. You can create your poem in a traditional form, with a rhythm and rhyme pattern, or in free verse—without a set pattern of rhythm or rhyme. If your poem is short and describes nature, look at an example of haiku. If your poem tells a story, look at a ballad. Many ballads include dialogue. Here's part of a famous poem that has dialogue. Notice the rhyming words.

Unsure about poetic forms? Take time for a quick review of different forms of poetry. **See page 152.**

from "The Walrus and the Carpenter"

"The time has come," the Walrus said,
"To talk of many things:
Of shoes—and ships—and sealing-wax—
Of cabbages—and kings—
And why the sea is boiling hot—
And whether pigs have wings."

"But wait a bit," the Oysters cried,
"Before we have our chat;
For some of us are out of breath,
And all of us are fat!"
"No hurry!" said the Carpenter.
They thanked him much for that.

— Lewis Carroll

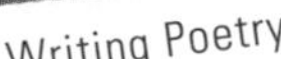

. . . you find its shape in lines and stanzas.

Pick Your Tools

Have some fun with your poem. Try out different tools or literary devices to give your poem special sound effects or a colourful or startling image. As you read the poem below, notice the shape, listen to the sounds, and watch for images.

If you want to know more about rhythm, rhyme, and poetic devices, see page 148.

Try These Poetic Tools

Use some of these tools to liven up your poem. Follow these tips.

Rhyme

Add *rhyme* by using words that have matching sounds, such as *things, kings, wings, chat, fat, that.*

Simile and Metaphor

What does the skateboarder compare herself to? In a *simile,* you use the words *like* or *as* to make a comparison between two unlike things. In a metaphor, two unlike things are compared without the use of *like* or *as*, such as, "I'm the sailor and the sail," "I'm the driver and the wheel."

The Sidewalk Racer OR On the Skateboard

Skimming
an asphalt sea
I swerve, I curve, I
sway; I speed to whirring
sound an inch above the
ground; I'm the sailor
and the sail, I'm the
driver and the wheel
I'm the one and only
single engine
human auto
mobile.

— Lillian Morrison

Alliteration

Use *alliteration,* or words that repeat the same beginning consonant sound, such as *sea, swerve, sway, speed.*

Repetition

Repeat words, phrases, or lines that build rhythm or emphasize a thought: "I'm the sailor," "I'm the driver," "I'm the one." Or you can pick words that repeat the same vowel sound, such as *swerve, curve, whirring.*

Here are two more tools you can try.

Personification

Introduce *personification*, or give human qualities to an animal, object, or concept. For example, in Lewis Carroll's poem all the oysters "are out of breath, And all of us are fat!"

Onomatopoeia

Use *onomatopoeia*, or words like *gurgle*, or *slap*, or *murmur,* in which the sound suggests the meaning.

"He's really nice!"

"He's a creative, fun-loving guy!"

REVISE

Sharpen the Meaning

If you've got a draft down on paper, you've made a terrific start, but you're not finished yet. It's time to take a closer look at your poem.

Ask
yourself

- What's the main image or idea I want my poem to communicate? Does the poem accomplish this?
- Would my point be clearer if there were fewer words or phrases? Which ones can I cut?
- Is each word the best possible word? Is it active? vivid? specific?
- Are there any words I could add or change to improve the sound of the poem?
- Does the poem end with force, surprise, or a message? How might I improve the ending?

Revise your poem until you feel that each word in the poem says just what you want it to say—no more, no less.

Hold a Peer Conference

Is your message coming across? Another reader might know. Show your poem to a partner or a small group of friends. What are their reactions? How do they respond to some of the questions you asked yourself? Think carefully about your friends' responses. Then decide what *you* want to revise. Advice is valuable—but it's *your* poem.

Choose a Title

Your title is the first thing your reader will see, so you'll want to take the time to think of a good one. It can be the main subject, an explanation, a line from the poem, a key phrase, a rhyme, or a tease.

inside INFO

Exact words are not easy to find—even for poets. The poet Eve Merriam said, "Sometimes I've spent weeks looking for precisely the right word. It's like having a tiny marble in your pocket; you can feel it. Sometimes you find a word and say, 'No, I don't think this is precisely it. . . .' Then you discard it, and take another and another until you get it right."

EDIT AND PROOFREAD

Fine-Tune Your Poem

Poems may require a special kind of editing because they often break the rules of capitalization, punctuation—even spelling. Read your poem through again. Is it clear and complete? Did you check the punctuation, spelling, and usage? Make sure that you have a good reason for breaking the rules. If you use a traditional poetic form, you might want to capitalize the beginning of each line. When you have made a final copy, give your poem a last proofreading. The way it looks is important.

Poems can follow their own rules.

I dreamed I was

falling, falling,
but then
I spread
my arms

and swooped up like
a bird into the sky.

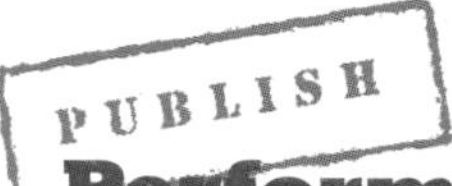
PUBLISH

Perform Your Poem

Poems are written to be shared. If you enjoy sharing, read your poem aloud to a group, or ask friends to help you present it as a choral reading. Before your oral reading, experiment with different speeds and volumes, and try emphasizing different words. Use a tape-recorder to hear yourself reciting. Some poems are very personal. You may prefer not to read your poem to the class. Instead, you may want to videotape your reading.

Need help with choral reading? Learn more about this way of performing a poem. **See page 176.**

BRIGHT Ideas

FOR PRESENTING YOUR POEM

Make an illustrated copy of your poem. Publish it in a class anthology or frame it for display.

Write out your poem, using calligraphy or a special writing of your own design. Present it as a gift to a friend or family member.

Enter your poem in a contest. Your library may have information about current poetry competitions.

Submit your poem for publication in a school newspaper or anthology. Or consider publishing your own poetry anthology with some friends.

Swap poems with a pen pal. Your school library should have information about how to find a pen pal.

WRITING

Persuasive Letters

A persuasive letter is a way to influence people. Your goal in writing a persuasive letter is to set forth your opinion about an issue or problem as convincingly as you can. First you want people to understand your view. Then you want them to agree with you. You may even want them to take some kind of action.

PREDRAFT

Find Your Issue

You need to ask yourself two big questions when you prepare to write a persuasive letter: What problem is most important to me right now? Who can help me fix it?

Major problems such as pollution, war, poverty, and injustice are issues too big for one person to solve. Try focussing on a small piece of a big issue. Or choose a smaller issue that bothers you in a big way.

Brainstorm for Ideas

Brainstorm alone to create a list of issues that are dangerous, unfair, or annoying. Then bounce your ideas around with a few of your friends. Knowing other people's opinions can help make your own ideas clearer.

Tired of brainstorming? Try clustering or looping to find an issue. **See pages 21 and 22** for help.

Sydney
joeys
marsupials
Australia
Perth
turtles
brainstorming

Prod Your Brain!

Here is a longer list of prompts to stir up your thinking. Freewrite about each one. Add to your list of possible issues.

Think about

. . . a promise made but never kept!
. . . a product that needs improving!
. . . a solution that could make a difference!
. . . an action that will make life better!

Make Your Choice

Look over your list of issues. Then ask yourself the questions below to decide which issue you will write about. Rate each issue depending on how many yes answers it gets.

Answer these questions

- Do I really care about this issue?
- Can I find strong reasons to support my position?
- Do I have an action to suggest?

Add up your yes answers and choose your issue. Then write a sentence or two clearly stating your opinion.

Target Your Audience

Who will be the audience for your letter? You'll want your message to go to people who can take the action you propose. The issue you've chosen, your opinion on that issue, and your purpose for writing determine to whom you should write. For example, check out the audiences in the chart below.

Your School

Issue: Students want to plan the next class field trip.

Your opinion: Students should make the choice of destination.

Purpose and audience: To persuade the teacher that students can make a good choice.

Your City

Issue: There's dangerous traffic on Main Street.

Your opinion: It's unsafe for bikes.

Purpose and audience: To persuade city council members to build a bike path.

The World

Issue: Hunger is a worldwide problem.

Your opinion: No one should be hungry in our community–there's plenty of food to go around.

Purpose and audience: To persuade friends to sponsor you in the Walk for Bread to raise money for a neighbourhood food bank.

Get Your Arguments Together

How will you support and defend your opinion? How will you promote your purpose? Jot down every reason you can think of that supports your opinion and any action you plan to suggest. Your opinions will need to be supported by facts!

Get the Facts

Does your mind go numb when you hear the word *research?* For help with locating information, **see page 231.**

You need information to build your arguments. It's not enough to say "Our town needs a food bank" or "We need a bike path." You'll need to convince your readers by providing answers to the questions in their minds. Start with the six basic questions—Who, What, Where, When, Why, and How—and make a list of questions that people might ask about your issue. Look for up-to-date answers in:

- The library
- The yellow pages
- Almanacs
- Newspaper and magazine articles
- TV and radio news programs

Advice from the Zone

Dear Z,

Help! I'm writing a letter to persuade our teacher to let our class decide where we should go on our next social studies field trip. Last year when she gave her class the choice, they really goofed. They all voted for a video arcade. Can you suggest some heavy-duty ways to convince her that we won't choose something that dumb?

—Anxious Letter Writer

Dear Anxious:

Here are three tried-and-true approaches:

Disarm your teacher. Overcome her objections in advance. Tell her you know field trips cost a lot, so you'll personally make sure the trip chosen is worthwhile.

State a precedent. That is, remind her of a time when your class made a responsible choice. (You *did* make a good choice once, didn't you?)

Predict success! Convince her that good things will result from letting you choose—more enthusiastic participation, better behaviour on the bus, and so on.

Good luck! Stay cool.

Z.

Put Your Arguments in Order

After you've listed your arguments, you need to put them in order. Two effective ways to organize your list are by:

Category: *How* a food bank will work. *Why* a food bank is easy to start.

Importance: Biking on a bike path is more enjoyable (less important reason). Some kid who bikes to school might get killed in that traffic (strongest reason).

inside
INFO

If you want your readers to follow your ideas easily, use introductory words and phrases like these: *First of all, Next, Another thing that, Finally.*

DRAFT

Get It Down

Try to visualize your audience's reactions to your arguments as you write your lead sentences. Once you have set the tone in the lead, keep it through the entire draft. This will help your arguments to build into a persuasive whole.

If you're writing to city officials or to a company, you will want to state your purpose or opinion in a businesslike way:

> On May 18 I plan to take part in the Walk for Bread, raising funds for our new food bank. I hope you will sponsor me.

If you are writing to family, friends, and neighbours, you can start off in a less formal, more attention-grabbing way:

> Picture me in the Walk for Bread on May 18: I'm on kilometre 15. My legs feel like lead weights. My feet are killing me. But I won't give up! I owe my best effort to the food bank—and to you, my sponsor. You will sponsor me, won't you?

Here's How To Draft Your Persuasive Letter

1. **State your purpose, opinion, or request.**

   Dear Channel 6:

   Recently you moved my favourite program, *Tales from Outer Space*, from 4:30 P.M. to 1:30 A.M. Please reconsider. Your audience will be asleep at that hour!

2. **Follow your plan for ordering your arguments or reasons: one reason or category in each paragraph.** For example, paragraphs might begin like this:

   First of all, this is my favourite program and . . . Furthermore, I am unable to tape the show because . . . You should know that our whole junior high school is upset . . .

3. **Restate your purpose. Ask for support.**

   We miss this show! Won't you please return it to its old time?

inside INFO

One draft seldom does the job! Major changes in a first draft mean a second draft will be necessary to sharpen up arguments. Then, when you get feedback from friends and editors, you sometimes have to revise yet again.

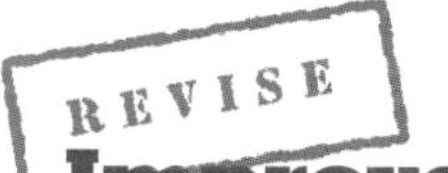
REVISE

Improve Your Letter

When you've finished the first draft of your letter, put it aside for at least a day so that you can come back to it with a fresher, more objective eye. Then, read your draft to yourself. Do your arguments make sense? How can you make your letter more persuasive? Remember what you want your readers to say:

GO FOR IT!

YEAH!

THAT'S RIGHT!

Look at Your Logic

Thinking logically means thinking clearly. Strong, logical arguments will best support your opinion. Here are some examples of weak logic. Watch for and avoid them:

Absolutes: "But everybody is going!" Words like *everybody, always*, and *never* weaken your argument. It's too easy to prove such absolute statements false. All the reader has to find is one exception to disprove your whole argument.

Irrelevant reasons: "Thirty kilometres is too long for a walkathon. We don't want to discourage people from joining us! The last time I wore these sneakers, I got blisters." Don't get sidetracked by statements (like that last one) that are irrelevant and don't directly support your opinion.

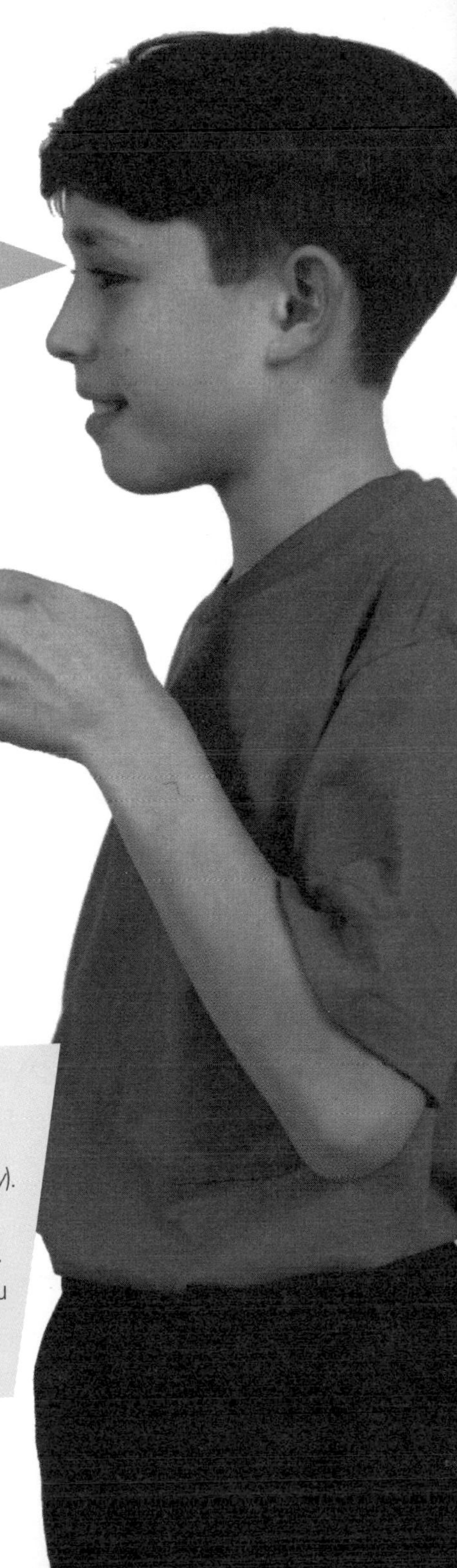

Get Some Feedback

Read your persuasive letter aloud to at least two other people to collect suggestions for improving your arguments.

"That is really persuasive because . . ."
"You could use more reasons for . . ."
"Someone might object that . . ."
"You could probably leave out . . ."

Then think carefully about the suggestions. Choose the revisions that you think will do the most to improve your letter.

Writing Persuasively: Do's and Don'ts

DO

- Do use words that appeal to readers' emotions and good sense: *vital, necessary, unjust, useful, important.*
- Do give specific facts: names, dates, numbers.
- Do use polite speech; be gracious. End by thanking your reader.

DON'T

- Don't use vague, unconvincing words (*nice, pretty, some, plenty*).
- Don't insult your reader ("No intelligent person believes . . .").
- Don't use slang, especially if you are writing for adults.

EDIT AND
PROOFREAD

Fine-Tune Your Letter

Feeling insecure? Help is at hand. For help with paragraph structure, **see page 356.** For help with revising, **see page 28.** For help with editing and proofreading, **see page 30.**

Your letter is going to represent *you* when you send it out into the world. So pay attention to details! Is it neatly written or printed on the best paper you could find? Have you used the correct name and address of the person you're writing to? If it's a business letter, check the format. **See page 372 for a sample of a business letter format.**

Check Your Paragraphs

Look over the middle section of your letter, where you've developed your reasons, arguments, and examples. Is it a jumble? Should you break it into new paragraphs? Do you need transition words, such as *in addition, another, also, finally*?

Proofread for Distracting Errors

You don't want misspelled words, confusing punctuation, or poor grammar to distract your reader from your persuasive logic! Correct errors now.

PUBLISH

Deliver Your Persuasive Letter

Put your neat, error-free letter in its matching envelope complete with neat, error-free address, plus adequate postage, and send it off.

RELATED
WRITING

More Ways to Be Persuasive

A letter is just one kind of persuasive writing. Whenever you want someone to understand your opinion, agree with you, or do what you suggest, you are arguing persuasively. Here are other forms you can use to persuade others.

- Write an editorial for a school newspaper.
- Compose a persuasive essay.
- Make an advertising poster.
- Write and deliver a speech.
- Review a book, concert, play, or video to let people know about your reaction.

WRITING

Personal Narratives

A personal narrative is a real story that you write about yourself. You tell that story using the first person, the word *I*. You write personal narratives when you want to share with others your thoughts and feelings about your experiences. That makes personal narratives different from private writing you may do in a diary or journal.

PREDRAFT

Look at Your Life

To get an idea of the extent of your experiences, try this: Multiply your age by three hundred. Multiply that answer by fifteen, the number of hours you are probably awake each day. Your answer is an estimate of the number of hours of experience you have had talking with friends, playing a sport or video game, watching TV, and so on. Some of these experiences can serve as the basis of a story about your life.

Advice from the Zone

Dear Z:

I want to write a story about my life, but I'm not sure what to write about. Nothing interesting ever happens to me.

—I

Dear I:

You must be kidding! Are you telling me you've never been angry, sad, scared, embarrassed, or excited? Start by making a list of experiences you felt strongly about. Which events were "the best thing" or "the worst thing" you experienced? Now imagine someone very different from you (maybe someone from the Zone!) observing you having those experiences. How could you explain your strong emotions to that observer? Use your feelings as a clue to finding your best stories.

Got my eye on you.

Z.

PREDRAFT

Choose an Event

Think of the thousands of hours of experience you have had. How can you select an event to write about? One way is to make a list of possible topics.

inside INFO

"The fascinating thing about writing is that it's a way of transforming the things you've experienced; it's like being able to live twice."

—Jacques Godbout

Develop Your Ideas

To decide which topic from your list will make the best story, you can do some predrafting. **For information about freewriting, brainstorming, and clustering, see page 21.** You may find the following questions helpful in making your decision.

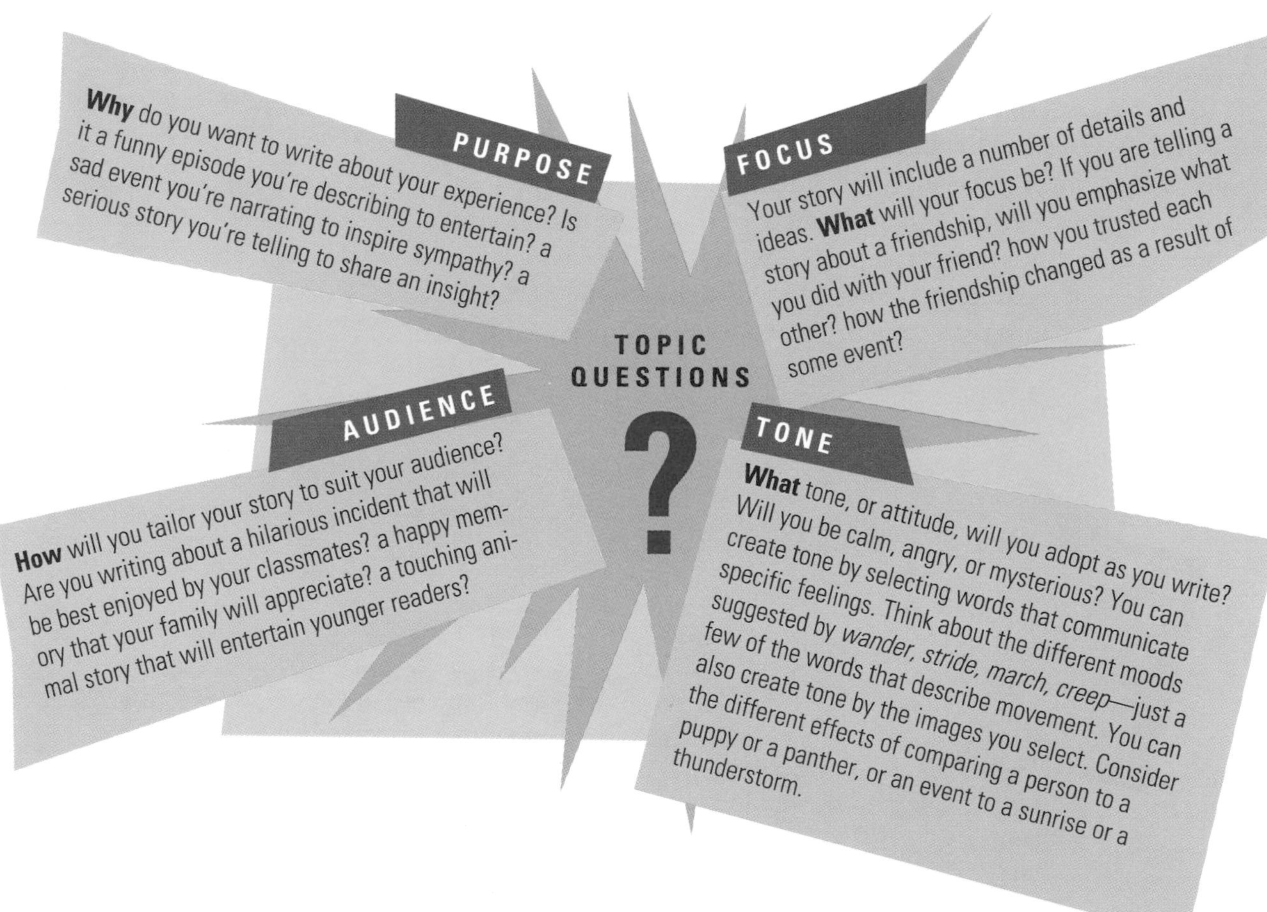
TOPIC QUESTIONS
?
PURPOSE
Why do you want to write about your experience? Is it a funny episode you're describing to entertain? a sad event you're narrating to inspire sympathy? a serious story you're telling to share an insight?
FOCUS
Your story will include a number of details and ideas. **What** will your focus be? If you are telling a story about a friendship, will you emphasize what you did with your friend? how you trusted each other? how the friendship changed as a result of some event?
AUDIENCE
How will you tailor your story to suit your audience? Are you writing about a hilarious incident that will be best enjoyed by your classmates? a happy memory that your family will appreciate? a touching animal story that will entertain younger readers?
TONE
What tone, or attitude, will you adopt as you write? Will you be calm, angry, or mysterious? You can create tone by selecting words that communicate specific feelings. Think about the different moods suggested by *wander, stride, march, creep*—just a few of the words that describe movement. You can also create tone by the images you select. Consider the different effects of comparing a person to a puppy or a panther, or an event to a sunrise or a thunderstorm.

Here's How

To Plan Your Personal Narrative

Remember that a personal narrative is a non-fiction story, so follow the steps for writing stories.

1. **Select the experience you want to write about, using your predrafting notes.**
2. **Outline events in the order in which they happened.** This process will help you decide what to include in the story and what to leave out. When you write the first draft, you can decide whether to organize the story by time, by space, or in some other way.
3. **List words describing how you felt during the experience.**
4. **Name the other people who were involved.** Write down any memorable words that people used and a few phrases to describe each person's character.
5. **Identify where and when the events took place.** Jot down notes on whether the place and time were special, for example, a first visit to Toronto during Caribana.
6. **Review your notes, and decide whether you have all the information you need.** If not, list what you need to know, and do research.

DRAFT

Write Your Story

You will probably find it helpful to refer to notes, lists, and an outline as you write your narrative. You can also think of a single person who represents your audience. Picturing that person will help you keep your story focussed.

inside
INFO

On writing non-fiction:

"My whole secret is to try and make it read like a novel."

—Pierre Berton

Pick a Good Lead

You can use the lead, or opening, of your personal narrative to do two things. First, grab the attention of your audience. Second, establish the tone of the story. One way to develop a lead is to freewrite, that is, to write down many ideas at once, without stopping to decide how good each idea is.

Suppose you decide to write about a contest you entered. It's boring to begin like this:

Last year, our town held a snow-sculpture contest.

Instead, you could begin like this:

I was surrounded by opponents and almost blown over by frigid gusts, but I was determined to win. My snow sculpture was going to get the prize for most creative idea.

Tips on Organization

Here are some ideas to consider as you decide how to organize your story. Why not imagine your experience told in each of these three ways, to see which would work best.

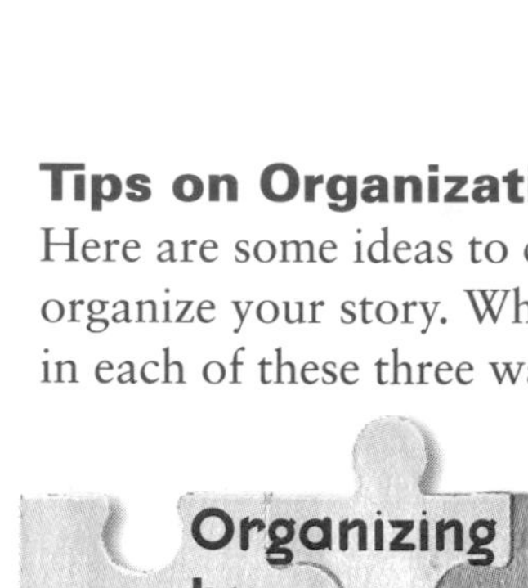

Organizing by Time

You can narrate events in the order in which they happened. You could vary this organization a little by using a flashback, which is an interruption presenting a scene from an earlier time.

Organizing by Space

You can describe what is happening in one location first, and then you can describe what is happening in another location. You could also alternate between two or more locations.

Organizing by Importance

You can begin with the least important event and end with the most important. You could also organize in the reverse order, starting with the most important idea and then following with less important ideas that support or explain the main idea.

"Show" Your Experiences

As you write, you may find it helpful to recall the advice often given to writers to "show, not tell." One way to "show" is to describe concrete details about a place, a time, or a person. Try to let your readers see what you saw and hear what you heard. You can also try to show your feelings instead of simply telling what they were. "I was inspired by the competition" could become "All around me, shapeless white blobs were turning into people, animals, and miniature ships and castles. My hands began to work faster and faster, as if fueled by magic."

The Last Word

What is the final idea you want to leave with your readers? You might choose an ending that allows different interpretations or leaves the reader to imagine what happens next. You could also let readers see how you felt about your experience or how your experience might affect your future.

> None of the prizes came my way, but I had no regrets. The three hours of the contest had felt like only minutes. When my sculpture was finished, I was soaked with perspiration and as hungry as could be. "Hey, folks," I shouted, "Does anyone know where there's a pie-eating contest?"

REVISE

Make Your Story Better

If you can, put your draft away for at least a day so you can read it over with a fresh eye. Then, you can make notes on your draft as you consider the questions below.

Want to improve your story-telling skills? Read good narratives that others have written. **See page 179** for some helpful tips.

Ask
these
questions

- Should you change or improve the lead?
- Can you make the ending more effective?
- Can you improve connections between ideas?
- Do your characters act and speak convincingly?
- Is the tone right for the story? Is it consistent?

Use the Best Words

You can polish your story by evaluating each of the words you used. Have you used general, vague, or abstract words that should be replaced by vivid, concrete words? Do some words produce a tone that's different from the one you intend? To find the right word, you may want to refer to a reference book. **See the sections on using the dictionary and the thesaurus on pages 328–331.**

Ask a Friend for Help

Of all the writing you do, you are closest to personal narrative. That can make it hard to see what can be improved. You may want to get feedback from a friend before revising further. **Suggestions for discussing your draft with a peer are listed on page 28.**

Ask these questions

- Did you enjoy it? Did it make you laugh or cry, or feel scared or excited?
- Were any parts puzzling or confusing?
- Do the people in the story seem real?
- Which parts did you like the best? the least?
- What would you like to know more about?

Then sift through your friend's comments and decide what to change in your story.

EDIT AND
PROOFREAD

Clean and Polish

Need help with editing and proofreading? Why not take time to review some helpful suggestions. **See page 30.**

Read your story aloud. Are there any rough spots? Do you need to improve the use of transition words and phrases? Can you cut out any repetition or unnecessary words? If a better word or image occurs to you, use it.

The Last Steps

Don't forget to fix any errors you find in mechanics and spelling. Also, edit for errors in usage and grammar, especially any mistakes using *I* and *me*. (Sometimes, however, you may wish to let your characters use speech patterns that do not follow the usual rules.) Make your final copy, and proofread a final time.

PUBLISH

Present Your Story

You can share your personal narrative in many creative ways, according to your purpose and with regard to the audience you had in mind.

BRIGHT Ideas

FOR PUBLISHING YOUR PERSONAL NARRATIVE

Illustrate your narrative with drawings or photos. Present a copy to a family member or friend, especially someone familiar with your story.

Create a class anthology of personal narratives. Such a collection will help you and your classmates remember yesterday's and today's events in years to come.

Read your narrative aloud to another class, to a community group, or to people in a nursing home.

Prepare an audiotape of your personal narrative. If your story includes different voices, do them yourself or ask friends to help.

Create a video that shows people and scenes from your story while you read the narrative as the audio portion.

Enter a contest whose subject matter, purpose, and audience seem appropriate for your story.

RELATED WRITING

Autobiography

Anyone can write a brief personal narrative about an event in her or his life. A person can also write a *long* personal narrative, which is called an autobiography. An autobiography is a type of non-fiction. It describes the writer's life, with real conversations, real events, real places, and other real people. (Sometimes an autobiographer changes other people's names to avoid embarrassing them or to protect them.)

Memoirs

A writer of an autobiography may have personal knowledge or specialized information about important people or events. A life story written by such a person is often called the individual's *memoirs*. Memoirs are written by entertainers, political leaders, and others who have been part of notable events.

"Memoir is a window into a life."

—William Zinsser

inside INFO

Writers use their experiences when they create. Author Phyllis Reynolds Naylor writes, ". . . after something I've read or something I've dreamed or something I remember from the past, I think, I could do something special with that idea!"

Short Stories

Do you ever tell a friend about something that just happened? You might tell a story to make sense of an event or just to make your friend laugh. When you write a short story, you can do the same things. You can also create a partly or entirely imaginary world and see what happens.

PREDRAFT

Search for Ideas

Stories can grow out of small moments that have personal meaning. Your experiences don't have to be earth-shaking to make interesting stories. Here's how to look for good ideas.

Ask "What If . . . ?"

Create a list of "what if" questions. The situations can lead to interesting stories.

What if

- . . . you woke up one morning to discover you were your favourite athlete?
- . . . one of your nightmares came true?
- . . . you received a letter from the future?
- . . . you were your mother or father?

The author Phyllis Reynolds Naylor once took a walk and came upon an abandoned dog. The image of the forlorn dog stayed with her, troubling her deeply. Eventually she turned her feelings into a book, the award-winning novel Shiloh.

Keep a Story File

Start a story file, or use a journal or writing folder to keep track of interesting moments in your life. Below are some things you might include. **For more ideas, see pages 19 and 34.**

Observations Write brief descriptions of events you've reacted to with curiosity, humour, wonder, anger, fear, pity. Later, those descriptions might prompt stories.

Quotations Jot down words and sayings you find in books or magazines and remarks you overhear. They may inspire you to create characters who say them.

Headlines Newspaper headlines can spark story ideas. *Lost Boy Found Alive in Cave!* What might have happened? Use your imagination.

What's Your Favourite Story?

The kind of story you like to read may be the best kind for you to write. Choose one of the types of stories described here.

In a **science fiction** story, you create a future or another world. What would you want to show about that world? Would the characters face a problem with advances in technology or with common things like dating?

Try retelling a *FOLK TALE* or making up an original one. You might show how a trickster fools someone or how a character with a pure heart gets what he or she deserves.

Use **contemporary realistic fiction** to show characters you know well because they're like your friends, your family, yourself. The problems your characters tackle might come directly from your life.

A **HORROR TALE** explores the fearful and the ghastly. If you like inventing creepy people or strange creatures, this story form is for you.

A **mystery** or **detective story** often revolves around a crime that has been committed. You can give your audience a suspenseful read by building the plot carefully and leaving plenty of evidence for the detective to find!

HISTORICAL FICTION is set in the past. You can make up characters (and use real historical people, too), but to make your story believable, you'll want to stick close to the actual events. Be sure to research the time period!

In a **modern fable**, you use fantasy characters to focus on social issues that matter to you—for example, how people respond to someone who is "different."

An **adventure story** is about an exciting accomplishment or the struggle to survive. Often the setting is important. If you describe it well, your readers will be able to travel there and share your character's experience.

PREDRAFT

Choose and Explore Your Idea

Being inventive can make writing a story exciting. You'll want to choose an idea that sparks your imagination. But to develop a believable story, you'll need to make sure that you know enough about your idea. If your main character is an acrobat with a fear of heights and you don't know about circus life, your story will ring false. You'll be more successful at writing about something you know well. Here are some other things to consider in choosing an idea.

inside
INFO

Even if you write about what you know, you still might need to do some research to add details or to broaden your understanding. Do what a professional writer would do: Look at books, check a computer database, and interview experts. **See pages 240, 246, and 249.**

Focus on Story Elements

To help you judge how workable each story idea is, ask questions about the four story elements: character, setting, plot, theme. **See page 135 to review these elements.**

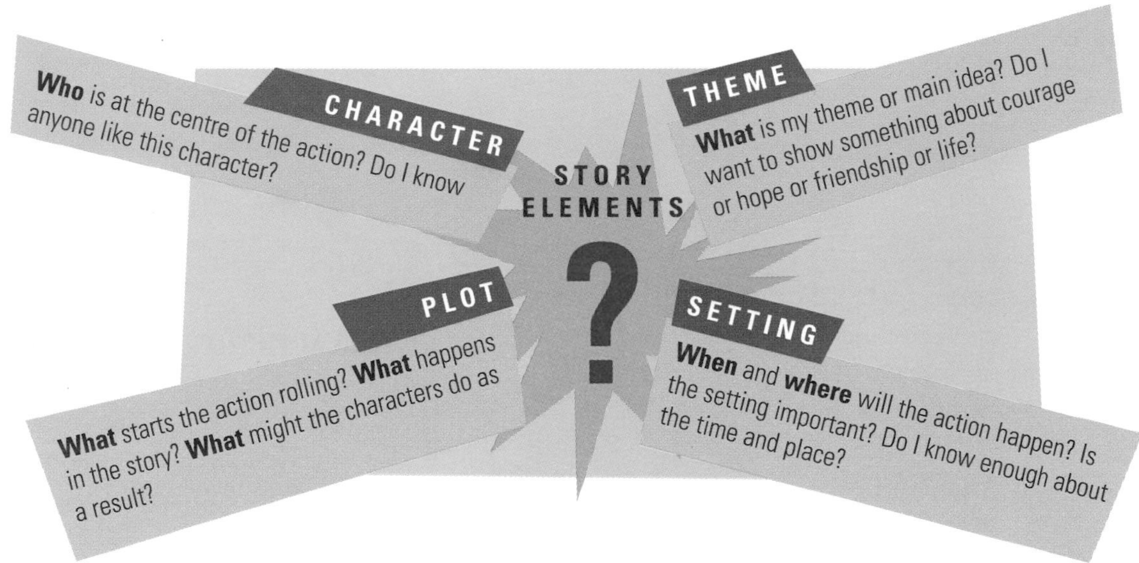
STORY ELEMENTS
?
CHARACTER
Who is at the centre of the action? Do I know anyone like this character?
THEME
What is my theme or main idea? Do I want to show something about courage or hope or friendship or life?
PLOT
What starts the action rolling? What happens in the story? What might the characters do as a result?
SETTING
When and where will the action happen? Is the setting important? Do I know enough about the time and place?

Unleash Your Imagination

Start with the main character, no matter how dimly you picture him or her. Or begin with the setting or with the plot. Write a word or phrase to identify one of these starting points. Then explore it by freewriting or by creating a cluster around it. **To refresh your memory, see page 21.**

PREDRAFT

Plan Your Story

Do you want to keep your readers turning the pages? A good way to do this is by building your story around a problem or conflict. Here is a model:

Beginning: Set up the problem or conflict.

Middle: Show how the main character struggles to solve the problem and how she or he changes as a result.

End: Resolve the problem, happily or not.

Creating a time line of events will help you plan the action. One way to present the events is in *time order*—the order in which the events happened. **To add flash-backs, see page 67.**

Advice from the Zone

Dear Z:
I have a great idea for a story about a girl who wants to do competitive cycling. This girl has a problem, though. The captain of the cycling team is her enemy. I think my story would be good at showing how people don't get along sometimes, but I don't know how to put the story together. Can you help me?

—Spokes Person

Dear Spokes Person:
Character is especially important in your story, so plan your story around your main character. Write a description of the girl, and see what you discover. What does she look and sound like? How does she feel about her problem? As you work out the plot, keep thinking about the problem as the girl sees it. Write back and let me know how things turn out for her!

Z.

Know Your Purpose and Your Audience

Who are you writing your story for? Do you want your readers to laugh, tremble, or sigh? The way you write your story will depend on your audience and your purpose.

Name the Narrator

If you want to tell the story from a character's point of view, the narrator will be limited to what that character knows. A *limited narrator* tells the story in the first person (using *I*).

limited first person

I knew I had to focus on the race, but I kept wondering why Nadia was angry.

A limited narrator may also tell the story in the third person (using *he, she, they*).

limited third person

Ahmed knew he had to focus on the race, but he kept wondering why Nadia was angry.

If you want to describe the thoughts and feelings of all the characters, make the narrator all-knowing, or *omniscient*. An *omniscient narrator* always tells a story in the third person and is not a character in the story.

omniscient

Ahmed's taunting had made Nadia furious, but she wasn't going to think about that now. The starting signal went off. Nadia took off like a shot, but Ahmed fell behind, distracted by Nadia's anger.

DRAFT

Follow Your Own Path

Now is the time to get your story down on paper. One way to get started is to create a rough draft. Write as quickly as possible. Don't think too much about any particular scene or conversation, and don't try to shape perfect sentences. If this approach doesn't work for you, try beginning with the scene that you picture most vividly. Then write the rest of the story, forward and backward, from that special scene.

inside
INFO

Don't follow your plan too rigidly. It will point you in one direction, so that's the path you should start on. But you'll make many more discoveries about your characters and events if you let your draft lead you down other paths, too.

Build a Strong Lead

Somctimcs just the first sentence can draw your readers in and make them hungry for more. Depending on your story, you might start with a dramatic moment, some dialogue, or the setting.

Dramatic Moment

Maria was just about to climb the stairs to the porch when the floor caved in.

Dialogue

"You'd better leave our stuff in the car. Something weird is going on," Maria called to her sister.

Setting

The old wooden porch, which usually seemed so welcoming, was covered with trash.

Use Dialogue

Story characters sound like real people, but their conversations usually come to the point faster. Use dialogue to show what your characters are like, but make sure that it also moves the story along.

Need help in punctuating dialogue? You may have a good ear for conversation but have difficulty putting it on paper. **See page 355 for helpful ideas.**

Dialogue Hints

Weak	Stronger	Why?
"Oh, really?" she questioned doubtfully.	"Oh, really?" she asked. "I doubt that."	The character's words should show how they're being spoken. Don't rely on adverbs, such as *doubtfully*.
"I saw you with Mark," Kevin argued. "But I was at home alone," she responded. He insisted, "I don't believe you!"	Kevin gave Romalda an accusing look. "I saw you with Mark," he said.	Verbs like *insisted* may clutter up the dialogue. Use the verb *said* most of the time.
"Where did this come from?" he frowned.	Ming frowned as he glanced at the letter. "Where did this come from?"	*Frowned* is not a verb of speech. To help readers picture a character, add details of description to the dialogue.

REVISE

Improve Your Story

Revising is part of creating a story. It isn't easy to get things just the way you want them, and revising can take time. But when you see a story begin to say exactly what you want it to say, then you know why writers write . . . and rewrite.

Don't tell your reader how a character feels! Let your characters show their feelings through their actions and conversations. **For tips on showing rather than telling, see pages 26 and 56.**

Review your story and ask these questions: Is the plot believable? Would the characters behave as they do if they were real people? As you reread your story, picture someone reading along with you. Have you included everything that person needs to know?

Here's How

To Revise Your Draft

1. **Look at your story plan.** Did it work for you? If you need to revise your story extensively, you may want to begin by creating a new plan.
2. **Look for weak places in your draft and make changes.**
   Cut unnecessary sections. Take out extra details that don't move the story along and may make it boring.
   Add specific descriptions of the setting. Let your readers know where and when events are happening.
   Add connections between events. If your hero begins battling a sea monster right after she wins a drag race, with no explanation given, your readers will be confused.
   Explain the motives of your main character's behaviour. Readers are more likely to sympathize with characters they understand.
   Move conversations and scenes to where they work best.

Hold a Peer Conference

Is the story you have written the same as the one in your imagination, or close to it? Read your draft aloud to a friend or classmate. Then ask this person questions about your draft.

Do you

. . . get pulled in by the lead?
. . . care about the main character?
. . . picture and understand the other characters?
. . . get lost, or can you follow the action?
. . . want to know more about anything?

Try a Flash-back

Writers use a flash-back to send a reader into the past. It shows the reader connections between what is happening now and what came before. You might want to use a flash-back if something in your story is not explained well. (Why *is* that character so afraid of the dark room?)

Or you might use flash-back if your story starts in the middle of the action and you need to show what came before. (So *that's* why they're all stuck in the tree.)

Check for Shifting Point of View

Without realizing it, a writer may switch from one point of view to another. The result is a confused reader. As you edit, pay special attention to who is telling the story.

Draft	What's Wrong?	Edit It!
Jorge was thinking about his missing mitt. "Have you seen it, Carmen?" he asked me.	The *me* shows that the narrator is Carmen. But the story character Carmen can know only her own thoughts—not Jorge's.	Jorge looked under the couch and behind the closet door. He scratched his head. "Have you seen my mitt?" he asked me.
She thought, "This is the worst day of her life! The missed bus and the torn jeans." And you haven't forgotten the caterpillar incident!	This appears to be written in the third person. The pronouns *her* and *you* are confusing.	She thought, "This is the worst day of my life! The missed bus and the torn jeans." And she hadn't forgotten the caterpillar incident!

PUBLISH

Go Public

Enjoy the pleasure of sharing your story. **To make sure you have a good title for your story, see page 27.** Then consider these possibilities for sharing.

- Send your story to a magazine that publishes writing from students.
- Publish an anthology with a group of friends or classmates, and include your story in it.
- Enter your story in a contest.
- Submit your story to a class or school publication.
- Prepare an oral reading for family or friends. **See page 179 to find out about oral storytelling.**
- Start a story exchange. Send your story to a pen pal and ask her or him to send you a story in return.

RELATED WRITING

Use Your Story as a Starter

Transform your story into a comic book. Take the characters, plot, setting, and theme of your story, but feel free to create dialogue and anything else! Focus on the most dramatic scenes, and use a narrator's voice occasionally to fill in any gaps. Look at comic books to see how the writers use action and conversation in just about every frame. Your drawings can be as simple or as elaborate as you wish.

Today a short story . . . tomorrow a book! Some modern novels are actually arrangements of loosely connected stories. Certain characters may appear in several stories. They may appear as children in one and as adults in another. Try creating new stories, using characters from the story you just wrote. You might focus on one of the minor characters or retell your story from a different point of view. You can also write a story in which your main character is older or younger.

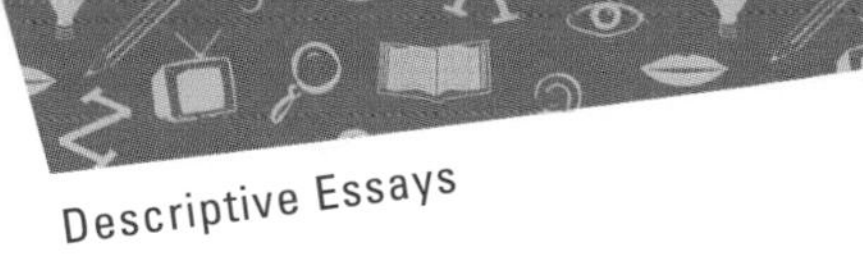

WRITING

Descriptive Essays

You use your senses, your memory, and your imagination to re-create a real-life experience when you write a descriptive essay. As you shape the introduction, body, and conclusion, you try to write so vividly that readers will feel as if they are standing in *your* shoes and seeing with *your* eyes.

PREDRAFT

Search for a Subject

What should you describe in your essay? If you can write about the giant insects and tropical heat on your trip down the Amazon River, that's wonderful. But if you can't think of any unusual experiences to share, don't worry. You can find plenty of possible subjects.

Freewrite Freely

All around you are people, places, living things, and objects that matter to you. The next page provides a swarm of ideas to help light up your imagination. Catch a few, and freewrite, cluster, brainstorm, or loop your way to the subject of your essay.

Need to practise your freewriting? You may want to review the information about freewriting, clustering, brainstorming, and looping. **See pages 21–22.**

It looks like

Look Around You

You can collect essay ideas as you go through your day just by sharpening your senses. Try these ways of looking at your world. Then choose some possible subjects.

Take a good look at the scenes around you: pictures, rooms, streets, closets, buildings, trees . . .

Close your eyes. Focus on what you smell, hear, taste, and touch as you stand near a playground, sit in the cafeteria, stop on a street corner . . .

Check out your feelings as you focus on events around you. Is something frightening or soothing? confusing or breathtaking? As you play with different ideas, think of the mood that each one suggests.

tRy it!

A small subject *can* be a good one! Examine a single pencil for five minutes. Think of it both as an object and as a tool. How would you describe it? What is it made of? What can it do? Freewrite a detailed description of your pencil.

Get Specific

What particular people, places, or things do the words below suggest? You can write an essay about anything from your uncle to an ocean to an orange. Pin down your subject and give it a name.

Who

neighbour
teacher
politician
relative
celebrity
enemy
hero
busybody
bully
expert
know-it-all

Where
a spot to get away to
a spot to get away from
a place full of memories
an attic
an elevator
a favourite place
a noisy place
a dangerous place
a swamp
a hideaway

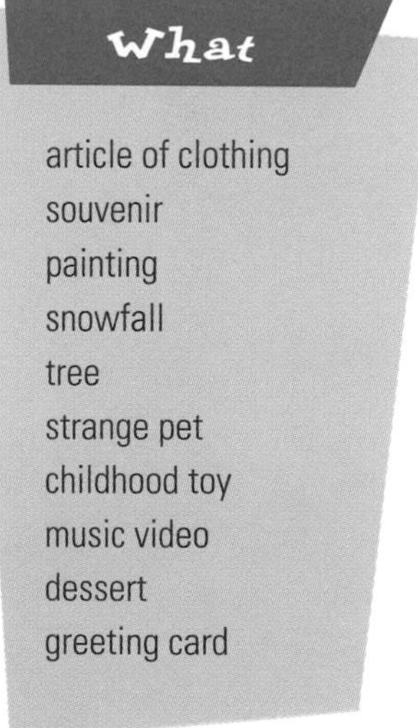
What
article of clothing
souvenir
painting
snowfall
tree
strange pet
childhood toy
music video
dessert
greeting card

DRAFT

Explore Your Subject

O.K., now you have a specific subject chosen from among your best ideas. Don't throw your other ideas away! They'll be useful another time. Keep a file of this valuable list of unused ideas.

Need a place to save your bright ideas? Find out how to set up a writing folder by turning back to **page 19.**

Think About Your Goal, Purpose, and Audience

Why are you writing a descriptive essay? And for whom? What do you want your essay to accomplish? The answers to these three questions will help you choose a subject and decide how you will present it.

A descriptive essay isn't just a series of vivid pictures. It has to have a purpose: an idea that you want your readers to see or experience by the time they get to the end of your essay. Your goal, purpose, and audience can affect the way you approach your subject. For example:

Subject: Favourite hangout—Ginger's Pizzeria

Suppose a writer's goal is to win the Mayor's Essay Contest. Her purpose is to show how Ginger's Pizzeria has contributed to the city. Her audience is readers around the city. She might take the following approach in her essay:

> Ginger's attitude has made her pizzeria a success—and a friendly place to visit.

Suppose another writer's goal is to try for the "Best in Town" page of the school newspaper. His audience is his peers and teachers, and his purpose is to show what a great place Ginger's is. The writer might then take a different approach:

> Sights, smells, and tastes combine to give Ginger's a special flavour.

Get Everything Together

How do you know that you've got a good subject for a descriptive essay?

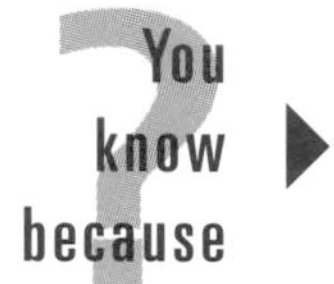
You
know
because

. . . you have a strong interest in it.
. . . you have a purpose and an approach.
. . . you think readers will be interested in it.
. . . you'll be able to include descriptive details.

It's time to get those descriptive details together.

BRIGHT Ideas

FOR GATHERING DESCRIPTIVE WORDS AND DETAILS

Draw your subject! Making a sketch, a diagram, a map, or even a portrait will help you spot easily overlooked details. Write captions for the different parts of your drawing.

Use the captions on your drawing. They can be starting points for brainstorming, freewriting, or building clusters of sights, smells, textures, tastes, sounds, and descriptive words.

Write recipes full of sensory details and descriptive words.. Exchange recipes with another writer. Then use your partner's recipe to draw a picture of her or his creation.

Order Your Details

Choose a way of ordering details that will lead readers from one part of your subject to another. Try these ideas for organization:

Spatial order: Take readers scene by scene through the space you are describing with words such as *at the top, in the distance, here, below.*

Categories: Lead readers through different aspects of your subject: from what you see to what you taste, from biggest to smallest, and so on.

Time order: If you're describing an event that takes place over time, use words such as *in the spring, back then, later that year,* and *now.*

DRAFT

Put It on Paper

In your first try at drafting your essay, keep in mind that an essay is organized in three sections: the introduction, the body, and the conclusion.

Here's How

To Build an Essay

Use Ginger's Pizzeria as a sample subject. The *goal* is to enter the Mayor's Essay Contest. The *purpose* is to convince people that Ginger's is a great place to eat. The intended *audience* is local kids and adults.

1. **Introduce your essay with a catchy first paragraph that does two jobs:**

   It gets the reader interested in your subject.

   It lets the reader know what point you will be making. The last sentence of the first paragraph is a good place to do this.

   I think of Ginger's Pizzeria as my second home. It's Ginger's attitude that gives me that feeling—the pizzeria is both a successful business and a great place to visit.

2. **Compose the body of the essay with paragraphs that tell about the subject. Most descriptive details go here.**

   First sentence of a body paragraph: *Walk in, and Ginger will give you a friendly wave.*

   First sentence of a body paragraph: *Sit down, and sniff the rich aromas.*

   First sentence of a body paragraph: *By the time you leave, the warm room seems to be a place you've always known.*

3. **End the essay with a paragraph that reminds readers of the point you made and leaves them with a closing thought.**

   Ginger's Pizzeria has succeeded where others have failed. The way Ginger treats her customers like family makes all the difference.

Essay

Get Some Distance

It's always a good idea to get some distance from your work before you revise it. And it's especially important with descriptive writing about a person, place, or thing that is important to you. Put your finished draft away for a day before you reread it. Tomorrow, with fresh eyes, you're more likely to notice rough spots, missing details, and confusing order.

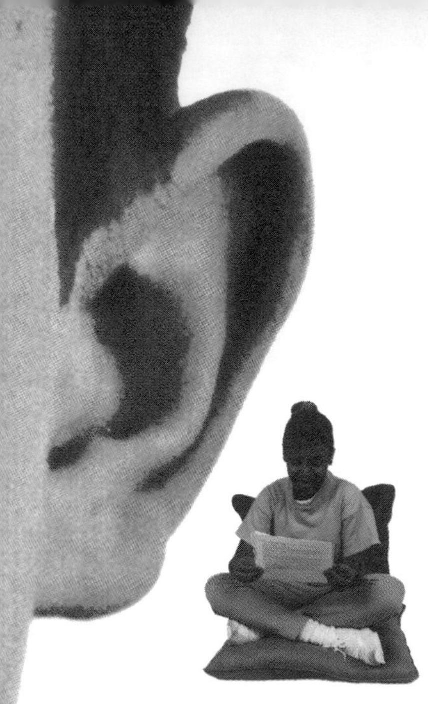

REVISE

Improve Your Essay

Now is the time to improve your writing by reworking your draft. To check the unity, or focus, of your essay, ask yourself some questions:

Answer these questions

- Does each paragraph add to the feeling about my subject that I'm trying to build?
- Does my essay lead readers from one descriptive detail to the next?
- Am I helping readers experience my subject with all their senses?

Listen to Your Editor

Ask someone to read your draft (or you can read it aloud to her or him). Make that person your editor and ask for reactions. For example:

Does your editor think that more details are needed?
Can your editor summarize the point you're trying to make?
What else would your editor need to know to share your experience more fully?

Make Your Writing Richer

If you want readers to feel they are "on location," replace general statements with exact information: not "The walls are covered with pictures," but "Jasmine Roy, a local artist and regular customer, has painted the walls with brightly coloured scenes of the town post office, cinema, and playground."

Get readers involved with your description. Replace vague nouns and verbs with precise ones. Rather than stating "The pizza is hot and inviting," zero in on the particulars: "A cloud of warmth rises from the steaming pizza."

Use a thesaurus to find exact words, but stick to synonyms that have the right connotation, or feeling. *Fragrant* and *smelly* are synonyms, but they have opposite connotations! **See page 330 for help with using a thesaurus.**

You can sometimes create a vivid image by comparing your subject to something it is not usually compared to: "Suddenly the kitchen was as noisy as a street full of jackhammers."

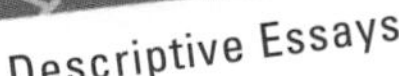

EDIT AND PROOFREAD

Fine-Tune Your Essay

In your revised draft, you chose the best descriptive words you could. Just be sure you haven't overdone it! Now is the time to edit out "adjective overload."

Cut redundant words.

Avoid words that mean almost the same thing. Pick the one you think works best:

He laughed **loudly** and **uproariously.**

Get rid of clutter

Too many adjectives can blur your picture:

Her mop of **long, shiny, wild, unevenly cut, flaming red** hair was tightly confined in a **brand-new jade green** hair net.

Proofread for Errors

Even the sharpest, clearest word becomes just a distraction if it's misspelled. So proofread carefully. **See proofreading marks on page 373.** You may also want help with the correct forms of adjectives and adverbs. **See pages 286 and 302.**

Do a final check for usage errors, too. A dictionary can help you make sure your connotations are on target.

inside
INFO

Occasional use only! It's O.K. to pack a description with an overload of adjectives for a special effect — but don't do it too often. Adjective overload is often useful in humorous pieces or tall tales.

PUBLISH

Present Your Essay

In addition to contest entries and pizza parlour promotions, you can find many ways to present your descriptive essays. Try writing a museum brochure or an article for a local or school newspaper.

Many Related Options

RELATED WRITING

You can use your ability to create vivid description in many kinds of writing. Descriptive paragraphs bring characters and settings to life in a fictional story or personal narrative. Or you might try one of these forms:

- Write a news report.
- Create a feature article.
- Try a travel article.
- Draft a restaurant review.
- Compose an art or music review.
- Write an advertisement.

WRITING

Scripts

Writing a script is like giving a party. You bring characters together and let them talk. But with a script, you can be sure everyone will say just what *you* want. A script has everything a short story has: characters, plot, setting, and so on. But instead of being read or told, it's written to be acted out. A script is a story meant to come alive. As a scriptwriter, you'll have a chance to learn, teach, and entertain all at the same time.

Scripts are used for . . .

soap operas
skits
sitcoms
movies
commercials
documentaries
plays

PREDRAFT

Spark Some Ideas

Want to describe a funny audition for the school band? Or the discovery of penicillin? Or a family in the year 2416? Write a script about it. You can take almost any situation, real or imagined, from literature or history or your own life, and turn it into a script.

You might not want to attempt a three-act play on your first try at scriptwriting. But you may feel comfortable writing a short scene, a skit, or an episode. You can find ideas all around you. Talk to people, read, watch movies and TV, check your journal, observe, recall. Here are some ideas to fire your imagination.

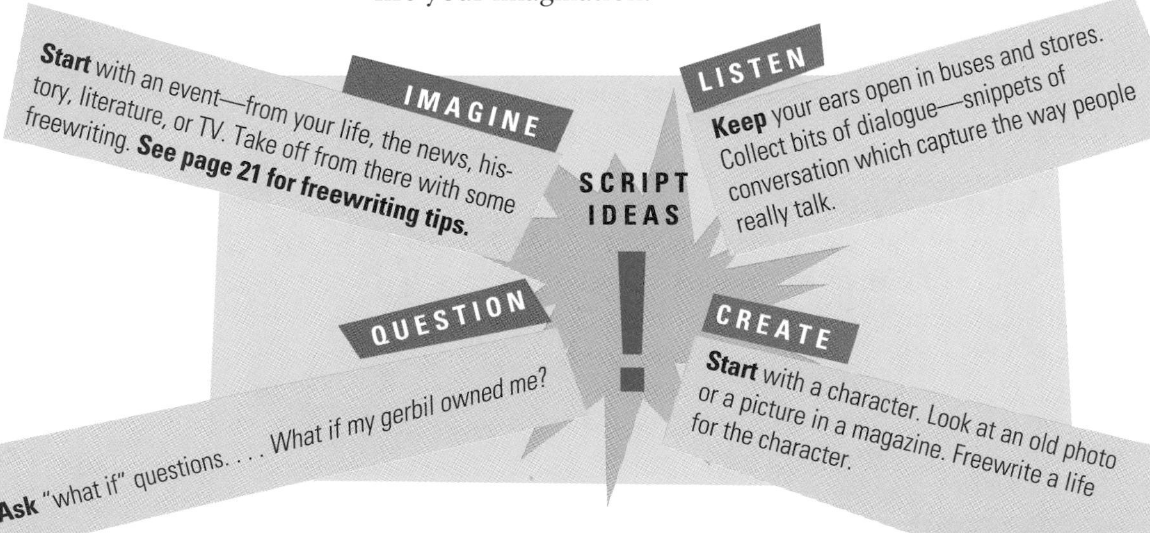

SCRIPT IDEAS
!
IMAGINE
Start with an event—from your life, the news, history, literature, or TV. Take off from there with some freewriting. **See page 21 for freewriting tips.**
LISTEN
Keep your ears open in buses and stores. Collect bits of dialogue—snippets of conversation which capture the way people really talk.
QUESTION
Ask "what if" questions. . . . What if my gerbil owned me?
CREATE
Start with a character. Look at an old photo or a picture in a magazine. Freewrite a life for the character.

Choose Your Script Idea

Remember that you can turn any set of circumstances, real or imagined, serious or silly, into a script. Anything goes, as long as you can make it *dramatic*. That is, you can tell the story through action and dialogue. Here are a few ideas:

what I saw through the microscope
a test of friendship
the party that never happened
the running shoes that got away
an audition to remember
a joke that misfired
the birth of a rap group

Once you have an idea, ask yourself questions about the characters, plot, setting, and theme. A script is a special kind of story, so you may want to review the information about story elements. **See page 62.**

What Makes It a Script?

Imagine you're sitting around gabbing with friends. If you write down what everybody says, will you end up with a script? Not really. The dialogue in a script has to build characters and action. It has to tell a story. *How* you tell the story is what sets a script apart from other kinds of storytelling. You build a script out of two parts:

Dialogue (the words your characters speak)

Sample Elsa: Oh come on, Peter. Why do you always have to make a big deal out of everything? It's only a little farther.

Directions

(your instructions to the performers about how to speak, sound, move, use props)

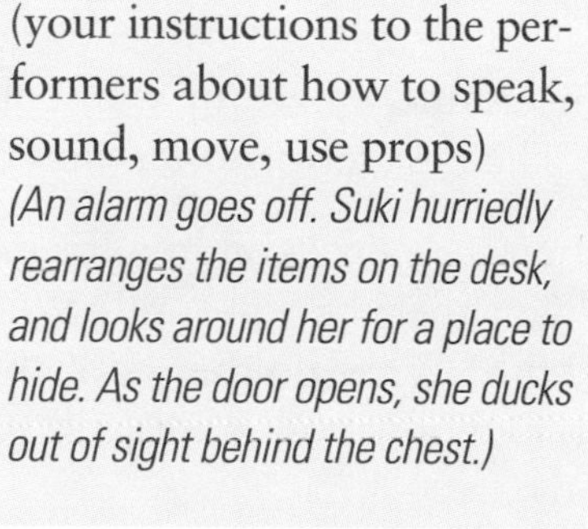

Sample *(An alarm goes off. Suki hurriedly rearranges the items on the desk, and looks around her for a place to hide. As the door opens, she ducks out of sight behind the chest.)*

Plan Your Script

There are several elements you'll need to consider as you begin to plan your script.

Characters

Your script will be easier to develop if you work with characters you feel you know—even if they're made up. You need to "hear" them talk so you can create believable dialogue. Your job will be more manageable if you limit yourself to three or four characters.

Setting

Choose a setting you know. Keep it simple. Your script isn't going to be produced on Broadway—not yet, at least! Think about what props and equipment you'll need, and about where and how you'll present your script. Such factors can make a difference in the kind of stage directions you give and how you set up a scene.

Plot

Decide on a plot or event that can be acted out. The simpler it is, the better. Rough out the order of the *actions* that will make up your plot. Figure out what will be the *climax,* or dramatic turning point of your story.

Exit, pursued by a bear.

—Stage direction in Shakespeare's *The Winter's Tale*

Who's in the House?

Your purpose in creating a script is to entertain people—to make your audience smile, shiver, or sob. You may want to inform them too. The best scripts often do both.

Who will be in your audience: children, teens, adults, or some of each? What's their background? What vocabulary are they familiar with? What do they care about? What you say in your script, and how you say it, will partly depend on your intended audience.

DRAFT

Build Your Script

You have your dramatic situation, your rough plan, and your intended audience in your head. It's time to get down to the nuts and bolts of drafting your script.

Here's How

To Develop a Script

1. **Create characters.** Make a chart for each character. Fill in details for categories like these: *physical appearance, voice, age, personality traits, style of dress, occupation, home, family, friends, behaviour, likes, dislikes.* Look at people on buses, in stores, in restaurants. Take notes on details that may help you round out your characters. You may find it helpful to visualize your characters by drawing sketches, especially of the main character.
2. **Get the "talk" right.** If the dialogue doesn't ring true—doesn't sound like real people talking—nothing else will work. So *listen* hard to people around you. Note or record words and expressions. Then listen as your characters begin to talk. Get into their minds, and practise talking like each one. Talk to a friend as if you were in your main character's shoes.
3. **Establish your setting.** Choose a specific place and time. It may help you visualize your setting if you draw a picture or a floor plan. Close your eyes and go there. See it in your mind's eye.
4. **Plot the plot.** Even a single scene needs a shape. Build your plot around the climax of your scene. In the *rising action* leading up to the climax, tell what your main character wants to have happen or to avoid. Reveal the dramatic *conflict*—what stands between your character and her desire, or what brings her face-to-face with the situation she feared. In the *falling action* following the climax, show how the problem is *resolved*, or worked out.
5. **Get in the mood.** Create an atmosphere that fits the events in the script. Does your story call for a spooky basement or a sunny beach? Think about what lighting, props, and sound effects you will need to set the mood.
6. **Write up your script.** Use a dramatic format to draft your dialogue and directions.

MOOD

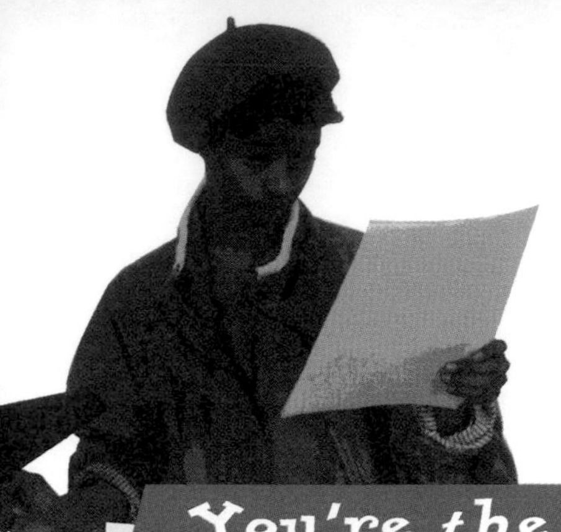

Every type of script has a special format, depending on whether it's for a live stage play, a movie, or a TV show. But you can just use an informal set-up like this as you write up your script:

ROSA *(in a frightened whisper)*: Are you really going in there?

MELISSA *(testing her flashlight)*: Sure. Why not?

You're the director, so . . .

. . . let your characters talk

Try to get to the point where you know your characters so well, you can just let them talk.

- Try starting in the middle. Beginnings can be hard.
- You may find that the characters begin to take on a life of their own. They will tell you what they would say next, and the scene will practically write itself.

. . . but control the action!

Guide your characters as you write.

- Stick to your rough outline, and check other prewriting notes.
- Tell *who, where, when, what* in the opening minutes.
- Picture the action. Put what you see and hear into directions.
- Become each character. Try speaking the words as you write.
- Don't like how things are going? Back up and try a different way.

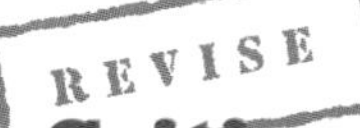
REVISE

Critique Your Script

Just rereading a script isn't enough. You have to find out how it "plays." Do the dialogue and the action work together to create the effect you're aiming for? To find out:

- Act it out by yourself. Move around the room as you read each character's part.
- Practise acting it out for an audience of classmates.

Ask Your Audience

Get comments from your classmates on your acted-out script. The following questions might be helpful:

Ask
these
questions

- Did the opening get your attention?
- Are the characters and dialogue believable?
- Could you follow the action?
- Were you satisfied with the ending?

Go over your own notes and your listeners' comments. Make changes you think will make the plot more exciting, the action clearer, and the characters stronger. Sharpen up those stage directions! Be sure they do the job.

Above all, keep working on the dialogue until it *sounds* right. Use contractions. Add pauses and interjections. Decide what kind of language a character would use: formal, with big words and long sentences? Or informal, careless, and slangy? Teens don't sound like their parents, and scientists usually don't sound like musicians. Keep these differences in mind as you revise your dialogue.

inside
INFO

"It's not wise to violate the rules until you know how to observe them."

—T. S. Eliot

EDIT AND PROOFREAD

Clean Up Your Script!

Keep these points in mind when you go over your script.

Edit the format

Check that every speaker is named and every direction is in parentheses.

Proofread all contractions

Dialogue is full of contractions. Check all of them to be sure they're really contractions and every apostrophe's in the right place. **Pages 283, 293, and 354 will help you with contractions.**

PUBLISH

Present Your Script

Here are ideas for sharing your script. Make as many copies of it as you'll need to do one of the following:

- Share your script with your class or the drama club.
- Arrange a broadcast over the school P.A. system.
- Audiotape or videotape a performance.

Let Me Entertain You!

RELATED WRITING

Your ability to write scripts can give rise to many different kinds of presentations. Here are a few you could try:

- Movie
- Sitcom
- TV show
- Documentary
- Commercial
- Radio theatre

Book Reviews

A book review gives you a chance to become a critic of someone else's writing. It's your personal response to a book, along with information about it and an analysis of its strengths and weaknesses. A review lets you share a neat book with friends or warn them about a time-waster.

PREDRAFT

Spend Time Browsing

You're going to spend a lot of time with your book, both in reading it and in writing the review. So if you have a choice, take time to choose a book you'll enjoy writing about.

Tips on Choosing Your Book

You can follow these guidelines when choosing a book:

- Sample the book: read the first paragraph and skim a few pages at random to see if you like the way it's written.
- Read the book jacket summary.
- Check the wording of the title for clues about the book.
- Choose an author whose work you like.
- Choose a genre you enjoy (mystery, science fiction, biography), or sample one you're curious about.

The kind of book you choose will affect the way you write your book review. For example, a review of a novel could include a look at characters, setting, theme, and plot; a review of a biography could include a discussion of how honestly and vividly the subject's life is presented.

Secrets for Successful Reading

Try to give yourself plenty of time to read the book once or even twice.

Try to read carefully and with concentration.

Try to take notes, write down page numbers, and place bookmarks at important points.

Avoid waiting until the last minute, rushing to the library, and choosing the thinnest book you can find.

Avoid skimming quickly or absent-mindedly .

Avoid trying to keep it all in your head, or you'll end up flipping frantically through the book.

Plan Your Book Review

Suppose you've chosen and read your book. What do you need to consider as you plan your review?

Respond to the Book You'll want to include your feelings and thoughts about the book in your review. Try freewriting about your impressions in your journal or in a reading log. Record any questions you may have. This can help you decide what to focus on in your review. For example, for the novel *Jasmin* by Jan Truss, you might write the following: The action of the story kept me wondering what would happen next. Will Jasmin survive in the wilderness?

Explore the Book What's really going on between the covers of your book? There are questions you should try to answer no matter what genre you've chosen. Is this book clearly written? well organized? Then, you'll need to look at any special features of your particular book. For a novel, you might explore the most important story elements. Your review could focus on one or more of these elements.

Need a new approach? Different kinds of books call for different kinds of reading. **See page 130** to learn some tips on reading different genres.

Story Elements

Setting

Where does the story take place? When is the story happening? Drawing diagrams or pictures of the settings in different parts of your book may help you visualize them.

Theme

What did the author want you to experience, feel, or understand through reading this book? A theme can be about specific people and particular situations or about life in general. Here is a possible theme for *Jasmin:* Living your life as you please isn't always possible because you have responsibilities to others as well as to yourself.

Characters

You learn about the characters who take part in a story through their thoughts, feelings, actions, and interactions with other characters. To learn about the main character in *Jasmin,* a reader might ask these questions: What were Jasmin's beliefs and feelings? What did she do? How did she change? Try answering similar questions for the most important characters in your book.

Plot

What happens in the story? What's the action, the sequence of events that grabs your attention as it builds to a climax?

Purpose and Audience

The purpose of your review is to inform readers about a book you have read and to provide your analysis and opinion of it. Think about who will read your book review—a fellow student, younger student, or parents? Think about what your readers would like to know about this book.

Focus on important Elements to get your slant!

What's Your Slant?

You've written down your impressions of the book. You've explored the story elements. Now you may want a *slant*—a way of approaching your review that will make your audience enjoy hearing or reading it. One or two story elements of your book may be more important to the overall work than others. Focus on those important elements, using quotations or specific examples as supporting details to give readers a "feel" for the book. You'll want to reread sections of your book to gather such supporting details.

The chart below, using the novel *Forbidden City* by William Bell as its example, focusses on plot as the important story element and offers details in support of this focus.

Story Elements		Supporting Details
Setting	busy streets and squares of Beijing, China	
Characters	Alex and his new Chinese friends are brave and loyal—they willingly risk their lives for each other.	
Plot	the suspense of wondering whether Alex will get arrested and killed	Alex wears a Chinese jacket, hat, and sunglasses so he won't be noticed in a crowd. (page 38) Alex witnesses the massacre at Tiananmen Square. "The tanks came on like obscene mutant insects in science fiction movies." (page 116)
Theme	People still need to work to bring about freedom and justice.	

Think About Organization

A good writing plan can help you draft your book review. Here is a plan that has three parts.

Introduction gives title, author, brief summary of the book.
Body focusses on one or two of the main story elements: setting, characters, plot, or theme.
Conclusion gives a response and makes a recommendation.

Here are some different ideas for writing plans. Check with your teacher about trying one of these creative forms.

Write a journal entry for a character.
Record an interview with one or more characters.
Dramatize an incident from your book.

DRAFT

Get Ready to Draft

Gather your pens, sharpen your pencils, have your paper ready. Gear up your computer, or turn on the tape-recorder if you prefer to tape your draft. Finally, gather all your pre-drafting papers and organizing schemes. Now you're ready.

Here's How

To Draft Your Book Review

As you write, remember these things:

1. **Let your thoughts flow.** There's no need to worry about errors just yet.
2. **Follow your writing plan.** But keep in mind that a mental detour may take you down pathways of thinking that can make your review more interesting. The drafting stage is a discovery stage. You may discover things that hadn't occurred to you before.
3. **Take a break if you get stuck.** Don't be afraid to rethink your writing plan.
4. **Try these tips for easier drafting.** *If you're writing by hand,* don't erase—draw a single line through unwanted material. You may want it later! Skip lines, leave margins. *If you're at the keyboard,* don't stop to correct errors. Double-space, leave margins. *If you're using a tape-recorder,* speak freely and let your thoughts flow. Don't worry about corrections. Wait until you're finished to rewind and listen.

REVISE

Improve Your Draft

Your first draft is a rough draft. Now it's time to smooth it out. You can use these questions as you reread your draft with a partner:

- Is there a beginning, middle, and ending to my review?
- Did I give the title and author in my first paragraph?
- Do I include enough supporting details from the book?
- Does my ending give a personal response?
- What do you like best about my review? List its strengths.
- What do I need to work on? List its weaknesses.

See page 28 for a revising checklist.

Rethink Your Book Review

Discuss your partner's reactions to your draft and look over the list of strengths and weaknesses that you created. Use the revising strategies in the chart to improve your book review. **(Look at the sample draft on page 87 to see how these changes strengthened this writer's review.)**

Revising Strategies	
Reword vague or awkward words, phrases, or sentences.	O.K.: Peter Dickinson's exciting novel *Eva* is a really great story . . . Better: Peter Dickinson's novel *Eva* is a clever, creative story about the future.
Add missing details.	O.K.: . . . about a teenager who awakens to find herself a chimpanzee. Better: Eva, a teenager, awakens after a car accident to find herself living in the body of a chimpanzee.
Cut unnecessary or irrelevant details.	O.K.: Without affecting the story by too much talk, this novel manages to raise many questions that we should all consider. Better: Without ruining the story, this novel raises important questions.

The following is a draft of a book review for *Eva*, a novel by Peter Dickinson.

Introduction

Peter Dickinson's exciting novel Eva is a really great story about a teenager who awakens to find herself a chimpanzee. She is able to communicate with other humans through a computerized voice synthesizer. She can also communicate with chimps.

Body

When the story opens, all chimpanzees are living in captivity and being studied by researchers. A few are also being used in advertisements shown on the shaper, a kind of TV. Eva learns that she too must appear on TV because the advertiser has paid all her hospital bills. At first, she co-operates with the humans. But she gradually becomes more of a chimpanzee. She finally decides to escape and lead her group back to the wild. After some exciting setbacks, she manages to set up the troop in a natural setting.

Conclusion

Without affecting the story by too much talk, this novel manages to raise many questions that we should all consider. For example, it asks us to think about how people should treat not just chimpanzees, but all animals. During one news confrence, Eva "tapped her chest. 'This belongs to a chimp called Kelly,' she said. 'You people stole it from her.'" (p. 143) The novel also makes readers wonder what kind of a future the people of today are building. Eva is an exciting book that should be read and discussed by both teenagers and adults alike.

Revise Your Draft

By now your rough draft probably looks like a tangle of words, circles, and arrows. You'll want to reread your marked-up draft to make sure your thinking is clear before you copy it on a clean sheet of paper. Keep any additional quotations and details nearby for easy insertion into your review. Look at the *Eva* review draft on page 87. The book review became much more likely to grab a reader's attention when the writer decided to begin with a quotation.

EDIT AND
PROOFREAD

Fine-Tune Your Book Review

Looking for more tips on fine-tuning your review? See page 30.

Once you think your draft is interesting and makes sense, it's time to polish it. Here are some points you might think about as you edit your review.

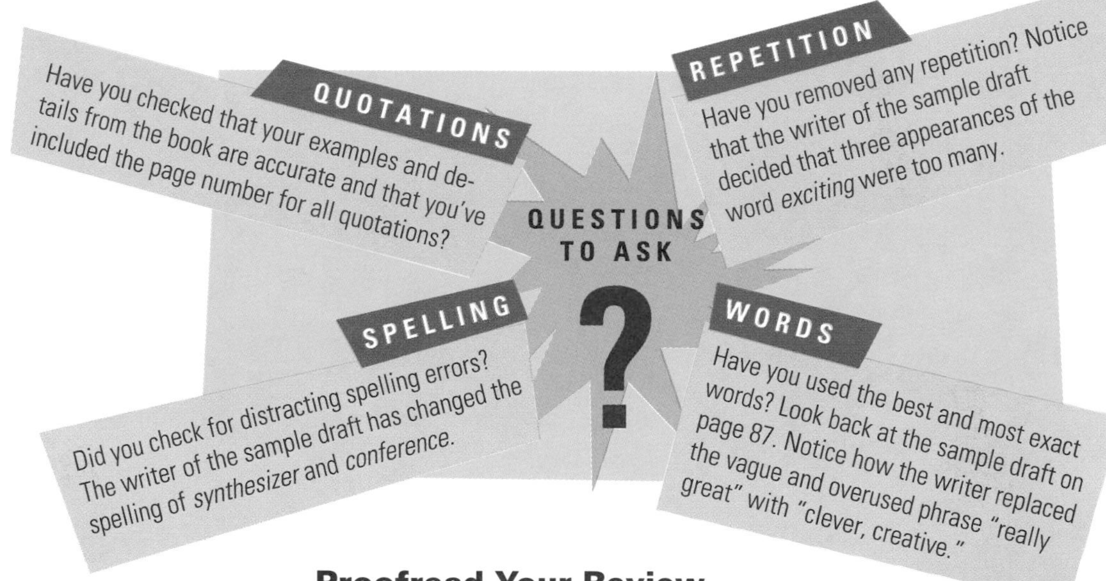
QUESTIONS TO ASK
?
QUOTATIONS
Have you checked that your examples and details from the book are accurate and that you've included the page number for all quotations?
REPETITION
Have you removed any repetition? Notice that the writer of the sample draft decided that three appearances of the word *exciting* were too many.
SPELLING
Did you check for distracting spelling errors? The writer of the sample draft has changed the spelling of *synthesizer* and *conference*.
WORDS
Have you used the best and most exact words? Look back at the sample draft on page 87. Notice how the writer replaced the vague and overused phrase "really great" with "clever, creative."

Proofread Your Review

Pay attention to your use of quotation marks, especially if you have used *a quote within a quote,* like the one in the last paragraph of the *Eva* review:

" . . . 'This belongs to a chimp called Kelly,' she said, 'You people stole it from her.' "

PUBLISH

Present Your Book Review

Here are some ways to share your book review.

Publication: Submit your review to a newspaper or magazine.

Bulletin board: Organize a bulletin board in the school library for posting book reviews.

Poster: Add maps and drawings to your text and create a poster about your book.

Book jacket: Find or draw a picture for the front cover, choose lines from your personal response for the back cover, and write your book review on the front and back flaps.

Pen pal: Start a book review exchange with pen pals in another school, city, or country.

RELATED WRITING

Beyond Book Reviews

Your ability to decribe your personal responses and to analyse strengths and weaknesses can be applied to situations other than book reviews. Why not try writing another type of review to help readers decide how they'd like to spend their leisure time, such as a concert, play, film, or video review.

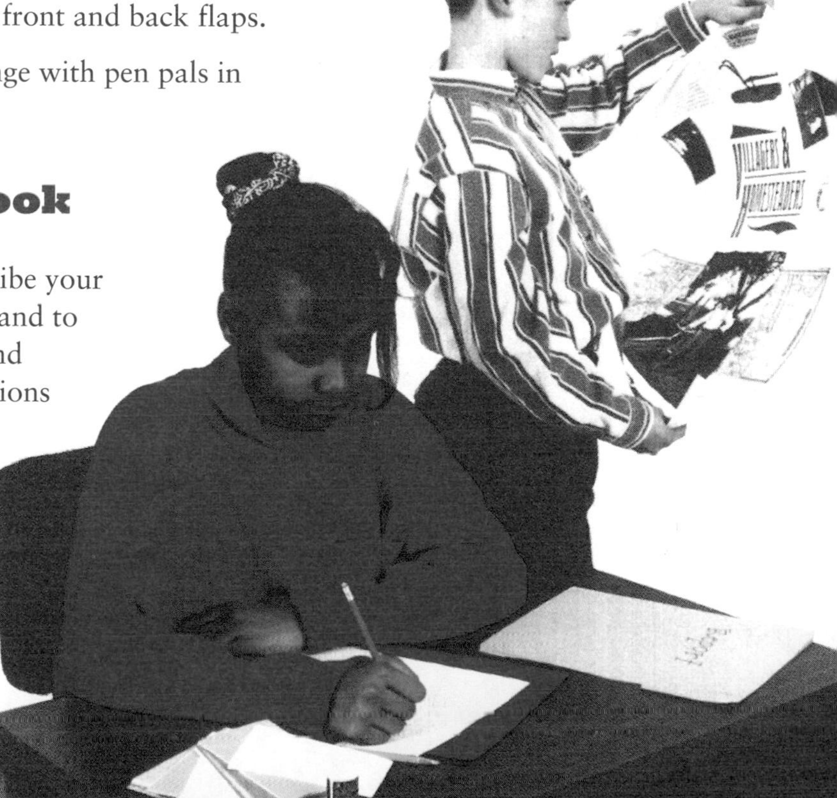
VILLAGERS &
HOMESTEADERS

WRITING

Research Reports

You're presenting information and your own ideas about a subject when you write a research report. You get to play detective as you gather information, organize it, think about it, evaluate it, and add your own thoughts. In presenting your report, you inform your readers by showing what you've learned.

PREDRAFT

Yikes! A Research Report

The focus of this section is just one kind of presentation, the kind that is often a school assignment: the written research report.

Do you have a different kind of research assignment? Help is at hand! See the section on researching that begins on **page 226.**

Recognize any of the following characters?

Panicky Pete

Report? How many pages? ... But I can't ... I don't know ... Due *when?* ... Help!

Blank Paige

Report? I don't have a single idea! Give me the topic—and the information too.

Last-Minute Lee

Report? Due in three weeks? No problem. I've got at least twenty days before I need to begin.

A research report assignment doesn't have to be a signal for panic or delay. Writing a research report can get you interested in new information and ideas. It's an opportunity for you to become an expert on a new subject—to hunt for facts, track down knowledge, and enrich your understanding.

Select a Subject

If you can choose the subject of your research report, think about what you *need* to know or *want* to find out. It's often the case, however, that a teacher assigns a general category (like ancient civilizations, vision, animal defenses) and then asks students to choose subjects within that area.

In choosing your subject, you'll want to consider several points.

It's a
help
if

. . . you can find information about it. You don't want to struggle just to locate a single book or article on a too-narrow topic.

. . . you are not overwhelmed by information overload. You don't want to stare at stacks of sources on a subject that's much too broad.

. . . you are personally interested in it. You don't want to spend time reading and learning about a subject you don't like.

Survey Some Sources

Check the library computer or card catalogue to see the range of topics that fall under your subject. Look these over and list some possible ideas. Besides such general sources as encyclopedias, almanacs, and non-fiction books on the subject, spend some time with magazines. Check the periodical index to see which magazines your library stocks. There are magazines on almost any subject you can name: travel, music, skateboards, history, computer games, astronomy. Find a magazine on your general subject. Then skim through several issues to see what kinds of articles are featured.

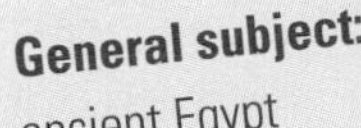

General subject:
ancient Egypt

Possible research ideas:
the step pyramids
everyday life on the Nile
the queen Cleopatra
the importance of cats
mummies

Checking in at the library? Learn detailed procedures for library researching. **See page 228.**

inside INFO

The three most important rules researchers follow while collecting information are: organize, organize, and organize!

Follow the Subject Trail

Once you've got a few subject ideas that you think might work, take a little time to check them out. Then pick the one you like best, and see whether it can be narrowed down any further.

Investigate

Investigate non-print sources. Include videos, museum visits, and interviews with experts in your research.

Question

Question the librarian. A librarian can help you find out what books and magazines are actually available. Ask one to direct you to new sources of information.

Talk

Talk with a knowledgeable person. You can gain special insight on your subject by talking with an expert. For example, Rehana's report will be about animals' defenses. She talks with a neighbour who is a bird-watcher and learns that birds have several interesting ways of protecting themselves.

Plan Your Attack

Think about your audience. Your main audience will be your teacher if this is a school report. But your report might also wind up being read by classmates or presented at a science fair.

Think about your purpose. You'll be presenting the information you've gathered and your own thoughts about your subject. You'll try to show what you've learned as clearly and as interestingly as you can. So ask yourself: Am I really interested in this subject? Can I make it interesting to my readers? Your own enthusiasm for your subject is what will hold your readers' attention.

Follow the Subject Trail . . . Investigate

What Would You Like to Know?

A list of questions you hope to answer in your report will help you gather your information. You may find it easier to limit yourself to six questions for starters. You can always add or change questions as you do your research. Try to focus on the essential information about your subject.

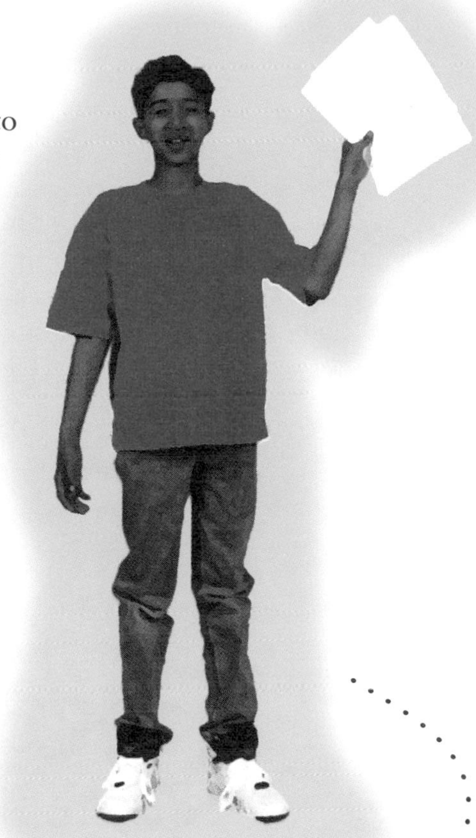

For example, on the subject of early animated cartoons, you might want to answer questions like the ones below.

Answer these questions ▶

- How were the first animated cartoons made?
- Who were the pioneers in the field of cartooning?
- What were the earliest animated cartoons like?
- Who were the first famous cartoon characters?
- Where were the first cartoons shown?
- What were audiences' reactions?

question ... and talk

Here's How To Gather information

The library is often the best place to start looking for answers. **For detailed help with research, see pages 228–239.**

1. **Get an overview of your subject** by looking at general reference sources, such as encyclopedias and almanacs.
2. **Use key words** to locate subject cards in the card catalogue or subject listings in the computer catalogue. They'll direct you to non-fiction books on your subject. *Subject:* Why the eye sees colours. *Key Words:* Vision; Colour
3. **Use the *Readers' Guide to Periodical Literature*** or a computer catalogue of periodicals to find magazines on your topic. (The library may have back issues on microfilm.)
4. **Look for videotapes** of television documentaries. Programs about science, cultures, history, and more are available at many libraries.

Keep Track of Your Sources

Have you ever torn your hair out, saying, "I know I saw that fact somewhere, but I can't remember where!" Create a system to track the information you find as you gather sources.

Source Card

3
Nielsen, Lewis T. "Mosquitoes Unlimited." *Natural History,* July 1991, pp. 4–6.

One tried-and-true way of keeping track is by using two separate sets of cards: *source cards* and *note cards.* Number each source card, and add the following information to each:

- the name of the author or authors
- the title of the work (and of the magazine or anthology if it's part of a collection of works)
- the publisher and place of publication
- the copyright date (and the date of publication if it's different from the copyright date)

On your note cards, write the answers you find to any questions you have as you read print sources, interview experts, watch videos, or visit museums.

Here's How To Store information on Note Cards

1. **Label each card with a key word or phrase that refers to one of your questions.** Your question is this, How do mosquitoes bite? Write *biting* at the top of the card.
2. **When you find an answer in a source, write the number of that source card on your note card.**
3. **Jot down the information that answers the question.** Try breaking up the question if you find that the answer has several parts. Label a separate card for each part.
4. **Write the number of the page in the book, magazine, and so on, where you found each fact or quotation.**

Note Card

Biting
(Source 3)
Cdn. researchers went unprotected into test area
Got 9000 bites per min
Could lose half of body's blood in 2 h p. 4

Tips for Using Note Cards

Save time and space by being brief. Use abbreviations and phrases rather than complete sentences where you can.

Use your own words. By *paraphrasing,* or using your own words, you'll be thinking, not just copying the information.

If you do want to copy a phrase or sentence exactly, remember to put quotation marks around it. **See page 355.**

For more suggestions on note taking, see page 261.

Organize Your Information

You've got a pile of note cards with information that answers your questions. Now how will you organize it? You can make a *working outline:* a list that shows how your facts and ideas are related.

You can organize your note cards by grouping together all the answers to each of your questions. Then use these groupings to make your outline. Move them around until you have an order that makes sense.

Each *main topic* (after a Roman numeral—I, II, III) can be turned into a paragraph or section of the report. *Subtopics* (after capital letters), can be divided into *subsections* (after Arabic numerals—1, 2, 3) and *details* (after small letters). These show what information will be included.

Topic: Mosquitoes

I. Kinds of mosquitoes
II. Life cycle of a mosquito
III. Biting behaviours
IV. Where mosquitoes live
V. Dangers posed by mosquitoes
VI. Useful things mosquitoes do

III. Biting behaviours

A. Only females bite
  1. Need blood to reproduce
B. Biting process
  1. How mosquitoes bite
    a. Six mouth parts pierce skin
    b. Damage small blood vessels
    c. Two pumps in head suck up blood
  2. Effect on victim
    a. Saliva causes itching and swelling

DRAFT

Get the Basics Down

Now that you've collected and outlined your information, it's time to begin your rough draft. But you've got so much to say! Knowing that you have a plan will help. Using a standard organization similar to that of a letter or essay will make writing easier and help make your information clear to your audience. The basics include three parts.

1. The *introduction* is usually a single paragraph. Tell your readers what the report is about and use a strong lead to get them interested.
2. The *body* of the report is made of several paragraphs, each built around one main idea. Follow the order of your outline.

Report

3. The *conclusion* is a paragraph that sums up the main points you made in the body of the report. Try to leave your reader saying, "This really is a fascinating subject."

You can begin by drafting the introduction or the conclusion or any of the paragraphs in between. The sentences don't have to be exactly right at this stage. You might even write yourself notes about the parts you need to work on later.

inside **INFO**

Feel free to improve your working outline as you draft. And plan illustrations. Note places where a drawing, graph, map, or diagram could help you explain an idea. You can draft the illustrations, too: make sketches that you'll later turn into finished pieces of art.

Let Your Outline Guide You

An outline will help you as you write your draft. Develop each subtopic into a paragraph, using the supporting details from your outline to construct the paragraph's supporting sentences. **See page 358 for more information about paragraphs.**

For example, you could turn this part of your outline...

III. Biting behaviours
- A. Only females bite
  1. Need blood to reproduce
- **B. Biting process**
  1. How mosquitoes bite
     a. Six mouth parts pierce skin
     b. Damage small blood vessels
     c. Two pumps in head suck up blood
  2. Effect on victim
     a. Saliva causes itching and swelling

...into this paragraph:

A mosquito bite is more than a simple sting. As a mosquito stabs its victim, six long mouth parts pierce the skin. Once under the skin, these parts drill tiny holes in small blood vessels. The mosquito's saliva keeps the blood from clotting while two pumps in the head eagerly suck up the blood. It's the saliva that causes the itching and swelling that makes the victim miserable.

REVISE

Reread, Rewrite, Refine

Now it's time to read your draft all the way through. You'll want to look for ways to rewrite and reorganize that will improve how it flows. Highlight your most interesting information. Just because a research report is factual doesn't mean it must be dull. Look for places to make vivid comparisons and to use lively language. Ask yourself the questions below to help you with your revisions.

Wondering how to make your subject interesting? Need help describing the sound of the arctic mosquito in flight? See **page 69** for tips on descriptive writing.

What if ▶
. . . I do more research about . . . ?
. . . I connect the ideas more clearly in . . . ?
. . . I cut the part about . . . ?
. . . I make my introduction stronger by . . . ?
. . . I make my conclusion more interesting by . . . ?

Confer with a Partner

Share your draft with a partner. Ask him or her these questions before you decide which parts of your report need fixing.

- What did you find especially interesting?
- Where is more (or clearer) information needed?
- Which points seem unnecessary or out of order?
- What else would you like to know about this subject?

Advice from the Zone

Dear Z:

I'm doing a research report on cats in ancient Egypt. Most of my info comes from encyclopedias, but I also found a great article by an archaeologist. Problem: She says everything I want to say in words I wish I'd thought of first. How much can I . . . well . . . borrow?

—Copy Cat

Dear C.C.:

Careful! This is *your* report, so the language in it should be *yours*. But there's another reason not to copy—it's against the law. If you put an author's exact words in your report without enclosing them in quotation marks and telling who said them, you are *plagiarizing*. And plagiarism is . . . well . . . stealing. Solution: Go ahead and jazz up your report by *quoting* a couple of great lines from that great article. Just be sure to credit that great writer in a footnote! Then *paraphrase*—that is, restate your information, using your own words.
O.K.?

Z.

Come to a Conclusion

Are you satisfied with the final paragraph of your report? Don't let your report come to a screeching halt or run out of gas with a weak sentence. Try to end with a general statement about the information and your ideas. A good conclusion will have an impact. It can also show your readers that you are knowledgeable and confident about your subject. Experiment with endings. The following examples show two ways to leave your readers feeling satisfied. Try them out in your report.

Conclude by stating the importance or value of your subject.

The mosquito has been responsible for more human disease and death than any other animal. This tiny, fascinating enemy continues to threaten the health of people all over the world.

Conclude by making a statement about the future of your subject.

Mosquitoes continue to thrive even though millions of dollars are spent each year to control them. And with species developing resistances to pesticides, we are a long way from winning our battle with mosquitoes.

EDIT AND PROOFREAD

Check for Accuracy

Be a considerate writer. Double-check the accuracy of your facts as you prepare a final version of your report, making sure to check as well for grammar, usage, and spelling. **See page 30 for tips on fine-tuning.** Go back to your notes, or original sources, to make sure that you've copied all dates, numbers, names, and terms accurately. As you edit your prose, remember the pictures! Check any maps, charts, time lines, diagrams, and other drawings you've included in your report. Ask yourself these questions about them:

- Does each drawing have a title?
- Are all labels and captions clear and accurate?
- Are the drawings neat, not smudged or crooked?

Make final versions of your illustrations on separate sheets, and cut them out. At the last stage of preparing your report, glue each piece of art securely on the page where it belongs.

Here's How

To Make a Bibliography

The last page of a research report is usually a bibliography, an alphabetical list of the sources you used. If you made separate bibliography cards, creating this page will be easy.

Assemble Your Sources

1. **Arrange the cards so that they are alphabetized by the authors' last names.** If there is no author, alphabetize by the first main word of the title.
2. **List your sources according to the styles below.** If you're typing, double-space. Indent under the first line of each entry.

1. Book with one author:

Blodgett, E. D. Alice Munroe. Boston: Twayne, 1988.

2. Book with more than one author:

Elwood, Ann, and Linda C. Wood. Windows in Space. New York: Walker, 1982.

3. Article in a magazine:

Daglish, Brenda. "A Matter of Interest." Maclean's, February 15, 1993, pp. 36–37.

4. Article in a newspaper:

Smith, Beverley. "Canadians Skate to Gold Medal." The Globe and Mail, March 11, 1993, p. A1.

5. Article in an encyclopedia:

Humber, William. "Bicycling." The Canadian Encyclopedia, 1988, ed.

6. Video or film:

Shooting Stars. Videotape. National Film Board of Canada (Toronto), 1987. 49 min., 30 sec.

7. Radio or television program:

"Haida Gwai—Islands of the People." Nature. PBS, December 19, 1992.

8. Interview:

Delaney, Daphne (musician). Personal interview. Toronto, April 10, 1992.

PUBLISH

Present Your Report

If your research report is a school assignment, then your teacher may have guidelines for preparing a final copy. Follow those guidelines, or use these:

1. Start with a title page. Centre the title of your report about ten centimetres from the top of the page. Write your name, your class, and the date beneath the title.
2. Number each page in the upper right corner.
3. Double-space if you're typing your report. Leave margins of at least two and a half centimetres on each side and at the top and bottom of the page.
4. Staple or fasten the pages to a cover. Write the report title and your name on the cover, and add an illustration if you wish.

For other possible presentations, see page 32.

RELATED WRITING

Informative Essay

Another way to share facts and ideas with readers is with an essay that informs or explains. Like a research report, an essay has three main parts: an introduction, a body, and a conclusion. In an essay you express your own point of view, or opinion (for example, elephants in the wild must be protected), and you support your idea with factual information.

WRITING

Feature Articles

A feature article is a slice of life served up by a newspaper or magazine. It takes its readers behind the scenes of a news event to meet the people, see the places, listen to the talk, and get a peek at what's really happening. Features often include photographs or illustrations—to give readers an added sense of the whole picture.

PREDRAFT

What Makes a Feature?

Are the Me2s playing tonight? That's news. How does a rock group get ready for a concert? That's the kind of "news behind the news" you'd find in a feature article. Your purpose is to inform and entertain when you write a feature. That doesn't mean you have to keep your readers laughing; just give them the facts and keep them interested.

In the chart below, the first column contains facts you would find in a news article about a baseball team. The second column contains the very different facts you might find in a feature article.

News	Features
Baseball score	What the star player is like
Who was playing	How the coach motivates the team
Who scored when	Why the team is on a winning streak
Where the game was played	Inside the locker room after the big win
How the crowd behaved	The history of the baseball team

MILLION SELLER
STEPS

News gets old fast. It's usually feature articles that hang on—that get clipped out, passed around, and saved. But writing *copy,* or text, for both news and features must be done quickly to meet a deadline. Your school magazine or newspaper can't afford to hold the presses!

Hunt for Subjects

Writing feature articles is a great way to investigate subjects you've wondered about and to spread the word to others. Features are about more than headlines—they're about life. So where do you look for topic ideas?

Can't think of a topic? Don't despair. **See page 20** for strategies for finding ideas.

You Can Find Subjects . . .

Around you: Observe and be curious. Ask *who, what, where, when, why, how,* and *how much* about the things you see and hear.

In newspapers and magazines: Think about the lives and stories *behind* the headlines. Look at the classified ads too: What are people buying? selling?

In conversations: Talk to people. See what interests them.

In your own head: Skim your journal and your writing folder. Take a look at your interests and hobbies. You're probably already an expert on a subject other people would like to read about.

To get your ideas flowing, try a few brainstorming exercises.

Create a list of "What if" questions.

What if ▶

. . . I could be invisible? Where would I want to be?

. . . I could follow someone around for a day? Whom would I pick?

. . . I could make people aware of a serious problem in my school? What would it be?

When you have a list of five or six possible subjects, look it over and decide which one interests you most. Keep the list, though—it may give you a jump start on future deadlines! Stow it away in your writing folder.

Feature This

Once you've found a subject you like, test it with these steps: Will you be able to get the facts you'll need? Check with friends. Are they interested in your subject? Most important of all, do you really want to write about it?

Narrow Your Subject

It is easier to write about a narrow topic than a broad one. To narrow a topic down to a manageable size, you could:

- write a few headlines.
- write an ending to see where you're going.
- write a single question your article will answer.
- write phrases that summarize your subject. Be tough on yourself. Get more and more specific.

Target Your Audience

Remember that your purpose in a feature article is to inform and entertain. Consider your audience—are they your school friends? the general public? young children? Thinking about your future readers now will help you decide what to put in, what to leave out, and how to illustrate your feature.

inside
INFO

"I find that a great part of the information I have was acquired by looking up something and finding something else on the way."
—Franklin P. Adams

Get the Facts

Feature articles are about the outside world. You have to go out into that world to find your material. Ask yourself these questions: What do I want to know about this topic? What will my readers want to know? Make a list of questions, and keep them handy as you search for information.

Do Research

Go to the library. Check newspapers, magazines, books, computer data banks. **See page 228 for tips on doing research.**

Interview

Find people in the know and talk to them. Ask them to refer you to other people who might add to your information. **See pages 164 and 249 for practical advice on interviewing.**

Observe

Hang out where the action is. Look. Listen. Take notes. Think about what you can "tell" by using a picture instead of words.

Put Your Facts Together

A bunch of facts, even interesting facts, does not make a feature article. You've got to pull the facts together and put your own special slant on them. The slant will grow out of choices you make at this point.

Here's How

To Find a Slant

1. **Talk about the subject with a friend.** What main points do you emphasize? Write them down and then circle the most important one.
   Subject*—How people choose running shoes*
   By discussing the subject, you find that many people buy running shoes in response to ads, fashion, and peer pressure; for prestige; or as a means of self-expression.
   Main point*—People choose running shoes for reasons that have nothing to do with sports.*
2. **Take time to think about your subject.** Figure out how you feel—amused, shocked, angry, serious, excited, sad, impressed—and how you want your reader to feel. Make a list of these words, and then circle one or two that best describe your feeling.
   Feelings*—amused, superior, curious, enthusiastic*
3. **Decide what point of view would best convey that feeling.** Should you approach your subject as a critic? a fan? a casual observer? Will you be discovering the facts along with your reader, or are you an expert explaining them? Write down the possibilities, and circle the one you think will work best.
   Point of view*—fan, trend-setter, critic, fashion rebel*
4. **Examine what you've done.** Combine your circled items from the three lists (main point + feeling + point of view), and you have your slant.
   My slant*—Non-sporting reasons why people buy running shoes + amused + critic*

Plan Your Strategy

Writing a feature article is like inventing something. There's no fixed way to organize your facts; you can arrange them in any way that makes sense. Your thoughts and angle can shape the facts into something new—and all yours. Just keep in mind that your article, like any invention, won't be very useful if it doesn't *work*. Whatever method you choose should order your feature so that it flows smoothly and develops your subject clearly.

Here are some arrangements you might try:

Organization	Topic
Time order	A day in the life of a firefighter
	How a gymnast prepares for a big meet
Spatial order	A tour of a harness-racing stable
	The new recycling centre
A series of scenes	Behind the scenes at a radio station
	A visit to city hall

Buried alive under a mountain of notes and details? See page 24 for help in digging yourself out and setting your ideas in order.

DRAFT

Write Your Copy

You've been assigned to write a feature article for the school newspaper. Your deadline is getting close. Your editor is getting nervous. It's time to write a first draft.

Advice from the Zone

Dear Z:

S.O.S.! I'm supposed to write a feature article on this year's swim team for my school newspaper. Right now my article is going under for the third time. Even I can't stand to read it all the way through! Can you rescue it?
—Feature Article Draftwriter

Dear F.A.D.:

Always remember Z's golden rule—never panic! Try these steps to administer CPR to your feature.

Start at an exciting moment—in the middle of a meet or near the end of a race—to hook your reader. Then you can flash back to earlier details.

Don't just string your notes together. Use your slant to shape your facts.

Think of your article as a conversation between you and your reader: use *I* and *you*.

Try using the present tense—"Dawn is just breaking as the swimmers, silent and serious, gather by the pool"—for a "You Are There" feeling.

Show action in your illustrations. Remember the old saying that a picture is worth a thousand words.

Hope this resuscitates your article and gets it back to shore.

Z.

Coping with Copy

Here are some tips for building a great article:

Herbert Melnick has changed the face of turtle racing for all time.

Melnick's mansion sits on a beautifully landscaped estate. Shrubs are pruned to resemble his favourite turtles from years past—Minky, Theo, and seven-time world champion Tina. "There'll never be another turtle like Tina," Melnick says sadly.

So, the next time you pass a turtle on the side of the road or behind a pet store window, remember that beneath that humble shell may beat the heart of a champion.

The Lead

The opening of an article is called the *lead.* That's because it leads the reader straight into the article—no turns or detours. You can use the lead to hook your readers, but don't tell them everything. That way they will want to keep reading until the very end.

For a different approach, try starting with a quotation or an action scene. An eye-catching illustration right up front also makes for a powerful opening.

The Body

Use lots of facts, but don't try to cram everything in. Picking and choosing facts that fit your article and your slant will help to keep your feature focussed. Even though you're writing about real people and real events, you can use techniques you'd use for writing fiction. Plot, setting, well-rounded characters, dialogue, and descriptive details will help you hold your reader's interest. **See page 62 for help with story elements.**

The Conclusion

Be careful that you don't just fade away. If you save an interesting tidbit for the end, or wrap up your article with a thoughtful summary, your readers will feel the way you do after watching a good game or a good movie—satisfied. Even better, leave your readers with something to think about.

Improve Your Copy

Read your article out loud to be sure it makes sense. Then ask someone else to read it to catch things you might have missed. Make that person your editor. Use the chart as you work on revisions with your editor.

Questions to Ask Yourself

1. Did I stick to my slant?
2. Did I get the facts right?
3. Have I included the important facts about my subject?

Questions to Ask Your Editor

1. Did my opening paragraph lead you into the article and make you want to read on?
2. Where do I need to add details?
3. Did I include enough facts to convince you that my points are correct?
4. Are there any details that are unnecessary or don't really fit in?

Look carefully at your notes and your editor's suggestions. Decide what you need to change to make your article better. Remember that some of the changes may send you back to the predrafting and drafting stages.

O.K.

The ride is quite popular.

Dr. Tsui said that the search for the cause of cystic fibrosis was long and difficult.

BETTER

Almost two million people shriek through the four-minute ride each year.

Dr. Tsui compares the search for the cystic fibrosis gene to looking for a single house in a city the size of Toronto or Montréal, without having an address or a map.

EDIT AND PROOFREAD

Mark Up Your Copy!

Read your feature slowly, a sentence at a time. Look for weak spots—generalizations, imprecise modifiers, and vague statements. In the student's writing on page 108, notice how adding facts, details, and a direct quotation makes the paragraph sharper and livelier.

inside INFO

If your article doesn't move smoothly from one part to another, cut out the paragraphs and put them back together in a different way. Or use a word processor to cut and paste.

This student's writing shows the editing changes she made at the revision stage.

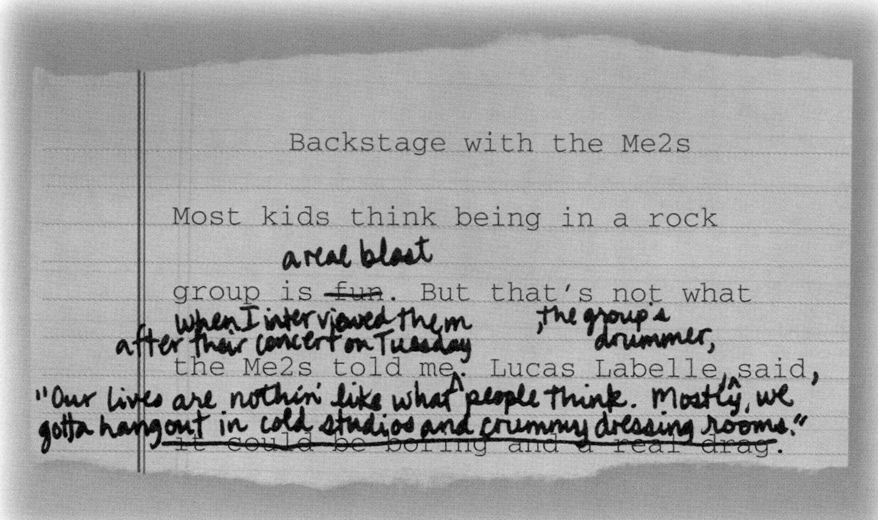

Backstage with the Me2s

Most kids think being in a rock group is ~~fun~~ a real blast. But that's not what the Me2s told me when I interviewed them after their concert on Tuesday. Lucas Labelle, the group's drummer, said, "Our lives are nothin' like what people think. Mostly, we gotta hang out in cold studios and crummy dressing rooms." ~~It could be boring and a real drag.~~

You're coming down to the wire. The clock is running out on your deadline, and it's time to take care of the last-minute details.

- Write a headline or title. Make it short. Recall your slant.
- Double-check your facts and figures. Because you're dealing with real people and events, it's extra-important that names, dates, and places be correct. Your readers are depending on you to give them accurate information.
- Check capitalization and punctuation. **See pages 28 and 30 for a revising checklist and fine-tuning tips.**

PUBLISH

Publish Your Feature Article

You made it! Put your article in an envelope and drop it on your editor's desk. Or you might try making your article even more attractive by using one of the following ideas.

Use Important Illustrations

Think about how you might add to the visual aspect of your feature. Is there information you could present in a chart? with a map? Readers might enjoy seeing photos of your interview subject. Think about writing short captions to go with the new illustrations—one or two sentences explaining what's going on in the photo or drawing.

Picture this: You too can be a photojournalist! **See page 206 for tips on photography.**

Videotape It!

Use your article as a script to narrate your feature on video. Live-action scenes and in-person interviews will add drama! **See page 216 for information on making videos.**

inside
INFO

Ever think of submitting your article to a local newspaper? Newspaper editors are always looking for fresh material. If you've found an interesting slant on something related to your community, there's a good chance your local paper would be eager to publish a well-written feature by a young writer.

Further Features

RELATED WRITING

Reading a feature article is a quick and entertaining way to get informed. That's why it's such a popular form—many of the TV shows you watch and the things you read for pleasure are really cousins of the feature article. Here are examples of specialized features:

The In-Depth Interview Present your subject's responses to a series of questions in a question-and-answer format. This approach allows your readers to form their own impressions of that person and to gain their own insights.

The Travel Feature On your next family vacation, explore hotels, restaurants, and tourist attractions. Then write a travelogue article to let readers enjoy a trip without leaving home or to help them decide if they want to follow in your footsteps.

The How-To Feature If you're willing to reveal your secrets about what you know how to do really well—from acing that video game to getting A's on science tests—people will line up to read about them.

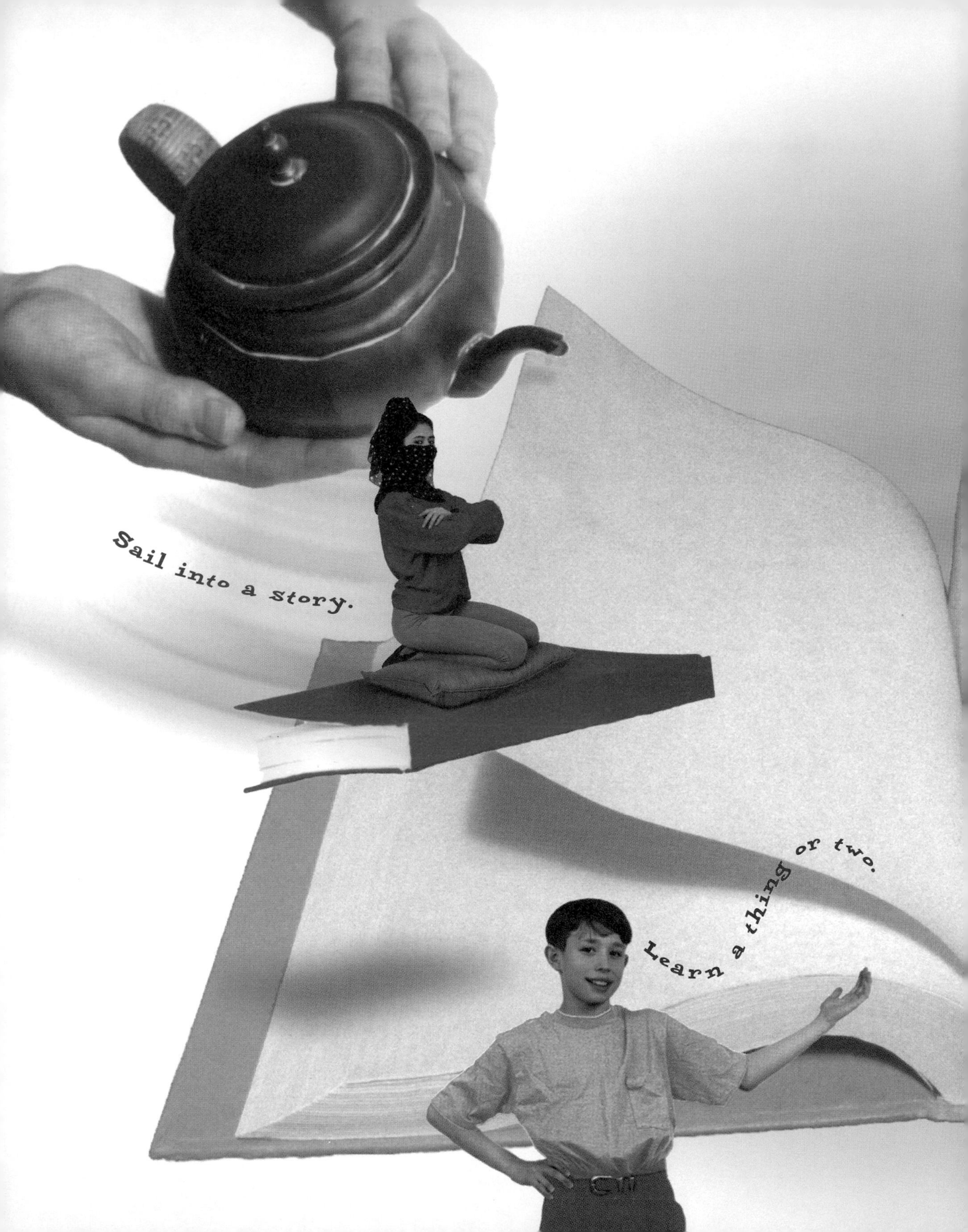
Sail into a story.
Learn a thing or two.

Reading

Reading can entertain you, make you smarter, help you plan a vacation—even show you how to tune up your bike. Here's how to get the most from your reading . . .

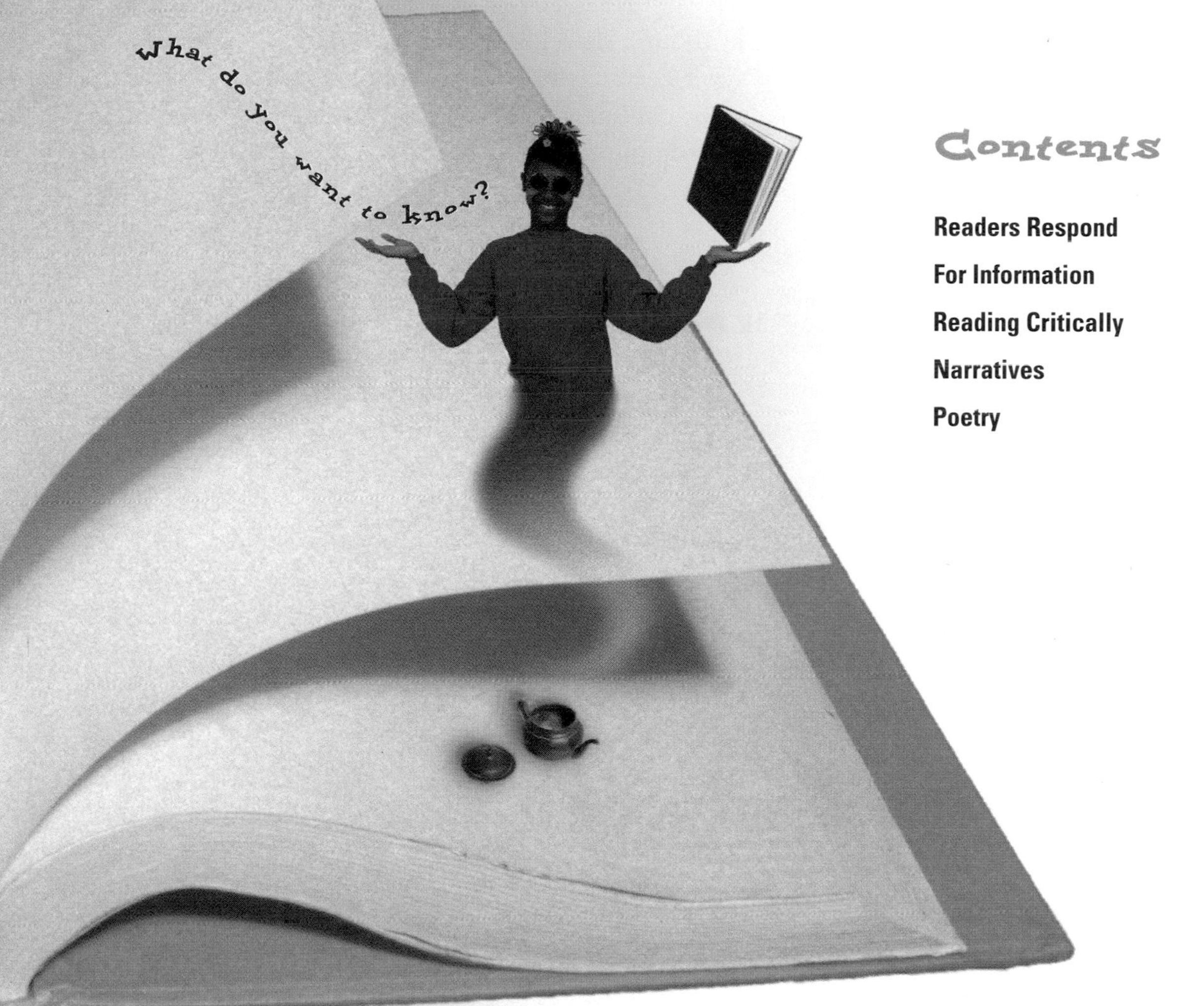
What do you want to know?

Contents

READING

Readers Respond

Some people think reading is like a one-way lecture—all you have to do is just sit there and take it all in. But reading is more like a discussion; you become an active participant in a two-way process.

Make It Personal

Reading becomes alive when you bring in your personal experiences and feelings. For example, you may be reading an article about a sled-dog trainer in the Yukon. Even if you've never been to the Yukon, you probably know what it's like to be cold or to care about an animal. Your experiences and thoughts help you understand what you read.

Respond

- Think about your reactions: "I guess I don't like this character. I'm not rooting for him."
- Make comparisons: "This character reminds me of my brother. They're both stubborn."
- Form opinions: "That baby-sitter has to work hard, even harder than I did when I baby-sat for the Wongs. He earns every cent he's paid."

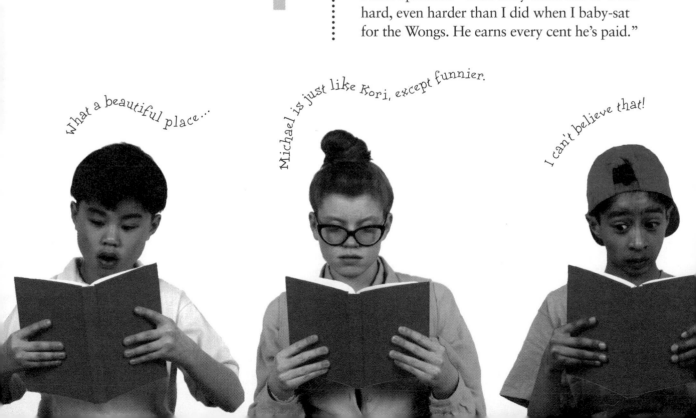

What a beautiful place...

Michael is just like Kori, except funnier.

I can't believe that!

Ask Questions

You can personalize what you're reading by asking yourself questions that interest you. Try questions like these.

What am I feeling? What images does this give me?

What surprised me the most?

Does this remind me of anything? anyone? anywhere?

Could anything like this ever happen to me?

What would I do if I were in the same situation?

What do I hope will happen to this character?

What would I ask the writer if I had the chance?

BRIGHT Ideas

FOR RESPONDING TO READING

Use pencils, pastels, or paints to: sketch the feelings you have, illustrate your favourite section, or design costumes, props, and sets for the story.

Use your voice to: improvise a conversation between characters, or read aloud the funniest, scariest, or most beautiful passages. **To perform a Readers' Theatre presentation, see page 183.**

Use a pen to: write a letter to a character, create a diary entry as if you were a character, or write an alternate conclusion.

So that's how it works!
Too cool!
This is great!

Responding in Style

Look for ways to express your responses. Get them down on paper. Tell them to a friend who has read the same thing, and then . . . listen. He or she may have a totally different reaction or a very insightful response. You can learn a great deal—and have quite a bit of fun—by sharing and hearing ideas about your reading.

The radio play "Frankenstein" is probably my favourite thing I've read so far. I am amazed at how different the story is from the film, and I actually think it's scarier to read than to watch. I love the passage "The dull yellow eye of my creature opened!"

Use a Response Journal

You can use a notebook to record your thoughts about what you read. Fill the pages with your feelings, opinions, questions, answers, and discoveries. Don't worry about spelling and punctuation. Instead, focus on exploring how you feel about the people and the events you're reading about. You might try two-column note-taking: writing quotes, facts, and images on one side of a page and noting feelings and responses on the other side. You can also jot down phrases that you think are especially interesting or well written.

Participate in a Discussion Circle

There are times when someone else's idea helps you see an issue in an entirely different way. That's why discussion circles can be so interesting. People who have read the same thing talk about their responses and listen to each other's ideas. You don't always agree, but that's O.K. There isn't one right answer to the kinds of things you talk about: whether you did or didn't like the book or what you would do in the same situation. Discussion circles work best when each member of the group makes a list of questions and ideas ahead of time. **For more on group discussion, see page 158.**

I liked it • I don't think so • I hated it • No way! • That was so funny • Cool! • Yes •

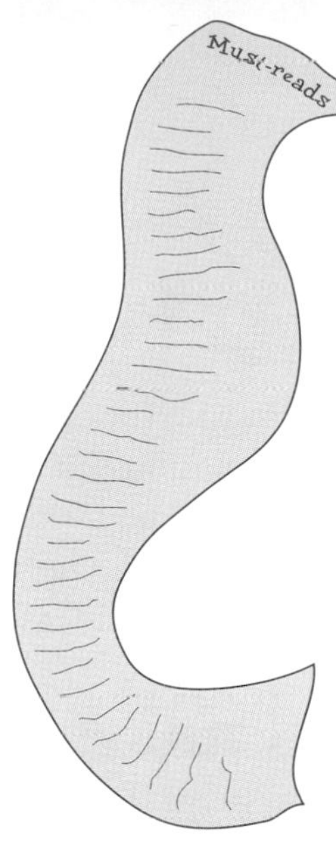
Must-reads

Compile a Future Book List

One good book can often lead you to another. The jacket flap or the back cover of a favourite book may list other books written by the same author. You can also ask your friends which books they recommend. Make a list of people and subjects that really interest you, and then search in the library for books on those subjects. You can also try "shelf shopping" while you're in the library. Just scan the book titles on the shelves and look more closely at those that sound interesting.

Sell a Book

Imagine that you are a salesperson and you want to sell the book you've just read. To convince your customers to read the book, you have to let them know what you like about it. You might describe a likable character, draw a poster of an intriguing setting, or compose an advertising jingle describing the story. Don't give away any surprises, though. If you do, your customers won't need to read the book. **For more on persuasive speaking, see page 169.**

Communicate Using a Dialogue Journal

In a dialogue journal, you share ideas with another person—a friend, teacher, relative, or anyone you wish—about what you're reading. The writing is informal and friendly, just like writing a note to a friend. Some people use computers instead of paper. They can discuss what they're reading with people all over the world through computer networks. **For more on journals, see page 34.**

I can't believe how sad the beginning of <u>A Child In Prison Camp</u> is. I also can't believe that Shichan isn't angrier. I would be totally upset if I found out, like she did, that I had to leave my home and all my stuff.

I agree! It is sad!!! I think Shichan is angry but also a little excited. She acted excited about her first train ride (page 14). I wonder what the prison camp will be like? (Shichan probably wondered the same thing).

READING

For Information

Written information is everywhere. It includes the facts in your textbooks and in the books, magazines, and newspapers you read. Information is also the on-screen instructions for a video game, the steps in a recipe, and even the list of ingredients on a cereal box. Information can provide an answer to a question, a path to a goal, or an open door to new experiences and ideas.

Information: A Need to Read

Will people ever explore beyond the solar system? To answer questions like this, you'll need information. Where do you find information? Stories have some information, but when your purpose is finding facts and information quickly, you'll probably choose non-fiction sources. The way you read is important, too. You might let the words flow past you when you read for entertainment. But when you read for information, you actively seek the knowledge you need.

ENGLISH
Encyclopædia
Encyclopædia

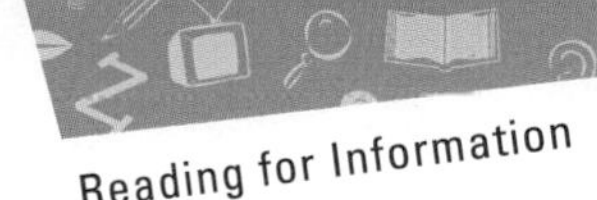

Get a Plan That Works

You can get more information, and spend less time getting it, by using a reading plan. Let's take a look at two plans.

What I Already Know • What I Want to Know • What I Learned

The KWL Plan

The letters *KWL* stand for What I Already *K*now, What I *W*ant to Know, and What I *L*earned. Before you read about a subject, label three columns *K*, *W*, and *L* on notebook paper. To fill in the K column, think about what you already Know. Next, think of what else you want to know, and list your questions in the W column. After reading the material carefully, write answers to your questions in the L column.

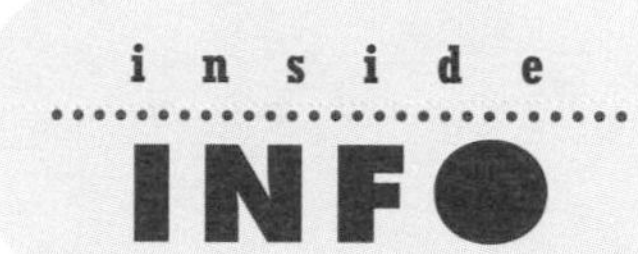
inside
INFO

"Outside of a dog, a book is a man's best friend. Inside of a dog, it's too dark to read."
—Groucho Marx

The SQ3R Plan

The letters of this plan called SQ3R stand for *S*urvey, *Q*uestion, *R*ead, *R*ecite, and *R*eview. Let's look at the plan briefly before examining it in depth on the following pages.

The SQ3R Reading Plan

1. **Survey** To get an overview, scan the pages to read titles, headings and subheadings, illustrations, and captions.
2. **Question** Before you read and as you read, ask yourself questions.Then, while you are reading, answer your questions, either to yourself or by jotting down notes.
3. **Read** As you read in depth, focus on what you read. Look up difficult vocabulary. Reread difficult passages.
4. **Recite** Talk about what you've read to make sure you really understand it.
5. **Review** Write brief summaries of what you read. Review the summaries and the answers to your questions.

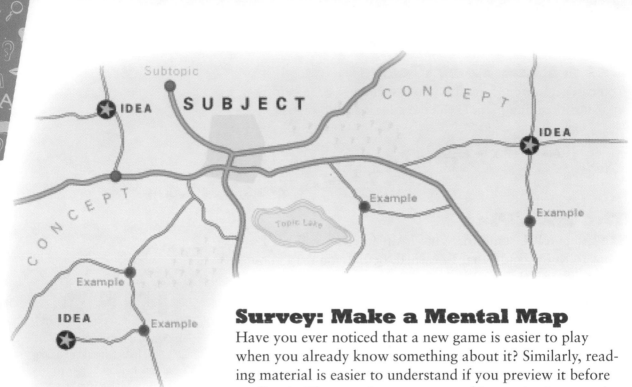

Survey: Make a Mental Map

Have you ever noticed that a new game is easier to play when you already know something about it? Similarly, reading material is easier to understand if you preview it before reading it. The ten minutes you spend in previewing may, in fact, be the most important minutes of your reading. As you preview the material, your mind makes an outline of the ideas. Even though you're *not* reading for understanding at this point, your mind prepares a mental map of the main ideas. Then, as you read in depth, it fills in the details.

Here's How
To Preview information

1. **Flip through the pages** to find the headings and subheadings. They signal major topics.
2. **Read the first paragraph** to find the author's slant on the information.
3. **Read any end-of-chapter questions or summaries *first*** to focus your thinking before you begin to read.
4. **Look at illustrations,** including graphs, charts, and pictures—and read the captions. They point out difficult or important concepts.
5. **Look for words or sections printed in bold or *italic* type.** This special treatment means these words and ideas are important.

Question: Get in the Game

When you play soccer, you don't just stand rooted to the spot and let the ball go by. When you read, you don't want to let the words just go by either. Asking questions lets you be part of the action. You'll be better able to understand what you read if you ask yourself questions *before* you read and *as* you read.

BRIGHT Ideas

TO GET A HANDLE ON WHAT YOU READ, ASK YOURSELF:

What questions do the headings suggest? For example, if you see the heading Continents Drift, you might ask: Why do continents drift? How do continents drift? Which continents drift? Find answers to your questions as you read—and you'll probably find the most important points.

Why are some words in boldface or italic type? If you can find the answer, you've probably mastered the key points and the new vocabulary.

Why might this be important? Where is this leading? Playing detective will keep you awake and focus your attention. Think of the *who, what, when, where, why,* and *how* of events and ideas.

What did I just read? Rephrase ideas, orally or in writing, every few paragraphs or so. Use your own words. If you can rephrase these ideas now, you'll probably be able to remember them later, when you need them.

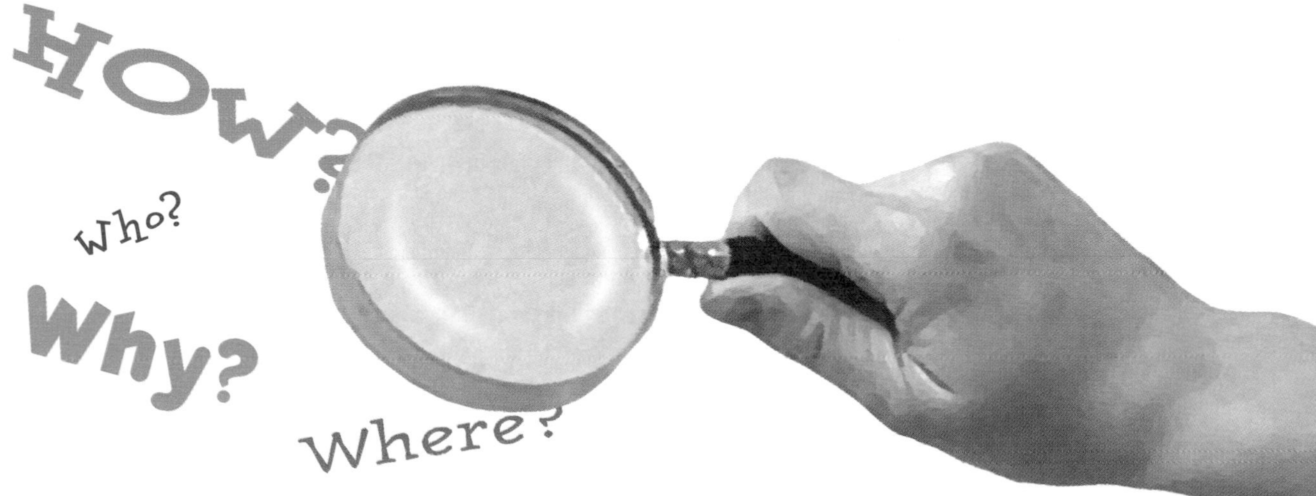
How?
Who?
Why?
Where?

Read in Depth

By slowing down your reading speed and carefully thinking about what you're reading, you're more likely to understand information the first time you read it.

Visualize What You're Reading

By visualizing what you read, you can make any subject more meaningful, more interesting, and easier to understand. For example, it's one thing to read about the Yukon Territory before the 1890 gold rush. But turn on your theatre-of-the-mind, and imagine you're there. You see a tired prospector, alone in a vast, frozen wasteland. He stoops to fill his canteen from a stream of spring run-off. He sees a yellow gleam . . .

inside INFO

If the directions come with drawings or diagrams, refer to them as you read each step of the written directions. They'll help you to see how all the steps fit together into a process.

Read the Directions

Suppose you spend a whole weekend writing a report and then on Monday morning discover that the assignment was to prepare an *oral* report, not a written one. Reading directions can save you more time than it takes.

Directions for Assembly

Here's How
To Use Directions

1. **Read the directions, all of them, all the way through.**
2. **Make sure you understand what you're expected to do.** If you're unsure, ask questions before you plunge in!
3. **Visualize each step in the directions.**
4. **Gather any reading materials or supplies that you'll need.**
5. **Go back to the beginning and complete the directions, one step at a time.** If the directions are long or complicated (as in a recipe), review them once in a while to make sure that you're on target.

Check In with Yourself

Are you keeping your mind on what you're reading? As you read a source, stop once in a while to give yourself a sort of mental nudge. Try this quiz to see how you're doing.

Self-Quiz

1. Can I state the main ideas in my own words?
2. What are the connections between the ideas that I've read so far?
3. What is the meaning of words in **boldface** or *italic* type?
4. How does each picture and illustration relate to the text?
5. What conclusions can I draw about what I just read?

So, how did you do? Don't hesitate to make another pass through the reading material to make sure you understand its content.

Don't let your reading get away from you!

Recite: Speak to Learn

What happens to your thought processes when you tell someone about a story you've read or a film you've seen? Have you noticed that telling someone about something forces you to clarify your thinking? Your brain does a sort of quick dash to organize the information and pick out the most important points. What happens when you tell a second person about the same story or film? Since your mind has already had a rehearsal, it's a lot easier, isn't it? Using the mind-to-mouth connection can help you understand and remember what you read.

Study with a Partner

To make the most of your time, you'll want to set goals and a time limit before you begin studying with a partner. Listing questions to ask each other about the material will help you focus your efforts.

Do you want to brush up on your study skills? Take a look at the ideas on **page 264.**

Advice from the Zone

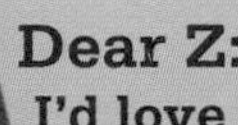

Dear Z:

I'd love to study with someone, but I have to stay home and watch my little sister while my mom is at work. How can I recite if I study alone? I'd feel stupid talking to myself.

—Lone Wolf

Dear Wolf:

Sometimes you just have to be your own wolf pack. Try this: Imagine that you're the teacher and you're telling the class about what you just read. You can stand up, imagine the class is in front of you, then whisper or move your lips silently. (Or, if you're really brave, try tape-recording yourself.) If that doesn't work for you, try using your built-in audience—your little sister. She may not be much of a listener, but hey, you still get to recite. Here's another idea: If someone else can watch your little sister for a little while, call a friend and study over the phone.

Good luck!

Z.

Review and Summarize

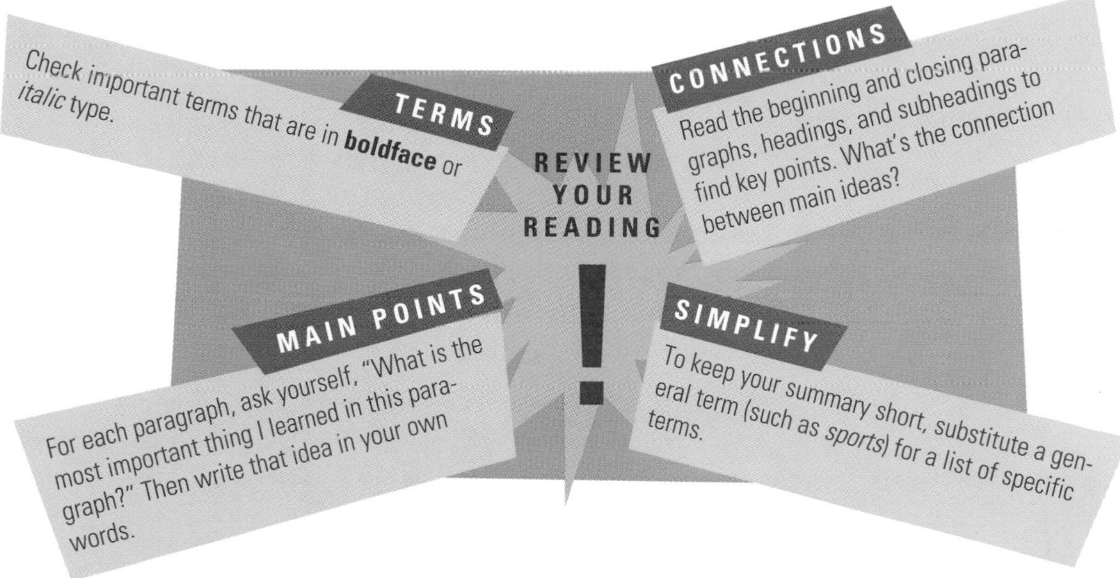
TERMS
Check important terms that are in **boldface** or *italic* type.
CONNECTIONS
Read the beginning and closing paragraphs, headings, and subheadings to find key points. What's the connection between main ideas?
REVIEW YOUR READING
!
MAIN POINTS
For each paragraph, ask yourself, "What is the most important thing I learned in this paragraph?" Then write that idea in your own words.
SIMPLIFY
To keep your summary short, substitute a general term (such as *sports*) for a list of specific terms.

You can remember important points by summarizing them. Writing a summary will help you find the main ideas and see how the details support them. To write a summary, choose only the most important ideas in a chapter or article, and rewrite those ideas in your own words. Of course, your summary should be much shorter than the original.

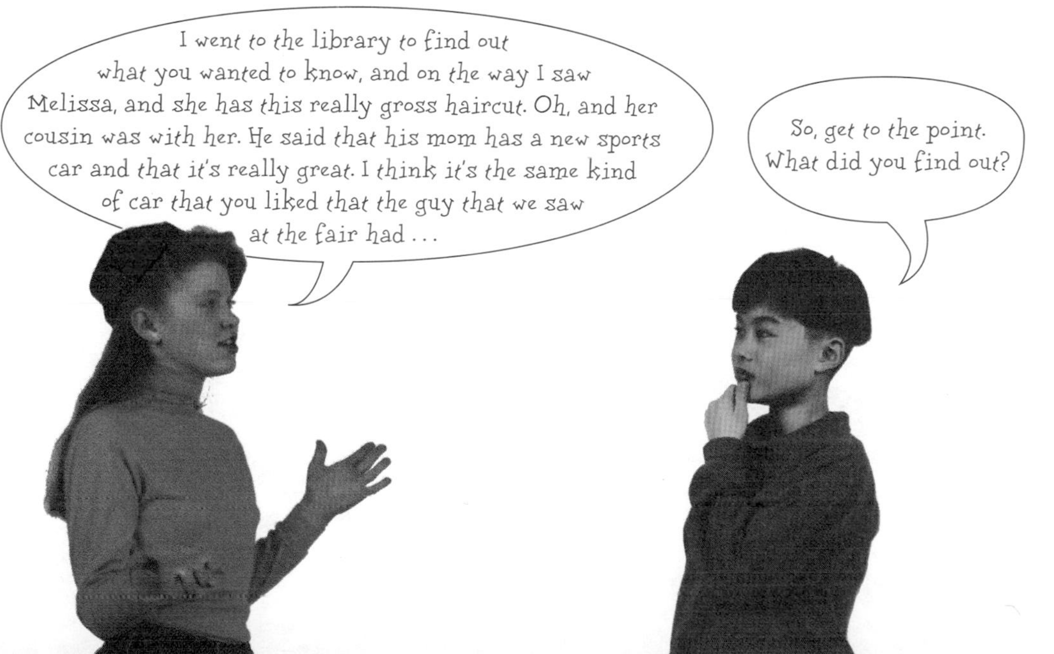
I went to the library to find out what you wanted to know, and on the way I saw Melissa, and she has this really gross haircut. Oh, and her cousin was with her. He said that his mom has a new sports car and that it's really great. I think it's the same kind of car that you liked that the guy that we saw at the fair had . . .
So, get to the point. What did you find out?

Original text to be summarized

Summarize this main point by using your own words.

Substitute a general term, *vegetables,* for this list.

These details are interesting, but for a summary, think of the point they make.

When Europeans first invaded the Americas, they set in motion an exchange that has dramatically changed the way in which people live worldwide. The exchange involved both plants and animals.

Spanish conquistadors arriving in the Americas brought with them strange creatures, horses! Horses had long been extinct in the Americas, and so the Aboriginal Peoples of the Plains had never seen these strange animals before. But within one generation, these people became expert at capturing, training, and riding the horses. Horses became a great aid in hunting bison.

Just as horses were strange creatures to the peoples of the Plains, so the tomatoes, squash, corn, and potatoes that grew in the Americas were strange vegetables to Europeans. However, these new plants became an important source of their nutrition.

Potatoes, in particular, became an essential part of the diet of the people in Ireland. Potatoes grew well, could last through a winter, and provided good nourishment. The Irish became so dependent on potatoes that when a terrible blight struck the potato crop, famine followed. From 1845 to 1848, at least one million people died in Ireland. More than that number immigrated to North America, changing the face of that continent's population.

student summary

Since their first contact, Europeans and the Aboriginal Peoples of the Americas have exchanged plants and animals. Aboriginal Peoples received horses from Spain, which changed the way they followed bison. Foods from the Americas went to Europe. The Irish grew to depend on potatoes so much that crop failures led to deaths and forced many to move to North America.

Patterns in Information

On the following pages you'll find a strategy you can use with any reading plan: Find out how information is organized. Once you identify the pattern of organization, you can better understand what you're reading.

Patterns of Organization

Information is often organized into these patterns:

- Main Ideas and Supporting Details
- Definition and Examples
- Description
- Classification and Lists
- Problems and Solutions
- Causes and Effects
- Comparisons and Contrasts

inside
INFO

Phrases such as *most remarkable, central concern, key idea,* and *main point* are clues to main ideas. Phrases such as *for example, for instance,* and *not only* are clues to supporting details.

Turning the pattern into a drawing, map, or diagram will help you see how one piece of information relates to another. Let's take a closer look at some of these patterns.

Main Ideas and Supporting Details

In this pattern of organization, one sentence tells the main idea of a paragraph or group of paragraphs. Sentences and phrases give details and examples that support that main idea.

When most people think of loons, they think of the bird's haunting cry, a sort of echoing, wailing laughter. The loon's **most remarkable** feature, however, is its rugged strength. **For example,** when a loon flies, its wings pump steadily 260 times per minute, minute after minute, hour after hour. With a strong tail wind, loons in flight can attain speeds of more than 160 kilometres per hour. Loons are powerful **not only** in the air, but also in the water. Loons diving for fish can stay underwater for five minutes and can dive to depths of 30 metres and more.

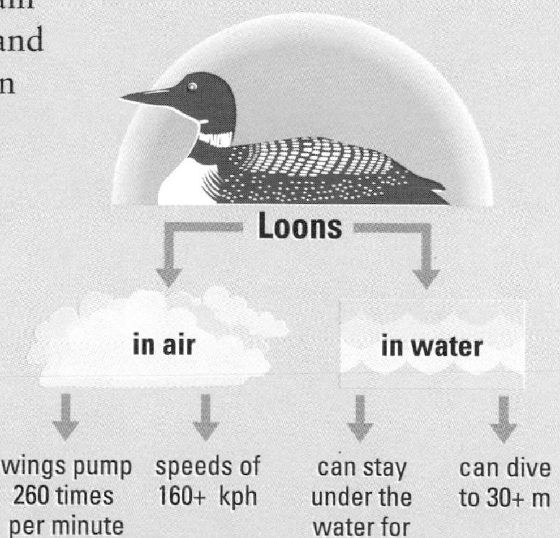
Loons
in air
in water
wings pump 260 times per minute
speeds of 160+ kph
can stay under the water for 5 minutes
can dive to 30+ m

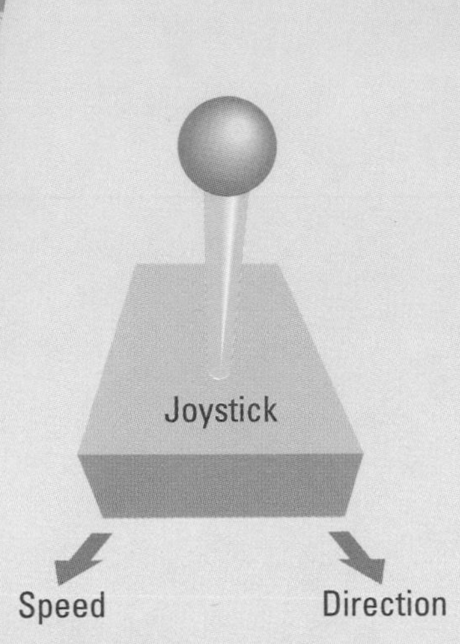
Joystick
Speed
Direction

Definition and Examples

This pattern is similar to Main Ideas and Supporting Details. The central idea is a definition, and the supporting details are examples.

Each player has a joystick, **which is** a box-shaped device with a movable stick. The joystick controls the speed and direction of each player's Galactic Warrior on the computer screen. **For example,** to make a character dodge Space Blob Devourers approaching from the left, move the joystick rapidly to the right.

inside
INFO

Phrases such as *which is, that is,* and *are called* are clues to definitions. Phrases such as *for example, such as, for instance, like,* and *including* are clues to examples.

Description

In paragraphs or passages of description, the author tells what something looks like, feels like, or smells like. You can target the most important aspects of a description by illustrating it with your own diagram.

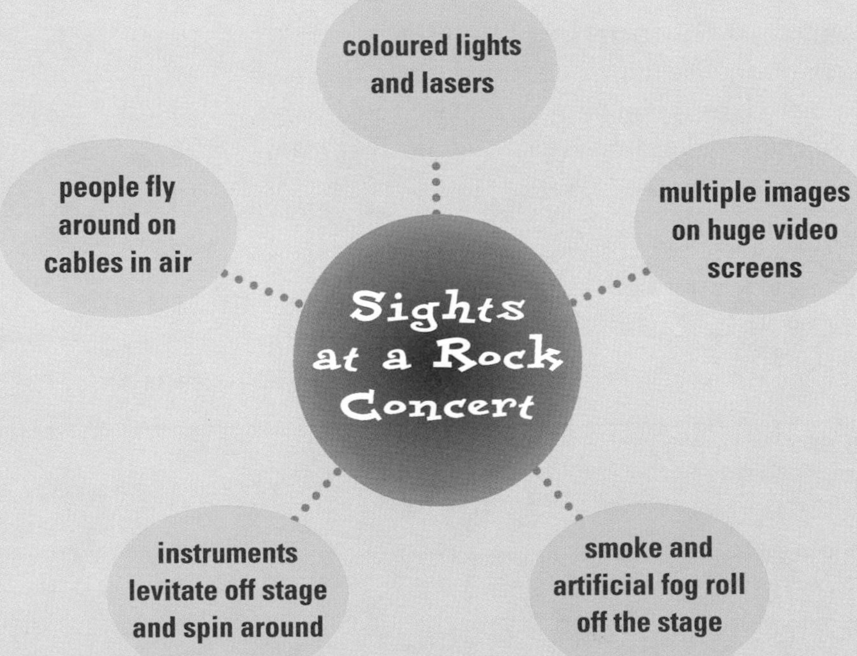
coloured lights and lasers
people fly around on cables in air
multiple images on huge video screens
Sights at a Rock Concert
instruments levitate off stage and spin around
smoke and artificial fog roll off the stage

Classification and Lists

Classification names the smaller categories that make up a large category.

The first horses, tiny creatures only 25 to 51 centimetres in height, evolved into several **kinds of** much larger animals. Workhorses, such as the Belgian draft horse, can attain 190 centimetres in height and weigh an impressive 1000 kilograms. Riding horses, such as the Morgan, the Arabian, and the Tennessee walking horse are average in height for modern horses, about 140 to 160 centimetres. Ponies, such as the Shetland pony, are the shortest horses at 120 centimetres.

inside INFO

Phrases such as *kinds of, types of,* or *categories of* are clues to classifications. Numerals, and words such as *first, next, then, materials, supplies,* and *contents,* are often clues to lists.

Early horses
Draft horses
Riding horses
Ponies

If you've ever gone shopping or have given someone "how-to" instructions for making, building, or doing something, you've made a list. Lists are useful for stating the parts of something or explaining steps in a process. Lists might—or might not—be numbered.

Cereal Ingredients:
oats
pecans
coconut
honey
soya oil

The Way to Wax a Car

Materials: mild detergent, running water, lint-free rags, car wax, a sponge, a chamois

Steps:

1. Wash the car with detergent and water.
2. Rinse it thoroughly, top to bottom, with a garden hose.
3. Dry it with rags so it doesn't spot.
4. Swirl on the wax with a sponge.
5. Buff the wax to a shine with a chamois.

Problems and Solutions

You might encounter problem-and-solution patterns in social studies or science books, magazine and newspaper articles, and other sources. You can boil down pages of information by drawing this kind of diagram:

PROBLEM
Teenagers want jobs, but many employers prefer to hire older workers.

SOLUTION 1
Lower the minimum wage so older workers who need to support themselves won't want minimum-wage jobs.

SOLUTION 2
The government should subsidize teenage workers by sharing the cost of their wages with employers.

inside

INFO

Phrases such as *a problem, a difficulty,* and *a dilemma* are clues to a problem. Phrases such as *a solution, another way of, to solve, to find out,* and *to find the key* are clues to a solution.
Words and phrases such as *because, when, as a result, therefore, since,* and *because* are clues to cause and effect.

Causes and Effects

If you throw a rock at a window, what happens? The cause, a thrown rock, will create an effect—a broken window. That effect might also lead to another effect, such as an angry parent. Writers use cause-and-effect patterns to tell why events happened or why things are as they are. One cause can lead to one or more effects. Or several causes can lead to one major effect. Also, an effect can become the cause of something else.

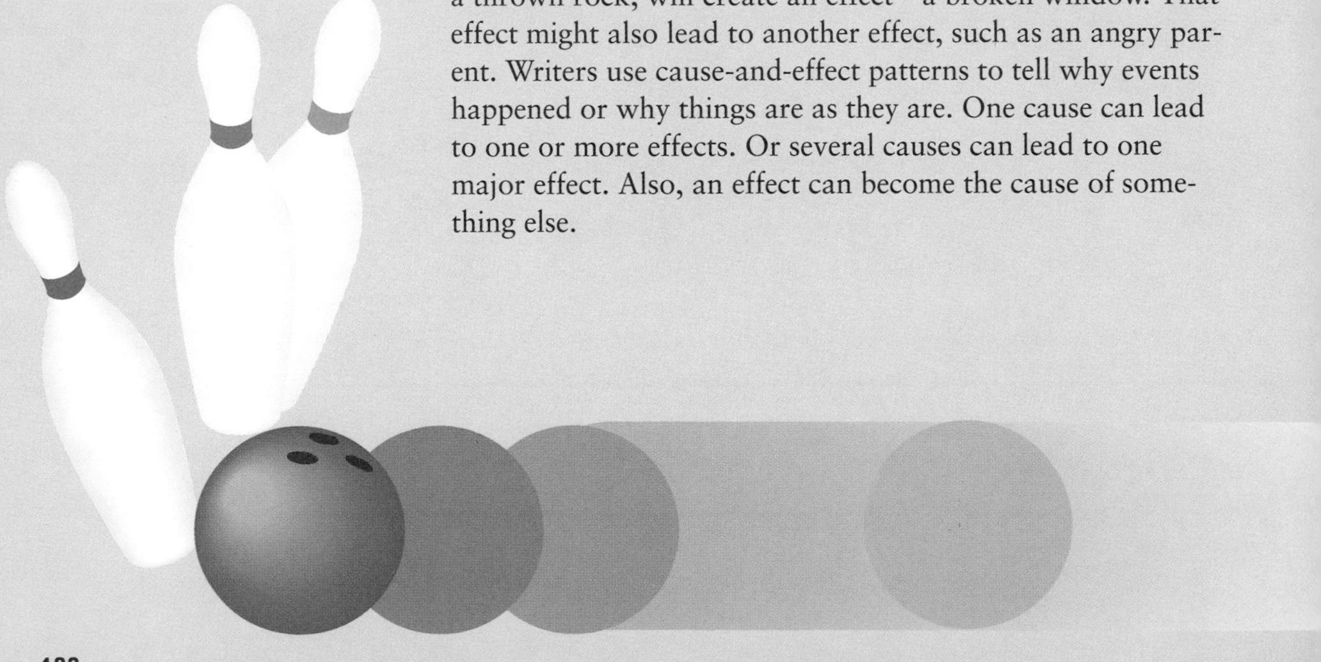

Comparisons and Contrasts

Writers use this pattern to show how things are alike and how they differ.

Margaret Atwood's poems "Snake Woman" and "Buffalo in Compound: Alberta" are **similar** in that the speaker in both poems recalls being a child and seeing animals. The poems are **unlike** in their tone and sensory images.

Tone | Subject matter | Images

Sometimes writers compare the unfamiliar with the familiar to help readers make a meaningful comparison.

Fleas can jump a distance that is 150 times their own length, **which is like** a person jumping to the top of a fifteen-story building. When a flea jumps, it accelerates at **the equivalent of** fifty times the speed of the space shuttle after liftoff.

inside INFO

Words and phrases such as *similar, which is like, the equivalent of, in the same way,* and *like* are clues to similarities. Words and phrases such as *unlike, but, in contrast to, however,* and *on the contrary* are clues to differences.

Advice from the Zone

Dear Z:

I'm so confused! Make that mega confused! I just read about the bubonic plague in my health class, and I think that my brain is plagued. I keep finding one pattern of information after another. First there are descriptions, then definitions, then causes and effects, then examples, then problems and solutions. Rats! What's wrong with me?

—Bub O

Dear Bub O:

You've got a cure, not a disease. Clever rascal that you are, you've discovered that a writer can use many methods of organization from sentence to sentence, from paragraph to paragraph. Sometimes writers don't even supply you with clue words to tip you off to what the pattern of organization is. You'll need to take notes and draw diagrams to find the patterns. Keep reading.

Z.

Reading Critically

When you hear the term *critical reader,* do you picture a person frowning and finding fault with every word? Being critical can mean finding faults, but being a critical reader means something else entirely. It means that you think about what you read. You analyse the content by looking at how it is written and what it is actually saying. You use your knowledge and skill to judge the truth and value of what is in print.

Think While You Read

Reading critically involves several kinds of thinking.

Recognizing: Identify main ideas, facts, opinions, and point of view.

Analysing: Make comparisons, link causes and effects, draw conclusions, and predict outcomes.

Evaluating: Form opinions about how well-written, logical, and interesting the work is.

The ways in which you recognize, analyse, and evaluate will vary with the kind of reading you are doing.

Not sure *what* you're supposed to recognize? Read about the different elements of fiction and nonfiction. **See pages 60 and 53.**

Informational article or book

Ask yourself:

What are the main ideas?

How has the writer organized them?

Does the writer offer support for those main ideas?

What is the writer's point of view and how is it supported?

Is this a useful source of information?

Essay, editorial, letter to the editor, advertisement, or other persuasive writing

Ask yourself:

What is the writer's point of view?

How has the writer presented this viewpoint?

Has the writer used valid reasoning to support this point of view?

Has the writer convinced me?

Short story or novel

Ask yourself:

How are the events in the plot organized?

What are the characters' personality traits?

Is the writer's point of view clear?

Have I gained anything by reading this?

Recognizing Facts and Opinions

What is the difference between these two statements?
Savitskava was the first woman to walk in space.
There should be more women astronauts.
The first statement can be proved and universally agreed upon. It is a fact. You can verify it in a book. The second statement is an opinion. It states someone's belief. No one can prove it in a way that everyone will agree upon.

inside
INFO

Opinions tell how people feel about things, how they view or judge them. They often contain words such as these: *best, interesting, should, important, helpful, beautiful.*

Finding Opinions

Though you may not always recognize them, opinions appear everywhere—ads, editorial columns, conversations, and textbooks (for an example, check the next sentence). Learning how to tell the difference between facts and opinions is an important skill for critical readers. If you mistake opinions for facts, you are likely to misjudge or misunderstand situations. You can recognize, analyse, and evaluate opinions by asking yourself certain questions:

Ask
these
questions

- Can this statement be proved and universally agreed upon?
- Is the opinion supported with examples and reasons?
- Might someone disagree with the opinion? Do I?
- Do I need to find out more?

Some of NASA's most interesting work is the research into voice-operated robots and machines. Recently, designers have tested a voice-controlled wheel chair. Well over one million people in the United States and Canada rely on wheel chairs for mobility; a voice-controlled chair would be a great help to those who also have limited use of their hands.

The word *interesting* means there's an opinion. I guess people could disagree that it's the space agency's most interesting work. Some people might think the space shuttle is more interesting. I'd better keep reading to see if I agree.

The number of people using wheel chairs is a fact. Someone could prove it by looking it up or by actually counting.

That "a voice-controlled chair would be a great help" is an opinion. Some people might disagree and think that such a chair would only be a minor help.

Does this make sense?

Test the Logic

When you find a sentence that expresses an opinion or argues a point, look carefully at the surrounding sentences. Identify the writer's reasons, and check to see if they make sense. The reasons should lead the reader, step by step, to an understanding of why the opinion or argument is valid. Be on the look out for faulty logic—reasoning that doesn't make sense. **See ideas on writing logically, page 51.**

Don't Get Trapped by Faulty Reasoning

Faulty Cause and Effect This occurs when event A is said to lead to event B, but no proven connection is given. For example: Every time I wash the car, it rains. (Though this may be the writer's belief, meteorologists know that there are other causes for the rain.)

Either/Or Fallacy This kind of reasoning falsely claims that there are only two options when there are actually more. For example: Either join this club or be a loner.

Overgeneralization Statements that reach beyond what the evidence supports are overgeneralizations; they often include words such as *all, never, always, must.* For example: *Everyone* loves opera.

BUY ACE SHOES!

All professional athletes know that the shoes they wear are the most important equipment they use.

They know the right shoe makes the difference in scoring that last-minute goal or clearing that final hurdle.

Of course, it's your decision: You can either buy Ace shoes, or you can get used to losing.

Overgeneralization
All is incorrect. Some athletes may think the kind of racket, ball, or glove they use is more important. Swimmers and divers don't even wear shoes for their sport.

Faulty Cause and Effect
Strength, skill, and timing have more to do with success in sports than the brand of shoe does.

Either/Or Fallacy
There are options besides buying Ace shoes or losing. Many athletes win while wearing no shoes.

Check the Point of View

Writers' experiences can affect the way they view and write about things. As a critical reader, you'll want to recognize a writer's viewpoint, or bias, and check for how the tone and structure of the writing may have been affected by that viewpoint. The newspaper articles below describe the same soccer match, but the writers had two very different views of the game. After you've read both articles, decide what a third, unbiased reporter might write.

inside INFO

As the reader, question the writer's point of view. Ask yourself: What is the writer saying? How is the point of view supported? Does the writing contain a bias? Do I agree with what the writer is saying? Do I see any things differently?

The Centreville Chronicle

The soccer championship was stolen from the Centreville Cleats by the Prattville Predators, who enjoyed the home-field advantage in yesterday's match. The Cleats outplayed the Predators during most of the game. Questionable referee calls in the last half gave the game to the Predators, who scored three goals in the last five minutes. Final score: Predators 6, Cleats 5.

The Prattville Press

The Prattville Predators are soccer champions for the third year in a row! The team celebrated its 6-5 come-from-behind victory over the Centreville Cleats, in which it scored three goals in the last five minutes. Everyone made a supreme effort all season, and it paid off.

Watch for Bias in Fiction

You can find bias in stories and poems, too. Look at the tone, word choice, setting, and character traits used. For example, in one story a soldier may be described as a brave hero. Another writer, however, might represent a soldier as a mean predator. Descriptions of the battlefield and enemy could also vary greatly.

READING

Narratives

Narratives are stories. You've been reading narratives all your life—poring over the comics or following the latest events in the life of your favourite singer, athlete, or film star. Fiction narratives are imaginary stories that often are based on real people and actual situations. Non-fiction narratives tell about true events and real people.

Pick Your Reading Experience

Do you have a favourite type of story that you like to read or watch on TV? Is it about animals? Does it have suspense? Or does it involve friends or romance? Which type of narrative would you choose for an escape? If you thirst for action, you might try a true-life adventure story. Or, if you're upset that you didn't make the soccer team, you might join someone else's team by reading the biography of a soccer star.

Stumped about which type of narrative to pick? Look at **page 143** for a description of the different kinds of narratives.

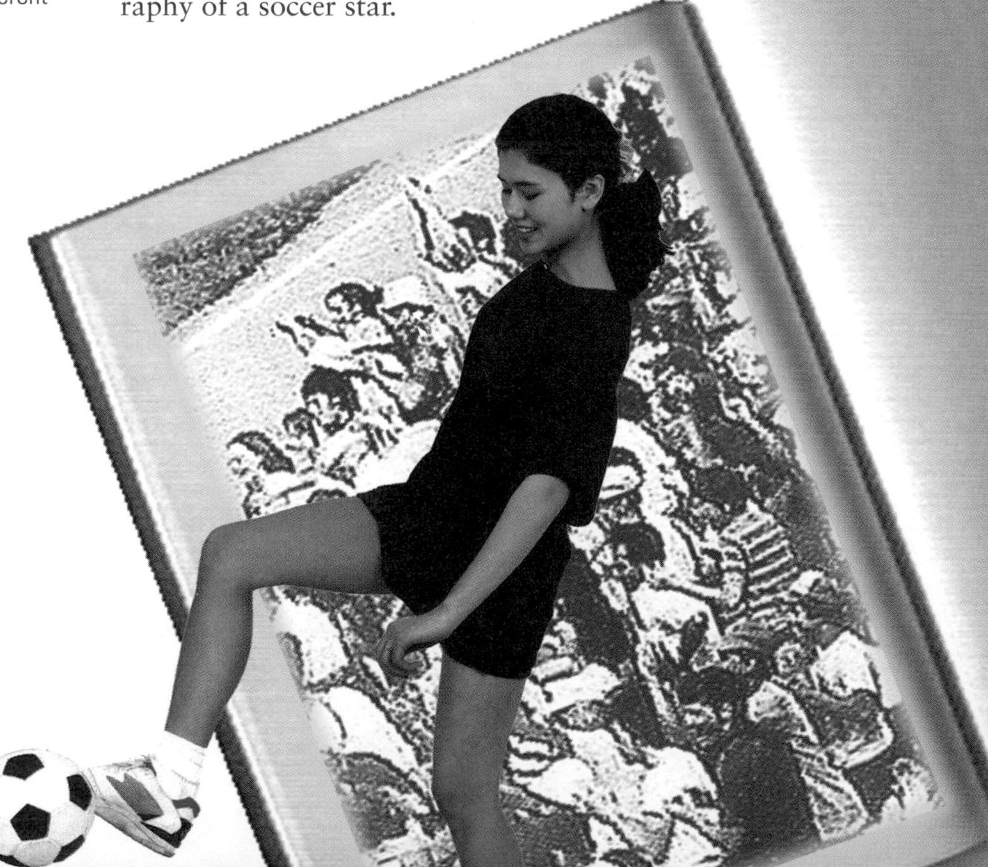

Find the Story Elements

You've chosen your book and settled down in a comfortable spot. You read three pages and—whoa—you decide this book isn't for you. Did you give the book a fair chance? If you stop too soon, you might miss the best story ever! A reading strategy might help you. As you read, think about these four basic elements: *setting, character, plot,* and *theme.*

Picture the Setting!

Picture the Setting

You are there. Is it midwinter in the Yukon in 1850? Or is it a sweltering day in downtown Calgary in the year 2020? Watch for details about time and place. Although a story always has a setting, it is not always described in detail.

Get to Know the Characters

How do you feel about the *major character* or characters in the story? Often the major character has some kind of problem. Have you gotten to know him or her? What do you think about the *minor characters*? Do they help the action, cause trouble, or just help move the plot along? How do you get to know a character?

Answer these questions

... What does the character look like?
... What does she or he talk about?
... What do others say about the character?
... What emotions does the character show?

Get to Know the Characters!

If you've decided to continue reading the narrative, notice the main character. Sometimes it's how he or she changes that keeps you turning the pages, or it may be the character's *problem* or conflict. Watch for conflicts like these:

- Character versus character: A bully is harassing Emiko.
- Character versus society: Kevin is outraged that a factory is polluting the river.
- Character versus nature: Sarita is the lone survivor of a plane crash in the Andes mountains.
- Inner conflict: Andrea wants desperately to get on the team. But to join, she has to tell a lie.

inside INFO

Many modern narratives, like science fiction stories, have a story plot that seems to take you in a circle rather than through a series of events leading to a resolution. Some folk tales and diary stories also loop back. As you read, notice if your story plot is circular.

Put Yourself into the Plot

Now imagine that you're right there with the characters. What's happening? What's the sequence of events? A good story will take you on a roller coaster ride, so hop on . . .

The *rising action* grabs your interest as the main character's problem begins to unfold.

The *story climax* is the turning point. You hang in suspense waiting to discover if the problem will be resolved.

Next, the *falling action* takes you through more ups and downs as the problem is attacked.

At the end of the story is the *resolution,* which may—or may not—resolve the problem.

Explore the Theme

O.K. What have you experienced? What is the main idea of the story? Is it to teach a lesson, to entertain, or to inform?

Put Yourself into thePlot!

Map Out the Story

Sometimes so much happens in a story that it can be confusing. Try filling in a story map. Watch for sequence.

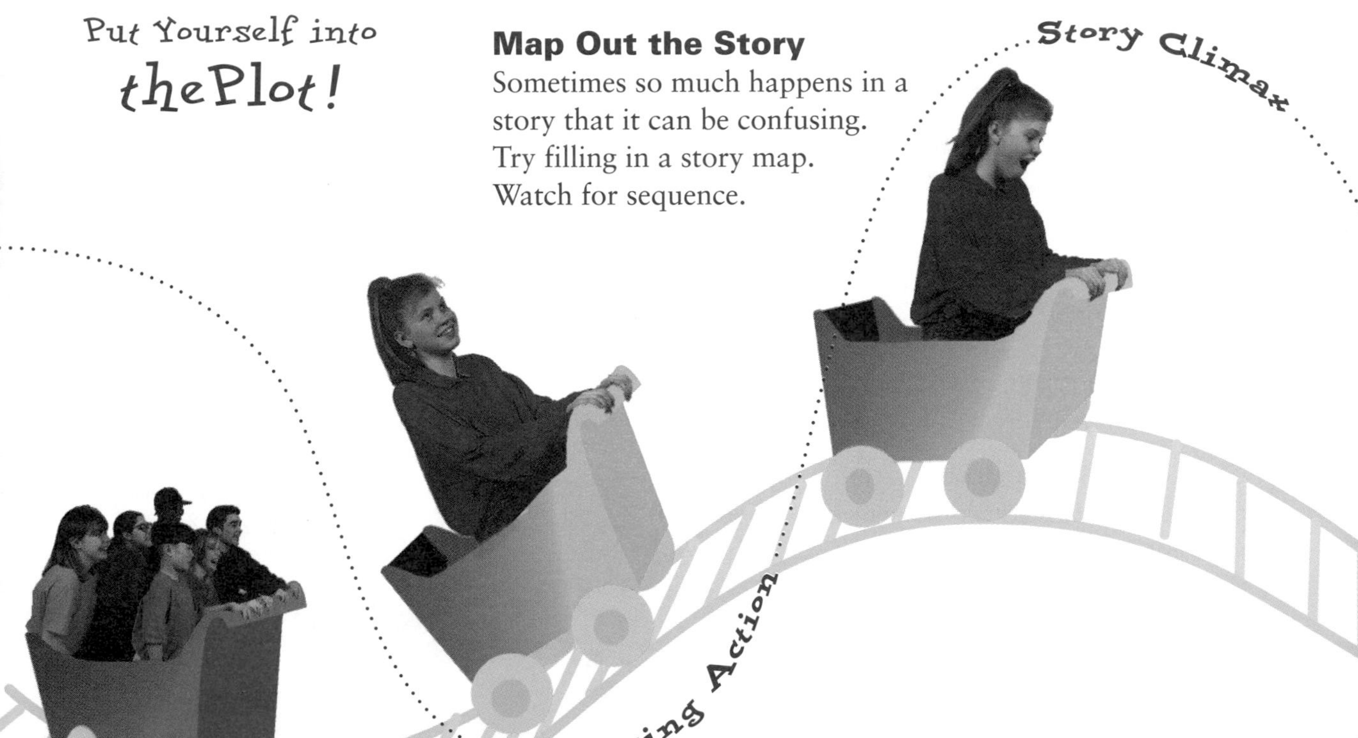
Story Climax
Rising Action

Here's How To Map a Story

1. **First discover the setting of the story.** Who are the main characters? When and where does the story take place?
2. **Next, recognize the problem.** What conflict do the characters face?
3. **Follow the sequence of events that leads to the resolution.** What situations occur that help to solve the problem?
4. **Then ask how the problem is resolved or *if* it is resolved.** What is the final result? Note that some of the most memorable stories are unresolved, with open endings.
5. **Finally, reflect on the main message of the story.** How did the story make you feel? What's the theme or lesson for you?

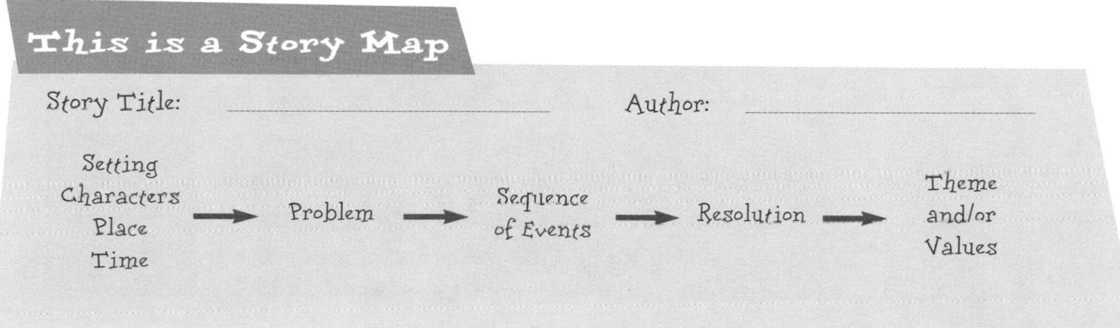
This is a Story Map
Story Title:
Author:
Setting
Characters
Place
Time
Problem
Sequence of Events
Resolution
Theme and/or Values

What's the Theme?

That's the author's message to you!

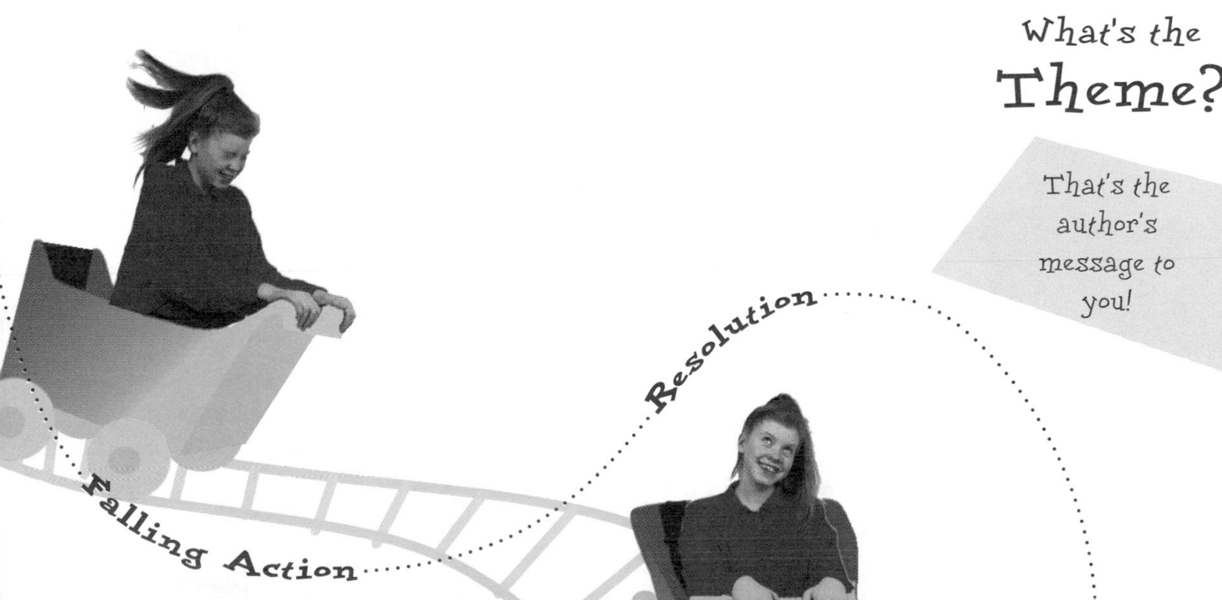
Resolution
Falling Action

Read Between the Lines

Authors don't always tell you everything. They carefully pick and choose which details are important to include in a story. They leave the interpretation up to you. That's called reading between the lines. The conclusions you make are called inferences. Here are some tips on reading between the lines:

Ask yourself

... what details are included in the story?
... what details have been left out?
... why did the author tell me that?
... why didn't the author tell me about this?

Here's the beginning of a story by Richard Peck called "Priscilla and the Wimps." As you read the dialogue, make some inferences and jot them down. Think about what you find out about the characters and situation without being told.

from: Priscilla and the Wimps

Listen, there was a time when you couldn't even go to the rest room around this school without a pass. And I'm not talking about those little pink tickets made out by some teacher. I'm talking about a pass that could cost anywhere up to a buck, sold by Monk Klutter.

> Passes! That sounds like our school—but not having to pay someone for them!

Not that Mighty Monk ever touched money, not in public. The gang he ran, which ran the school for him, was his collection agency. They were Klutter's Kobras, a name spelled out in nailheads on six well-known black plastic windbreakers.

> Monk must be smart and also a real bully to have so much clout.

Monk's threads were more . . . subtle. A pile-lined suede battle jacket with lizard-skin flaps over tailored Levis and a pair of ostrich-skin boots, brassed-toed and suitable for kicking people around. One of his Kobras did nothing all day but walk a half step behind Monk, carrying a fitted bag with Monk's gym shoes, a roll of restroom passes, a cash-box, and a switchblade that Monk gave himself manicures with at lunch over at the Kobras' table.

> His own gang must be afraid of him if they carry his things around and do his dirty work for him.

Speaking of lunch, there were a few cases of advanced malnutrition among the newer kids. The ones who were a little slow in handing over a cut of their lunch money and were therefore barred from the cafeteria. Monk ran a tight ship.

I admit it. I'm five foot five, and when the Kobras slithered by, with or without Monk, I shrank. And I admit this, too: I paid up on a regular basis. And I might add: so would you.

This school was old Monk's Garden of Eden. Unfortunately for him, there was a serpent in it. The reason Monk didn't recognize trouble when it was staring him in the face is that the serpent in the Kobras' Eden was a girl.

Practically every guy in school could show you his scars. Fang marks from Kobras, you might say. And they were all highly visible in the shower room: lumps, lacerations, blue bruises, you name it. But girls usually got off with a warning.

Except there was this one girl named Priscilla Roseberry. Picture a girl named Priscilla Roseberry, and you'll be light years off. Priscilla was, hands down, the largest student in our particular institution of learning. I'm not talking fat. I'm talking big. Even beautiful, in a bionic way. Priscilla wasn't inclined toward organized crime. Otherwise, she could have put together a gang that would turn Klutter's Kobras into garter snakes.

The author is exaggerating here, but this guy does sound really scary.

I like the narrator. He's not afraid to admit that he's scared.

It sounds as if some girl is going to cause trouble for Monk.

This guy sounds really mean. I can see why everyone in school pays money to him.

Priscilla must be important here. She's big and her name is in the title of the story. I wonder who "the wimps" are?

Explore the Writer's Tool Box

How is a writer like a carpenter? They are both builders. Good story writers use a variety of tools and techniques, called literary devices, to build something that didn't exist before. Think about your favourite stories. They probably use some of the techniques described below:

Inspired? Try writing a sequel to a story you've read–or write your own short story! **See page 60.**

. . . I sat back in my chair, just listening to the wind

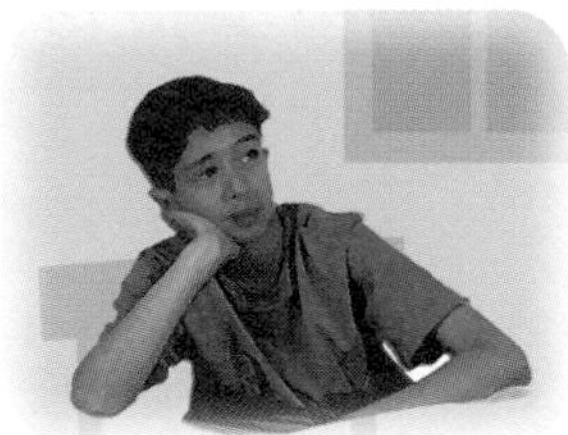

Point of View

Point of view is the "voice" of the story. First-person point of view is told by one story character, using *I*. Third-person point of view is told by a character outside the story, using *he, she,* or *they*.

Flash-back sends you back to an earlier event. The writer may use words or phrases such as *I remember when* or *a few years earlier.*

Figurative language builds comparisons and creates special effects that help you understand characters, places, and ideas. **See simile, metaphor, and personification on page 151.**

Mood is the feeling or atmosphere you get from the story. It may be peaceful, scary, gloomy, funny, weird, or sad.

Symbolism is the use of an object to represent an idea or feeling, such as a raven to represent death or a dove to stand for peace.

Sensory language helps you to share sights, sounds, and other sense experiences with the characters.

Foreshadowing is a clue that may create suspense by hinting at things to come.

Characterization is the description of a character's looks, behaviour, motives, emotions, and personality.

Suddenly I remembered that August night. . .

Flashback

Test Out the Tools

Few stories—especially short ones—use all of these literary devices. But here's a story that uses many of them.

Or Was It Something Else Out There?

I was so tired that I sat back in my chair, just listening to the wind. POINT OF VIEW Suddenly I remembered that August night of long ago FLASH-BACK:

The dark clouds that night raced across the sky. The wind whined and moaned through the cracks in the cabin. FIGURATIVE LANGUAGE: PERSONIFICATION The waves crashed upon the shore. I waited and watched and listened on that stormy night. MOOD

Suddenly a flash of light cast the shadow of a raven upon the wall. SYMBOLISM The air smelled damp and musty, and the rain beat against the window and seeped under the sill.SENSORY LANGUAGE The crying of the wind increased—or was it something else? Something outside? FORESHADOWING

I leapt to the door and peered outside just as lightning filled the sky and revealed an overturned boat and a man being tossed out to sea. I told myself to keep cool and not to panic, as I rushed out in my motorboat to rescue him. CHARACTERIZATION Soon after I reached him, he fell unconscious.

I hauled him to shore. Trying to keep calm, I pumped and pressed him—I kneaded him like a piece of dough FIGURATIVE LANGUAGE: SIMILE until one eye opened, and he gasped for air.

. . . a flash of light cast the shadow of a raven on the wall.

Symbolism

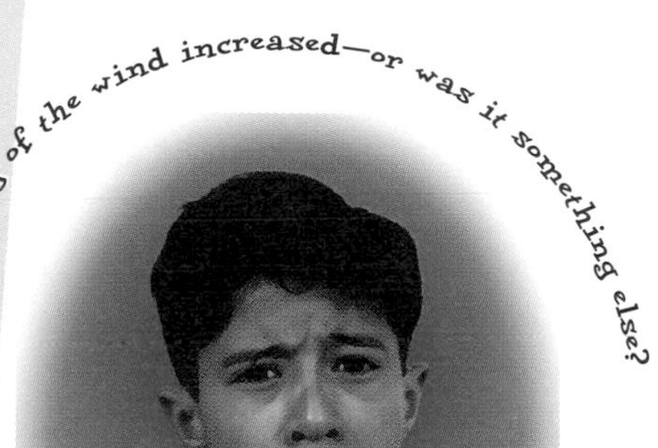
The crying of the wind increased—or was it something else?

Foreshadowing

Here's How To Read a Narrative

Now that you know the elements and tools that build narratives, you're ready to pull your knowledge together to work for you. Here's a three-step plan of action.

Before You Read

1. **Preview the book**. Do you want to read this book? Check out the title, author, jacket flaps, illustrations, contents, and copyright date. Give it the once-over. Do you know of other books by this author?
2. **Make predictions.** What is this book going to be about? Is it the kind of book you usually find interesting and challenging?
3. **Set a purpose.** What do you hope to get out of this story?

While You Read

1. **Summarize.** Stick to the key points of the story here. Who are the characters? What's their problem? How might it be solved? If you need help, try creating a story map first. Then summarize.
2. **Note the sequence.** What's the order of events in the story? Are you confused about shifts in time? Watch for words and phrases like *before, later,* and *I recall.*
3. **Make predictions.** Stay involved in the story by asking yourself what will happen to the characters. Read on. Did your predictions come true?
4. **Assess.** Do you understand this book? Are you enjoying the story? If not, switch to another book.

After You Read

1. **Respond.** How did the story make you feel and why? Did you like the main character? Does he or she remind you of anyone? Would you recommend this book to a friend? Write your reponses in a journal, create a new story ending, or construct a collage. **For more creative ideas for responding to narratives, see page 113.**
2. **Go beyond the book.** Find another book by the same author or on the same topic. Or pick a passage that you really liked—a funny conversation, a character description, a tense scene. Reread it to yourself, or share the passage with a friend!

Before you read ...While you read...After you read

Choose Your Narrative

Narratives come in many forms—short stories, novels, plays, film scripts, magazine articles, and others. Here's a list to pick from.

Adventure stories are action-packed tales in which the characters—either fictional or real—come into conflict with nature or a dangerous enemy.

Biography is the life story of a person other than the author. *Bio* means "life," and *graphy* refers to writing.

Autobiography . . . What do you think an autobiography is? *Auto* means "self." It's the story of the writer's life.

Fantasy deals with the non-existent, the unreal, and the incredible.

Science fiction creates future or other worlds and imaginary characters. These stories frequently deal with today's issues and problems in futuristic settings.

Mysteries, thrillers, detective stories, and horror stories are suspense-filled stories that keep you guessing about what will happen next. The ending may come as a surprise.

HISTORICAL FICTION takes you back in time, putting you in touch with actual events and people of the past.

Myths, legends, and folk tales have been handed down from past cultures. These stories of heroes and gods often explain events or natural phenomena.

Contemporary realistic fiction takes place in the present or recent past. These narratives deal with people—like those you know—and their problems or achievements.

READING

Poetry

What can send a chill creeping down your spine or cause a catch in your throat? What can beat a rhythm in your head? A poem. That's because it taps into your memories and your emotions.

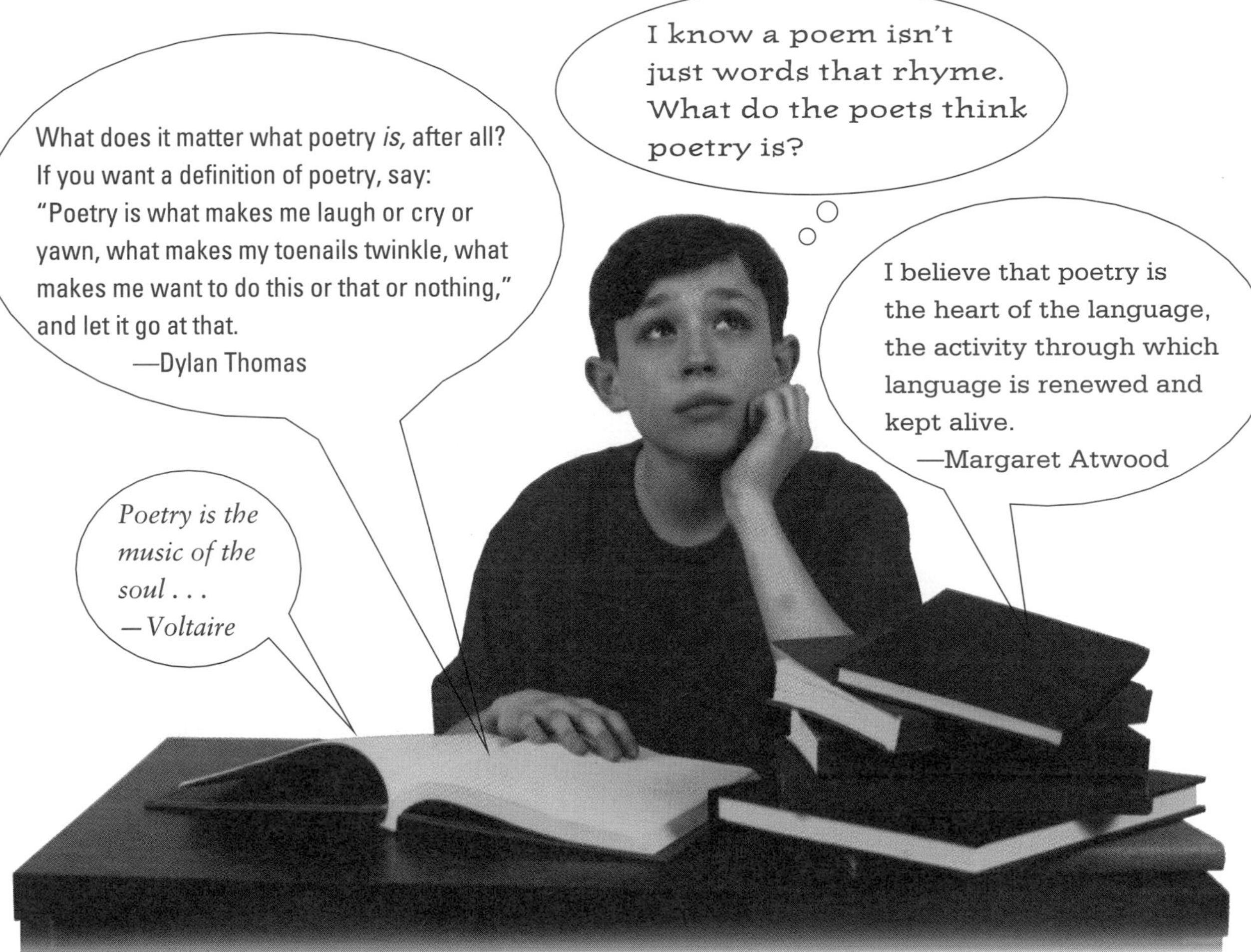

I know a poem isn't just words that rhyme. What do the poets think poetry is?
What does it matter what poetry *is,* after all? If you want a definition of poetry, say: "Poetry is what makes me laugh or cry or yawn, what makes my toenails twinkle, what makes me want to do this or that or nothing," and let it go at that. —Dylan Thomas
I believe that poetry is the heart of the language, the activity through which language is renewed and kept alive. —Margaret Atwood
Poetry is the music of the soul . . . —Voltaire

Even the poets don't agree on a definition! But just because poetry is hard to define doesn't mean that it's hard to read. Reading poetry does take some practice, though. A reading strategy will help you!

Experiencing a Poem

What makes you remember a poem? Is it the poet's use of sounds, images, and rhythm? Poets choose and arrange their words very carefully. The language of poetry, or the images, metaphors, sounds, pauses, and rhythms, creates the meaning of a poem. In a way, the language of poetry *is* the meaning of the poem. The poet John Ciardi believed that readers should concentrate on the *how* of a poem—the way its parts work together—instead of on what a poem means. Look at these two poems about the crescent moon.

The Path on the Sea

The moon this night is like a silver sickle
Mowing a field of stars.
It has spread a golden runner
Over the rippling waves.
With its winking shimmer
This magic carpet lures me
To fly to the moon on it.

—Inna Muller (age 13)

Winter Moon

How thin and sharp is the moon tonight!
How thin and sharp and ghostly white
Is the slim curved crook of the moon
tonight!

—Langston Hughes

Did you notice that Langston Hughes uses cold, cutting words and images, such as *thin* and *sharp, ghostly white,* and *curved crook*? Did you feel the difference in the mood of Inna Muller's poem? The words and images of *silver sickle mowing, rippling waves,* and *golden runner* are soft sounding and call forth rich, pleasant images.

It's the tree in our yard

Reading a Poem

Relax! Enjoy! Reading a poem involves spending time with it, listening to it. Discover how the poem connects with your feelings. Experience what it means to you. Responding to poetry is not an exercise in finding the hidden meanings.

Here's How

To Read a Poem

Begin by reading the poem several times, simply to enjoy it. If the meaning puzzles you, try this process:

1. **First read the poem all the way through.** If you come to a word or phrase you don't understand, just keep going. Think about your reactions to the poem. Ask yourself, "What images do I see? How do I feel? What do I think of?"
2. **Read the poem again.** Concentrate on the parts that seemed unclear. Use context (surrounding words) to unlock the meaning of unfamiliar words, or use a dictionary.
3. **Read the poem a third time, aloud.** As you listen, think about how the sounds in the poem affect you.
4. **Tell what the poem is about.** What is happening in the poem? What does the poet see, think, or feel?
5. **Connect with the poem.** Which feelings, situations, or images remind you of events or emotions in your own life?

Advice from the Zone

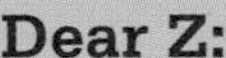

Dear Z:

Whenever we talk about poetry in class, hands wave in the air, and everyone talks at once. But not me! I scrunch down behind the person in front of me. I don't have a clue what the poet is saying. It's totally frustrating. What should I do?

—Clue Less

Dear Clue:

Have confidence in your instincts. React honestly. Try blurting out the first thought that pops into your head—even a question. You probably will be on the right track. Or bounce your response off one of your hand-waving classmates. Remember, poetry is personal, so there are lots of possible responses.

Spontaneously yours,

Z.

Discussing a Poem

Is your response to a poem often different from those of your friends or classmates? Probably it is. Reading poetry can be a very personal experience. Even so, pooling your reactions—in a discussion with your classmates—can make the experience of the poem richer for everyone. You will get more out of a poem if you share your thoughts and feelings, using specific examples from the poem to point to what you mean.

Unclear about how to lead a group discussion? Learn all about the art of team talking. **See page 158.**

Here's How

To Discuss a Poem

Stumped on how to begin? Although there's no single way to discuss a poem, here are some steps to get your group started.

1. **Listen to the poem as it's read aloud.** Ask your teacher, a group member, or someone else familiar with the poem to read it to you. Or listen to it on the audiotape.
2. **Read the poem to yourself.** Does it remind you of an experience or emotion that you've had?
3. **Take turns stating reactions to the poem.** Each group member should answer these questions, "How does the poem make you feel? How does it sound to you? What images does it bring to mind?" You'll get more ideas if everyone speaks without interruption.
4. **Discuss the first round of comments.** After everyone has responded once, ask "What related ideas occurred to each of you as others stated their reactions?"
5. **Open up the discussion.** Try to cover some of these points: Is anything unclear to you? What questions would you want to ask the poet? What's happening in the poem? How do the words and phrases affect you?
6. **Reread the poem aloud.** Try to clear up any confusing points that came up in the discussion. Have a volunteer report on the findings of your group.

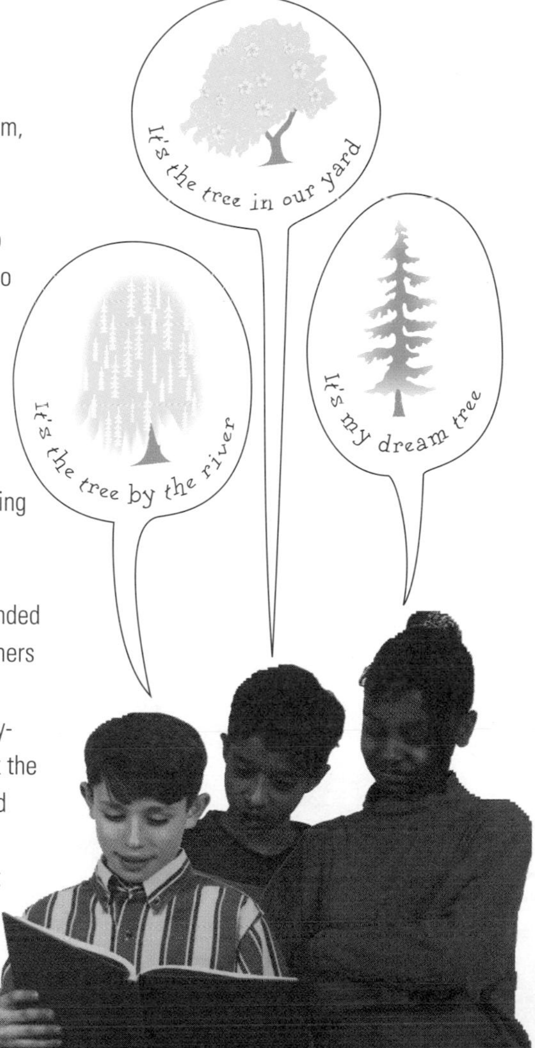
It's the tree in our yard
It's the tree by the river
It's my dream tree

. . . . The sound of poetry is the music of poetry. It's got rhythm, it's got a beat, it's got a pulse!

The Sounds of Poetry

What makes a poem different from other forms of writing? Do rhythm and rhyme come to mind? Not all poems use both these elements, but most poems have a music of their own. Listen for the music in this poem. How does the arrangement of sounds help to create feeling and meaning?

Something Is There

Something is there
there on the stair
coming down
coming down
stepping with care.
Coming down
coming down
slinkety-sly.
Something is coming and wants to get by.

—Lilian Moore

Beat Out the Rhythm

You react to rhythm every day—in the music you hear and the sports you play. In poetry, rhythm is the beat of the lines. Some poems have a predictable rhythm, called *metre*. Here are some tips to figure out the rhythm pattern of a poem.

Find the Metre of a Poem

Here's part of a poem with a strong, regular metre. Try *scanning,* or reading the poem to find the rhythm pattern of stressed and unstressed syllables.

Listen to the beat and mark each syllable. Mark the lighter or unstressed syllables this way: ˘

Mark the heavy or stressed syllables this way: ´

Now listen again to the beat of the lines: duh-DAH, duh-DAH, duh-DAH, duh-DAH.

Th̆e sún / th̆at brief / Dĕcém/bĕr dáy
Rosĕ chéer/lĕss óv/ĕr hílls / ŏf / gráy,
Ănd, dárk/lў̆ cír/clĕd, gáve / ăt nóon
Ă sád/dĕr líght / thăn wán/ĭng móon.

—John Greenleaf Whittier

After marking the beat, look for the pattern. Usually, the rhythm pattern repeats

It rhymes, it sings, it repeats. Listen to the music, listen to the rhyme.

Locate the Rhyme

You've been listening to rhymes for years! Rhyme is the repetition of the same sound in different words. Poets use rhyme for the same reason they use rhythm—to help organize the poem and to suggest meaning and emotion.

On Being Much Better Than Most and Yet Not Quite Good Enough

There was a great swimmer named Jack
Who swam ten miles out—and nine back.

—John Ciardi

The most common type of rhyme in poetry is called *end rhyme*, which occurs—you guessed it!—at the end of lines, like *Jack* and *back* in the poem above. *Internal rhyme* occurs within a single line. For example: See the *mean gleam* in his eye and *deep crease* in his *cheek*. Often poets repeat a rhyme scheme or metre pattern within a four- or five-line stanza. A *stanza* is something like a paragraph in prose. It's a group of lines standing together.

Of course, some poems have no rhyme at all! Check out the rhyme scheme in the following stanzas.

Find the Rhyme Pattern of a Poem

Dust of Snow

The way a crow—a
Shook down on me—b
The dust of snow—a
From a hemlock tree—b

Has given my heart—c
A change of mood—d
And saved some part—c
Of a day I had rued.—d

—Robert Frost

Mark each line according to the sound at the end. Mark the first line with an *a*. If you find another line-ending sound that rhymes with the first line ending, mark that with an *a* also. Then mark the next line-ending sound with a *b*, and so on.

Mark the rhyme pattern of the next stanza. Watch for a pattern as you mark the next stanza. Each new line-ending sound should be marked with a new letter.

Look for Repeated Words

Why do parents repeat the same comments? Is it to make sure you get the point? Look at the repetition in this poem.

Poetry

What is Poetry? Who knows?
Not a rose, but the scent of the rose;
Not the sky, but the light in the sky;
Not the fly, but the gleam of the fly;
Not the sea, but the sound of the sea;
Not myself, but what makes me
See, hear, and feel something that prose
Cannot: and what it is, who knows?

—Eleanor Farjeon

inside
INFO

Alliteration is not always the repetition of a beginning consonant sound. Sometimes the sound is hidden within the words. For example, listen for the repetition of similar consonant sounds in the words *sad, uncertain, bustle,* and *symbol*.

Why does Eleanor Farjeon repeat words and phrases in her poem? What effect does the repetition have?

Note the Line Breaks

Line breaks help set the pace and rhythm of a poem. They tell you where to pause and where to take a breath. Try reading "Poetry" to see where you pause. Poets arrange their poems carefully. Try to follow the signals given by line breaks, rhythm, and rhyme.

Listen for Alliteration

In the poem below, listen for the *l* sound in *like* and *licorice,* and the repetition of the *t* sound in *twisting, traffic,* and *taste*. Can you taste the rain? The taste image travels all the way through the poem, strengthened by *alliteration,* the repetition of the consonant at the beginning of words.

rush hour in the rain

wet streets
shiny black like licorice
twisting through the city
traffic tastes its way home

—Tiffany Stone

The Language of Poetry

Imagery is language that creates pictures and sensory impressions. Often you remember a poem because its images appeal to your sight, sound, touch, taste, or smell.

Can you see the giant, rolling sea-dog in this poem? Hear the clashing of teeth and jaws? Touch the greasy paws?

from The Sea

The sea is a hungry dog,
Giant and gray.
He rolls on the beach all day.
With his clashing teeth and shaggy jaws
Hour upon hour he gnaws
The rumbling, tumbling stones,
And "Bones, bones, bones!"
The giant sea-dog moans,
Licking his greasy paws.

—James Reeves

Simile

The sea is like a hungry dog.

Metaphor

The sea is a hungry dog.

Figurative language uses images that cannot be taken literally. If your dad says, "Your room looks like a cyclone hit it!" what do you think of? You will have a personal reaction—but it won't be fear that a big storm has ruined your room! Figurative language suggest similarities in things that are not usually compared. A comparison using the word *like* or *as* is called a *simile*. In a *metaphor* the comparison is made more directly, without either of those words—"The sea is a hungry dog. . . ."

In *personification,* an animal, object, or concept is given human characteristics, as in this poem, "Eclipse."

Eclipse

I looked the sun straight in the eye.
He put on dark glasses.

—F. R. Scott

The Forms of Poetry

Poetry has been growing and changing since ancient times, and there are many different poetic forms. All over the world, people of all ages have enjoyed singing, chanting, reciting, writing, and listening to poetry. The roots of modern poetry go back to prehistoric songs, chants, and prayers.

Do you ever wonder how poets decide which poetic forms to use? Sometimes they create new forms to fit what they want to say. But poets may also choose a particular poetic form for the fun and challenge of fitting words, sounds, and meaning into its structure. You will find examples of some common poetic forms below. See if you can figure out how the structure contributes to the meaning of the poem.

Haiku

Haiku, a three-line form that captures a moment in nature, originated in Japan. Its seventeen syllables are arranged in three lines in a five-seven-five syllable pattern.

Tips for Finding Other Sources
Look for haiku collections, such as *The Haiku Anthology*, edited by Cor Van Den Heuvel.

Haiku

In the bent birch tree
wind ruffles the fur and quills
of a porcupine.

—Bruce Meyer

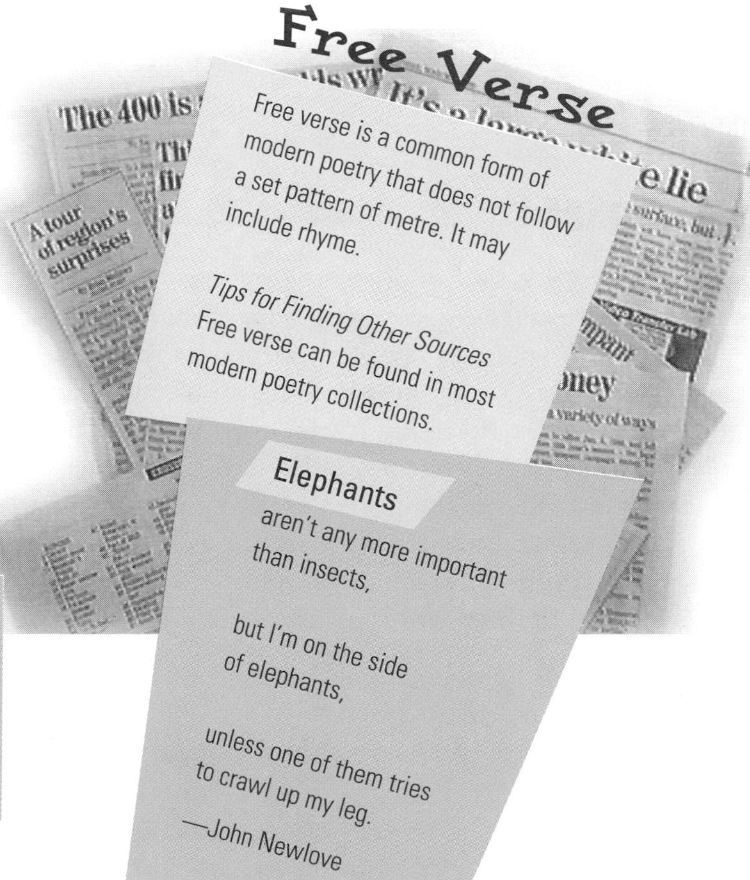

Free Verse
The 400 is
A tour of region's surprises
Free verse is a common form of modern poetry that does not follow a set pattern of metre. It may include rhyme.
Tips for Finding Other Sources
Free verse can be found in most modern poetry collections.
Elephants
aren't any more important
than insects,

but I'm on the side
of elephants,

unless one of them tries
to crawl up my leg.

—John Newlove

Sonnet

A sonnet is a fourteen-line poem that usually follows a set rhyme scheme and metrical pattern.

Tips for Finding Other Sources
Look for collections of works by the famous sonnet writers—William Shakespeare, John Keats, Elizabeth Barrett Browning, and Edna St. Vincent Millay.

If I should learn, in some quite casual way,
That you were gone, not to return again—
Read from the back-page of a paper, say,
Held by a neighbor in a subway train,
How at the corner of this avenue
And such a street (so are the papers filled)
A hurrying man, who happened to be you,
At noon today had happened to be killed,
I should not cry aloud—I could not cry
Aloud, or wring my hands in such a place—
I should but watch the station lights rush by
With a more careful interest on my face;
Or raise my eyes and read with greater care
Where to store furs and how to treat the hair.

—Edna St. Vincent Millay

Ballad

A ballad is a short narrative poem told in songlike form. Many ballads have been passed down as folk songs that tell love stories or tales about heroes or historical events.

Tips for Finding Other Sources
Look in collections of folk ballads for well-known ballads such as "Frankie and Johnny" or "The Cremation of Sam McGee." To learn what happens to Annabel Lee, find the entire poem in a volume of the works of Edgar Allan Poe.

ANNABEL LEE

It was many and many a year ago,
In a kingdom by the sea
That a maiden there lived whom you may know
By the name of ANNABEL LEE;
And this maiden she lived with no other thought
Than to love and be loved by me. . . .

—Edgar Allan Poe

Speaking
Use the right words to get your message across !

Two heads are better than one.
I always have lots of questions
What does he really mean?
Express yourself in performance!
Can you convince me?

and Listening

Are the words that leave your mouth not what you intended to say? When you listen, do the speaker's words seem to be on fast-forward? Here's help!

Contents

SPEAKING AND LISTENING

What was that you said?

Person to Person

Do you express yourself differently depending on whom you're talking to? Most of us do. Even if you know a person well, what you *mean* to say may not be what he or she *hears* you say. But there is hope! We can all practise ways to speak and listen better.

The Drama Club

Let me express my thanks to all of you, club members, for letting me have this role. I hope to be the **best** Romeo ever!

Yawn!

You're welcome! You're going to be great.

Good speakers speak in a style and vocabulary their listeners will understand.

Good listeners are respectful, polite, and interested. Their behaviour helps the speaker feel more confident.

Guess what, Grandpa, I'm gonna be **Romeo** in the play!

It's noisy here! Did you say you'll be in a **rodeo** today? That sounds dangerous!

Good speakers talk clearly, not too fast, and loudly enough for their listeners.

Good listeners pay attention. If they can't hear, they let the speaker know.

Yo Beth! I just got a **wicked** big part in the school play! Cool, huh?

Awesome. Way to go!

"Wicked"?

Good speakers use language that expresses how they feel. They use slang that's familiar to the listener, but only in informal situations.

Good listeners listen closely before drawing conclusions.

Did I overhear you say you'll be a **villain** in the play?

Huh? What did I say to make her think that?
No. I'm the tragic hero—Romeo!

In a Group

Listen, can we talk?

Discussion IS . . . sharing ideas with others . . . considering other viewpoints . . . thinking out loud . . . helping one another to learn . . . solving problems and making decisions together.

Discussion MEANS . . . listening carefully . . . speaking clearly and thoughtfully . . . making sure everyone gets a chance to talk . . . being open to new ideas and ways of looking at things . . . treating one another with respect.

Learn the Art of Team-Talking

	HOT	NOT!
To agree with a group member	☛ Smile and nod. ☛ Say, "I agree!" ☛ Say, "That's a good point." ☛ Look encouraging.	☛ Clap wildly and cry, "Yes, YES!" ☛ Say, "Let me interrupt to say that I agree with you completely, Sarah, . . . (blah, blah, blah)."
To disagree with a group member	☛ Look puzzled. ☛ Say, "But have you thought about . . .?" ☛ Say, "I have another suggestion."	☛ Roll your eyes and sigh. ☛ Shake your head violently. ☛ Mutter, "What a stupid thing to say!" ☛ Shout, "You don't know what you're talking about!"
To get more involved in the discussion	☛ Listen to what others are saying, and think of ways you can add to what someone else has said. ☛ Say, "That's a good point, Gerardo, because . . ." Or say, "But there might be exceptions to that rule. For example, . . ." ☛ Jot down some notes on the discussion. Read one aloud and comment on it.	☛ Mutter, "Well, I guess no one here cares what *I* think!" ☛ Slump in your chair and refuse to make eye contact with anyone. ☛ Wait for someone else to ask you what you have to say. ☛ Try to get the group's attention by stretching, clearing your throat, and tapping the table.

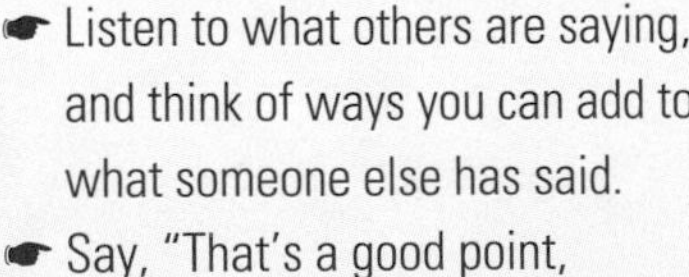

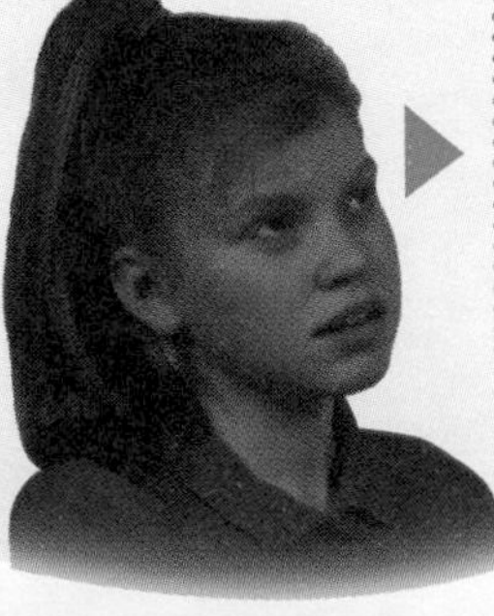

	HOT	NOT!
To keep one member from hogging the discussion	☛ Hold up your hand and say, "I have something to add when you're finished, Kim." ☛ Say, "Interesting point, Kim. Can we discuss that? Mashid, what do you think?"	☛ Make "oink-oink" noises. ☛ Stare angrily and hope the person takes the hint. ☛ Exclaim, "Kim! Would you shut up and give someone else a chance!"
To make sure you and your group understand something	☛ Check to see if anyone looks confused or puzzled. ☛ Ask, "Are we all clear on this?" ☛ Say, "Excuse me, Kyoko, I want to make sure I understand what you just said."	☛ Sit back and hope everything will become clear later. ☛ Cry, "What on earth are you talking about, Kyoko? You've got everyone confused!"
To deal with group members who interrupt you while you're speaking	☛ Make sure *you* aren't hogging the discussion. ☛ In a pleasant voice, say, "Could you give me another second, Sam? I'm almost done."	☛ Get angry. ☛ Hiss, "Thanks, Sam. I'll finish my thought when *you're* done."
To keep group members from being rude	☛ Be a good example. ☛ Keep your tone light but firm to avoid bad feeling. ☛ Direct a rude person toward the issue. Ask, "Do you have something to add to the discussion, Josh?"	☛ Let someone get away with rudeness. ☛ Shout, "What makes you think *you're* so great?" ☛ Cry, "Hey! You want name-calling? Here's a name for you!"
To reach group agreement	☛ Say, "Let's keep talking this out. I don't think everyone agrees." ☛ Say, "I think we need to get more information before we can agree." ☛ Ask, "Has everyone had a say?" ☛ Say, "We're ready. Let's vote!"	☛ Move around restlessly. ☛ Announce, "I say we go with Sergei's proposal. And that's that!" ☛ Demand, "We've got two minutes to agree—starting *now*."

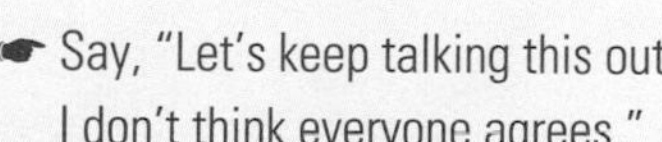

In Discussion

Team-talking is only part of what goes on in a good discussion group. Different kinds of discussion groups have different goals, and group members may have different roles and responsibilities. Here are "what's what" and "who's who."

What's What

Pairs

Roundtables

Group Investigation

Group Investigation

3–5 Members

Goals and Uses
- do a research project
- learn about an assigned or chosen topic
- share responsibility for learning

Roles and Responsibilities
- The team has a topic to investigate or a project to complete.
- The team divides the topic into subtopics to investigate or divides the project into tasks to accomplish.
- The members share what they learn or accomplish.

Pairs

2 Members

Goals and Uses
- brainstorm or exchange ideas on a topic
- learn or study together
- tutor each other
- hold a peer conference

Roles and Responsibilities
- Take turns speaking and listening.
- Alternate taking the roles of teacher and learner. One or both might be the recorder.
- Go through the material together or separately, then quiz each other.
- In a peer conference, one asks to hear the other's thoughts about the topic or asks for help learning or understanding it.

Roundtables

5–8 Members

Goals and Uses
- discuss all sides of an issue to reach group agreement
- think critically; analyse
- problem-solve
- make decisions

Roles and Responsibilities
All members are expected to contribute. The roles of leader, clarifier, recaller, recorder, and reporter may be assigned.

Literary Circles

3–8 Members

Goals and Uses
- examine critically a piece of literature
- share personal responses to a reading
- compare critical responses to a literary element

Roles and Responsibilities
Each member reads the same piece of literature. Or each reads a different piece—on a similar topic, or in the same genre, or by the same author.

Buzz Groups

3–5 Members

Goals and Uses
Brainstorm or exchange ideas on a topic—this is a fast, creative way to come up with ideas.

Roles and Responsibilities
All members are expected to contribute. The roles of leader, clarifier, recorder, and reporter may be assigned.

Jigsaw

3–5 Members

Goals and Uses
- discuss the material in a textbook chapter
- learn about an assigned topic
- share responsibility for learning

Roles and Responsibilities
- Each home team learns or explores the same topic or the same subtopics.
- Assign each home team member a different subtopic to learn.
- Members go to their subtopic "expert" groups to learn their subtopics.
- "Experts" go back to teach their subtopics to home-team members.

Who's Who

Leader—Keeps discussion on topic.

"Good point. What does that teach us about the rain forest?"

Clarifier—Makes sure everyone understands what a speaker has said.

"Alice, do you have a question about how trees produce oxygen?"

Recaller—From time to time, summarizes what has been learned or discussed before the group decides to record something.

"We've learned that there are important medicinal plants that live in the rain forest."

Recorder—Writes down the main subjects of discussion.

"Why the rain forest is important: medicinal plants, . . . oxygen. . . ."

Reporter—Shares the group's findings with others.

"In addition, our group learned that the oxygen produced by the rain forest . . ."

Can you tell if you're coming or going?

To Inform and Persuade

You want to tell someone how to get to a theatre, or you want the class to vote for you. You have to give a report or take part in a debate. How do you do it? You use the forms of oral communication that have the purpose of giving information or persuading someone to do or agree with something.

Oral Directions

If you're writing directions, it's easy to check how accurate your information is. But when you're getting or giving oral directions, that can be harder to do. These tips can help.

Tips for Giving Oral Directions

Give it some thought. What are you explaining to someone? Directions to a particular location? Instructions for programming a VCR? Whatever it is, think it through. Imagine the whole process as a series of steps.

Give it your best shot. Explain each step, in order, as clearly and simply as possible. Pause after each step to make sure your listener is following you.

Give it a second chance. Ask your listener to explain the process back to you.

Give your listener a break. Consider how much your listener already knows and what ideas and language he or she is likely to understand.

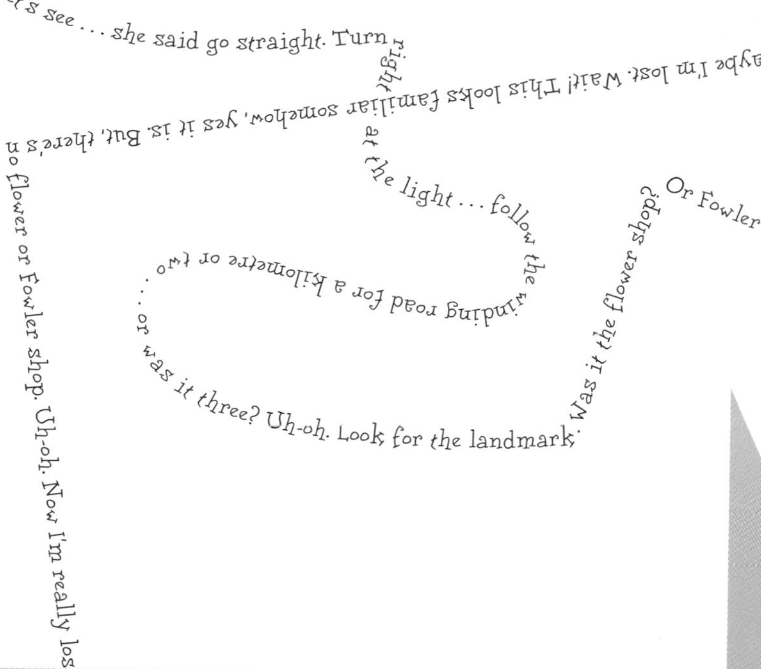
Hmm. Let's see . . . she said go straight. Turn right at the light . . . follow the winding road for a kilometre or two . . . or was it three? Uh-oh. Look for the landmark. Was it the flower shop? Or Fowler's Hardware Shop? Hmm. I thought I saw it back here . . . Uh-oh. Maybe I'm lost. Wait! This looks familiar somehow, yes it is. But, there's no flower or Fowler shop. Uh-oh. Now I'm really lost

Tips for Getting Oral Directions

Get the picture. As you hear the directions, try to picture yourself performing each step of the process.

Get a clue. Listen for clue words that tell you when one step ends and another begins. Some common clue words are *first*, *next*, *after*, *before*, *while*, *then*, and *last*.

Get it straight. How many steps do you have to complete? Do you have them all? Are they in the proper order? Go through the complete process in your head. If possible, act it out.

Got it? Check to make sure you have all the information you need. Don't be afraid to ask questions if something is unclear to you.

I guess it's time to call her and find out where I went wrong. . .

Interviews

People can be wonderful sources of information. But conducting a good interview requires careful planning. Suppose your research topic is recycling, and you want to interview Dr. Uzita Genn, a supervisor at a local recycling plant. What do you do?

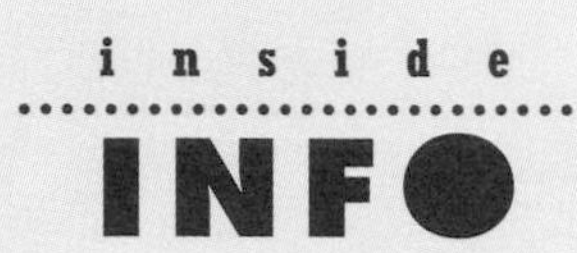
inside
INFO

If you plan to use a tape-recorder, practise turning it on and off, changing tapes, and replacing batteries. Don't forget to bring extra tapes and batteries to the interview in case you need them.

Conduct an Interview

Before

Know something about your topic. You won't be able to fully understand Dr. Genn if you know nothing about recycling. Do a little research.

Decide what you want to find out. What kind of information do you want? How much? When you first contact Dr. Genn, give her a general idea of what you want to know and how long the interview will take.

Make an appointment. Introduce yourself. Explain your project and invite Dr. Genn to talk with you. Ask when and where she'd like to meet. Write down the time and location. If you plan to use a tape-recorder, ask Dr. Genn's permission.

Write a list of questions you want to ask. Make them clear and simple. Avoid questions that can be answered with just "yes" or "no."

Ask for information

Question: Dr. Genn, do you agree that recycling is necessary for our planet to survive?
Answer: Yes.
Better question: Dr. Genn, why is your work necessary? What will happen to our planet if we don't recycle?

Q: What will happen to our planet if we don't recycle?

During

Get off to a good start. Introduce yourself again. Remind Dr. Genn of the purpose of your interview.

Be responsive. Look and act interested. Make eye contact. Ask questions clearly and politely.

Take careful notes. If you aren't taping, write down the most important points, words, and phrases. If you are taping, take notes to remind yourself of your unspoken thoughts.

Be polite, but follow up. In answering a question, Dr. Genn mentions a topic worth pursuing. Don't interrupt her; just jot a note to yourself to go back to it.

Get it right. If you don't understand something Dr. Genn says, ask her to explain. Check your notes to make sure everything is clear. If you want to quote Dr. Genn, ask her permission and check the wording of quotations.

To Quote . . . or to Paraphrase?

A *paraphrase* is a summary of a direct quotation.

DIRECT QUOTATION:	PARAPHRASE:
"I am concerned," Dr. Genn said, "that we are using up our non-renewable resources."	Dr. Genn is concerned that this country is using up its non-renewable resources.

After

End it right. Thank Dr. Genn for her time. Ask if she would like a copy of the interview.

Take some time. As soon as possible, organize your notes. Make a word-for-word copy of your tape. If you're unsure of something, ask Dr. Genn before including it.

Publish your work! Send a copy of the interview, with a persuasive letter, to the editor of your school or local newspaper. Explain why you think readers will enjoy it.

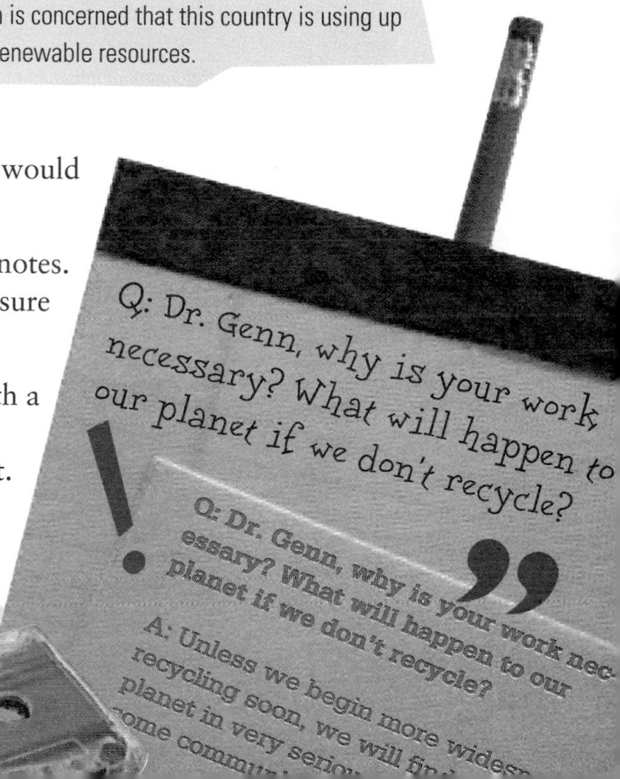

Q: Dr. Genn, why is your work necessary? What will happen to our planet if we don't recycle?
Q: Dr. Genn, why is your work nec-essary? What will happen to our planet if we don't recycle?
A: Unless we begin more wides recycling soon, we will fi planet in very serio

Oral Reports

Oral presentations are part of every student's life and part of many working people's lives, too. They may include displays, models, charts, or other visual aids; or they may rely on words and gestures.

Need help giving a talk? Is it an informal talk about your own experiences? Is it a speech that expresses your viewpoint on an issue—a viewpoint you want others to share? **For tips on storytelling, see page 179. For more about giving a speech, turn to page 172.**

Mateo asked his friend Isha to help him practise giving his oral report. He prepared a checklist of things to do and remember. Isha agreed to make up a checklist of things the audience might watch and listen for during Mateo's presentation. Here are their checklists.

Things to Remember for My Oral Report

Ahead of time

- ☑ Make notes of main points to cover.
- ☑ Organize notes. Print large so I can read fast and not lose my place.
- ☑ Mark places to show pictures & charts.
- ☑ Write interesting—dramatic!—opening.
- ☑ Do a trial run to check time (I only have 15 minutes).
- ☑ Practise using slide projector. Do slides look OK?
- ☑ Get organized. Is projector set up? Are slides & notes in order?

As I speak

- ☑ Relax! This can be fun!
- ☑ Don't slouch!
- ☑ Keep hands below shoulders so they won't be distracting.
- ☑ Glance at notes only now & then. Don't read everything. Use my own words too.
- ☑ Sweep eyes over audience. Then look up at people often.
- ☑ Speak up. Can everyone hear me?
- ☑ Speak slowly! (Listen to voice—am I racing?)
- ☑ Sound interested. (Who else will be interested if I'm not?)
- ☑ At the end, don't run away. Give people time to ask questions.

How long will I speak?

My notes are handy . . .

Take a deep breath . . .

Advice from the Zone

Dear Z:

I hate giving oral reports! They always turn out so boring! What should I do?

—Bored Silly

Dear Silly:

If *you're* bored, imagine how your audience must feel! (YAWN) Try these ways to keep everyone awake.

Start with a very short story. It can be true or made up.

Begin with a series of questions your audience might ask, or ones they'd never think of.

Deliver your report as if you're an expert on the topic: a famous scientist, an artist, or even an animal or a plant!

Present part of your report as an interview. Have a friend play the person you interview.

Create a soundtrack of prerecorded sound effects to go with slides or overheads. Or do your report set to music.

Come up with a better idea.

Z.

What I Looked for in Your Oral Report

Opening

Got audience's attention?
(Yes) No

Presentation

Was clear and easy to follow?
(Yes) No

Covered topic well?
(Yes) No

Made information interesting?
(Yes) No

Delivery

Good appearance?
(Yes) No

Voice clear and natural?
(Yes) No

Speed good?
Yes (No)

Sounded interested/interesting?
(Yes) No

Looked at audience often?
(Yes) No

Comments: Mateo, you started out talking a little fast. When you slowed down, it was easier for me to take in all the information you were giving. But you really made me feel like I was there in the Rockies. Thanks for the trip!

Your friend,
Isha

TRY it!

If you have access to a camcorder, ask someone to videotape you as you practise giving your oral report. See how you look and sound. You may have a speech or gesture habit you weren't aware of and could avoid. Or you may look and sound just great!

Is It Logical?

It's hard to contradict an argument that you build logically. Logical ideas are like steps leading to a conclusion that really makes sense. But faulty logic is like a staircase with some of the steps missing. What sounds logical at first may not be convincing when you really think about it. Knowing what to avoid and what to listen for can help you make your case or help you avoid being fooled. Here are some common examples of faulty logic.

Irrelevance: "And that reminds me . . ."

Sometimes, instead of giving reasons to support a main idea, a speaker wanders into another idea:

Marta says, "Our community centre needs more funding. The sports equipment is old and in poor shape. We only have one basketball. I saw some basketballs at Speedy's. Speedy's has the best prices in town."

Irrelevance gets off track.

Speedy's prices have nothing to do with why the community centre needs more funding. Make sure your reasons lead back to the main point—not away from it.

Incomplete Comparison: "It's better!"

Better than what? Better than whose? Incomplete comparisons say less than they pretend or mean to say. Advertisers often use them to make you think their product is best. Here's another incomplete comparison:

Kay says, "In the old days, students learned more than they do today. Teachers made kids work hard. When they graduated, they knew how to read and write. So those students definitely learned more."

Half a comparison isn't a comparison.

Kay begins to compare how much students used to learn with how much they learn today. But she never describes how much students learn today. The incomplete comparison makes her conclusion illogical.

Wrong Conclusion: "The sky is falling!"

In the popular tale, Chicken Little gets hit on the head with an acorn and concludes that the sky is falling. Here's another illogical conclusion:

Joe says, "Animal-rights activists are against hurting animals in medical experiments. Medical experiments have brought us cures for certain types of cancer. These animal-rights activists are against finding a cure for cancer."

Wrong conclusions don't add up.

Joe begins by stating two separate facts that have nothing to do with each other. The two facts don't lead logically to any conclusion. So Joe's conclusion is wrong.

Are you listening critically?

Can you tell whether the speaker is knowledgeable about the subject? Has the biologist done her research? Does the actor understand his lines? Can you separate the speaker's facts, which can be proved, from the speaker's opinions, which can't? Listening critically doesn't mean trying to find fault with everything someone says. It means evaluating what you hear before deciding what you think of it.

Persuasion—or Propaganda?

"Smart people know . . . , so you must agree. . . ." Sound familiar? You've heard manipulative reasoning such as this in speeches, ads, and conversations. It uses generalizations, false information, or other devices to persuade you to do or believe something without asking why. Sometimes it's called *propaganda*. Critical thinking can help you spot it.

But not all persuasive techniques are designed to trick people. To make a point sound stronger, try the ones below.

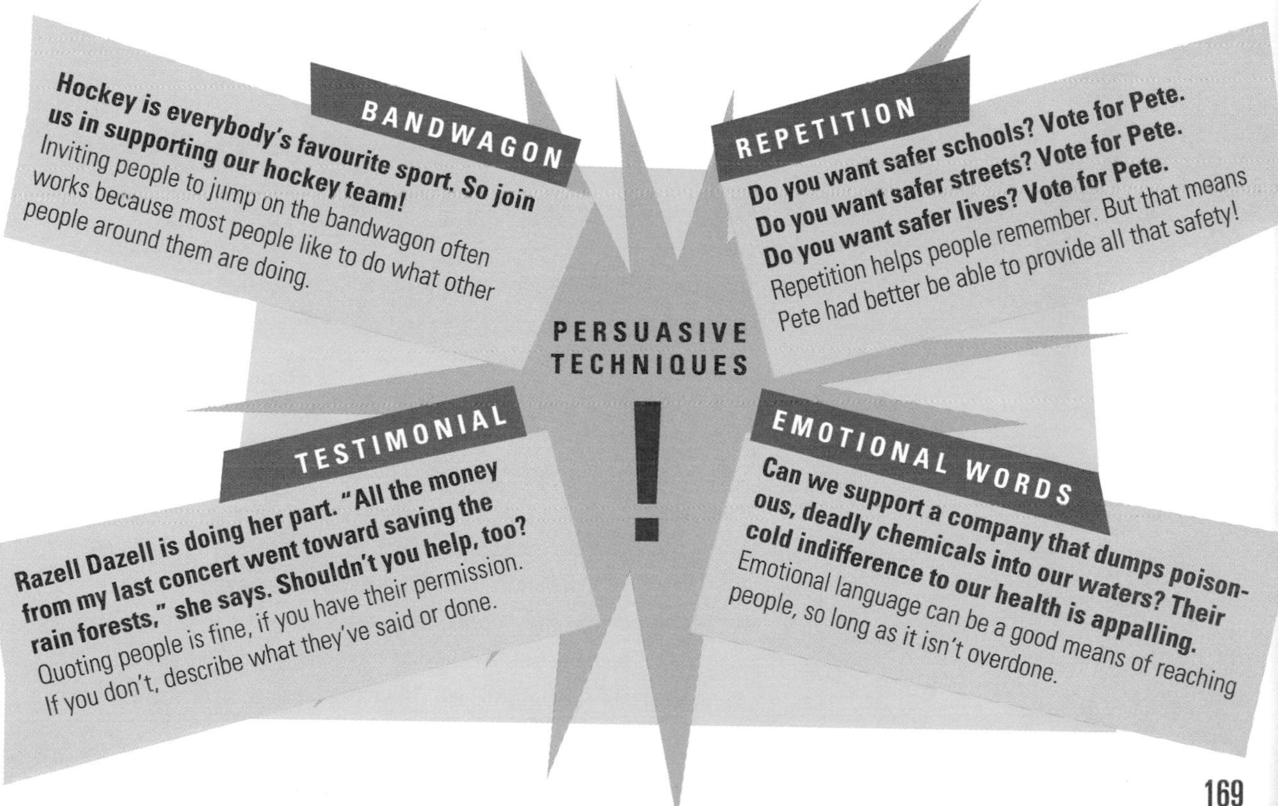
BANDWAGON
Hockey is everybody's favourite sport. So join us in supporting our hockey team!
Inviting people to jump on the bandwagon often works because most people like to do what other people around them are doing.
REPETITION
Do you want safer schools? Vote for Pete.
Do you want safer streets? Vote for Pete.
Do you want safer lives? Vote for Pete.
Repetition helps people remember. But that means Pete had better be able to provide all that safety!
PERSUASIVE TECHNIQUES
!
TESTIMONIAL
Razell Dazell is doing her part. "All the money from my last concert went toward saving the rain forests," she says. Shouldn't you help, too?
Quoting people is fine, if you have their permission. If you don't, describe what they've said or done.
EMOTIONAL WORDS
Can we support a company that dumps poisonous, deadly chemicals into our waters? Their cold indifference to our health is appalling.
Emotional language can be a good means of reaching people, so long as it isn't overdone.

The facts show . . .
On the other hand . . .

Debates

In a debate, two individuals or teams present opposite sides of an issue before an audience or judges. The debate topic is called a *proposition*. It's a single idea that can have strong arguments for it (an affirmative side) and strong arguments against it (a negative side).

Examples of propositions

- Extending the school year would improve the quality of education.
- If more politicians were women, would the world be more peaceful?
- Free housing should be provided for everyone.

During the debate, each side is allowed the same amount of time to make one "constructive" speech (for its own position) and one "rebuttal" speech (against the opponent's position). The judges time the speeches and decide which team wins.

Here's How To Learn the Art of Debate

What if you're assigned to be on a debate team? In a formal debate, things might go something like this.

1. **Talking.** Team members discuss arguments both for and against the proposition. They zero in on the main issues. Teams also discuss how to go about collecting evidence for their side.
2. **Gathering of evidence.** Each team looks for facts that support its argument. Team members refer to books and magazines, call agencies and organizations, and talk to professionals. As they collect evidence for their case, they also note evidence that might be used by the other side.
3. **Planning.** Team members meet, sharing the information they've collected. The team puts together its case, backing up each main point with evidence—maybe a few strong facts, the results of a study, or a quotation from an expert. They discuss the arguments the other team is likely to make and how to refute them. Then they check their own arguments for any weak or faulty reasoning.

4. **Practising.** Each team picks a team captain to present the team's constructive speech. Team members help that person make notes of the team's arguments and backup evidence. Then the captain practises in front of the team to make sure he or she can meet the time limit and present the case convincingly.
5. **Presentation.** In timed constructive speeches, each captain has one turn to present the team's points and supporting evidence. The captain concludes by confidently reminding the judges and the audience how strong the team's case is. Team members listen carefully.
6. **Rethinking.** Team members huddle to consider the other side's arguments. They discuss flaws in the other side's reasoning. They plan new ways to show that their own case is stronger.
7. **Rebuttal.** In timed rebuttal speeches, each team's captain has one turn to explain the weaknesses of the other side's arguments. The captains are calm, avoiding sarcastic comments and name-calling. They remind the judges and audience why their own team's case is stronger. Team members listen without interrupting.
8. **Judges' decision.** The judges decide which team has won the debate by presenting its position more persuasively.

This information proves . . .
We think you'll agree . .
In conclusion . . .

Will You Be on a Panel?

Panel members are both speechmakers and informal debaters. Panels usually consist of three or four people who explain their ideas on a certain subject. This is the speechmaking part. After all their positions have been presented, panelists are invited to join in a general discussion, responding to one another's comments. This discussion may become an informal debate.

Speeches

What makes speeches so challenging—and nerve-wracking? A speech is delivered by you alone, in front of an audience. It's about *your* thoughts, *your* opinions, or *your* experiences—and it's in your own words.

Has speech writing got you stumped? See the chart on the next page. Also, review persuasive writing. **See page 46.**

Determine the Basics

Who will the audience be? Your peers? Adults? A mix? Who they are may affect what you say and how you say it.

Where will you speak? Outdoors? In an auditorium? Will you have a microphone? If so, learn how to use it.

How big will the audience be? Smaller audiences pay closer attention. It's harder to keep a large group interested.

How long will you have to speak? You don't want to run out of time—or end too soon and be left with nothing to say.

Plan the Speech Itself

Decide on a topic and a goal. Your speech could inform your audience about something you know ("My Cambodian Heritage"). It could persuade them to agree with you ("Why I Should Be President"). Or it could entertain them with your experiences ("The Thrill of Windsurfing").

Make notes. They're handy for an informal speech. On separate index cards, write a sentence to introduce each important point. Below, jot down details. Write out any jokes, quotations, or statistics you plan to read.

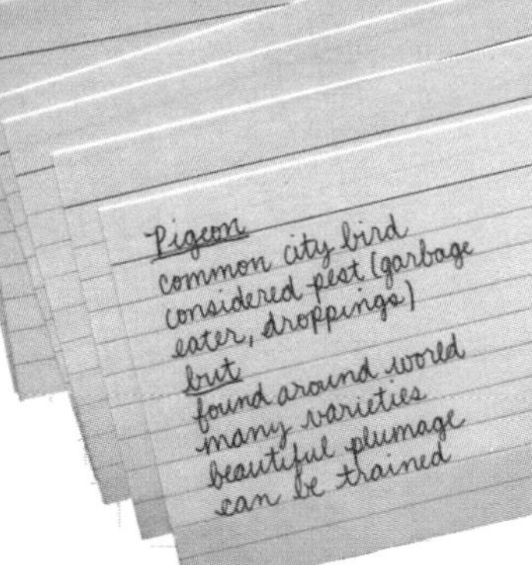
Pigeon
common city bird
considered pest (garbage
eater, droppings)
but
found around world
many varieties
beautiful plumage
can be trained

Write the whole speech. If it has to be formal, or if you're worried about the time limit or afraid you'll leave something out, this way is best. Print or type, so the speech is easy to read. Number the pages and put them in order, unstapled.

Polish your delivery. Practice is the only way.

Plan Some Visuals

Visual aids get an audience's attention and help get your point across. Use a chalkboard, posters, charts or diagrams, slides, or a video. Be creative.

Be Cool

Wear clothes that will make you *and* your audience comfortable. Walk confidently to your speaking spot. Smile and look around before you begin. Use language and humour that won't turn off your listeners. Relax. *Be yourself.*

Nervous? Petrified? Learn how to deal with stage fright. **See the next page.**

WOW THEM WITH YOUR SPEECH TECHNIQUE

SPEECH PART	TECHNIQUES TO TRY	FOR INSTANCE...
Introduction: First, get their attention. Then tell them what you're going to tell them about.	Open with a quotation by a famous person.	"Roberto Alomar, the second baseman for the Blue Jays, once said . . ."
	Start with a dramatic example or statistic.	"Do you know how many people died last year in car accidents?"
	Tell an anecdote (a short personal story).	"Two weeks ago, for the very first time, I talked to a homeless person."
Body: Tell them what you want to tell them.	**Repetition:** Repetition emphasizes an idea and helps people remember. But be careful: enough is enough.	"They asked us for money. But no one gave. They asked us for help. But no one came."
	Rhetorical questions: Set up the body as a series of questions that you ask and answer.	"How can such a plan work? Let me explain. . . . What would it cost? The figures may surprise you . . ."
	Emotional words: Use words that people react to strongly, but don't overdo it. Avoid stereotyping.	"Our public road system is in *crisis*. Our city streets are *choked* with cars . . ."
	Humour: Jokes can backfire. Ask yourself the questions at the right. If you can answer yes, the joke should work.	Will the joke fit my topic? Will my audience get it—and like it? Is it short and easy to deliver? Is it fresh or probably new to my audience?
Conclusion: Remind them of what you've told them. Then end with a bang!	End with a quotation, a dramatic example or statistic, or an anecdote.	"Yesterday, I was reminded of how common this experience is. A woman at the bus stop turned to me and said . . ."
	End by going back to the beginning of your speech and briefly adding a point.	"I began my speech by looking with hope toward our future. I end it by asking you to join me in . . ."
	End with an emotional plea.	"And that's why we can't survive without your help!"

Don't Be Afraid, Speak Up!

Do you feel nervous when all eyes are upon you? At such times it may help to remember that your audience is on your side to begin with: they want to enjoy what you have to share. If remembering that doesn't help, then try this: what you're feeling is normal! Even the coolest speakers and performers have had sweaty palms! They've just learned some tricks to relax and gain confidence.

Tackle Stage Fright

Who says it has to be perfect? Mistakes happen even to professionals. If you make a mistake, don't stop. Improvise! **See page 181.**

Practise, practise, practise! The more you practise, the better you do; and the better you do, the bolder you feel. Try talking in front of a mirror to see how you look and move and talking into a tape-recorder to hear how you sound. Ask some friends to be your practice audience. This might feel awkward at first, but it'll help you get used to having listeners. Practise in the place where you'll be speaking, if possible. See how loudly you have to speak to be heard.

Exercise your fear away before you speak or perform.

Go off alone. Run in place or jump up and down to let off steam.

Take deep breaths and exhale slowly. Do slow stretches at the same time.

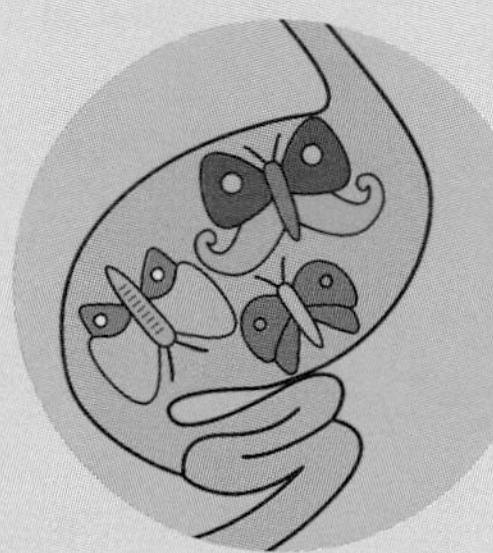

Figure out which part of you feels tense, and tighten it. Then relax it. Repeat.

Swing your arms—together, one at a time, together.

Think good thoughts. Close your eyes and remember a wonderful experience. Let the good feeling fill you up.

Reassure yourself. Remind yourself, "I know what I'm going to do. I've done it all before."

Visualize. Picture yourself speaking and your listeners responding positively to you. Vividly imagine the whole experience, step by step, just the way you want it to be.

SPEAKING AND LISTENING

In Performance

The curtain goes up. The spotlight comes on and finds an inventive person, working magic with the spoken word: reading a nature essay to a writing club, performing a rap, mesmerizing a group with a story, ad libbing in a radio comedy, reciting a soliloquy in a school play. Who is it? It's YOU, using your voice in performance!

One Voice Reading

The best part of reading aloud is that you get to bring a piece of writing to life for others. Often you can hear them respond—laughing at humour, gasping at suspense, even crying at something sad. And reading aloud is a skill. You can make money at it—as a disc jockey; a TV or radio news anchor or sports commentator; a reader of literature for the blind; a narrator of documentaries; a voice in TV or radio ads; or even as the voice of a character in an animated film.

Here's How
To Read it Aloud

1. **Select a written piece you think your audience would like to hear.** It shouldn't be very long or complicated. It should keep you interested from beginning to end.
2. **Use your understanding of the writing.** What's the general mood of the piece—humorous? tense? thoughtful? sad? Decide what you want your audience to understand about it from your reading.
3. **Practise.** On a photocopy of your piece, mark pauses and passages you want to read in a certain way. In a dictionary, check the pronunciation and meaning of any words you aren't sure of. Then read the piece aloud a few times. Try different ways to express the mood. Use your voice comically as you read something funny. Use it dramatically as you read a suspenseful passage. Read some passages slower or faster, louder or softer than others.
4. **Captivate your audience.** Make eye contact with them. Read clearly and with feeling. Don't rush: the audience is probably hearing this piece for the first time. Take time to use the techniques you practised! Pause at special points to give your listeners a chance to react.

Voices Together

Have you ever gotten together with a partner or a group to perform a rap or a choral reading of a poem? If so, you already know that a choral presentation can be as much fun to perform as it is exciting to hear.

When you put together a choral reading, you're like a composer arranging the music for a show. The poem is the music. Your voices are the instruments.

Give a Choral Reading

Pick a poem you'll all enjoy working with. It should have such things as strong rhythms, repeated lines, dramatic passages, rhymes, and places where switching from one voice to another would add to the effect.

Experiment with sounds. Try these ways to "play" your voices as instruments:

Adjust the *volume.* Should words or passages be louder? softer? Change your volume, gradually or abruptly.

Play with the *tempo.* Some lines work best when they're read rapidly or slowly.

Bring out the *rhythm.* The poem already has rhythm; your voices can use ***stress,*** or emphasis, to help others feel it. You may also want to give extra stress to certain words because they're important to the meaning of the poem.

Change *pitch.* Try using high voices for humorous or playful parts and low voices for serious, sad, or scary parts.

Use *pauses* and *stops.* These are good places to switch voices. Remember, a poet may expect readers to pause in the middle, and not at the end, of a line.

Arrange your voices. Decide whether you want each line to be spoken *solo* (by one voice), as a *duet* (by two voices), or *in unison* (all together). (You will probably find that speaking in unison is hard to do for very long.) In most choral readings, two or more voices or sets of voices take turns speaking lines. In another pattern, one voice after another joins in, until all voices are reading together. You may want to use a combination of patterns. Experiment.

Score the reading. A composer scores music with special marks and words to show how the instruments should play each musical "phrase." In the same way, you can use special marks to score your choral-reading piece.

Indicate who says each line. Use your names, or call yourselves Voice 1, Voice 2, Voice 3, and so on.

Make copies of the score. Give a copy to everyone in the group.

Scoring System

/	= a pause
//	= a full stop
~	= no pause
>	= softer
<	= louder
´	= accent word or syllable

Two Choral-Reading Scores

Here is a poem by Langston Hughes, marked for a choral reading using three voices. You can also read the poem alone or experiment with using a different number of voices. Sample scoring marks have been added.

Voice 1	Dream Dust by Langston Hughes
Voice 1	Gáther out of stár-dúst /
Voice 2	> Éarth-dúst, /
Voice 3	> Clóud-dúst, /
Voice 2	> Stórm-dúst, /
Voice 3	And splínters of háil, /
Voice 1	One hándful of dréam-dúst ~
	Nót fór sále. //

TRY it!

Add gestures and movement to your choral reading for dramatic flair. You might try stepping forward a bit when it's your turn to speak.

RAP IT UP!

What we know as rap *is a kind of "talk singing." Like some poetry, rap uses rhyme, repetition, and other patterns that "play" with word meanings and sounds. Here is an excerpt from the rap "Our Time Has Now Come" by Soul II Soul. It has been scored for choral reading to show how it was recorded.*

Voice 1

Take my time to create this rhyme /
Words of inspiration drew me time after time /
I was flowin' ~
Goin' / on and on /
Inducin' motivation, knowin' made me strong /
So clear in my mind with intentions and thoughts ~
Like the ones / that brought us here /
Here to this place /
So now you gotta gain ~
Your own time and space ~
By movin' / in the right direction /
Aided by a selection of actions ~
Enrich your positivity /
There's no time for negativity /
It's prosperin', developin', ~
And we're envelopin' /
And I'm here ~
Showin' you all something ~
Flowin' ~
Goin' on and on /
Our time has now come /
Our time has now come //

All Voices **[Sing refrain twice]**

Refrain
Our time has come
to be together and live as one
Forever livin' free, happily
Our time has come, yeah

Storytelling

Thousands of years ago—before TV, even before books—people gathered to hear their storytellers. They listened to learn—about their ancestors, about nature, about themselves. And they listened just for the fun of hearing a well-told tale. Today, from Saskatoon to San Salvador, for the same good reasons, people are still telling and listening to stories. Are you about to try the ancient craft of storytelling? Of course, there's no one "right" way to tell a story. But here are some tips.

"To be a good teller one must also be a good listener. . . . to be able to tell stories you must have an ear for the story, an ability to take in people's emotions, especially those feelings you haven't experienced yourself."
—Connie Regan-Blake, storyteller

Find a Tale to Tell

The first thing is personal: You, the storyteller, must really *like* the story. Beyond that, the story should have these elements:

A good plot: A good opening will draw in the audience. Story events shouldn't be too complicated or be in a confusing order. The ending should be interesting, too.

A good length: A relatively short story is easier for you to learn and less likely to bore your audience.

Interesting language: The story might have vivid descriptions, humorous or very realistic dialogue, or a dialect. The language might build a suspenseful or magical mood.

Where do you find such a tale? Go to libraries and bookstores. Skim picture books, folk-tale collections, and story anthologies in the fiction sections. Ask relatives and neighbours to tell you their favourite tales (ask if you can tape them!). Or look through your own writings. After all, storytellers don't just tell other people's stories.

Learn the Tale

There are two basic ways. When you just *get the gist* of a story, your goal is to learn its plot, characters, and general language so you can bring them to life in your own way, with your own words. When you *memorize* a story, your goal is to use the author's or previous storyteller's exact words. Pick the way that works best for you.

"I don't memorize my stories. In fact, I'm not a good memorizer. Instead, I see images. . . . I know that I'm never going to go blank as long as I know the topic and focus on it, because I'm describing an inner film running through my mind as I go through the story."
—Spalding Gray, monologuist

Make the Story Your Own

Maybe you think it sounds most natural to tell this story in a conversational tone. Or to have the villain tell it, in a hoarse whisper. You may decide to leave out an unimportant story event. Or to shorten the ending. Maybe you want to add more dialogue. If the language is old-fashioned or too hard for your audience, you can substitute other language or define the hard words. As the storyteller, you can do anything you (and your audience) like!

Bring It to Life with Your Voice and Sounds

Once there was a craggy land . . .

You can tell the whole tale in your own voice or in the voice of a character who is the narrator.

And the witch cackled,
"The wolf will . . ."

Use a different voice and manner for each character.

HOWL!

Use sounds to create mood and express emotion. Howl like a wolf. Moan like the wind. Sigh. Make the door creak. ***For more ideas on using your voice, see page 183.***

Move with It

Some storytellers like using hand gestures. Others avoid any movements that might distract the listeners from what they're "seeing" in their imaginations. Experts know that a single dramatic movement at the story's climax (maybe you *LEAP* forward) can electrify an audience like nothing else. There's no rule about how much you should move. Just concentrate on *feeling* the emotion and mood you're telling about. The rest will probably come naturally.

"Any movement in storytelling will be born out of the story itself."

—Steve Sanfield, author/storyteller

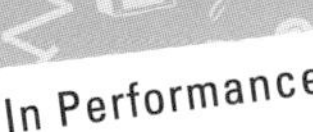

Keep Your Listeners with You

You know when your listeners are "with" you—when they're laughing, or wiping their eyes, or hanging on every word. You also know when they're restless, or whispering, or dozing off. If you're losing them, try moving more quickly through that part of the story—by leaving some of it out, *not* by speeding up. Or pause. Add a gesture or a sound effect.

> **"To enhance the stories I tell, I often stop for a moment . . . to give a twinkle of the eye, a slight smile, an expression of disbelief that helps reinforce and make powerful the statements I've just made. And during those pauses, I'm thinking ahead, to my next words, and my listeners are given time . . . to build the mental images of the story."**
>
> **—Doc McConnell, storyteller**

BRIGHT Ideas

FOR IMPROVISING

To *improvise* means to invent, recite, or do something spontaneously, without planning it. Storytellers—as well as actors, dancers, and other performers—sometimes like to improvise. To practise, try some of these exercises:

Talk to music. Put on a tape or CD of instrumental music (without voices). Close your eyes and move your body to the music. Then begin saying things that come to mind as you're moving, until you're talking non-stop. (The words don't have to make sense. Just keep talking!) Try many kinds of music, including classical, jazz, and music from unfamiliar cultures.

Become a machine. Be a can opener (solo), an alarm clock (duet), or a chain saw (group). Express yourself with sounds and motions.

Ad lib a dialogue. With a partner, invent the conversation between two people in a particular situation—a salesperson and a customer, two strangers stuck in an elevator, an art critic interviewing a rock star, two residents of a nursing home, a parent and a teenager having a talk. Don't discuss beforehand what the people would say (and no scripts allowed!).

Do an impression or a parody. Choose a serious or a humorous imitation. Pretend to be a famous or familiar person. Stand in front of the mirror and talk for five minutes straight, as though you're that person. (Don't pause. Don't be shy. Pretend you're Robin Williams.)

Tape your improvisations. Record some short narratives, monologues, or dialogues that you think up as you go along, using different characters' voices. (You could pretend they're telephone answering messages.) Then listen to the tape. What works? What doesn't?

Voices on Stage

In this era of TV, video, and virtual reality, some people might be surprised to learn that radio and readers' theatre performances are still done. But it isn't really so surprising. Most of us—in fact, nearly all of us—use our voices dramatically, at times. And we enjoy listening to music, stories, and drama. So maybe the surprising thing is that *more* people aren't radio and readers' theatre professionals!

Radio Play

Good radio shows depend on actors who can use their voices well, narrators who explain what can't be seen, vivid sound effects, and mood-making music. To create a radio play, you *don't* need scenery, props, or costumes. You only need one or two tape-recorders, and dramatic voices.

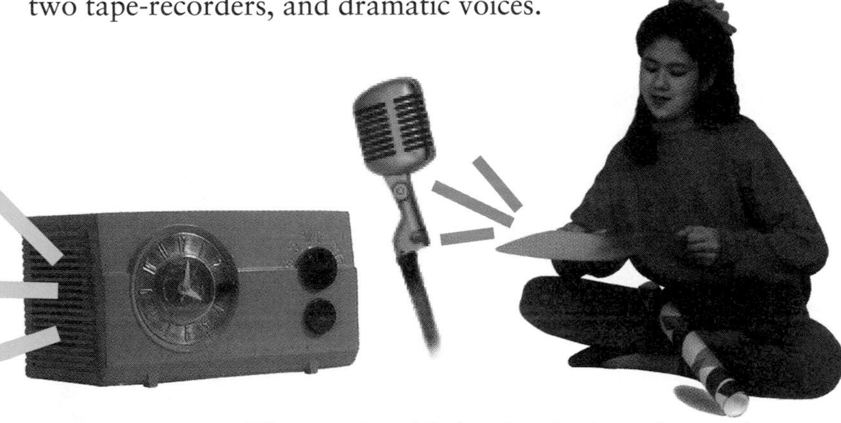

Get used to the tape-recorder and microphone. How close must you be to get good sound? If you have only one mike, put it where all the actors can easily reach it. Or designate a "mike mover," someone to quickly take it to each actor.

Sound effects: The train's whistle, the ringing phone, the echoing footsteps, the crack of thunder: you can take them from sound-effects recordings at a library or (for more fun) make your own. Unless you want to make the sound effects as you're taping the play itself, use a second tape recorder. For a sound-effects tape, record sounds in the order in which you'll use them. Designate a "sound person" to play parts of the tape as each effect is called for in the script.

Music: Does the play have dramatic episodes? sad or frightening ones? Find some background music that will add to the mood. You can have musicians play it, live. Or make another tape, combining your musical selections in order, and have the "sound person" play each selection on cue.

Act With Your Voice

When you're portraying a character, give him or her a special way of speaking. Does she sound as though she's racing to finish each sentence? Does he nervously say "uh" before every phrase, then clear his throat? There are many vocal techniques you can use to convey your character's personality and emotions.

USE THIS	TO EXPRESS CHARACTER	TO EXPRESS EMOTION OR PURPOSE
volume	Shy people often speak softly. Confident characters may have booming voices.	Angry people may yell or stress their words in a lowered voice. People giving orders may talk loudly. Those who are scared, menacing, or telling a secret may whisper.
rate	Thoughtful individuals may talk slowly. An energetic or aggressive person may speak fast.	People speak fast when excited or in a hurry, slowly when tired or trying hard to be understood.
pitch	Adult male voices tend to be lowest. Older people usually speak lower than young people.	Angry or excited people often speak at a higher pitch. Frightened, sad, or quiet people usually speak in low tones.
rhythm	A character from a particular region or country may speak with a distinctive rhythm.	Someone feeling unsure may speak in a halting, stop-and-start pattern. A happy person may speak in a bouncy, laughing manner.

Pauses can be very effective. They can show that a character is thinking, or hesitating, or in shock. They can also be used to draw attention to an important point or to . . . create . . . suspense.

Readers' Theatre

This is a dramatic reading, with a minimum of fuss. The readers typically sit or stand together, facing an audience. Each reader reads from a script or text but often looks up to make eye contact with the audience. Readers do not move or gesture. They rely on their voices for expressiveness. Readers may wear regular clothes. Or they may dress alike, in something simple—such as dark sweat shirts and jeans. They may also use a few "character props," such as hats or eyeglasses. No scenery is necessary, though a simple curtain or backdrop may be used to create a mood or set a scene.

inside
INFO

Experts warn readers and actors to avoid using any foreign or regional accent unless they *know* they can do it well *and* it's right for their character. A fake-sounding accent can spoil an otherwise good performance. (So listen, and practise.)

Stage Play

As an actor in a stage play, you have numerous tools for communicating with an audience. Like the storyteller, you have your voice, facial expressions, posture, and hand gestures to help you express a character's personality, thoughts, and feelings. But you will rely more than the storyteller on dramatic body language and movement. You can use make-up and costumes to tell even more. And you can take advantage of stage props and lighting.

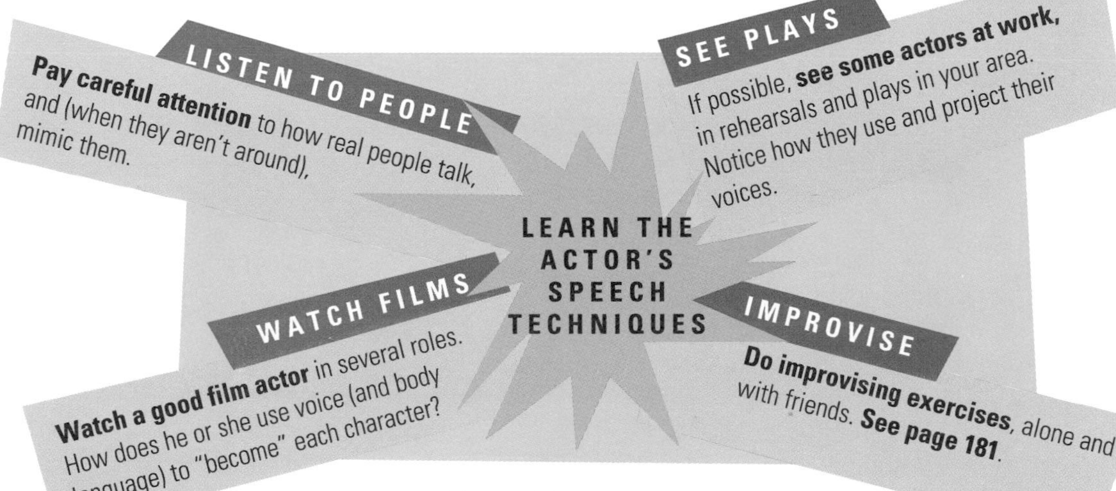
LEARN THE ACTOR'S SPEECH TECHNIQUES
LISTEN TO PEOPLE
Pay careful attention to how real people talk, and (when they aren't around), mimic them.
SEE PLAYS
If possible, see some actors at work, in rehearsals and plays in your area. Notice how they use and project their voices.
WATCH FILMS
Watch a good film actor in several roles. How does he or she use voice (and body language) to "become" each character?
IMPROVISE
Do improvising exercises, alone and with friends. See page 181.

Learn Your Lines

Read the lines *aloud,* over and over, until you can say them with your eyes closed. If you have a big part, memorize your lines one scene or one act at a time.

Visualize what your character will be doing as you speak each line.

Practise your lines "in character," with all the expression and gestures you plan to use on stage. Remember, you aren't just memorizing words; you're memorizing how your character speaks, feels, and behaves.

Don't learn only your own lines and cues. Instead, read the entire play several times. Get a sense of what the other characters do and say in each scene.

Attend *every* rehearsal, because just hearing the lines again and again will help "set" them in your mind.

tRy it!

Read your lines—or the whole play—into a tape-recorder. Listen to it, over and over, while you're brushing your teeth, waiting for the bus, and walking. Pretend you're learning a song!

Really Use Your Voice

This is drama, so use it dramatically. **For tips on using your voice, see page 183.**

Project it. Even though you're supposedly talking to the other actors on stage, you're actually hoping to reach the person in the last row of the audience. Project your voice as if you're speaking to someone there—but don't shout. It takes practice. When the theatre's empty, get a friend to sit in the back row while you experiment with your voice on stage.

Pronounce words clearly. An audience may hear you but not understand your words. Slow down (if you're at all nervous, you're probably speaking faster than you think). You may have to exaggerate your consonants at first.

Remember the Others

Play to the front. This means keeping your face turned toward the audience, even when you're talking to another character, beside you. It looks and sounds better.

Don't "upstage" another actor. When it's another actor's turn, don't distract everyone with actions or ad libbing that will draw attention back to you.

Watch your timing. Delivering your lines late or early can throw off the other actors. But if you really listen, your timing will take care of itself. *Bad* timing usually occurs when someone's attention (yours?) has wandered.

inside
INFO

"Break a leg!" This is an actor's way of saying "Good luck!" Some actors are superstitious. Wishing someone good luck would be asking for bad luck, they think. So wishing for *bad* luck should bring *good* luck!

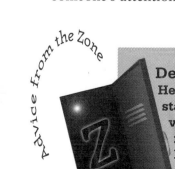

Advice from the Zone

Dear Z:
Help! I'm afraid to get back on stage because one time my voice cracked as I was saying my only line. If you can't help, I may never act again.
—Mortified

Dear Mort,
Don't give up! You may still be a star. Here's my advice: Warm up before you go on stage. Warm up your voice by singing some scales, like a singer does. Warm up your acting by running through a few of your character's speeches. Break a leg!
Z.

Creating

Contents

and Viewing

So, who are you? Try creating a work of art—or interpreting one. By expressing ideas, you'll learn to express yourself. Begin by discovering what inspires you.

Visual Arts

"Beautiful!" "Yuk." "That's sad." "Hmmm. I don't know . . ." Why do some works of art make you smile and others make you feel sad? Why are you sometimes not sure if you even *like* a work of art? Becoming familiar with the basic elements of art will help you to understand the "why" of your feelings—whether you're viewing art or creating it.

Where Feeling Begins

Any work of art begins with one or more of these four elements: line, shape, form, and colour. Together they can create powerful emotional effects.

Line

Any image begins with a line.

Straight lines suggest order and direction.

Jagged lines, like lightning bolts, can suggest power or fear or confusion.

Curved lines may suggest motion, like waves, or softness, like a smile.

Shape

When a line turns, it creates a shape. Shapes are flat, with only two dimensions: height and width. Believe it or not, you can show almost anything using three basic shapes: squares, circles, and triangles.

When shapes are balanced, they create a feeling of harmony.

When shapes are not symmetrical, they create tension.

Form

The illusion of three-dimensional forms having height, width, and depth can be created on a flat sheet of paper. Size can create a sense of depth, called perspective. Things that are far away look smaller than things that are nearby.

When one object overlaps another, the object shown in full view seems to be in front of the other object.

Colour

Colour can communicate many things. It can represent the way things really look. Many dark colours together can create feelings like mystery or sadness.

Shading a colour can create an illusion of curves.

What Creates Interest?

When you look at a work of art, ask yourself "What's happening in this work?" Once you've identified the subject matter and how the artist felt about it, you can probably figure out why you have the emotional response that you do.

M EMILY CARR

"Memalilaqua, Knight Inlet," Emily Carr, 1912

Ask these questions

- What feelings does this painting arouse in you? Why?
- What is shown in this picture?
- What "story" does this painting suggest?
- What do you think the artist's attitude toward the subject was?
- What are the clues?

People Are Interesting That's why people are often the subjects of songs, works of art, and conversations. When you look at a work of art, look at the people in it. What are they doing? How are they relating to each other? to their surroundings? If the people look sad, they may make you feel the same way.

Beauty Draws Us In Everybody likes a beautiful picture. If a work of art presents a beautiful subject or scene in a new way, you'll probably appreciate it.

The Unusual Sparks Curiosity Unusual subject matter presents a mystery that makes us pause, take a second look, and try to figure it out.

Some Subjects Guarantee Certain Responses Most people react the same way to certain subjects. For example, images of mothers and babies or happy homes create warm feelings. On the other hand, images of danger, death, and hostile weather create apprehensive feelings.

The Art of the Art Critique

A written opinion of a work of art is called a critique. The word *critique* comes from a Greek word meaning "to criticize." In English we often use the word *critic* in a negative way. But a critique looks at the positive as well as the negative aspects of a work of art.

Art isn't like spelling or math. There are no right or wrong answers when you give your opinion about art. Yet some people consider some works of art to be better than others. That's where criticism comes in.

"Patriarche," by Mickael Bethe-Selassie, papier-mâché sculpture, 205 cm high, 1991

Student Art Critique

At first I didn't like "Patriarche" very much. It sort of weirded me out. The colours are intense, and the guy is shaped like a refrigerator. It reminded me of one of those costumes in an Iron Lemon video. Then I looked again. The guy's head is really big, and he's wearing a crown. Actually, the crown doesn't exactly look like a crown, but somehow you just know it's a crown. So, that made him seem like a king. The crown and the king's outfit are covered with little figures of people. Maybe the artist is saying something like we're all made up of the people who are part of our lives. Now the sculpture seems friendly—maybe even happy.

Drawing

Do you doodle when you're on the phone? From the humble telephone-pad squiggle to the most elegant expression, drawing is something nearly everyone does. A drawing can be an end in itself. Or, it might be a preliminary sketch for a painting or sculpture.

Draw What You Feel

Realistic drawing is great for planning creative work or to show things as they really appear. But you can also draw an object in a way that expresses how you feel about it, not how it actually looks. You could draw a pile of homework ten times as tall as yourself! Or you might draw something that could exist only in your imagination. Remember, there is no wrong way to draw when you're drawing what you feel.

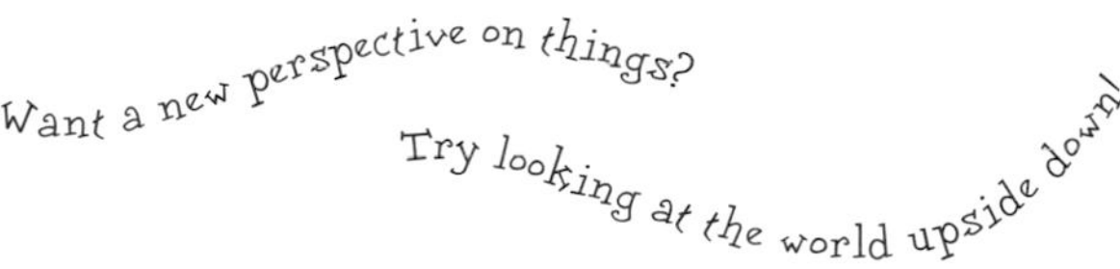
Want a new perspective on things?
Try looking at the world upside down!

Here's How

To Draw from the inside Out

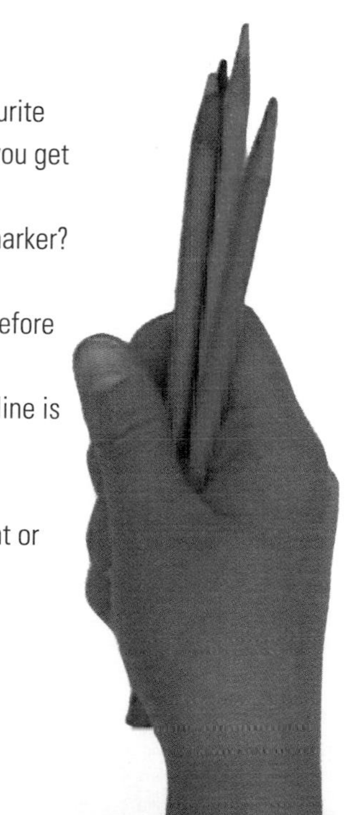

1. **Think of something that you have strong feelings about.** It could be a pet, a favourite pair of boots, or a special place. Or it could be that awful old lawnmower that you get stuck pushing around the yard every summer.
2. **Pick a drawing tool.** Be adventurous. If you've always used a pencil, why not try a marker?
3. **Focus on how you feel about your subject.** Ask yourself what it means to you.
4. **Close your eyes and imagine** just where your first line will begin and end. Do this before you start drawing.
5. **Begin drawing** so as to express what you feel. As you draw, ask yourself what each line is going to represent, and draw only the lines you need.
6. **Don't stop if you make a mess!** Go with the flow, and see what happens.
7. **Stop once in a while and step back.** What do you think? Remember, there's no right or wrong way to draw your feelings.

Compare Two Drawings

Look closely at the two drawings on these facing pages. How do you think the artists' personalities come through in their drawings? What is the feeling you get from Kathë Kollwitz's thick charcoal lines? Why do you think Henri Matisse made his drawing so simple?

Comparing drawings can help you to better understand each one. When you look at two drawings together, observe the kinds of materials, colours, and techniques used by each artist.

Ask
these
questions

- What does this drawing make me feel? Why?
- What was the artist trying to express?
- How well did the message come across?
- What materials did the artist use? How did the artist's choice of materials affect the drawing?

Consider the lack of detail. No line is wasted.

What do you think Matisse had in mind when he drew this figure? Do you think this was a completed drawing, or a sketch for another work?

What would be the effect of this drawing if it were sketched with a felt-tip pen? If it were shaded?

A drawing by Henri Matisse, 1944

"Self-Portrait," Kathë Kollwitz, 1933

What effect did Kollwitz create by drawing just the subject's head and arm?

Artists decide how much of a subject to show in order to focus our attention on what they feel is important.

What a Line!

Compare the lines in the drawings on these two pages. Notice how Kollwitz used charcoal to create her drawing. How would you describe the lines in her drawing? thick? dark? smudgy? What would be the effect if Kollwitz had used a fine-point pen? Notice the kind of lines Matisse used. What kind of lines would make each drawing look more forceful? more gentle?

Colour

Have you ever been green with envy? Red with anger? Colour is often linked in our minds with feelings. That's one reason why colour in a work of art can bring out a viewer's feelings. Shades of blue can be calming and soothing. Yellows and reds are often exciting. Combining colours and using certain colours next to each other can create almost any effect the artist wants. Some colours are comfortable together. Think about the colours you pick to wear together or to decorate your room. What effect are you creating?

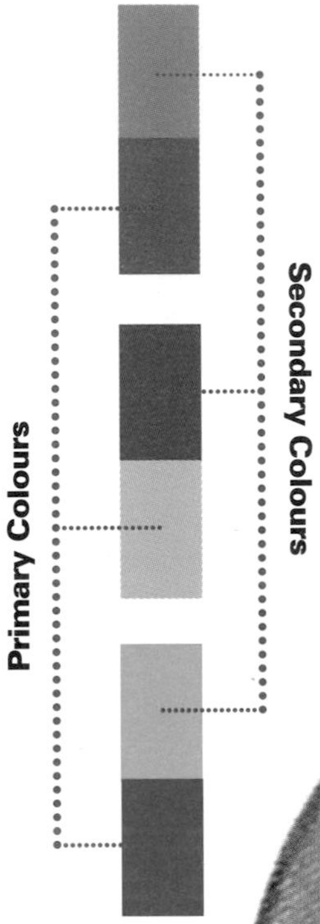

Primary Colours

Secondary Colours

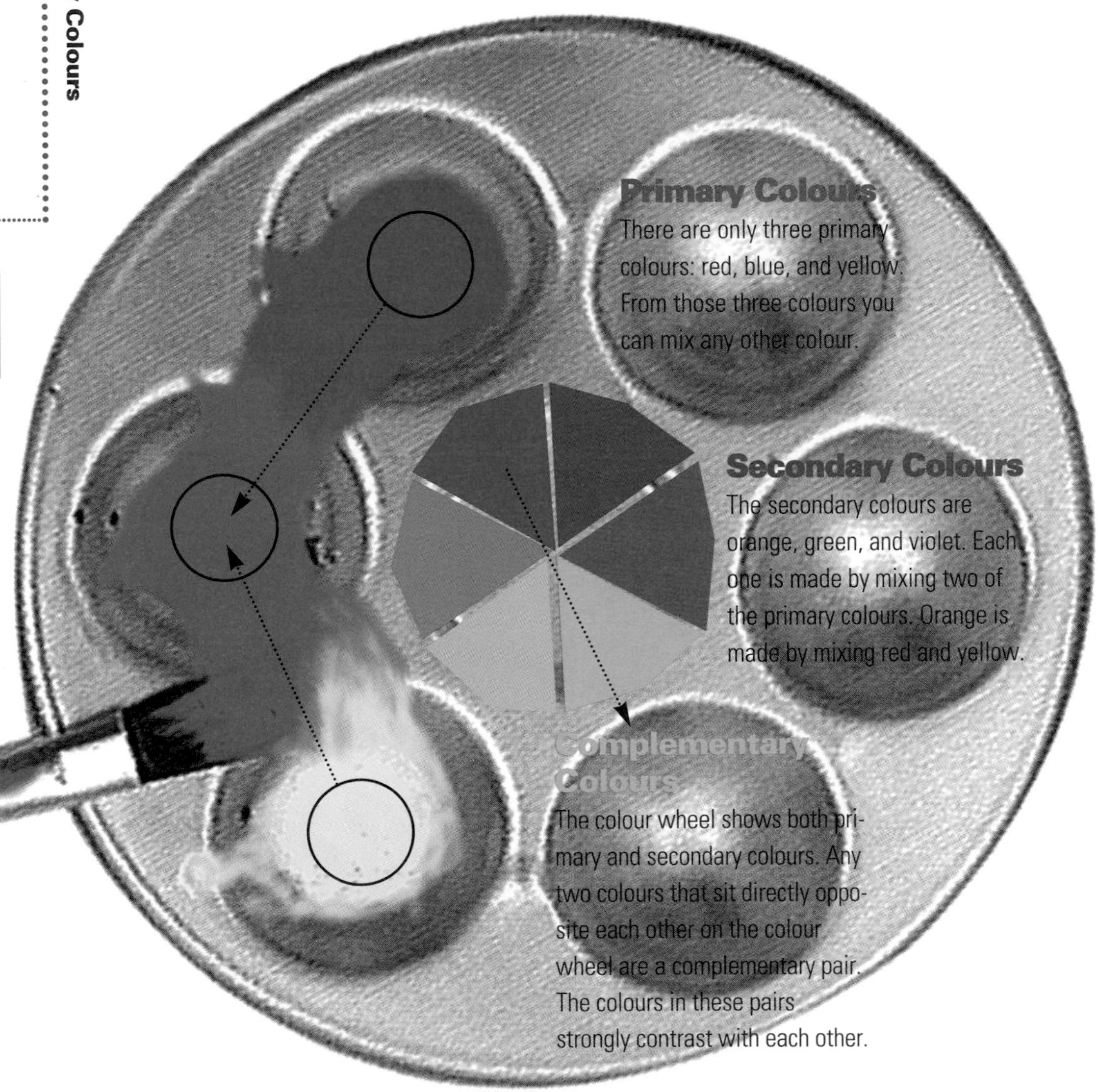

Primary Colours

There are only three primary colours: red, blue, and yellow. From those three colours you can mix any other colour.

Secondary Colours

The secondary colours are orange, green, and violet. Each one is made by mixing two of the primary colours. Orange is made by mixing red and yellow.

Complementary Colours

The colour wheel shows both primary and secondary colours. Any two colours that sit directly opposite each other on the colour wheel are a complementary pair. The colours in these pairs strongly contrast with each other.

Painting

You can use painting to capture your feelings, memories, or thoughts and communicate them to an audience. In the painting below, Marc Chagall used strong colours; large, basic shapes; and playful, curving lines to express childhood memories of his village. What did he gain by making his painting unrealistic rather than showing the village as it really looked?

"I and the Village," Marc Chagall, 1911

TRY it!

Throughout history, painters have used all kinds of materials for painting. Before oil and acrylic paints were invented, artists used to grind coloured minerals and mix them with fluids like egg yolks that would later harden. Try to find natural things you could use as paint. How about berries? grass? coffee? mud?

"Spring Salmon," Roy Henry Vickers, 1979

Need some help in focussing your responses? Check out responding to reading. **See page 112.**

Responding to Paintings

How do you respond to a painting? Do you respond to it in the same way you'd respond to a poem? If you do, you probably begin by just examining your emotional reaction to it. Then, you give the painting a second look to see what it reminds you of and what it could mean. A third look might focus on the painter's artistry.

Advice from the Zone

Dear Z,

I've never been to an art museum, but we are supposed to go to one as a homework assignment for art class. I wish I could get out of it! The last thing I want to do on the weekend is go see a bunch of paintings by dead people. Who cares? I want to go to a film instead. What should I do?

—Art-Is-a-Drag

Dear Art:

You want to just go to a film? Why settle for the small stuff? When you go to an art museum, you can be in a film—your own. What you do is wander around the museum and just see what's there—you're scouting a location. Choose a few paintings that really grab you. Then for each painting, imagine you're stepping into the picture. What's in the scene? What's beyond the scene? What's the mood? What action just happened? What happens next? When you "get into" paintings, you'll discover that they're anything but dull.

Oh, and another thing. You might be surprised to know that some of those "dead people" expressed ideas and feelings that you have. Check it out.

Z.

Questions to Ask Yourself

Sometimes when you see a painting for the first time, you can tell when it was done, by whom, or even why. These clues help you to understand what the artist tried to express. The artist intended the painting on the facing page to represent his family, who for generations have fished for salmon. The faces represent past generations. The eggs represent the generations still to come. But what if you don't have that kind of information about a painting?

Ask yourself questions to discover your feelings.

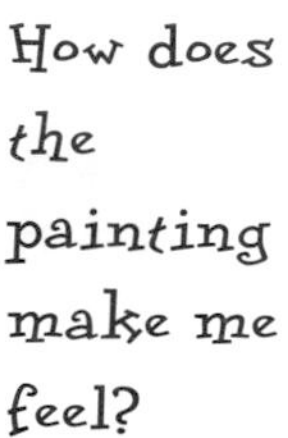

How does
the
painting
make me
feel?

Does the painting remind me of something?
an idea?
a feeling?
an experience?

What objects are in the picture?

Why are they there and what do they say?

What
story
does
the
picture
suggest?

Do I like it?

Collage

Painting and drawing create images on flat surfaces. If you don't like to paint or draw or don't feel confident about your skills—then you might try a collage. You make a collage by gluing various materials to a firm, flat surface. You can use magazine clippings, swatches of fabric, photographs, sports programs, buttons, pressed flowers, and even garbage!

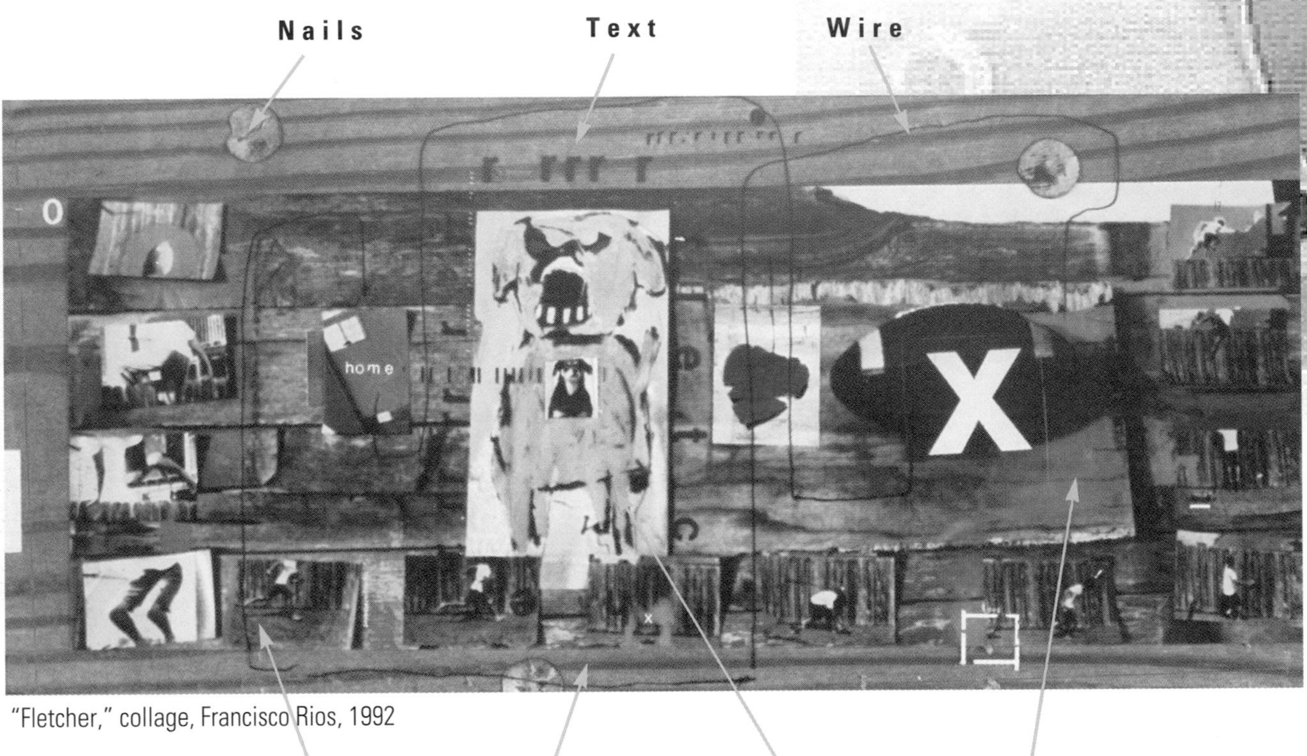
Nails
Text
Wire
home
X
Photographs
Wood
Drawing
Paint

"Fletcher," collage, Francisco Rios, 1992

Looking at Collage

Look at the collage above and take note of the materials the artist has used. This collage was created by Francisco Rios, a university art student. His assignment was to tell a story in a collage. Look carefully at the objects in the collage. What do the photographs show? What words did Rios include? What is your response to the whole collage? The incident Rios described in this collage involved playing ball and an angry dog named Fletcher.

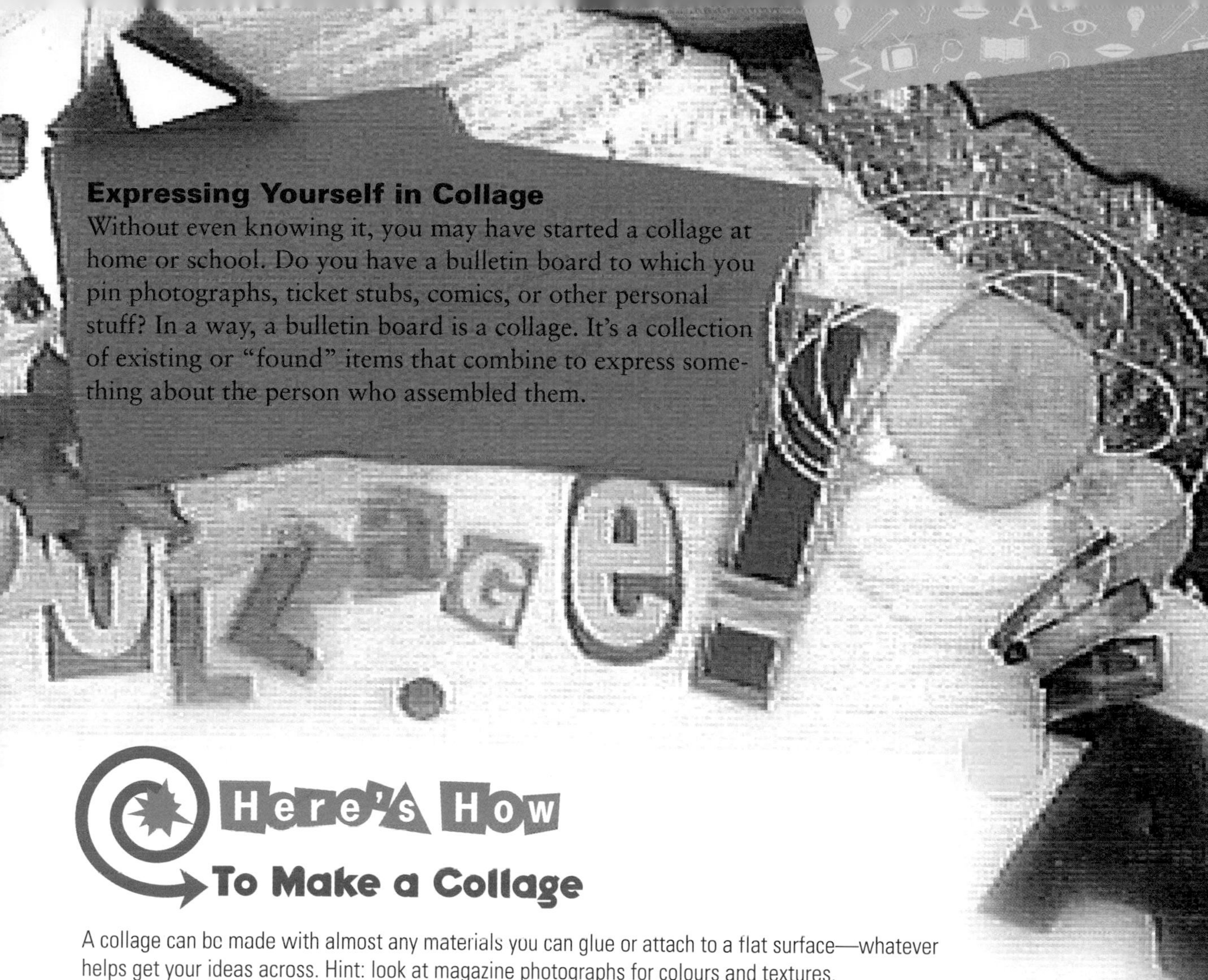

Expressing Yourself in Collage

Without even knowing it, you may have started a collage at home or school. Do you have a bulletin board to which you pin photographs, ticket stubs, comics, or other personal stuff? In a way, a bulletin board is a collage. It's a collection of existing or "found" items that combine to express something about the person who assembled them.

Here's How
To Make a Collage

A collage can be made with almost any materials you can glue or attach to a flat surface—whatever helps get your ideas across. Hint: look at magazine photographs for colours and textures.

1. **Choose a person, idea, or topic as your subject.** You might choose your grandmother, an idea such as friendship, or a topic such as dogs.
2. **Think about what makes up your subject.** What does the person wear? What are the elements of friendship?
3. **Think about colours and textures.** Which ones best express your subject?
4. **Collect magazines, newspapers, and other objects.** You'll want materials that you can cut up or add to your collage.
5. **Make a few sketches or photographs of your subject.** Then you'll have a reference as you create your collage.
6. **Make a final sketch of your subject on heavy paper.**
7. **Cut up your materials to the size and shape you want.** Paste them on your sketch, overlapping the layers as needed.

Sculpture

Sometimes paintings, drawings, collages, and other two-dimensional media seem too flat for what you want to express. Then you may find yourself reaching for clay, papier-mâché, wood, soapstone—anything that allows you to create in three dimensions.

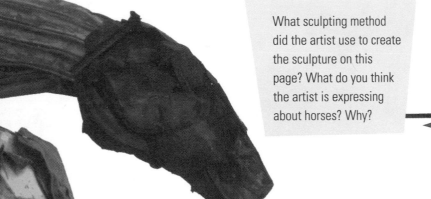

What sculpting method did the artist use to create the sculpture on this page? What do you think the artist is expressing about horses? Why?

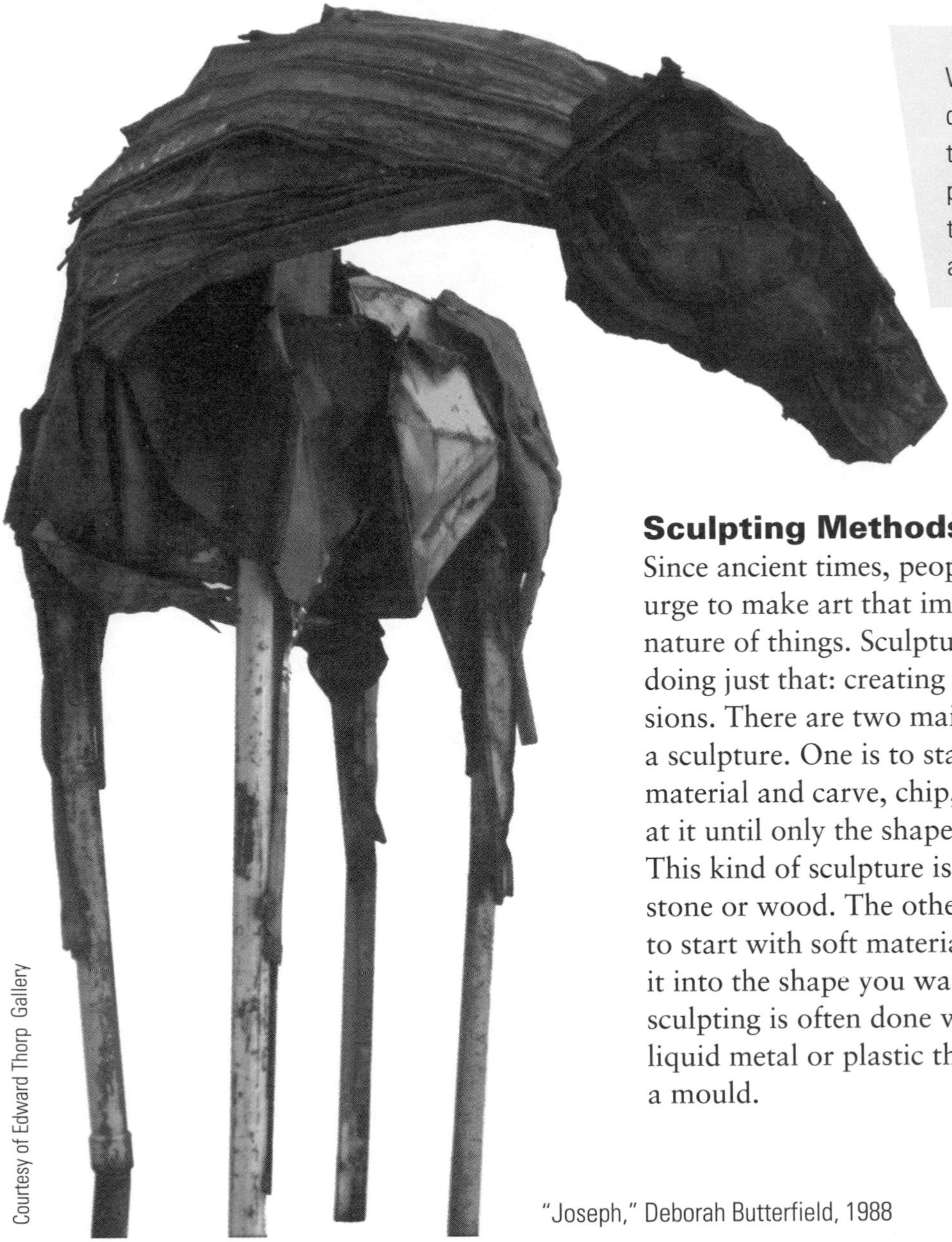

Sculpting Methods

Since ancient times, people have had the urge to make art that imitated the solid nature of things. Sculpture is the art of doing just that: creating in three dimensions. There are two main ways to make a sculpture. One is to start with a block of material and carve, chip, or scrape away at it until only the shape you want remains. This kind of sculpture is often done in stone or wood. The other way to sculpt is to start with soft material and then mould it into the shape you want. This way of sculpting is often done with clay, or with liquid metal or plastic that hardens inside a mould.

"Joseph," Deborah Butterfield, 1988

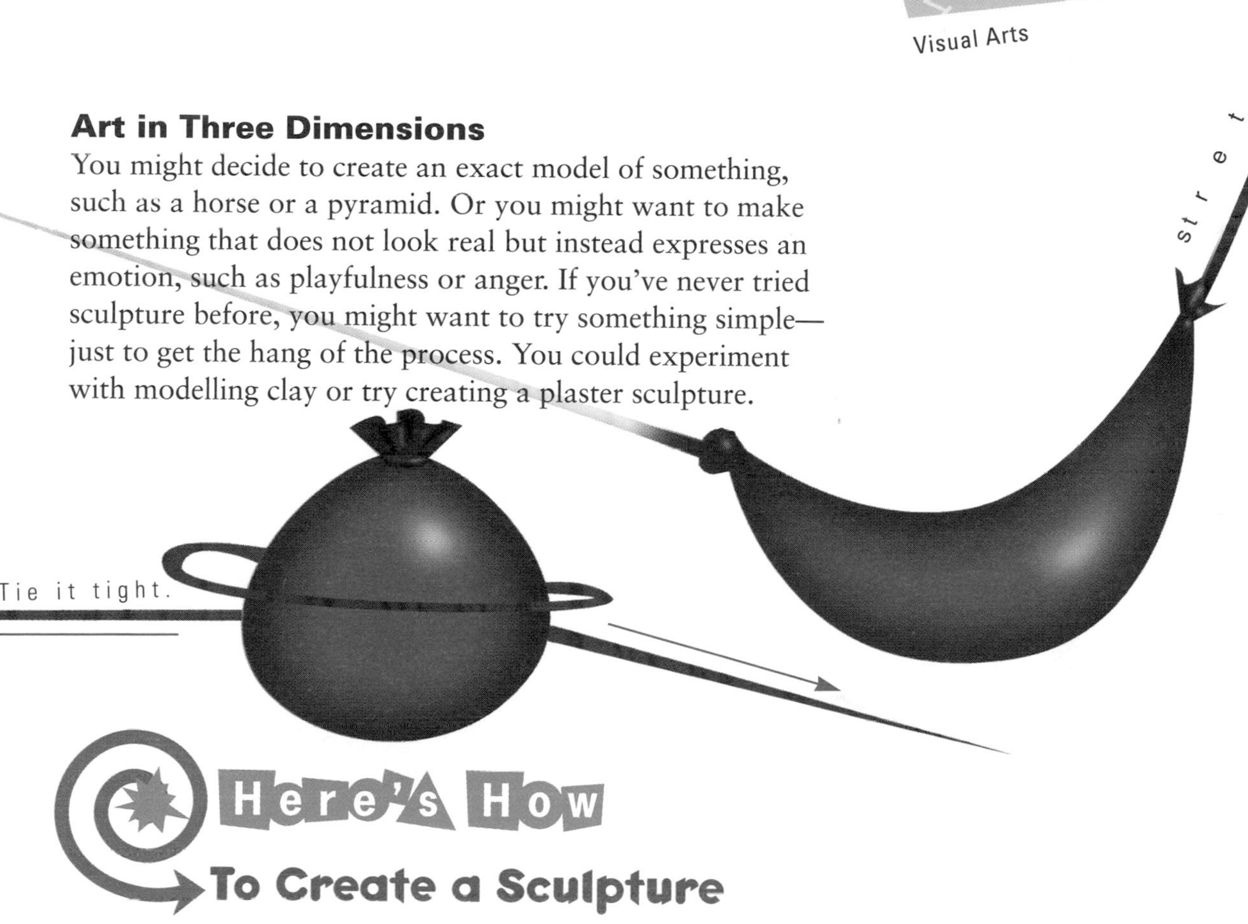
stretch
Tie it tight.

Art in Three Dimensions

You might decide to create an exact model of something, such as a horse or a pyramid. Or you might want to make something that does not look real but instead expresses an emotion, such as playfulness or anger. If you've never tried sculpture before, you might want to try something simple—just to get the hang of the process. You could experiment with modelling clay or try creating a plaster sculpture.

Here's How

To Create a Sculpture

Here's one way to make a plaster sculpture, using a balloon. As you work with the material, see what feelings you can express and what shapes you can produce.

1. **Mix up a batch of plaster.** Follow the directions on the package. You'll need about 750 mL to 1L (3 or 4 cups) of plaster per balloon.
2. **Stretch your balloon.** Blow it up and let the air out a few times.
3. **Pour the plaster into the balloon using a funnel.** Fill it as full as you can.
4. **Tie a knot in the open end of the balloon.**
5. **Shape your balloon sculpture while the plaster is still soft.** Think of different ways you can alter the shape of the plaster-filled balloon. Tie it in several places with twine, stretch it, squeeze it, drape it over a ledge, press heavy objects into it. Be careful not to pop the balloon.
6. **Let the plaster harden overnight.**
7. **Cut away the balloon and admire your sculpture.** Be sure the plaster has thoroughly hardened first.

Materials

- Plaster mix
- Water
- Funnel
- Bucket
- Balloons
- Twine
- Tempera paints
- Carving tools

Is it finished? You may want to add to your sculpture by carving into it or by painting the surface with tempera paints.

Printmaking

Many works of art, such as paintings and sculptures, are meant to be one-of-a-kind works. But sometimes you may want to have a number of copies of the same work of art. Today a photocopier can make lots of identical copies of any flat image or text. But another method, called printmaking, has existed for 1000 years. It allows you to make as many copies of your work as you like, and each print—unlike a photocopy—is considered an original work of art.

The Basics of Printmaking

Many different methods have been developed for making prints. Most methods start with a firm surface of wood, metal, or linoleum, on which carving is then done. This carved surface is called the plate. Once the artist has carved a design or image, ink is applied to the surface of the plate. The plate is then pressed against paper, leaving the image on the paper. The paper with the image is the print. Rubber stamps use this same method.

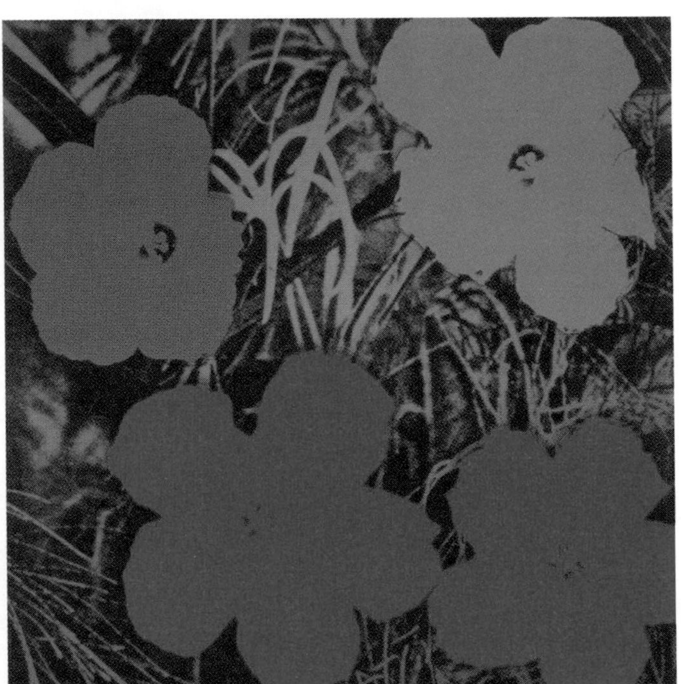

"Flowers," Andy Warhol, 1970

Silk-screening

Another method of printmaking is called silk-screening. In this process an artist first makes a fine screen by stretching silk or other material across a frame. The artist then applies a stencil of a design to the screen. The stencil masks out parts of the design that are not to be printed. The paper to be printed on is placed beneath the stencilled screen. The artist then rubs ink across the top of the screen. Because of the stencil, the ink can only pass through certain areas, creating the design. This flower print was silk-screened by artist Andy Warhol. Each colour was printed separately. How many screens did Warhol use?

Sign and Number

To make each print more valuable, artists often limit the number of prints they make from one plate. You can do the same thing. Once you have made all the prints you want, sign and number each one. After the print number, put a slash mark followed by the total number of prints you made.

Here's How To Make a Potato Print

If you want to try your hand at printmaking, why not start with a simple potato print? You can carve a potato to create the design and then use your potato "plate" to make prints.

1. **Get a large, firm, raw potato.**
2. **Think of a shape or design that you'd like to print.** Make practice sketches on paper. Your design can't be very detailed or larger than the potato.
3. **Slice the potato in half.** Then carve your design on the flat, cut surface. Remember, you are carving away what you *don't* want to show of your design and leaving what you *do* want to print. Try to leave a raised surface that is at least six millimetres higher than the background.
4. **Blot the surface of your plate after carving.** Use a paper towel to absorb any potato juice.
5. **Coat the raised surface of your plate with ink, paint, or food colouring.**
6. **Press the plate surface on paper or cardboard.** Repeat steps 5 and 6 to make more prints.
7. **Stand back and admire your spud art!**

Illustration

There you were, minding your own business, drawing a pair of ice skates to go with a poem written by another student for the school paper. You are now an illustrator. What kind of artist is that?

What Do Illustrators Do?

Illustrators are visual artists who draw and paint in order to enhance written information. They use their art skills to communicate. Illustrators often work on assignments from publishers and writers who ask them to create art for books, magazines, and newspapers. Often an illustrator has a style that is better for one kind of book or article than another. Here are some examples of assignments for an illustrator:

- Create a map for a news article.
- Draw a cartoon for a magazine.
- Draw the surface of Venus based on scientific data.
- Depict a scene in a children's storybook.
- Draw a crime suspect based on an eyewitness description.
- Show the steps in baking beans for a cookbook.

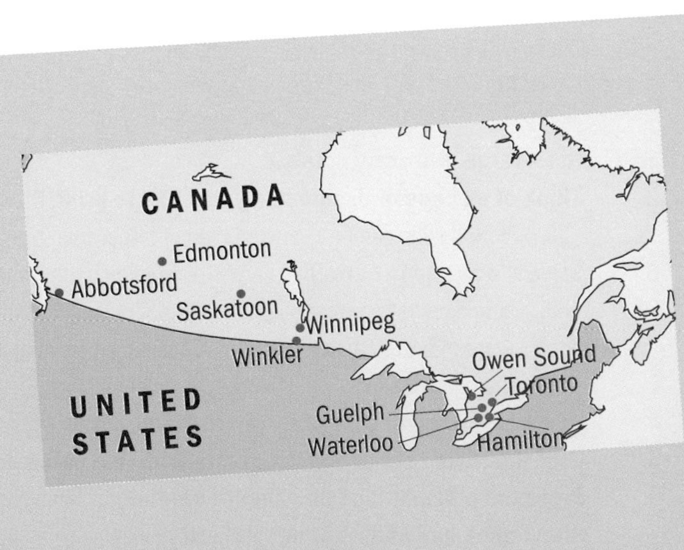
CANADA
Edmonton
Abbotsford
Saskatoon
Winnipeg
Winkler
Owen Sound
Toronto
UNITED STATES
Guelph
Waterloo
Hamilton

Here's How
To illustrate

When you need to create illustrations, try following this procedure.

1. **Choose a newspaper or magazine story that interests you.** Cut out the article.
2. **Reread the piece, and choose a detail or idea that you would like to illustrate.**
3. **Decide if your illustration should show a person, process, place, or event described in the story.** You might even express an idea or opinion through your artwork.
4. **Choose the materials that will be best for your purpose and style.** A fine-point pen works well for a detailed illustration, while markers and watercolour paints can make great cartoons.
5. **Make a few sketches of your illustration in pencil.** Do the sketches show what you want to express about the story?
6. **Make the final illustration.** Use a fresh sheet of paper. Colour the illustration if you choose.
7. **Paste the article and your illustration to a piece of heavy paper or cardboard for your final display.** Does the illustration help make the story clearer, more interesting, or more fun to read? If it does, you're a successful illustrator.

Photography

Think of all the pictures you have been in: baby pictures, birthday pictures, school pictures. There are probably some you like and some you wish had never been taken. Do you have any photographs of friends or family members that are special to you? Do you decorate your room with pictures of film or sports stars?

Pictures, Pictures Everywhere

We are surrounded by photographs everywhere we go. They are used in newspapers, books, and magazines to help illustrate facts or ideas, and to sell products. Some photographs capture a moment, such as a runner crossing the finish line, or a friend's familiar smile. Other photographs are considered art. They stand alone as expressions of an artist's feelings or interpretation of reality. But whether the purpose is personal, persuasive, informational, or artistic, a photographer makes choices to create the best possible photograph.

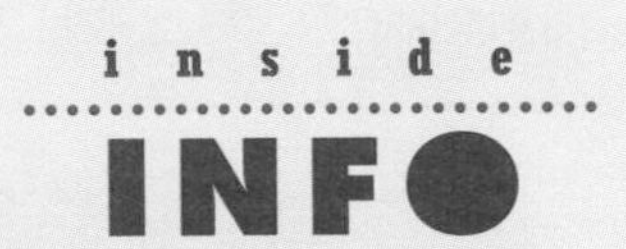
inside
INFO

You can ask your art teacher or parents for help in choosing the right camera for your photography. Ask a salesperson at the photo store to help you pick the right film for your subject.

Decide What to Photograph

The first thing to decide when you're planning to take a photograph is what you want the picture to show. It could be your sister's basketball team or a dog that lives on your street. Once you've picked a subject for your photo, look at it through the camera. If your subject is a dog, do you want to show it in a particular setting, present just the dog, or focus on the dog's face? Think of the final product you want to create: Is it a detail, a portrait, or a whole scene?

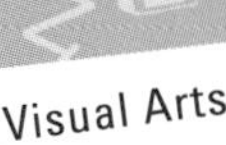

What's Your Point of View?

Now that you've decided on your subject and how much of it to show, it's time to consider your angle, or the point from which you'll view it. For example, where will you place your camera when you shoot your picture?

High-angle Climb up above your subject and point your camera down. Your subject will appear smaller than life.

Eye-level Shoot straight at your subject. You can take an eye-level shot when you want others to see the subject as they normally would.

Low-angle Crouch or lie down and shoot up at your subject. Your subject will appear larger than life—and very dramatic.

Shed Some Light on Your Pictures

You've got your subject and camera angle worked out; now you need to check the lighting before you snap the picture. Is there enough light around your subject to reveal all the details you want to show? Look through the camera: Are shadows covering part of your subject's face? Do you want more shadows or more bright spots? You can use a flash unit or portable lamp to add light.

Here's How To Create a Photo Essay

A photo essay uses a series of images, and sometimes words, to communicate ideas to viewers. The process for creating a photo essay is similar in some ways to writing an essay.

1. **Choose a subject you care about.** You also want a subject that you feel will carry a strong message to viewers.
2. **Think about your purpose.** What effect do you want to achieve? Do you want to inspire people? Shake them up? Fill them with wonder?
3. **Consider your audience.** Whom do you want to reach? Your peers? Teachers? Community?
4. **Review your options.** Your photo essay might tell a story—with a beginning, middle, and end. Or it could be a collection of images to be viewed in any order.
5. **Collect photographs.** You can use existing snapshots, cutouts from magazines and other sources, or take new photographs. As you select your pictures, keep asking yourself this question: How will this photo add to my essay? Keep in mind your subject, purpose, and audience as you choose each photo. Try to show different aspects of your subject.
6. **Make a display.** Arrange the photos on a large piece of poster board. Add a few of your own words, or perhaps some lines of poetry, if these would strengthen your essay.

TRY it!

The topic of a photo essay can be almost anything, such as:

- **Making Music** Images of people singing and playing instruments as they make music
- **Being the Best You Can Be** Images of people of all ages and talents achieving a moment of success
- **Helping Hands** Images of people in your community working together to help others

Graphic Design

Imagine yourself on the committee that creates information signs for the Olympic games. Thousands of people are coming from all over the world. Which languages would you use? Even if you used a hundred languages, it still wouldn't be enough. Instead of language, you could create a symbol for each event that will mean the same thing to all the viewers. You could show them rather than tell them.

Years ago
I was an
I'd pretend
I fell in love

Designed by Tibor Kalman and Emily Oberman for the music video "(Nothing but) Flowers" by Talking Heads, 1988

"(Nothing but) Flowers" by Talking Heads. Produced by M & Co., directed by Tibor Kalman, designed by Tibor Kalman and Emily Oberman.

Showing Rather Than Telling

You're surrounded by illustrations, sometimes called graphic design, all the time. Some of the time, graphic designers use visual forms to send clear messages to specific audiences. What are some things that graphic designers create?

They design ▸
- . . . movie posters
- . . . subway maps
- . . . book covers
- . . . video graphics
- . . . brochures
- . . . product advertising
- . . . fashion illustration

©Ⓜ

©Ⓜ

©Ⓜ

What Goes into Graphic Design?

The Olympic symbol and the CBC (Canadian Broadcasting Corporation) symbol are examples of graphic design that communicates without words. Depending on the audience you want to reach, you might use symbols or a combination of symbols, words, photographs, and illustrations in your design. Most graphic designers use both words and images.

Designing with Type

Designers work with printed words and images the way painters work with paint or sculptors work with stone. When a design includes words, the designer must choose a style for the printed type. Each style is called a typeface.

This typeface is called Keedy.

This typeface is called Bodoni.

This typeface is called Sabon.

This typeface is called Univers.

This typeface is called Rockwell Condensed.

This typeface is called Journal.

CHOOSING TYPEFACES

?

How many different typefaces are there on this page?

How does the choice of a typeface affect the way you react to each written message?

Why do you think the designers of this book chose several different typefaces to use throughout the book, instead of sticking with just one?

Making Thumbnails

If you're creating a design, you'll select a typeface, or faces, and images for your design. You'll also want to create a "thumbnail," which is a miniature sketch of your final design. You can sketch one by hand or use a computer. Here is a thumbnail a designer created for these two pages.

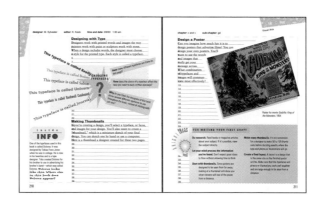

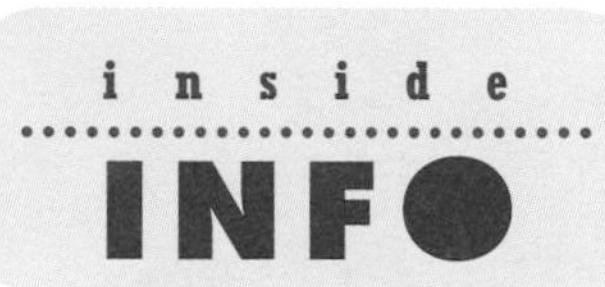

inside
INFO

One of the typefaces used in this book is called Dolores. It was designed by Tobias Frere-Jones when he was in college. He is now in his twenties and is a type designer. Toby created Dolores for his brother to use in advertising his brother's band—which was called Dolores. Dolores looks like this. Where else in this book does Dolores appear?

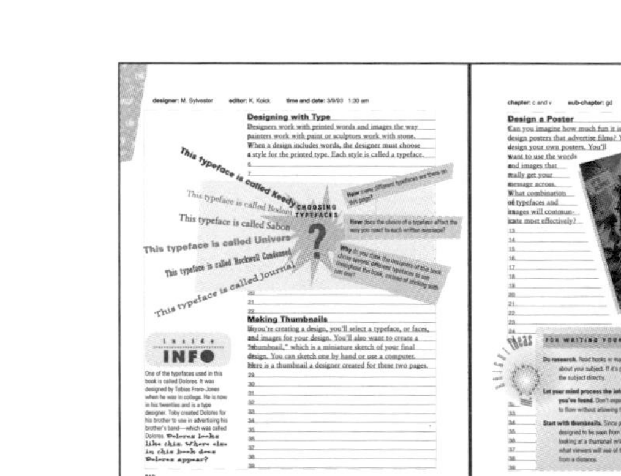

Designing with Type
Making Thumbnails
Design a Poster
GODZILLA KING OF THE MONSTERS

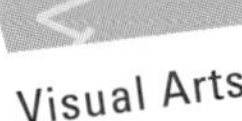

Design a Poster

Can you imagine how much fun it is to design posters that advertise films? You can design your own posters. You'll want to use the words and images that really get your message across. What combination of typefaces and images will communicate most effectively?

AN ENRAGED MONSTER WIPES OUT AN ENTIRE CITY!
IT'S ALIVE!
GODZILLA
KING OF THE MONSTERS!
RAYMOND BURR
Directed by TERRY MORSE and I. HONDA ... A TRANS WORLD Release

Poster for movie *Godzilla: King of the Monsters,* 1954

BRIGHT Ideas

FOR WRITING YOUR FIRST DRAFT

Do research. Read books or magazine articles about your subject. If it's possible, view the subject directly.

Let your mind process the information you've found. Don't expect great ideas to flow without allowing time to think.

Start with thumbnails. Since posters are designed to be seen from far away, looking at a thumbnail will show you what viewers will see of the poster from a distance.

Make many thumbnails. It's not uncommon for a designer to make 50 to 100 thumbnails before deciding exactly where the type and photos or illustrations will go.

Create a final layout. A layout is a design that is the same size as the finished poster will be. Make sure that the typefaces and photos or illustrations work well together and are large enough to be seen from a distance.

CREATING AND VIEWING

Film and TV

What's in a name? The old names for film, "moving picture" and "motion picture," point out the basic difference between film and photographs. A photograph is a *still* (unmoving) picture. A film uses many still photographs to show things in motion. The photographs are in small rectangular *frames* on a long strip of film wound onto a reel. When the reel is rolled, the film moves quickly in front of a light, and the images, projected onto a screen, make one big picture that moves. A movie!

These days, it's hard to imagine our world without the "big screen" and the "small screen." But actually, they haven't been around for long.

Flash-back

Filmmaking began in the late 1870s in California when a young British photographer, Eadweard Muybridge, wanted to capture on film the motion of a running horse. He placed a series of cameras at equal distances along a race-track. Then he attached a separate string to the lens shutter of each camera and stretched the strings across the track. As the horse ran by, it ripped the strings, making the cameras take pictures only instants apart. Muybridge's experiment paved the way for modern filmmaking. The time line starting on this page traces this and other highlights in the history of film and TV.

1877–1878 Eadweard Muybridge creates the first moving pictures.

Flash Forward

As you can see, a lot has changed since the invention of moving pictures. Today most of our homes have at least one TV. Many people rely on film and TV for entertainment and for information about everything from local sports to international politics. In fact, these media may now be the major influences on how people spend their spare time and what they learn. What do you think of this development? You can use the following questionnaire to focus on the roles film and TV play in your life.

What Do You Watch?

Write your answers to these questions.

1. What are your three favourite TV shows?
2. Think carefully about the TV shows you've watched during the past week. Make a list of every show you recall viewing. Rate each program according to how good you thought it was: Awesome, Pretty Good, O.K., Lousy. Which of these ratings did you use most?
3. Using the list you created for question 2, jot down the length of time you spent watching each program. Add up the times and divide the total by 4 to find out approximately how much time you spent watching commercials. For example, 8 viewing hours divided by 4 = 2 hours of commercials. (Note: If you watched some TV on a station with no commercials, subtract that amount of time from the total before dividing by 4.) Are you surprised by these numbers?
4. Make a list of the first ten TV or film characters that you think of. Beside each character's name, write your main feeling about him or her. For example: John Connor (*Terminator 2*)—*Admire him* or *He's not that great.*
5. Make a list of your three favourite films. Below each, write a short explanation of why the film had a big effect on you.
6. Most TV programs and films are designed to get an emotional response from viewers. Write down the three things you have recently seen on TV or film that made you feel most inspired, amused, sad, or afraid. Consider all genres, including news, music videos, and cartoons, as well as dramatic programs. Then write whether you'd watch this film or program again.
7. Pick one film whose ending you would change if you could. Write a persuasive letter to the film's director suggesting the new ending. Explain how you think the new ending would improve the film.

1904 The first movie theatres, called nickelodeons, are built. Entrance fee: five cents.

1909–1927 The silent film era brings such stars as Mary Pickford to audiences everywhere.

What's On Tonight?

Now that you've given some thought to your viewing habits, you may have noticed patterns. Do you mostly watch sit-coms (situation comedies) or crime dramas? Do you prefer to have film and TV take you to places you might never go, such as the rim of a smouldering volcano or backstage at a rock concert? Film and TV producers know that viewers have different interests. But despite the many kinds of programs mentioned below, most of them share one goal: to entertain you. Some may also hope to inform you or to persuade you of something—or to do all three.

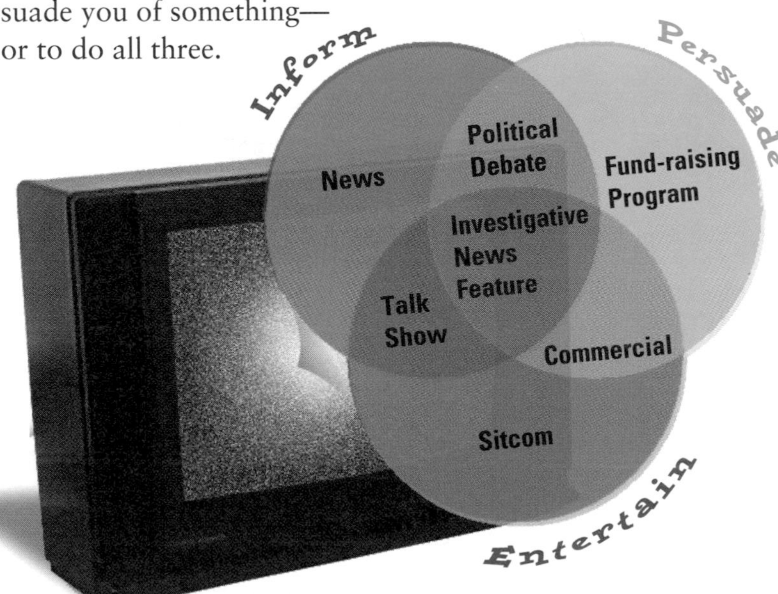
Inform
Persuade
Entertain
News
Political Debate
Fund-raising Program
Investigative News Feature
Talk Show
Commercial
Sitcom

Try it!

On a separate sheet of paper, draw a Venn diagram like the one shown on this page. Use the same labels as the ones given. Then think of five of your favourite television programs, and write their titles on your diagram. Do you tend to prefer a certain kind of program?

Focus on Animation

One of the oldest kinds of films is the cartoon, which is a form of animation. The word *animate* means "give life to." Like all motion pictures, an animated film or video is made of single frames, or images, on a reel of film or videotape. Animators have three main techniques for creating those images: drawing, photography, and computer art.

1927 The film *The Jazz Singer* is the first "talkie"—a film with sound.

1928 The Walt Disney Company produces an early Mickey Mouse cartoon film.

Cel animation. A set of background scenes is drawn. Then animators make separate drawings of each character's actions. (One action may require many drawings, each slightly different from the one before.) The drawings are traced onto cels, which are sheets of transparent plastic. Colour is added on the reverse side of each cel. Cels are then photographed against the appropriate background scene.

Puppet animation and claymation. Three-dimensional figures such as puppets or other objects are photographed, moved slightly, and photographed again. Claymation uses clay figures. The photographs are then made into a film.

Computer animation. Pictures are created, coloured, and moved around on the colour monitor (screen) of a computer. Instead of being filmed, the animation is recorded by the computer's memory onto a disk. The information stored on the disk can later be transferred onto film, videotape, or laser disks by a special laser printer.

inside
INFO

"All great cartoon characters are based on human behavior we recognize in ourselves."
—Chuck Jones, animator of Bugs Bunny and Daffy Duck; creator of Road Runner

Here's How

To Animate Your Own Cartoon

To see how a series of still pictures can "move," make a flip book.

1. **Cut out a set of 30 square pieces of lightweight paper, 8 cm or 10 cm on a side.** Or use a Post-it™ note pad.
2. **On the first square,** near the edge you plan to flip, draw a simple figure that is doing something simple—such as a fish swimming toward the surface of a fishbowl.
3. **On the next square,** in the same location, draw a fish the same size, but show it swimming closer to the surface.
4. **On the next square,** draw the same fish getting nearer to the surface of the bowl.
5. **Continue using the squares** to draw the fish swimming up to the surface and then swimming back down to the bottom of the fishbowl.
6. **Arrange the sheets in order,** facing upward, with the first picture on top. Staple them together on the side opposite the figures you have drawn. Running your thumb top to bottom along the edge closest to the figures, flip through the pages, and watch your fish swim.

1939 The first regularly scheduled telecasts in the United States take place on the NBC network.

Lights! Camera! Action!

Have you been bitten by the video bug? Maybe you'd like to make a short film or video about a person or a place—or even about a feeling. Maybe a music video would be more your style—or a documentary about your school. Since you are the director, the choice is yours! Once you decide, this section can help you with the technical aspects of making a video.

Plan It

Make a storyboard . . . A storyboard is a series of sketches with captions that describe what scenes you plan to shoot, what camera techniques you'll use, how long the parts of each scene will last, and where the dialogue will go. (Not artistic? Don't worry. Stick figures are fine.) The example below could be part of a storyboard for a TV ad:

LS:

V/O: *It feels like it's 50 degrees. You're hot and tired. You thought you hated winter. But right now you wouldn't mind a little snow and cold.*

MS:

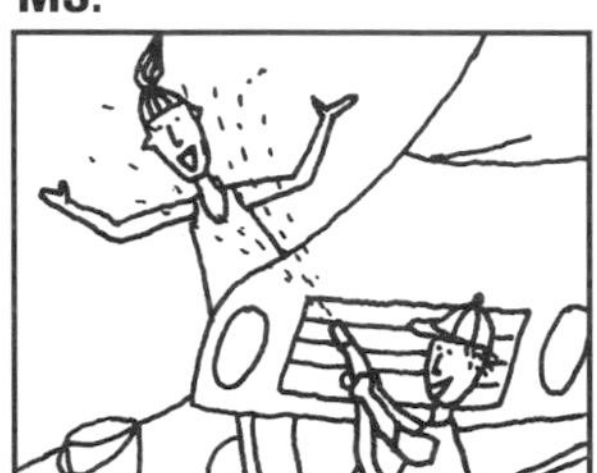

CS:

V/O: *We can't make it snow in summer, but we can help cool you down.*

Terms: Use these abbreviations to indicate what is to happen in each scene:
LS: long shot (shows the setting)
MS: middle distance shot (shows persons in the setting)
CU: close-up (head and neck of one person)
MCU: medium close-up shot (body of one person)
POV: point of view (where—or who—camera eye seems to be)
V/O: voice-over (unseen narrator)
SFX: special effects

1953 The first colour TVs appear on the market.

. . . write a shooting script. Unlike a storyboard, a shooting script doesn't use any drawing. But it includes the same technical terms and information about each scene as a storyboard. The example below shows part of a shooting script for the same TV ad planned in the storyboard on page 216:

Scene: Exterior: driveway, middle-class neighbourhood. Soapy car in driveway, hose, pail, etc.; woman leaning against car—hot, exhausted.

V/O: *It feels like it's 50 degrees. You're hot and tired. You thought you hated winter. But right now you wouldn't mind a little snow and cold.*

MS: We see child pick up hose and start to spray mom. Zoom in to CU of woman's face—smile appears as water turns into flakes of snow.

Dissolve and slow zoom-out to MCU: Woman lying in snow making snow angel.

V/O: *We can't make it snow in summer, but we can help cool you down.*

1962 For the first time, a TV program is broadcast across an ocean. It is watched in the United States, Great Britain, and France.

inside

INFO

Remember: your storyboard or shooting script is just a guide to help you keep track of where you're going. But you're not stuck with it. You may find that you can't shoot a scene exactly as planned. Or you may get a better idea while "on location." In that case—go for it! (Just don't forget the big picture: keep in mind what comes next.)

Make
Your
Own
Video

Shoot It

Make your movie move. Movement shouldn't be only *in front* of the video camera. Try moving your camera too.

Pan it

—to reveal a panorama or to build suspense.

A terrified girl edges into the shadowy room and looks around. The camera pans slowly, showing you what she sees.

Zoom it

—to move in close or back away. Use the automatic zoom button to do this slowly and steadily. For a sudden zoom, you'll have to move the lens yourself.

The detective is looking for clues. The camera zooms in on a gardening glove on the sofa.

Track it

—to stay with a moving person or thing. This is easiest to do by putting your camera on a cart or by sitting on a moving vehicle.

The camera tracks beside the runner. The background is just a blur. But we can see the runner clearly—her face determined, arms pumping, legs churning.

Tilt it

—to create interesting angles and effects.

A little boy, running around a corner, crashes into a man. The camera tilts to show what the boy sees as he looks up.

Switch scenes with style. Scene changes, or transitions, can be done in various ways.

CREATE SMOOTH TRANSITIONS

USE THE ON/OFF SWITCH

To make a transition from one scene to the next, simply turn off the camera and turn it on again for the new scene.

USE A BLACKOUT

To do this variation on a fade-out, use the fade dial or the exposure part of the lens to darken the scene. Return to normal light before shooting the next scene.

FADE OUT AND FADE IN

If your camera has a fade in/out dial, turn it to darken the picture until the image disappears. Turn it the other way to slowly lighten the picture until the image of the next scene is clear. You can get similar effects using the exposure setting of your lens.

DO A DISSOLVE

Make one scene blend into another. Turn the focus ring on your camera lens to blur the last image in a scene. Keep the focus where it is while you position your camera for the next scene. Then start shooting, turning the focus ring until the new image is clear.

1965 The world's first commercial communications satellite is launched, making worldwide TV broadcasting possible.

Make
Your
Own
Video

Edit It

The final process in making a video is selecting and arranging your scenes so they create the effects and the message you want. Here are two ways to edit:

Field editing: edit as you go. You shoot each part of your video in order, beginning with shot 1, scene 1. This method requires careful planning. You'll need to think through every shot *before* you start filming, to make sure you'll be satisfied with the way the scenes flow into one another. Suppose you're doing a documentary about your school. You want to open with a shot of the school building before anyone has arrived, and dissolve to a stream of students entering. You know your first shot will have to be on a weekend or early in the morning. You'll wait for your next shot until school opens.

Post-production editing: edit after shooting. With this method, you're free to experiment with shots, using your storyboard or shooting script as a guide. For example, to create your school documentary, you might shoot all or most of your outside shots at the same time. You can experiment with shooting from different angles, maybe using different lighting. When you've finished shooting, you use an editing machine to select your shots and arrange them in the order you think works best.

inside
INFO

You've probably seen those high-energy TV ads and music videos that flash from one image to another. This is called *quick cutting*. It's done during editing. Each image may be on the screen for less than a second. The viewer can't see each image clearly, but gets a strong impression from the quick changes.

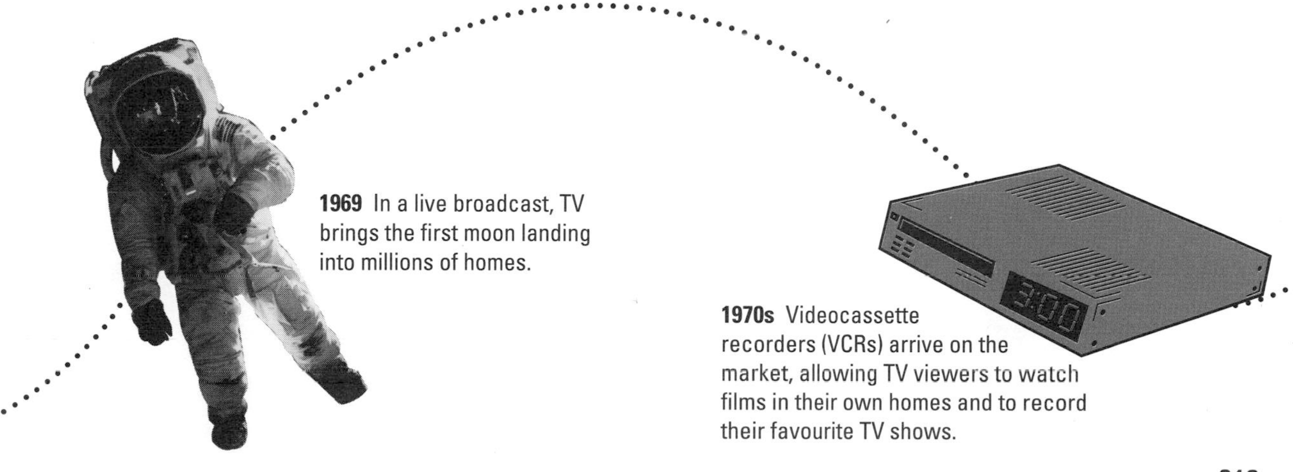
3:00

1969 In a live broadcast, TV brings the first moon landing into millions of homes.

1970s Videocassette recorders (VCRs) arrive on the market, allowing TV viewers to watch films in their own homes and to record their favourite TV shows.

Pros and Cons of Editing Processes

	Advantages	Disadvantages
Edit as you go (closely following your storyboard or shooting script).	You don't need an editing machine. The process takes less time. You use less videotape (no extra shots).	You have less freedom to experiment with different shots on location. If a shot doesn't work as planned, you can't just improvise—you must start over.
Edit after shooting (using your storyboard or shooting script as a guide).	You can experiment on location. You can shoot scenes out of sequence. You can take new approaches that occur to you as you review the videotape.	You may have so much fun experimenting that you end up with a confusing jumble of ideas and images. You use more videotape than you need. You need patience and time for editing.

Make
Your
Own
Video

Present Your Video

Now for the best part! Once your video is finished, you can show it. Your audience might be your friends, your family, or your class. Maybe they're a group you filmed. Afterward, invite them to let you know what camera effects they liked best or what message they thought your video expressed. (And don't forget the popcorn!)

tRy
it!

Shoot the title and a list of the people who worked on the production. You can write the information on a poster and film that. Or you might spell it out in pebbles on the sidewalk and shoot that. Any format is possible, so be creative!

1980s Two cable networks—MuchMusic in Canada and MTV in the United States—are first to entertain viewers with music videos.

MTV
MUSIC TELEVISION

THENATION'SMUSICSTATION

Have Your Say

Now that you know more about the video-making process (basically the same process that's used for film and TV), you're better qualified to evaluate a film or TV feature created by the pros. So speak out!

inside
INFO

"To many people dramatic criticism must be like trying to tattoo soap bubbles."
—John Mason Brown

Here's How

To Write a Film Review

Before you go to a film, keep an open mind. Try not to make judgments about a film based on its director, cast, or genre.

1. **Be prepared.** Take a large note pad and several pencils.
2. **Watch the film.** View the film with a critical eye: Does the beginning draw you in? Does the rest of the film hold your attention? What works well? What doesn't? Be aware of the various aspects of the film as you evaluate it—the acting, directing, camera work, sound quality, musical score, special effects, lighting, costumes, make-up, editing.
3. **Take notes.** It's not easy writing in the dark, so write big and jot down short phrases to remind you of key thoughts. Watch the opening and closing credits, recording the names of the director, actors, and anyone else you want to single out.
4. **Develop your notes in detail.** As soon as you get home, you need to write all your thoughts while they're still fresh.
5. **Write the review.** A film review should mention the film's title, year (unless it's new), director, and cast. It should tell a bit about the plot—but without giving anything important away. Your overall recommendation (see it, don't see it) has to be supported with convincing reasons. They don't have to be brilliant reasons; sometimes the best are common sense: "If a comedy keeps you laughing, it must be good" or "I never believed the main characters cared about each other."
6. **Share your review.** Give it to some friends to read. Post it in your classroom, or submit it to your school paper. If you enjoyed writing the review, offer to do more of them for your paper. Or offer to review films for people your age for your local newspaper.

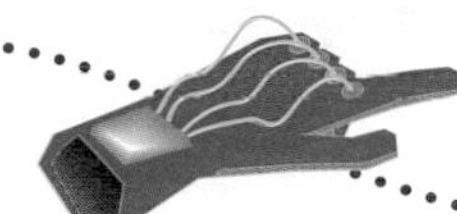

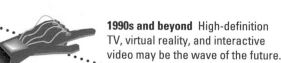

1990s and beyond High-definition TV, virtual reality, and interactive video may be the wave of the future.

Advertising

An advertisement has just one purpose: to sell something. It may be selling a product (cereal ad), a service (house-painting ad), an idea (public service ad against drug abuse), or a person (political ad). A successful ad grabs your attention and then persuades you to buy.

Ads Are Everywhere

How many advertising slogans or jingles can you remember? How many ads do you see in an average day? Everywhere you look—billboards, car bumper stickers, T-shirts, locker posters, TV commercials—someone's trying to sell something. In one high school, an Australian teen even rents his head for advertising space, shaving an ad into his hair each week.

Who Will Buy?

Who reads all these advertisements? You do, for one. You don't see them all, of course. Advertisers just hope you'll see the ones targeted specifically at you, and you probably will. They make it their business to find out as much as possible about people like you: what you watch on TV and when, where you shop and why, what you listen to and when, what you read and why. Using this information, advertisers can then target ads to specific audiences, or *markets*, such as teens. It's no coincidence that the commercials aired during your favourite TV program advertise things *you* might buy: jeans, shampoo, snacks.

inside
INFO

Advertise comes from the Latin root *vertere*, meaning "to turn." When an advertisement *turns* your head, it's already done half the job. Once it has your attention, it may *turn* your ideas about what to buy, think, or do.

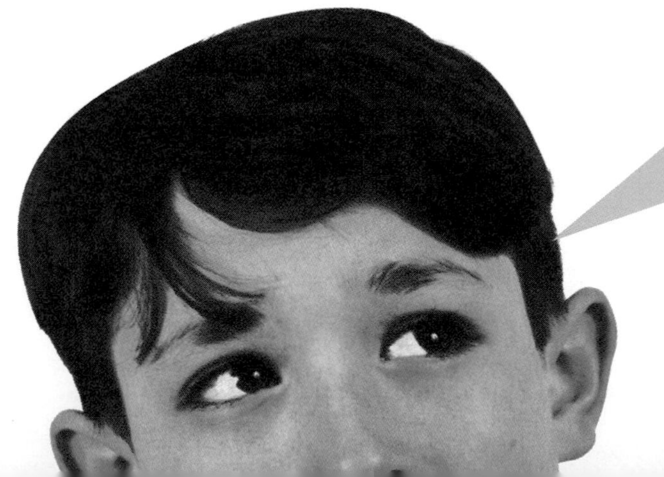

Advertising Tricks

A Name to Remember

A clever name links certain ideas with the product. "Yummy Power Nuggets" suggests a high-energy, delicious food.

WOW!
20% FREE
EXTRA
YUMMY
POWER
NUGGETS
NEW!
NATURALLY AWESOME
BUY ME
DELUXE JUMBO BOX
AUTHENTIC ACTION SUBMARINE INSIDE!
PROOF OF PURCHASE
TOTALLY COOL "T-SHIRT" OFFER
ONLY 12 BOX TOPS
INGREDIENTS

Let the Customer Do the Advertising

Are you a walking advertisement? Do you have brand names on your jeans, running shoes, or T-shirts? Not only do you pay for "free" offers like this one by having to buy a large quantity of the product (eleven more boxes to get this T-shirt), but every time you wear the T-shirt or use the mug or pen, you become an ad for the product.

Sweet Talk: Using the Right Words

Advertisers know which words are fashionable. That's why they put *naturally* in large type and hide the sugar by calling it "sucrose" or "dextrose."

An Appealing Image When advertisers photograph food, they may use anything from gelatin to window cleaner to make the product look appetizing. The cereal you prepare won't look nearly as crunchy as the cereal shown on the box.

The Power to Persuade

If someone covered the label on your usual brand of shampoo or pop, could you tell it apart from another well-known brand? It's hard to tell the difference (if there is one) between various brands. That's why ads often make emotional appeals, associating a product with something the target audience wants: popularity, beauty, security. If you stop to think about an ad, you can often see it's offering something a product could never actually provide—happy relationships, a trouble-free life. It's when you don't think, but simply respond to the ad's emotional appeals, that an ad has the most power to persuade.

Making an Impact

Think about the words used in ads: "Just do it," "Take the plunge." Do they suggest buying on impulse, without thinking carefully about the ad—or the product? Think about the visual images used: slam-dunks, business suits, mountain streams, cozy fireplace settings. They associate a product with qualities such as success, freshness, and security. Advertisers choose words, colours, and photos very carefully. Each word and design element focusses on the message. Type and photography reinforce each other to give the message maximum impact. Design features like the following help get a message across:

A striking contrast between black and white is easy to see.

Simple, uncluttered forms are easy for people to identify and read.

Black and white with a third colour can emphasize key information.

Complex uses of type and image become a puzzle the viewer must solve.

Photographs of people can make a message more real and believable.

Use of colours—warm or cool—can bring out specific emotions.

When Is an Ad Not an Ad?

All the advertising done on TV isn't in commercials. Music videos help sell CDs and concert tickets. A product may be mentioned or displayed on a show; for instance, a character may drink a recognizable brand of pop. Actors and authors on talk shows are often trying to sell their newest film or book. Infomercials are entire programs devoted to selling a product, service, or idea.

Need some tips on being persuasive? Refresh your memory about writing a persuasive letter and speaking persuasively. **See pages 46 and 168.** Check out the information on using colour and typefaces. **See pages 194 and 210.**

Here's How

To Create an Advertisement

1. **Choose a product, service, or issue to advertise.** Give it a catchy name.
2. **Decide on a target audience.** Who would be most interested in your product or idea?
3. **Choose a medium.** What is your target audience most likely to see: a poster, a newspaper ad?
4. **Plan a strategy.** Keep your plan simple. The best ads are often those that create a simple, appealing image for the product.
5. **Think of an attention-getting headline.** If the large headline of your ad attracts people's attention, they may take the time to read the smaller type.
6. **Write strong, persuasive body copy.** Body copy is the small type in an advertisement. It gives the details, explaining why and how to follow through—where the store is located, for example, and when the sale begins.
7. **Choose eye-catching visuals.** That's a good way to grab the reader's attention.
8. **Use your design skills.** Experiment with the impact of larger type, lots of empty space, bold contrasting colours. See the design ideas on page 224.
9. **Does your ad persuade?** Test it on friends. Does it get their attention? Is it clear? Experiment with your ad until it works.

Researching

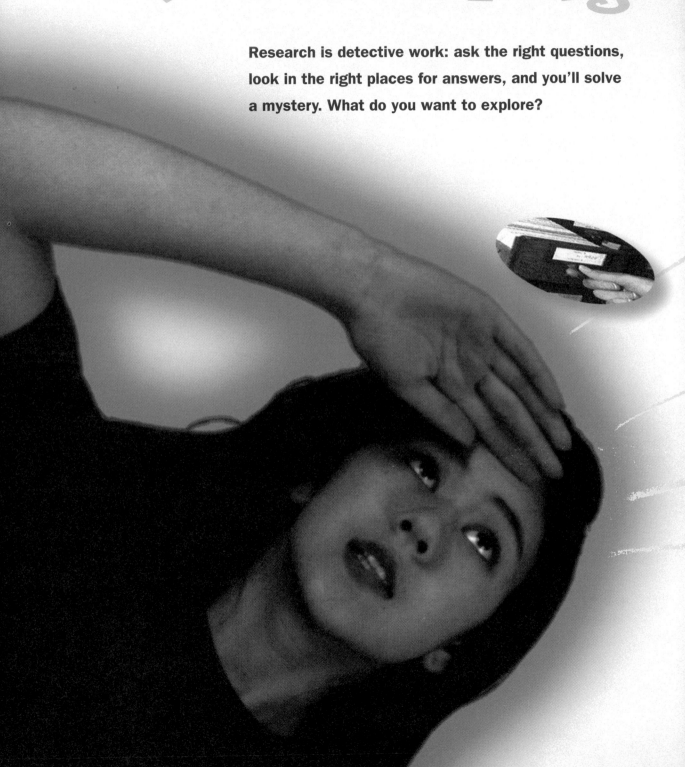

Research is detective work: ask the right questions, look in the right places for answers, and you'll solve a mystery. What do you want to explore?

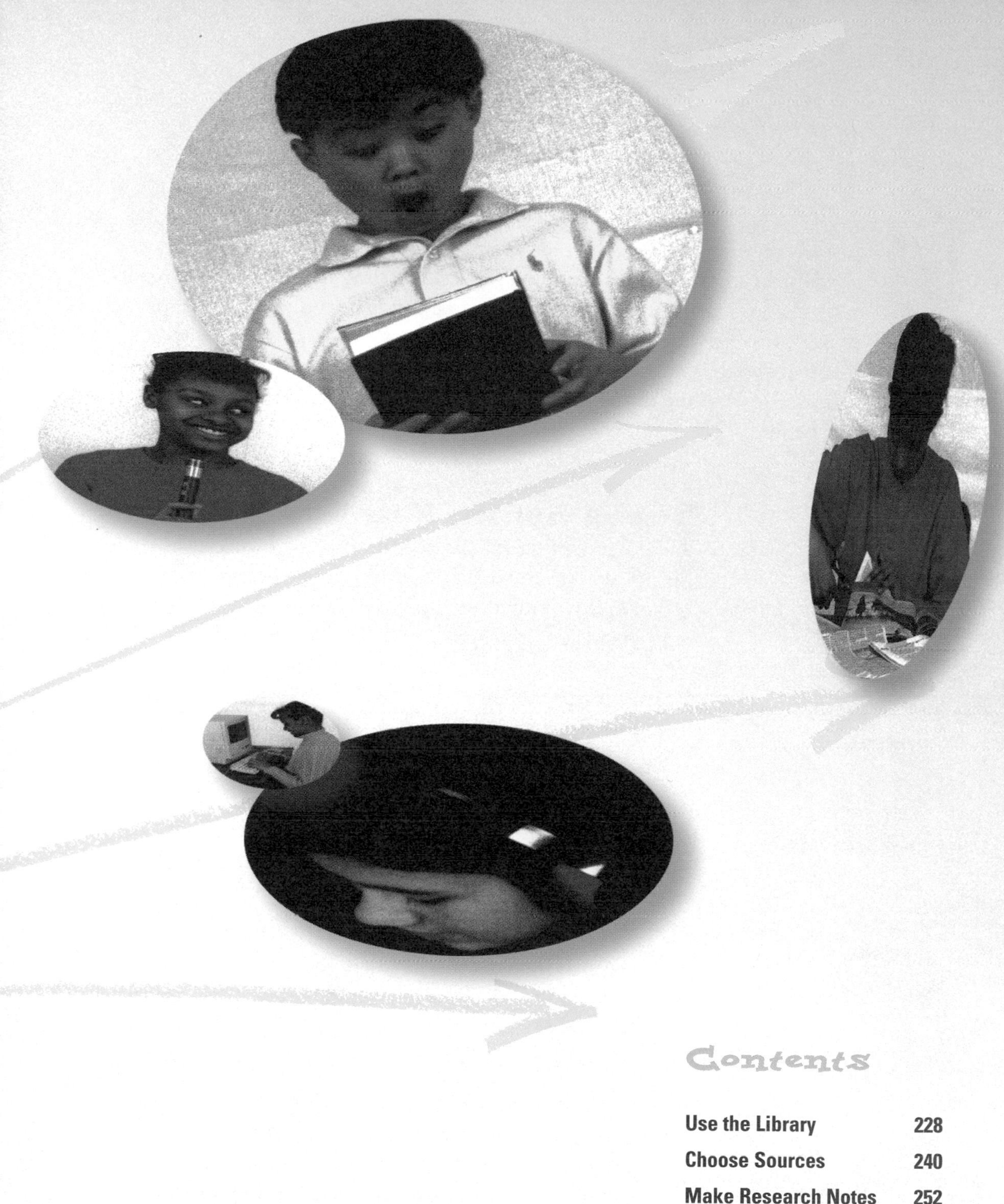

Contents

Use the Library

Inside every library are hundreds of imaginary secret passages leading to adventures of every kind. Gripping stories, startling investigations, eyewitness accounts, and amazing photographs hide upon library shelves. Countless opportunities await—chances to discover new interests, visit new worlds, and find answers to many questions. You'll never be bored in the library if you learn to do just one thing: get your hands on what interests you and leave the rest behind.

Think Before You Go

Thinking about a few simple things before you rush to the library will make your adventure there even more rewarding. Otherwise, your enthusiasm may dwindle as you become overwhelmed with choices.

Need to back up and find a topic? Now's the time to do it, before you hit the library! For help in zeroing in on the topic that will inspire the researcher within you, **see page 91.**

Know Your Needs

To figure out a game plan for how you'll spend your library time, ask yourself a few questions:

• What brings you to the library? Are you satisfying your own curiosity, or do you have an assignment? If you decide on your mission before you arrive, thumbing through interesting magazines and books won't cloud your thinking or make you forget why you came.

• How much time do you have? If you plan your library visit well, you won't spend too much time on one stage of the research process and have to scurry around the library to make up for lost time.

• How much leeway do you have to change your topic if research proves too difficult? Are you researching for yourself, or for an assignment? If you're working on an assignment, but you're not sure how closely you have to stick to your original plan, find out.

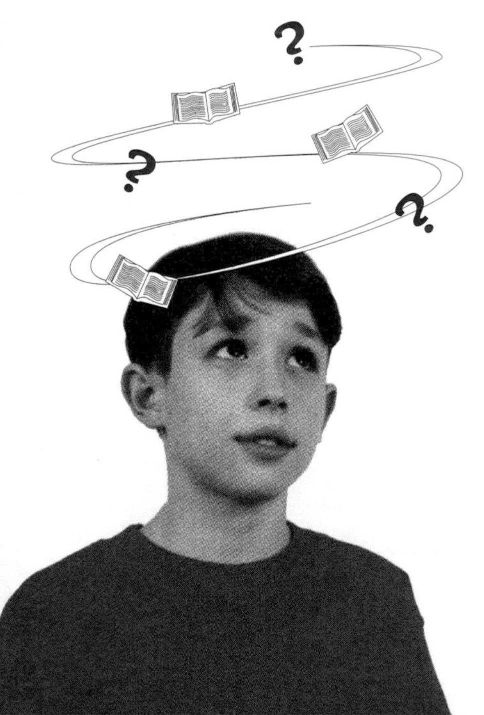

Keep the End in Sight

What will you be doing with your research? Will you be turning it into a report that you present to others? In what form will you present it? Although you'll make your presentation later on, thinking about it now will keep you from having to backtrack to the library for extra materials. Planning ahead will save you from trying to give a slide show when all you've collected is newspaper clippings.

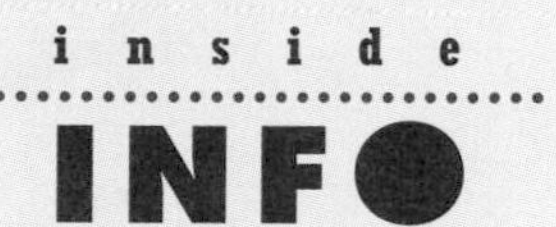
inside
INFO

If you're bored with your topic, anyone who has to read or listen to your presentation will probably doze off after the first paragraph. If your topic seems dry, try looking at it from different angles until you find an interesting twist. For example, ask yourself how it connects to your own life.

Presentation Possibilities

As you plan your end product, consider these presentation ideas.

Posters—Use splashy headings, colourful drawings, and even 3-D objects. Make every word count.

Minimuseum—Put interesting objects on tables, or hang up artwork and let people walk around while listening to an audiotape. You can record explanations of what they're seeing, interviews with experts, sound effects, and music.

Docudrama—Take an actual event (the *documentary* part), and write a short play about it (the *drama* part).

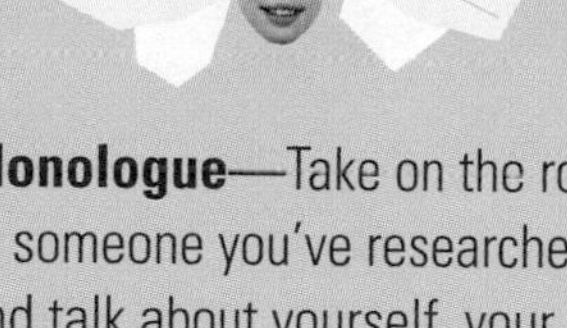

Monologue—Take on the role of someone you've researched, and talk about yourself, your times, or your culture. While you're at it, wear a costume.

Model—Build a model and caption the parts. Your model could show the earth cut in half, a bee flying with its tiny wings, or the parts of a pulley working together.

Need some advice on giving presentations? This *Survival Guide* is all yours. For more presentation ideas, including lessons on how to wow audiences with your incredible performance, **see page 174.**

Here's How

To Combine Forces

The key to researching in groups is making sure everyone participates. Besides lightening the load, combining brain-power can produce great ideas that might never have surfaced if members were working on their own.

1. **Team up.** You may find that a manageable group has three to five members, including a leader to track jobs and keep discussions moving.
2. **Brainstorm for areas to investigate.** Make a giant list of questions about the topic—welcome all suggestions. Then choose three or four questions to research.
3. **Discuss presentation possibilities.** The way you'll gather information may depend on your presentation plan, so shape some ideas now. Should everyone be looking for photographs or for relevant quotations?
4. **Set up a research strategy.** You could divide the team according to the sources you plan to use (one person covers newspapers, another checks magazines, and so on), or each person could pursue one of the research questions the group has chosen.
5. **Make a schedule.** Write down each person's job, and arrange a few meeting times to review progress; list what should be completed by the time of each meeting.

Advice from the Zone

Dear Z:
I have always wondered why bee stings hurt so much. I'll have some spare time after school next week, so I could go to the library and find out. I might also use the topic for an assignment coming up in one of my classes. Do you think there's enough information on this for a seven-page paper?

— Stung Once Too Often

Dear SOTO:
Sizing up your topic before tackling it is always a good idea. You may have a hard time filling seven pages with why bee stings cause pain, but you also wouldn't want a topic as big as "Bees." Maybe you should spread out just a little more. If you add a few more questions to the one you already have (is it true that bees die after stinging? do all bees sting?), seven pages on "bee stings" should be about right. Also, you'll have alternatives if you hit some dead ends.

Z.

What's in the Library

After an evening of gathering library materials for a report on bee stings, you settle down at home for a good night's sleep. Your dreams take you to a classroom where someone is reading a research report. As the reader drones on, students begin to doze. One student wakes herself up with a loud snore. As you zoom in for a closer look at this unlucky reader, you gasp—it's you! What happened to the videotape you found today of a magnified bee stinging somebody's arm in slow motion? Where's the TV you planned to ask permission to use? What about that fascinating magazine article you found?

You wake up when the teacher yawns loudly. What a nightmare! Calm down, you tell yourself. You've been finding some good resources; your report will be informative and interesting. But maybe tomorrow you'll ask the librarian if there are any other resources you've overlooked. . . .

inside
INFO

One of the most helpful library resources is the living, breathing person who is there to help you: the librarian. Librarians won't do your work for you, but they can guide you in finding good answers—especially when you've thought ahead and know what you're looking for.

The map below gives a general idea of services and sources that can be found in many libraries.

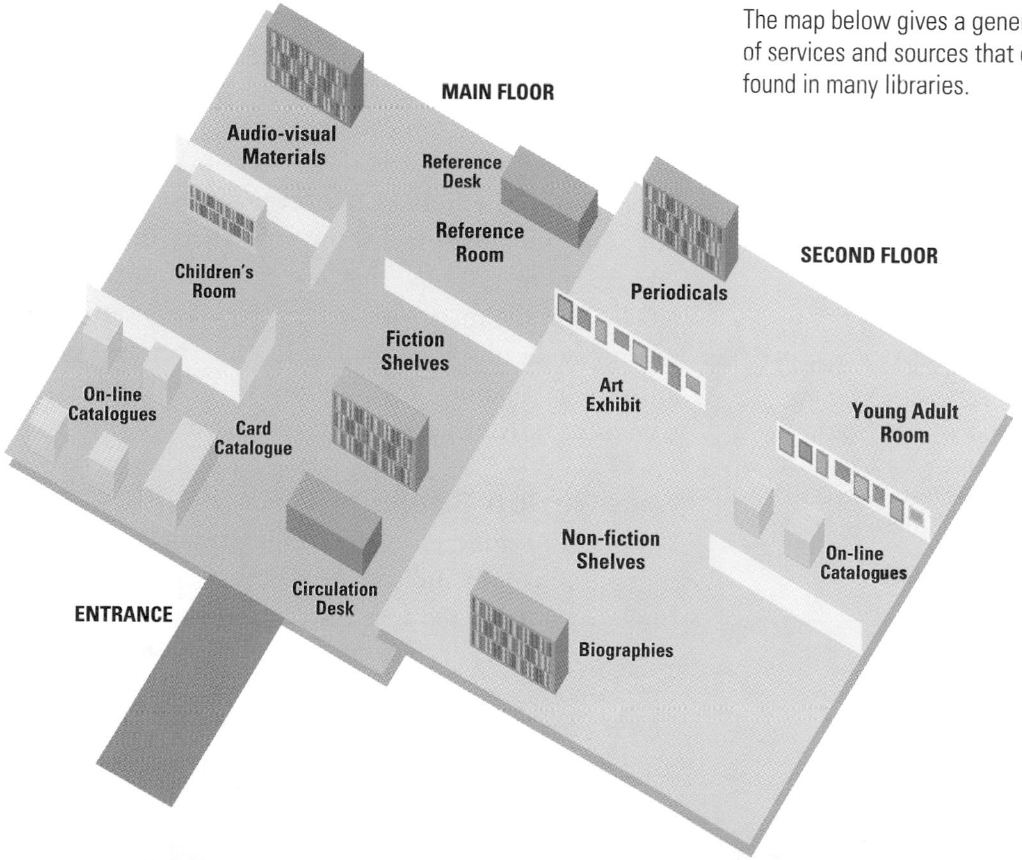

MAIN FLOOR
Audio-visual Materials
Reference Desk
Reference Room
Children's Room
Fiction Shelves
On-line Catalogues
Card Catalogue
Circulation Desk
ENTRANCE
SECOND FLOOR
Periodicals
Art Exhibit
Young Adult Room
Non-fiction Shelves
On-line Catalogues
Biographies

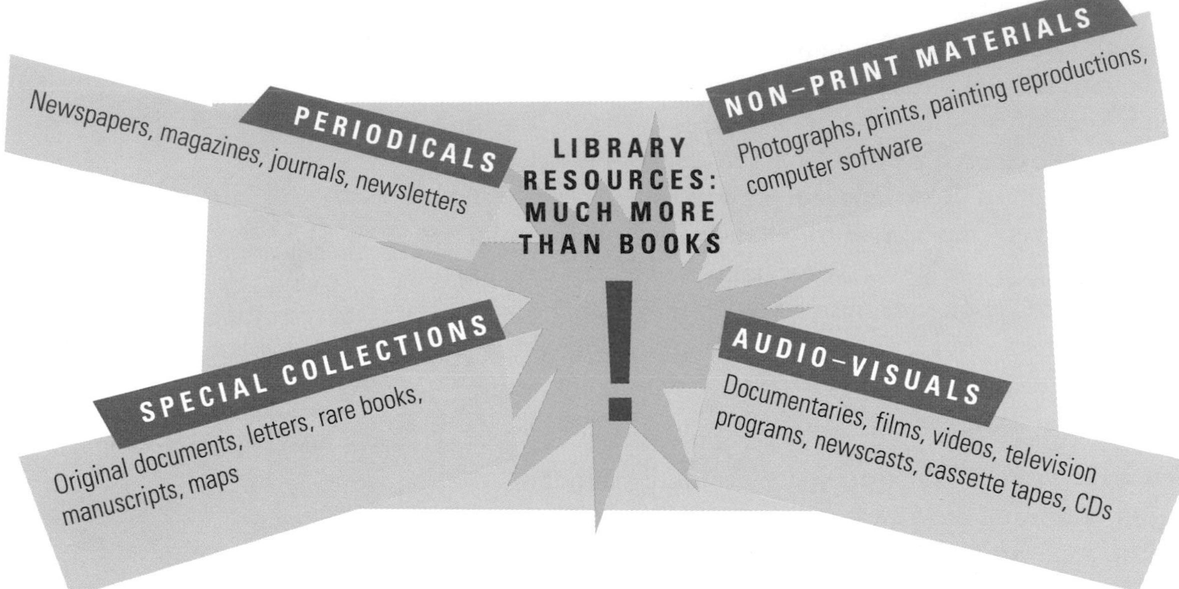
PERIODICALS
Newspapers, magazines, journals, newsletters
LIBRARY RESOURCES: MUCH MORE THAN BOOKS
!
NON-PRINT MATERIALS
Photographs, prints, painting reproductions, computer software
SPECIAL COLLECTIONS
Original documents, letters, rare books, manuscripts, maps
AUDIO-VISUALS
Documentaries, films, videos, television programs, newscasts, cassette tapes, CDs

How Books Are Sorted

Even though it may not be obvious at first glance, library books are arranged in categories that make a lot of sense. The quickest way to decode the system is to get a library floor plan. If the floor plan isn't posted, ask the librarian for one. The floor plan will show you where the different resources are and how they are arranged. If the shelves are labelled on the map with letters only (for example, *E–F*), that means the books are arranged in alphabetical order by authors' last names. Fiction books—for example, mysteries, romances, adventures—are usually ordered that way.

inside
INFO

You can use the way books are organized to help you narrow your research topic. First look up two or three books about a subject that interests you. When you go to the shelves that carry those titles, you will find many other books covering different aspects of the same topic. Look through these until you find a topic you like.

Non-fiction Books

Numbers or number-letter combinations (known as call numbers) usually indicate non-fiction books. Non-fiction books are organized by subject, so once you find the category you want, you can camp there without having unrelated books in your way. Biographies (non-fiction stories about people's lives) are sometimes kept in a separate section, alphabetized by the subject's last name.

Non-fiction books are organized according to one of two systems. Most Canadian and U.S. libraries use the Dewey decimal system; only large libraries tend to use the Library of Congress (LC) system.

Dewey Decimal System

000	General works
100	Philosophy
200	Religion
300	Social sciences
400	Language
500	Science
600	Technology
700	Fine arts
800	Literature
900	History and Geography

Library of Congress System

A	General works
B	Philosophy, psychology, religion
C	History and related sciences
D	History: general and Old World
E-F	History: the Americas
G	Geography, anthropology, recreation
H	Social sciences
J	Political science
K	Law
L	Education
M	Music
N	Fine arts
P	Language and literature
Q	Science
R	Medicine
S	Agriculture
T	Technology
U	Military science
V	Naval science
Z	Bibliography and library science

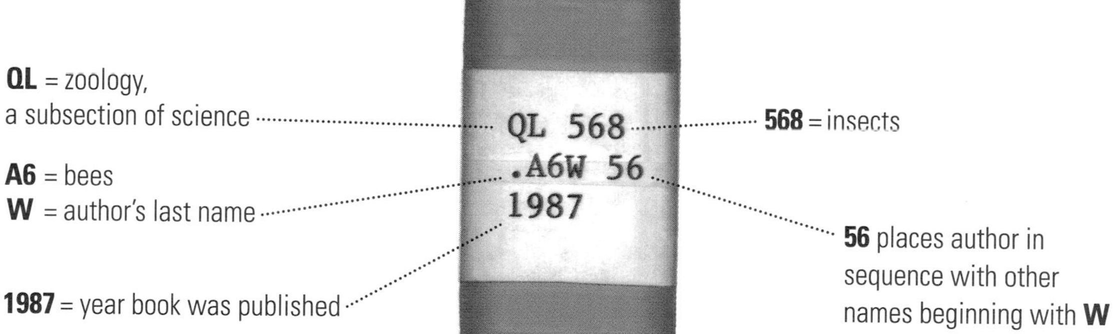
QL = zoology,
a subsection of science
A6 = bees
W = author's last name
1987 = year book was published
QL 568
.A6W 56
1987
568 = insects
56 places author in sequence with other names beginning with **W**

To find *The Biology of the Honey Bee* by Mark L. Winston, you would look in numerical order among the **QL** shelves for **568**. Then you would look in alphabetical order among the listings under **QL568** for **A6**. Finally, you would look among the listings under **QL568.A6** for **W56**.

Search with Library Catalogues

Now that you've made yourself familiar with the library's offerings, it's time to slide up to the catalogues and begin your search. The catalogues will look like rows of little drawers, or they will look like computers. As more libraries computerize their listings, the drawers may one day be seen only in antique stores, where they may be sold as storage containers for floppy disks or perhaps for socks.

Three Paths to Your Book

Whether you're flipping cards or tapping keys, you always have three choices of how to look things up: by subject, by author, or by title. When beginning your search, you will probably start with subjects, unless you already have the names of authors or books. The catalogue will lead you to books.

The Card Catalogue

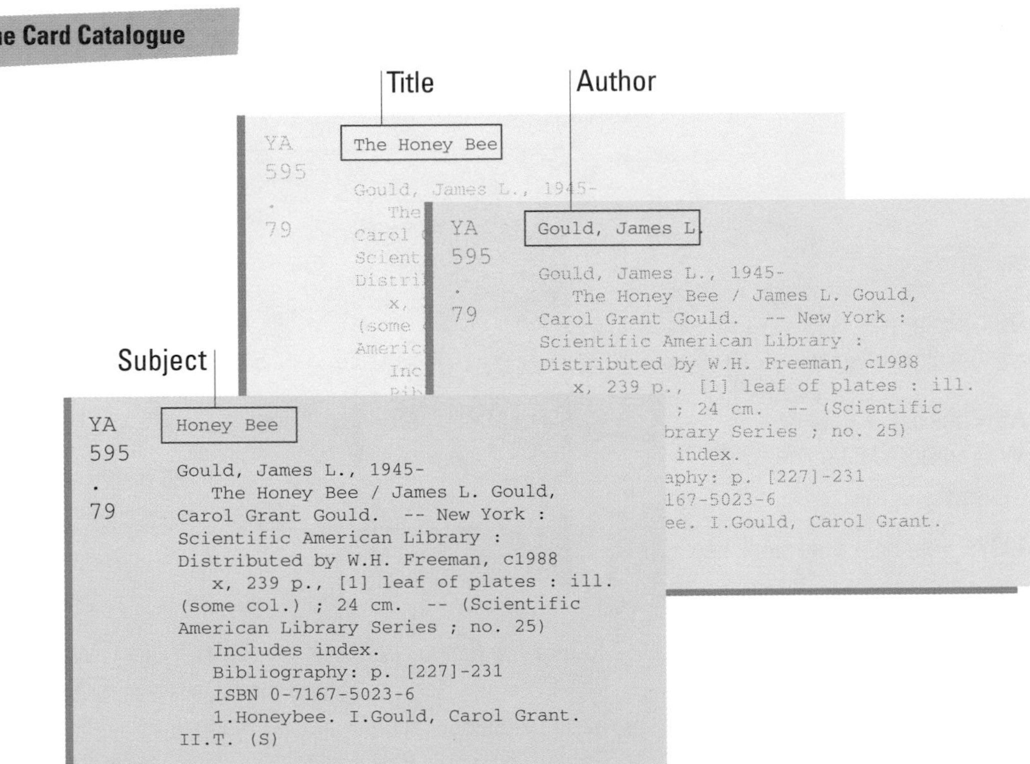

Title
Author
Subject
The Honey Bee
Gould, James L
YA 595 . 79
Honey Bee
Gould, James L., 1945-
The Honey Bee / James L. Gould,
Carol Grant Gould. -- New York :
Scientific American Library :
Distributed by W.H. Freeman, c1988
x, 239 p., [1] leaf of plates : ill.
(some col.) ; 24 cm. -- (Scientific
American Library Series ; no. 25)
Includes index.
Bibliography: p. [227]-231
ISBN 0-7167-5023-6
1.Honeybee. I.Gould, Carol Grant.
II.T. (S)

The Computer Catalogue

Computer catalogues have simple commands that carry you from screen to screen.

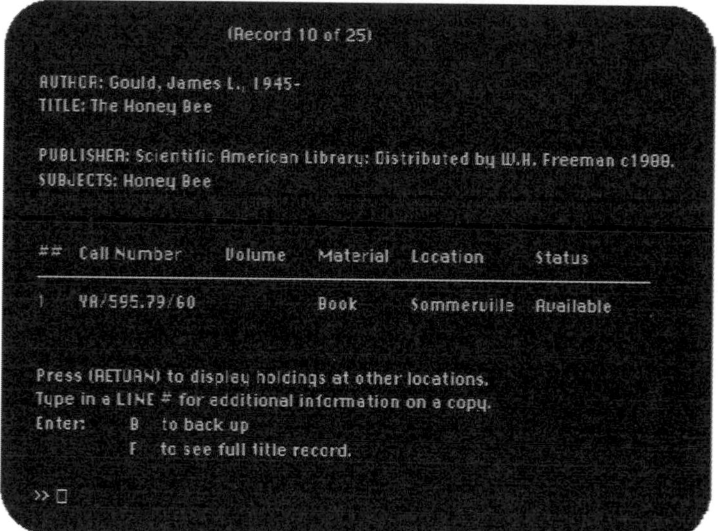

(Record 10 of 25)

AUTHOR: Gould, James L., 1945-
TITLE: The Honey Bee

PUBLISHER: Scientific American Library: Distributed by W.H. Freeman c1988.
SUBJECTS: Honey Bee

##	Call Number	Volume	Material	Location	Status
1	YA/595.79/60		Book	Sommerville	Available

Press (RETURN) to display holdings at other locations.
Type in a LINE # for additional information on a copy.
Enter: B to back up
F to see full title record.

>>

Computer Catalogue Extras

Computer catalogues, with simple commands that carry you from screen to screen, have a number of features that are not available with card catalogues.

Keywords—Keywords enable you to focus your search by using more than one identifying term at a time. Typing *Bees and Hum* will bring up Hum Bug's book titled *Bees I Have Known*. Typing *insects and habitats* will bring up all the titles with those two words in their entries.

Alternative suggestions—When you arrive at a list of sources on one topic, a "see also" list will often appear on the screen, recommending related categories to search.

Location identification—Computer catalogues tell whether your library owns the book and whether it is on the shelf or out on loan.

Library listings—Some computer catalogues list nearby libraries that have books your library doesn't own.

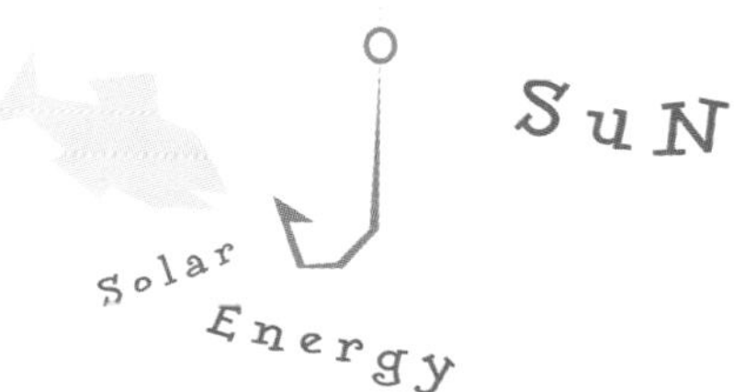
SuN
Solar
Energy

inside
INFO

Sometimes you'll need to fish for a keyword. Don't give up—keep trying all related words that come into your mind. If your topic is "Getting Power from the Sun," you may not find much until you stumble upon the magical combination *renewable and energy and sources.* Don't get too specific, though; remember that you're looking for entire books.

LOOK
HERE!

inside

INFO

Many encyclopedia publishers are creating computerized encyclopedias. Find out if your library offers any. There are also computerized sources of information on everything from films and sports to politics and science. Most of these databases are continually updated. To read more about **computerized encyclopedias, see page 246.**

Rummage in the Reference Section

Many people know where the reference section of their library is because that's where the encyclopedias are found. But numerous other research shortcuts await those who spend some time in the reference section. Consider, for instance, indexes. If you are interested in bees, all you have to do is look in the *B* encyclopedia, right? Well, that's a start, but you might find more if you use that last book in the row, called the Index. There you can find all the references to bees in the entire set of encyclopedias.

BRIGHT Ideas

FOR FACT-FINDING

Investigate biographical dictionaries. Many are specialized, offering biographies of authors, artists, musicians, scientists, and so on. *Current Biography* and *Canadian Who's Who* give short biographies of notable living people.

Examine almanacs and yearbooks. Books such as the *Information Please Almanac* or the *Canada Year Book* collect amazing varieties of information, ranging from census results to world records.

Skim specialized encyclopedias. How about an entire encyclopedia devoted to your topic? See if something like the *Penguin Encyclopedia of Popular Music* exists for your topic.

Make use of directories. Directories list addresses, associations, members, or other types of information about a topic. *Bowker's Complete Video Directory* lists all kinds of videos and tells what they're about and where to get them.

Note the publication date when consulting reference books. Entries can sound as if they were written a week ago even though they are years old and out of date.

Use Periodicals

What a waste it would be if the thousands of magazine articles published every month were tossed away and forgotten—including the articles with up-to-date information about your research topic!

Fortunately, libraries save issues of many periodicals. What's more, some companies specialize in keeping records, called indexes, of magazine and journal articles. Some indexes cover a wide variety of publications, while others list magazine articles dealing with one field of interest (such as the social sciences). Each index begins with a list of the publications they track. The *Readers' Guide to Periodical Literature* is the most commonly found index to magazine articles. It covers about two hundred popular magazines, beginning with the year 1900.

BEES
See also
Bee culture
The African advantage [honeybee research: cove
Weiss. il *Science News* 137:328-9+ My 26 '90
African bees make U.S. debut. R. Weiss. il *Scien*
138:261 O 27 '90
Africanized bees near Texas border. il *Science*
19 '90
The antifreeze of bees. [Ellesmere Island] B. I
Natural History p52-9 Jl '90
Bee cool [Himalayan cliff bee's strategy for
winter without being eaten] B. A. Under
History p50-7 D '90
Bee police [cooperation among honeybees
Scientific American 262:28+ Mr '90
Bumblebee energy: what's the buzz? [stu
Ellington] R. Cowen. *Science News* 1
Dance of the electronic bee. M. W. Mof
Geographic 177:134-40 Ja '90
How African are "killer" bees? M. Ba
250:628-9 N 2 '90
Stinging criticism [honeybee dance la
Scientific American. 263:29+ N '9
A wing and a prayer [condensed fro
G. Wasson. il *Readers Digest* 136
Diseases and p
Mites and killer bees. B. Sletto. il
Ja/F '90
Identificatio
Bee billiards [photograph] S. Car
p120-1 Ap '90
Photograp
Bee billiards. S. Camazine. il N
'90
BEES, GEOGRAPHY *See* Ge
BEES, SPELLING *See* Spellin

Dance of the electronic bee. M. W. Moffett. il *National Geographic* 177:134-40 Ja '90

To Use a Magazine index

1. **Decide which time period you want to explore.** The most recent? The time when a particular event occurred? A five-year time span? Select the volumes covering the time period you want.
2. **Choose a word that covers your topic and look it up.** If you already have an article title or author, you can use that to find where and when the article appeared.
3. **Make note of each listing.** Use the directions at the beginning of the index to interpret abbreviations you don't understand.
4. **Follow up on any "see also" listings that appear.**
5. **Repeat steps 1 through 4 for each question or subtopic you have.**

Computerized Magazine Indexes

The *Readers' Guide to Periodical Literature* is also available in electronic form. Many libraries have this or similar computer catalogues of magazines. These electronic indexes allow you to search for articles by subject, author, or title. The prompts that appear on the screen at every step make it hard to go wrong. The computers often come with printers, so you can print out each helpful entry.

Wondering if an article will be useful? Some of the steps used in judging a book can be applied to judging an article, too. For instructions on skimming for information, **see page 241.**

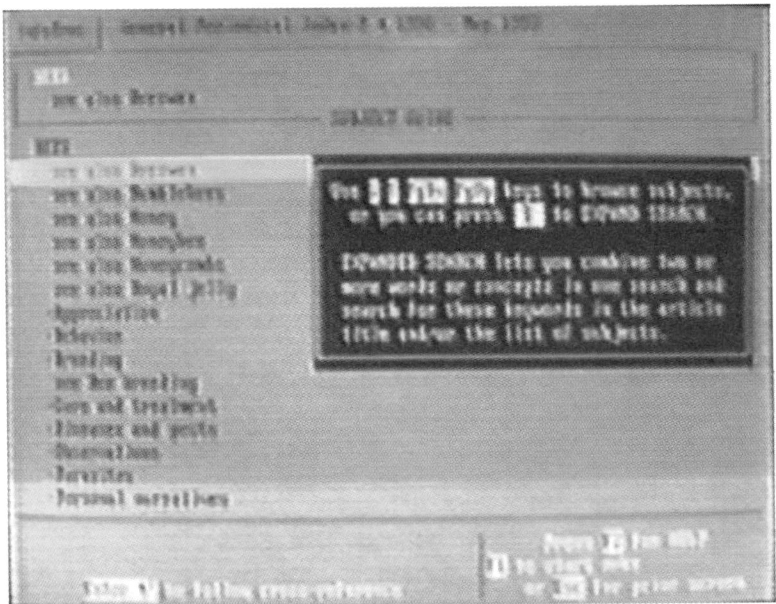

Find Newspaper Articles

Newspapers are not as well indexed as magazines. Most small newspapers are not indexed at all. Larger papers may be indexed through computer services such as Infomart, CBCA (Canadian Business and Current Affairs), or through databases produced by individual newspapers (such as the *Toronto Globe and Mail*'s Info Globe). Some computer indexes show where articles appear, while others display entire articles. Some libraries have more access to computerized newspaper indexes than do others. Call libraries in your area to learn what your choices are.

BRIGHT Ideas

FOR FINDING USEFUL NEWSPAPER ARTICLES

Try the *Canadian News Index.* C.N.I. has been indexing seven large Canadian newspapers since 1977 and is available at most libraries in Canada.

Look in computerized periodical indexes. Some may include a few major newspapers in their listings.

Ask for any newspaper index. Your library may have indexes for one or two major newspapers. Because many events are covered by more than one paper, finding the right date in one paper can lead you to helpful editions of other papers.

Close In on Your Article

There's nothing like putting the indexes down and setting off to find the actual articles, only to discover that you forgot to copy vital information. Before you leave the indexes, make sure you have the periodical titles, dates, and volume numbers, as well as the article titles and page numbers for each article you hope to find.

With library floor plan in hand, head toward the appropriate shelves. Look for a listing of the periodicals the library holds, and find out in what form the periodicals are stored. Unless someone has beaten you to it, you can search the shelved periodicals immediately. Older issues might be bound into books or saved as miniaturized photographs, called microfilm or microfiche, to be read on a machine that magnifies the photographs. Once you find the pages you need, you can usually print a copy for a small fee.

If your list contains periodicals that the library doesn't own, you may be able to request the articles from other libraries. Your librarian can help you do this. Be sure to find out when you can hope to receive the articles.

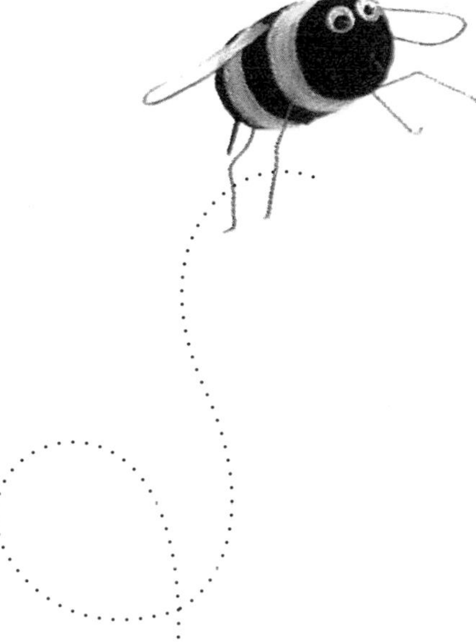

The next best thing to knowing something is knowing where to find it.
—Samuel Johnson

Choose Sources

Say you're working on a research report about bees. If you were to collect every resource in the library that discusses bees, it could take months to read them all. You'd be ready to write your own book about bees by the time you finished. A good researcher has to be selective. Knowing how to shop for sources can save hours of time as you pass over unhelpful information and pull exactly what you need from the sources that remain.

Preview Books

When you're researching, why read an entire book when you may need only some of what it offers? By looking first at five key parts of a book, you can figure out how much of it will be useful for your research. Then you can rearrange your collection of resources while you're still at the beginning of your project.

Copyright Page

An entry like this appears among the first few pages of a book. The date after the © symbol indicates when the book was published.

Do I need information that was written more recently, or will these facts still be true?

Table of Contents

The table of contents shows how the book is organized, which aspects of the topic are covered, and how much space is devoted to each aspect.

Is this book likely to have the information I need? Which chapters should I skim?

Does this book have enough information on the specific facts I'm looking for?

Index

The index gives a complete list of the topics covered in a book; it is much more thorough than the table of contents. The index also gives a page number for every appearance of the topics listed.

Author Information

Often found inside the back cover of a book, the description of the author usually reveals why he or she is qualified to discuss the subject.

Should I use only technical books by scientists, or can I use other authors too?

Extras

Scan the rest of the book to see if it has any other features that could be useful to you.

- **Notes** explain more about certain points in a book.
- **Bibliography** lists the sources the author used.
- **Recommended Reading** suggests other research sources.
- **Maps and Charts** help you picture information.

BRIGHT Ideas

FOR PREVIEWING A BOOK

Learn the author's plan. To get a feel for the author's intentions, read the introduction and last few pages of the book. Does the plan match your needs?

Survey each chapter. To get a better idea of what's in each chapter, read the first and last paragraphs.

Skim the chapters that interest you. For a chapter you know you want to use, read the first and last sentences of each paragraph. Skimming will show you what subjects are covered and where you'll want to take notes when it's time to read more thoroughly.

Time how long it takes you to read a full page. If you're working under a deadline, knowing your reading speed will help you plan how many pages you can read thoroughly.

When was this map drawn? Is there any reason to believe the information may have changed?

Decode Maps

Maps can communicate in one glance ideas that would require pages of description. Maps can also be studied. For example, you might compare different types of maps (a political map for national boundaries and a population map for bee populations) and combine the facts gathered from each one. You can also use maps as a visual aid when it's your turn to communicate information.

Kinds of Maps

Political maps show boundaries inside and between nations.

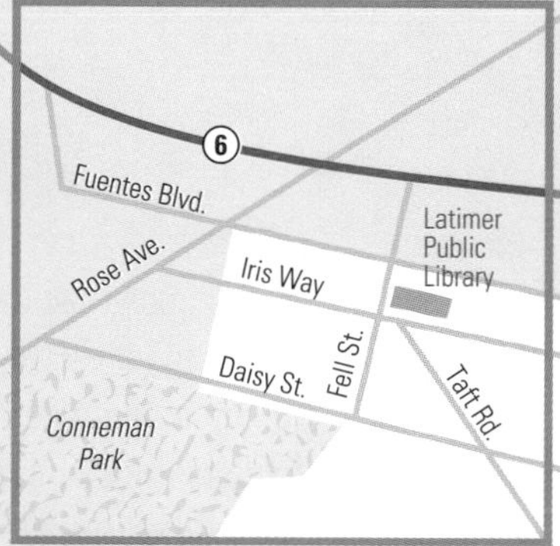

6
Fuentes Blvd.
Rose Ave.
Iris Way
Latimer
Public
Library
Daisy St.
Fell St.
Taft Rd.
Conneman
Park

Road maps show how to get from here to there.

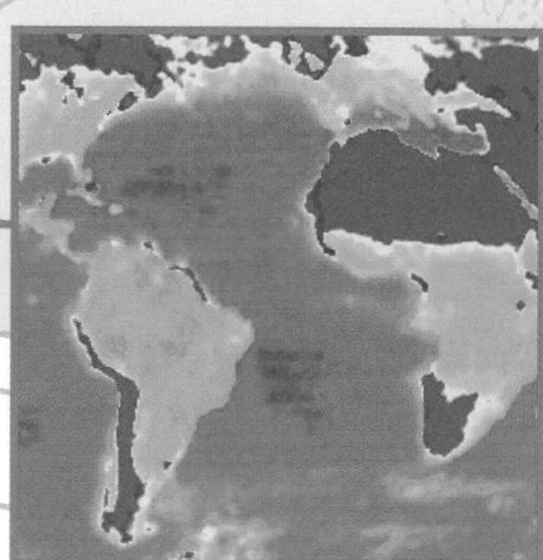

Specialized maps show particular features, such as mountains, climates, or populations.

Map Indexes

Maps with a lot of locations marked on them are usually supplied with indexes, which allow you to look up the places alphabetically. A number-letter combination appears next to each entry in the index. This combination refers to numbers and letters printed along the vertical and horizontal borders of the map, forming a grid. Follow the grid with two fingers to find the segment where the number and letter meet, and you will have the location you want.

Index

Goodman Centre for the Arts **H-4**
Hannah Provincial Airport **D-11**
Latimer Public Library **D-4**
Marshall High School **A-14**
O'Mara Convention Centre **B-13**
Queen Ella-Bee Mansion **A-10**
Westside Mall **A-12**

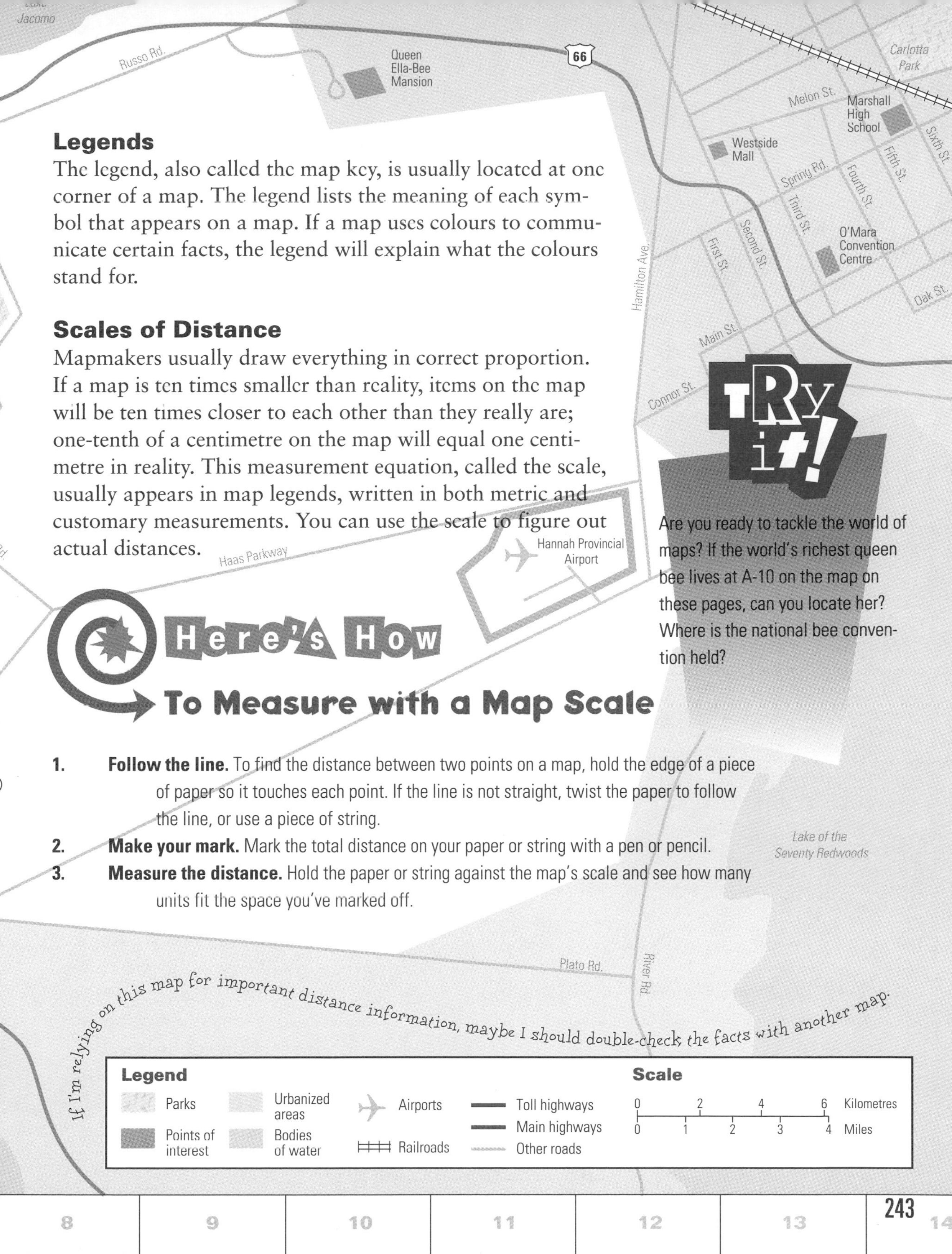

Jacomo
Russo Rd.
Queen
Ella-Bee
Mansion
66
Carlotta
Park
Melon St.
Marshall
High
School
Westside
Mall
Sixth St.
Fifth St.
Spring Rd.
Fourth St.
Third St.
Second St.
First St.
O'Mara
Convention
Centre
Hamilton Ave.
Oak St.
Main St.
Connor St.
Hannah Provincial
Airport
Haas Parkway
Lake of the
Seventy Redwoods
Plato Rd.
River Rd.
6
If I'm relying on this map for important distance information, maybe I should double-check the facts with another map.
Legend
Parks
Urbanized areas
Airports
Toll highways
Points of interest
Bodies of water
Railroads
Main highways
Other roads
Scale
0 2 4 6 Kilometres
0 1 2 3 4 Miles

Legends

The legend, also called the map key, is usually located at one corner of a map. The legend lists the meaning of each symbol that appears on a map. If a map uses colours to communicate certain facts, the legend will explain what the colours stand for.

Scales of Distance

Mapmakers usually draw everything in correct proportion. If a map is ten times smaller than reality, items on the map will be ten times closer to each other than they really are; one-tenth of a centimetre on the map will equal one centimetre in reality. This measurement equation, called the scale, usually appears in map legends, written in both metric and customary measurements. You can use the scale to figure out actual distances.

TRY IT!

Are you ready to tackle the world of maps? If the world's richest queen bee lives at A-10 on the map on these pages, can you locate her? Where is the national bee convention held?

Here's How To Measure with a Map Scale

1. **Follow the line.** To find the distance between two points on a map, hold the edge of a piece of paper so it touches each point. If the line is not straight, twist the paper to follow the line, or use a piece of string.
2. **Make your mark.** Mark the total distance on your paper or string with a pen or pencil.
3. **Measure the distance.** Hold the paper or string against the map's scale and see how many units fit the space you've marked off.

8 9 10 11 12 13 14

Interpret Charts and Graphs

Drawings can sometimes show connections among pieces of information far more clearly than words can. If you hear that the number of bees living in the Northwest Territories has decreased by twenty percent, this may not impress you as much as a drawing might. How many bees were there before? Is this a noticeable change? If you saw a line on a graph slanting down sharply from last year to this year, you'd understand more quickly.

Are the categories clearly different from each other, or might they be divided in another way? If divided differently, would the facts change?

Pie Charts

In pie charts, also known as circle graphs, the whole circle represents 100 percent of something. This total is then divided into wedges that represent the different parts of the whole. Instead of having to subtract and add, you can see immediately how much space each part takes up.

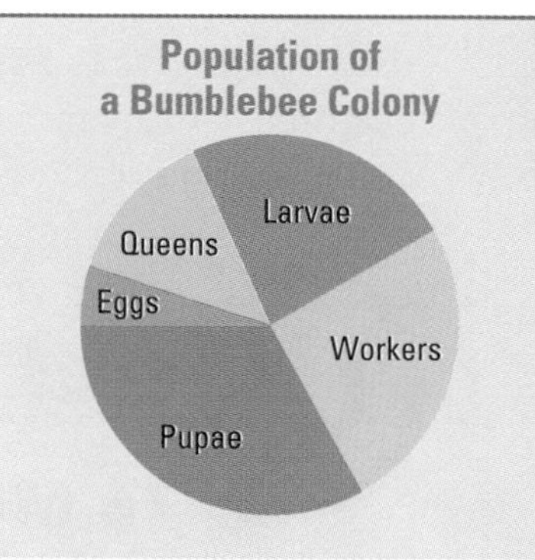
Population of
a Bumblebee Colony
Larvae
Queens
Eggs
Workers
Pupae

How was this information collected? How many people or instances were counted?

Line Graphs

Line graphs often show trends over time. Segments of time are marked along one side of the graph, and amounts of a certain item are marked across an adjoining side. Points are marked where the two categories meet. A line drawn to connect the points will reveal trends. Upward lines show increases, downward lines show decreases, and level lines show no change.

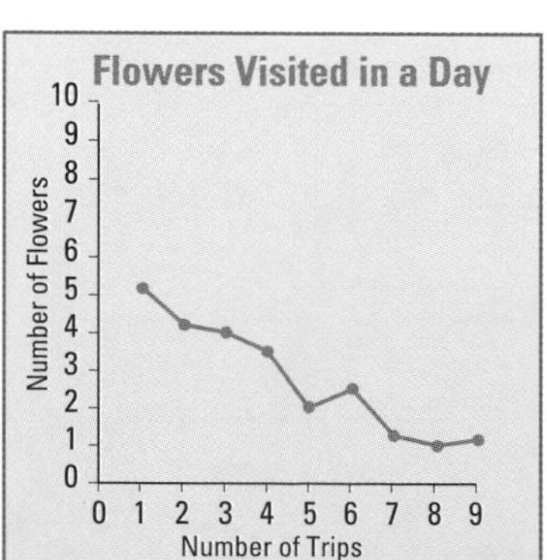
Flowers Visited in a Day
Number of Flowers
0 1 2 3 4 5 6 7 8 9 10
0 1 2 3 4 5 6 7 8 9
Number of Trips

inside INFO

Reading the fine print near a chart may throw new light on it. Asterisks (*) are clues that lead you to more information. Look also for words like *estimate*—it tells you that a number is only a good guess; by now a more exact number may be available.

LINE GRAPH ALERT!

Sometimes graphs can be misleading. A queen bee has designed the graph below to give the impression that her workers have been slacking off. Although both graphs below show the same information, she has made the line drop more dramatically by spreading out the vertical numbers in the left graph.

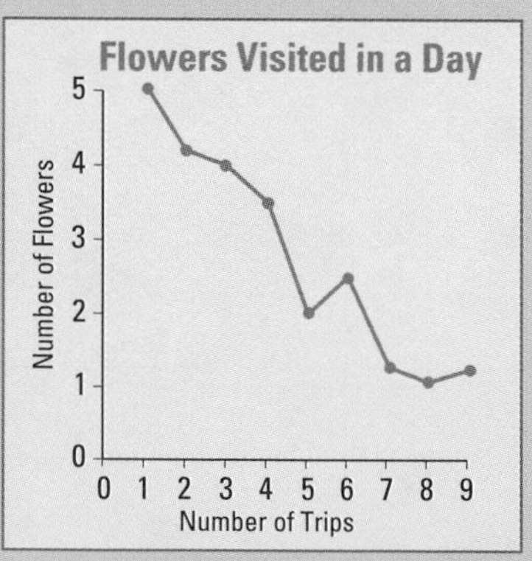
Flowers Visited in a Day
Number of Flowers
0 1 2 3 4 5
0 1 2 3 4 5 6 7 8 9
Number of Trips

Did this diagram aid my understanding of the information? Should I use it for my own presentation?

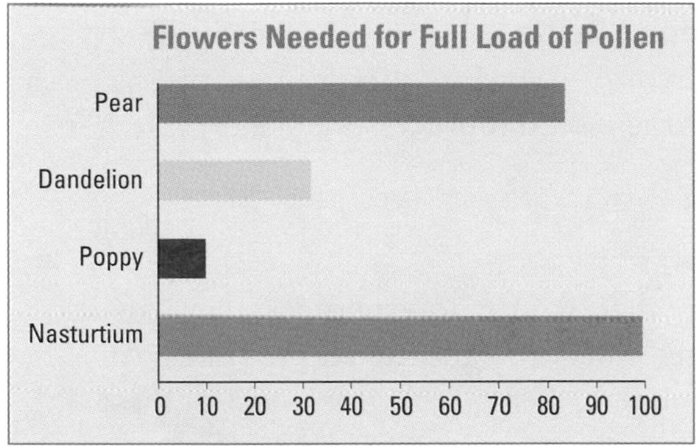
Flowers Needed for Full Load of Pollen
Pear
Dandelion
Poppy
Nasturtium
0 10 20 30 40 50 60 70 80 90 100

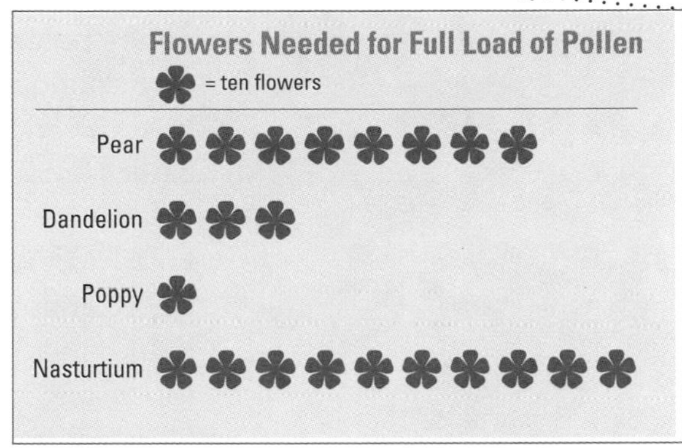
Flowers Needed for Full Load of Pollen
= ten flowers
Pear
Dandelion
Poppy
Nasturtium

Bar Graphs

Bar graphs show several thick lines that represent amounts. Seeing the bars lined up allows you to compare them easily. To understand what a bar graph is showing, you need to read the title and the information along the sides of the graph.

Pictographs

A pictograph is similar to a bar graph, except that it uses symbols (instead of bars) to stand for quantities. Instead of measuring the bars, you add up the symbols. Each symbol stands for a given amount, usually specified on the graph.

Diagrams

A diagram is a drawing of an object or process. Diagrams show objects in a simplified way so that you can understand things you might not see in real life. Diagrams often include labels or arrows to help explain functions or parts.

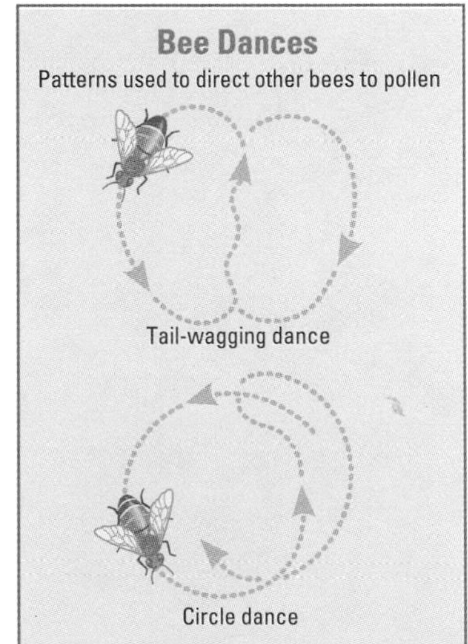
Bee Dances
Patterns used to direct other bees to pollen
Tail-wagging dance
Circle dance

Try Computer Resources

Not long ago, a researcher might not have sat at a computer until it was time to begin writing. Recently, however, computers began providing help earlier by speeding up library card catalogue searches. Now computers are starting to pitch in at the middle of the research process, helping researchers gather facts.

CD-ROMs

CDs can hold more than your favourite tunes; they can also hold books, pictures, indexes, educational programs, cartoons, and much more. Called CD-ROMs, most of these CDs won't sound like much in your CD player. They work like computer disks, except that you cannot change or add to their information—hence the initials ROM (Read-Only Memory). The most popular library CD-ROM holdings are encyclopedias and indexes to articles.

On-line Computer Searches

Several years ago, a few companies began collecting information about sports, the stock market, health, travel, books, and hundreds of other topics—all on computer. When they had piled up enough facts and figures, they offered their giant catalogues of information to the public. Anyone with a computer, a telephone line, and a modem (a device that lets computer data be transmitted by telephone) could pay to hook up to continually updated files, called databases.

Response to the idea has skyrocketed, and the databases continue to grow. Hundreds of thousands of computer users are now members of these on-line information services.

ON-LINE RESEARCH OPTIONS

- Encyclopedias
- Consumer Reports
- Weather Maps
- News Summaries
- Newspaper Articles
- Magazine Articles
- Biographical Profiles
- Country Profiles

Use Audiovisual Sources

As videocassette recorders (VCRs) become more common, opportunities abound for you to learn about a topic in new ways. Even if you don't own a VCR, many libraries and schools do, so there's no reason to limit yourself to books and periodicals when researching.

Videotapes

Interested in travelling with a mountain climber through the Himalayas? Want to watch a beekeeper collect honey—from a safe distance? Check at the library or the video-rental store. Some videotapes show experiences or discoveries in science, history, foreign cultures, or the arts. Others fall into the "how-to" category and can teach you about anything from playing basketball to setting up computer software. Take a look at video catalogues to see what you might be able to borrow, rent, or order.

Who published this video? A professional association, or an entertainment company?

Television Programs

TV can occasionally be a good source of information—especially if you watch public broadcasting. Check listings to see if any programs might meet your research needs. Keep an eye out for travel stories, science programs, special news reports, and documentaries. If you decide to take notes, write down the station, date, and time of the program you watched, including the title, if there is one. This information can be difficult to track down later.

inside INFO

Try TV and radio talk shows! Sometimes, especially on smaller or public channels, you can find intelligent interviewers asking good questions of knowledgeable guests—possibly about your research topic. Some talk show hosts invite several guests who will disagree with each other, allowing the audience to hear different viewpoints.

Visit Places

What if you could walk inside a book and experience all of its sights, sounds, smells, and surfaces first-hand? Visiting places that relate to your topic is like having that chance.

SOLO FIELD TRIPS YOU CAN TAKE

Museums
Are there any museums close enough for you to visit? If so, ask them to mail you notices of the different exhibits they have throughout the year. You can visit shows that interest you and turn them into the beginnings of research projects.

Tourist Attractions
Call your town or city hall for a listing of points of interest in your area. You might find old photographs of your neighbourhood, collections from archaeological digs, or famous landmarks under your very nose.

Homemade Tours
Why wait for an invitation? If you're interested in a type of job, or in how a product is put together, arrange a behind-the-scenes tour. You could ask to visit a TV studio, a factory, or many other business places.

Here's How

To Request a Visit

Mailing your request will help it get into the right hands and increase your chances of receiving a thoughtful reply.

1. **Call the place you'd like to visit.** Ask for the correctly spelled name and address of the person who will handle your request.
2. **Draft a short letter.** Explain who you are, what you'd like to learn, and why. If you have a deadline, include it.
3. **Ask someone else to read your request.** If the person thinks it's clear, type it. **See page 372 for a sample business letter.**
4. **Send it off.** Include your phone number and a self-addressed, stamped envelope for a reply.
5. **Be persistent.** If you receive no reply within two weeks, follow up with a phone call. Ask for the person to whom you addressed your request.

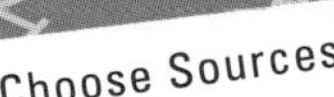

Ask People

As a researcher absorbed in your books and other sources, you can easily forget that there are people in the world who are interested in your topic and have even devoted more time to it than you have. These people may work in a job related to your topic, have made a hobby of it, or in some other way pursue their interest in it. Why not talk with them and enjoy a new view on what you're researching?

inside INFO

Spread the word when you're looking for helpful people to talk with about your topic. Perhaps someone knows someone who knows someone who can help.

PEOPLE TO INTERVIEW

Professionals have special knowledge and experience. Who would know something about your research topic—a veterinarian? a firefighter? a journalist? an artist? Even someone who can't talk for long might suggest other resources.

Travellers often enjoy telling about their experiences. If you are researching a place, do you know of people who have visited there? Do they have slides or photographs? You can learn a lot by looking at pictures of a place and hearing it described.

Narrators are simply people who like to tell stories. A narrator could be anyone—from a citizen who has served on a jury to an immigrant who came to this country at the age of ten. If you were researching bee stings, you might look for a bee keeper with stories to tell.

How long has this person been involved with my topic?

Members of organizations have reasons for being members, such as support for a cause or enjoyment of membership activities. Find out what types of societies and organizations meet in your area, and see if any relate to your research topic. You might find a whole group of people to interview.

Successful Interviewing

Phone ahead. Don't assume the person is ready to talk when you call—ask for a good time to call back. If you'd like a face-to-face interview, set a date and time—don't just walk in.

Come prepared. Have your questions written down and your note-taking gear (pen and pad, or tape-recorder) ready.

Let your interest show. Make the person you're interviewing feel that his or her knowledge is valuable to you. This helps people talk more openly.

Is there more than one side . . .

Form good questions. Do enough research before your interview so that you know what to ask. Questions that can be answered yes or no won't get you too far.

Advice from the Zone

Dear Z:

I have two friends from different parts of Sri Lanka, and they both remember being stung by bees there. But my map shows no bees in Sri Lanka. What's going on here?

—Baffled

Dear Baffled:

Have time for a trip to Sri Lanka? One thing here is for sure: you can't always believe what you see in print. This won't be the last time you come across conflicting stories when you're researching. When this happens, you have to use your best judgment. Is one source more reliable than the other? Can you find a third source or a fourth (try the Sri Lankan embassy!)? Are you sure everyone's talking about the same thing? You're the judge!

Z.

Give the person time to talk. Don't rush from one question to the next—allow pauses. Let the person's comments spark new, unplanned questions from you.

Boost your confidence. Still feeling shaky about interviewing? **Read more about it on page 164.**

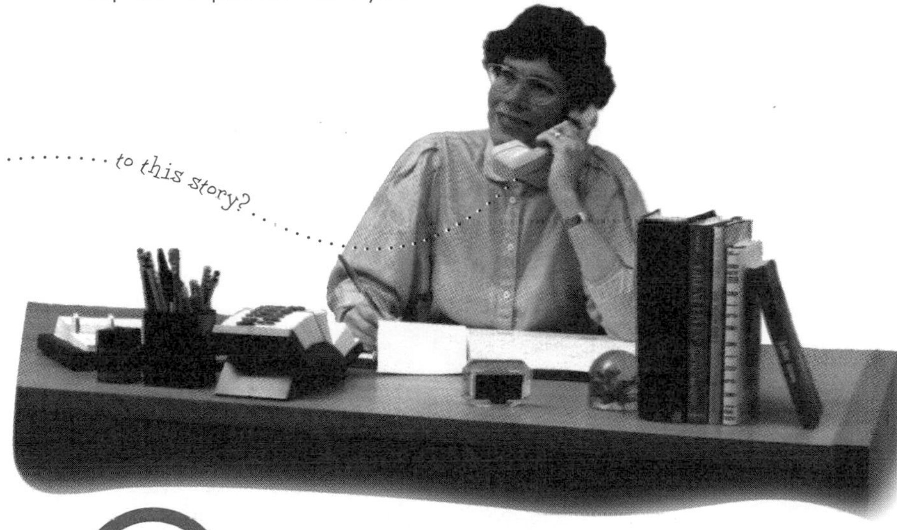
to this story?

inside

INFO

When looking for people to interview or poll, the telephone yellow pages can be your research assistant. Use your imagination to think of experts you might call. Are you researching insects? You could look up *Pest Control* or *Extermination.* Researching plants and trees? Look up *Garden Centres* or *Nurseries.* Researching trash and recycling? Look up *Rubbish Removal.* And keep an ear open for good quotations to use!

Here's How

To Take a Poll

Knowing that everyone's story is a little different, you may decide to collect information from many different people and combine the results for a broader picture.

1. **Decide exactly what you want to know.** Then make a list of questions. Do you want yes/no or multiple-choice questions that are easy to add up? Or do you want open questions that give more detailed answers?
2. **Decide whom you'll poll.** Students? Working people? People of all ages? It depends on whose answers you want.
3. **For each person you poll, decide what information you need:** age? sex? eye colour? name? Include space for this information on your question list.
4. **Conduct your poll.** Ask the questions yourself or pass out copies of your question list for people to fill out.
5. **Organize the results and see what you find.** Always include a description of the type of people you polled whenever you share your results. Sometimes graphing the results will show trends in the most readable way. **For examples of different kinds of graphs, see page 244.**

RESEARCHING

Make Research Notes

Once you've collected enough research material on your topic, what will you do with it? How will you coax your brain to remember what you read? The harder you make your mind work, the more you'll remember. You could decide which parts of your research material are the most important and copy them out; this forces you to think about them longer. Better yet, you could put the important parts into your own words, involving your brain even more.

Use Your Own Words

Being able to repeat what you've heard or read doesn't mean you understand it; it only means that you can repeat the words, just as you might repeat a bird call. However, to put information into your own words, you really have to understand it.

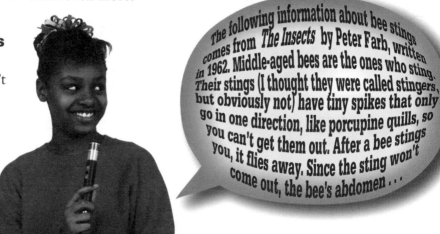

The following information about bee stings comes from *The Insects* by Peter Farb, written in 1962. Middle-aged bees are the ones who sting. Their stings (I thought they were called stingers, but obviously not) have tiny spikes that only go in one direction, like porcupine quills, so you can't get them out. After a bee stings you, it flies away. Since the sting won't come out, the bee's abdomen . . .

The Insects - Peter Farb 1962

STINGING
Done by m-aged B's.
Sting = porcupine quills/barbs = can't pull out
Abd. tears off when B flies away
Cont. 2 pump poison. Pulling = squeeze ++ poison
Losing few lives > losing +++

Invent a Shorthand

Use abbreviations, symbols, and your own shorthand to help you quickly write down what you're learning. Make sure your shortcuts are clear enough to make sense when you read them later!

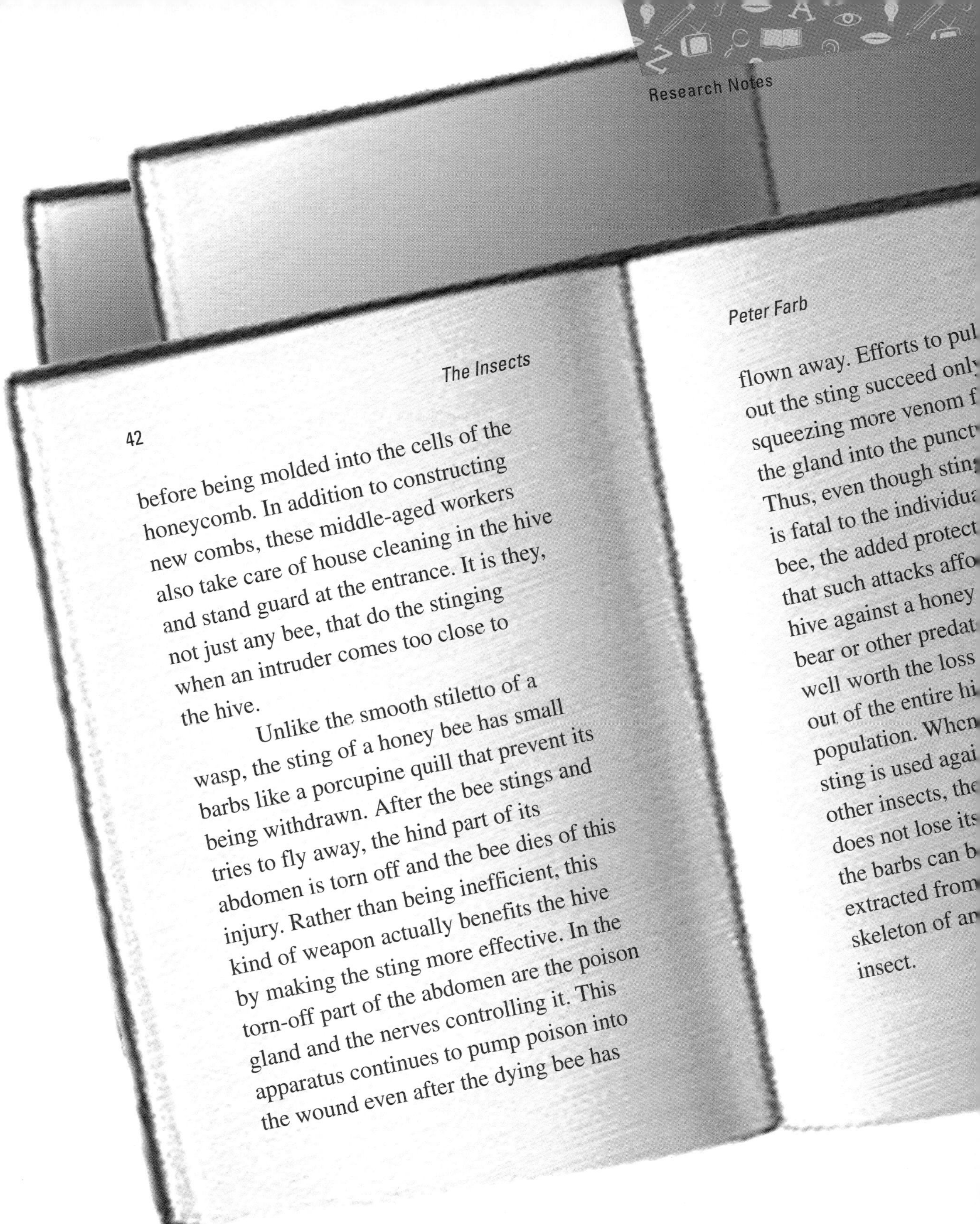

The Insects

42

before being molded into the cells of the honeycomb. In addition to constructing new combs, these middle-aged workers also take care of house cleaning in the hive and stand guard at the entrance. It is they, not just any bee, that do the stinging when an intruder comes too close to the hive.

Unlike the smooth stiletto of a wasp, the sting of a honey bee has small barbs like a porcupine quill that prevent its being withdrawn. After the bee stings and tries to fly away, the hind part of its abdomen is torn off and the bee dies of this injury. Rather than being inefficient, this kind of weapon actually benefits the hive by making the sting more effective. In the torn-off part of the abdomen are the poison gland and the nerves controlling it. This apparatus continues to pump poison into the wound even after the dying bee has

Peter Farb

flown away. Efforts to pul
out the sting succeed onl
squeezing more venom f
the gland into the punct
Thus, even though stin
is fatal to the individu
bee, the added protect
that such attacks affo
hive against a honey
bear or other predat
well worth the loss
out of the entire hi
population. When
sting is used agai
other insects, the
does not lose its
the barbs can b
extracted from
skeleton of a
insect.

23

SCIENTIFIC AMERICAN

To discover how the message is passed on we conducted a large number of experiments, marking individual bees with colored dots so that we could recognize them in the milling crowds of their fellows and building a hive with glass walls through which we could watch what was happening inside. Briefly, this is what we learned. A bee that has discovered a rich source of food near the hive performs on her return a "round dance." (Like all the other work of the colony, food-foraging is carried out by females.) She turns in circles, alternately to the left and to the right. This dance excites the neighboring bees; they start to troop behind the dancer and soon fly off to look for the food. They seek the kind of flower whose scent they detected on the original forager.

The richer the source of food, the more vigorous and the longer the dance. And the livelier the dance, the more strongly it arouses the other bees. If several kinds of plants are in bloom at the same time, those with the most and the sweetest nectar cause the liveliest dances. Therefore the largest number of bees fly to the blossoms where collecting is currently most rewarding. When the newly recruited helpers get home, they dance too, and so the number of foragers increases until they have drained most of the nectar from the blossoms. Then the dances slow down or stop altogether. The stream of workers now turns to other blossoms for which the dancing is livelier. The scheme provides a simple and purposeful regulation of supply and demand.

The round dance works well for flowers close to the beehive. Bees collect their nourishment from a large circuit, however, and frequently fly several miles from the hive. To search at such distances in all directions from the hive for blossoms known only by scent would be a hopeless task. For sources farther away than about 275 feet the round dance is replaced by the "tail-wagging dance." Here again the scent of the dancer points to the specific blossoms to be sought, and the liveliness of the dance indicates the richness of the source. In addition the wagging dance transmits an exact description of the direction and distance of the goal. The amount and precision of the information far exceeds that carried by any other known communication system among animals other than man.

"Dialects in The Language of the Bees"
by Karl von Frisch, 1962

Round Dance (for food closer than 84 m)	• B turns in circles, other bees watch, smell flower type, go look • Richer the food, rowdier the dance • When others return, they do same until source runs out
Wagging Dance (for food farther than 84 m)	• More specific, gives exact direction and distance • Most specific animal communication known (in 1962, anyway—have dolphins outdone this record by now?)

inside INFO

If you like the way something is worded and you want to quote the author, go ahead! Just make a note of the source (including the page number), and use quotation marks.

Write in Two Columns

This method works like a file drawer. Brief summaries in the left column are like tabs on file folders, noting the main ideas. The supporting details line up on the right side.

How much information do I want? Do I need more or fewer details?

Make an Outline

Creating an informal outline of what you're reading can put you on the author's train of thought and help keep your eyes on the big picture. Group the ideas you're writing down by indenting each time you get more specific.

"Dialects in the Language of the Bees" by Karl von Frisch, 1962

1. von Frisch & colleagues had been studying Bs for 20 years.
    - —Started by noticing Bs were communicating
    - —Tried to learn language
2. Observation set-up
    - —Marked Bs with coloured dots
    - —Built hive with glass walls
3. Noticed two kinds of dances
    - —Round dance
        - —for food near hive
        - —excites other bees, who smell the scent and go look
        - —the richer the food source, the more vigorous the dance
    - —Tail-wagging dance
        - —for food over 275 feet (= 84 metres) away
        - —gives exact description of distance and description of food
        - —tempo and number of moves = distance
        - —direction told in two ways
            - —outside hive: B uses sun as compass
            - —inside hive: B uses gravity as compass

Studying

Here's how to save time, do better on tests, and remember more of what you learn.

ncyclopedia
clopedia

STUDYING

Winning Tips

Think about the things you have learned: at least one language, how to play games, and lots more. Why not take time now to think about *how* you learn so that you can get to know new things more easily.

Picture the Way You Learn

Did you learn to ride a bike the same way you learned to multiply and divide? People learn in different ways, and the same person might learn one thing in one way and another thing in another way. Consider the ways of learning described below.

Logic Lover

Do you like doing science experiments, figuring out how nature works, solving problems, and playing with numbers? If you're a logic lover, you will find it helpful to break topics down into parts or steps, put ideas into categories, find relationships, and look for patterns such as similarities, differences, and cause and effect.

Word Whiz

Do you enjoy playing with language—reading, writing, telling stories, solving word puzzles, and reciting poetry? If you're a word whiz, you probably learn best by taking notes, following written directions, memorizing, and explaining ideas out loud.

Space Specialist

Do you like art and engineering—painting, sculpture, architecture, figuring out how objects are put together, and playing with machines? If you're a space specialist, you are helped by drawing diagrams and maps, making charts and models, visualizing information, and imagining yourself in a scene.

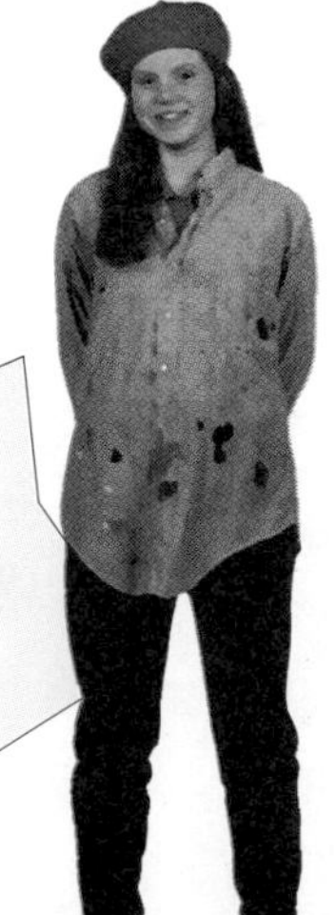

Inward Individual

Do you like to work alone? Do you enjoy coming up with original projects and pursuing your own interests and hobbies? Inward individuals learn best by setting their own goals and their own pace for reaching them.

People Person

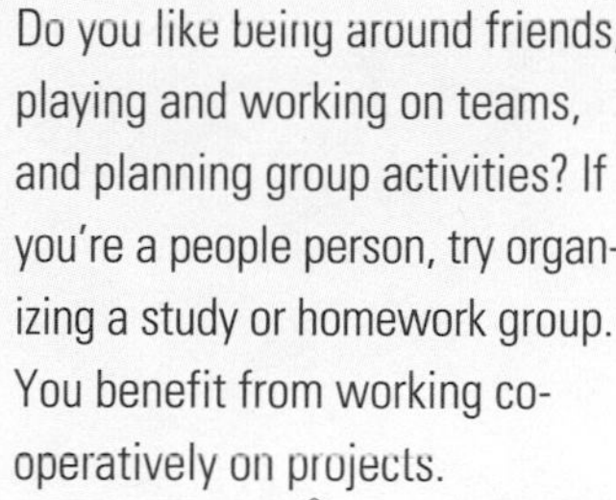

Do you like being around friends, playing and working on teams, and planning group activities? If you're a people person, try organizing a study or homework group. You benefit from working cooperatively on projects.

Movement Master

Do you need to keep moving? Do you like sports, gymnastics, acting, cooking, using tools? As a movement master, you like working with your hands and body. You learn best by taking action and getting involved—building something, taking it apart, acting out a process.

Music Maker

Do you hum tunes and tap out rhythms frequently? Are you fond of singing, listening to music, dancing, or playing an instrument? Then you're a music maker. You might try learning by setting ideas to music, putting information into rhymes you can chant, or finding the rhythm in a process.

Do you fit in more than one category? Try making a list of the strategies that work best for you.

Consider All Dimensions

Suppose you need directions to get somewhere you've never been. Your destination is about a kilometre away, and you plan to walk. How would you prefer to be given directions? Remember, there is no "correct" answer to this question.

WHICH WAY ?

SPOKEN I'd like to hear someone tell me the directions.

ILLUSTRATED I'd like to examine a drawing or map with the route drawn in.

WRITTEN I'd like to see the directions written out.

DICTATED I'd like to write down the directions as someone gives them to me.

After you've made a decision, consider whether your answer would change in any of these situations: the person giving the directions wasn't good at using the method you prefer; you were getting the directions a week ahead of time; you were getting the directions for a friend. As you see, you can adapt your strategies to suit each new learning situation.

Take Charge

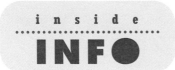

In school and elsewhere, you have to handle information according to certain expectations. You have to absorb new ideas, recall them, and use them. Such learning may sometimes seem difficult, but you *can* make it happen. You can try out the strategies and techniques described here and keep track of which work best for you. You will soon become an expert on your own learning process.

inside INFO

On average, people today change careers about five times during their lives. Such career changes usually require additional education, retraining, and so on. A person with a variety of learning skills always has an edge!

How to Learn from a Speaker

Think about the best way to learn from someone who is talking. Begin by mentally preparing to listen *actively:* for example, by comparing new information with what you already know. Then you can keep focussed by taking notes.

Here's How

To Make Notes When Listening

1. **Get your mind ready for the topic.** If a speaker says, "Today we'll be talking about how Mayan society worked," write a heading that captures that idea: *Mayan society.*
2. **Listen for the order of ideas.** A speaker usually has a plan for presenting information in an organized way. Your notes can mirror that plan. You hear this: "The first important thing is . . . Second, . . ." You might write this: *Important things: 1., 2.*
3. **Summarize information in your own words (paraphrase).** Be brief: use abbreviations, phrases, and your own shorthand. The idea is to think about what you're hearing, not to get it down word for word. You hear this: "The Maya put a high value on jade, and archaeologists have found many beautiful jade items carved by the Maya more than 1000 years ago." You might write: *M valued jade. Btful carvings, 1000 yrs old.* Reminder: Don't forget to write a translation for any abbreviations you might forget later!
4. **Copy down information that is displayed.** The speaker may write on the board or show information that is important in another way. Also, be sure to get a copy of any handouts.
5. **Add your own remarks.** These might be questions to yourself, points you agree or disagree with, associated ideas, or things you find surprising, confusing, or interesting.
6. **Review your notes afterwards.** First, make questions out of your headings. *How did Mayan society work?* Then circle or highlight information that answers the questions. Also, if the speaker is available, you might ask her or him follow-up questions based on your notes.

Taking notes is important, but it's not the only way to get yourself involved with a talk or other presentation. You might try tape-recording a class to listen to later, or making a chart to keep track of a discussion. If visual aids help you to remember information, sketch diagrams and drawings in your notebook. Think about how you learn best, and prepare to process information in whatever way is most comfortable for you.

Looking for information about flow charts? Learn how to interpret and use charts and graphs. **See page 244.**

Be an Information Processor

You know that it's important to concentrate on information to absorb and remember it. That's easy if the subject is one of your favourites. But what if it's a subject you don't find interesting? What if your mind doesn't focus on the subject automatically? Don't give up. There are strategies that can help you stay focussed on any new information.

Information in

knowledge
Knowledge out

Information Processing Strategies

Compare it. Ask yourself, "What is this like?" If you're learning about an influential leader, you could compare that person with other leaders you know about. What characteristics made people follow each leader? What impact did each leader have on events? You could make a list of similarities and differences.

Make it personal. Connect new ideas or information to your personal experience. Is *lethargic* an unfamiliar word? Visualize someone you know who's sleepy and slow moving, and caption your imaginary picture "lethargic."

Do something with it. If you're learning about volcanoes, try making a model. Learning about solid geometric forms? Build pyramids from triangles or cubes from squares.

Own it. To make new information yours to keep, discover everything you can about it through sight, sound, and touch (and maybe even taste and smell). Learning about the parts of the heart? Examine pictures and captions. Say the parts aloud as you point to each one. Trace or draw a diagram. Hold a model and name each part, telling what it does.

inside INFO

When you plan how to use your time, don't forget to consider your less-obvious time-consuming activities: eating, cleaning, talking on the phone, standing in line, watching TV, and so on.

Be an Expert Time Manager

Do you know any people who always get a lot of jobs done? Those people are probably well organized. They know how to make short-range and long-range plans and how to budget their time to accomplish those plans. If you'd like to be better organized, try some time-management techniques. They'll turn you into someone who can get all required jobs done and still have free time to do other things you enjoy.

Keep an Assignment Notebook

Keeping track of assignments and jobs to be done will help you become a successful time manager. One tried-and-true method is to log assignments in a pocket-size notebook. But you'll need to carry the notebook with you all the time! Once you've got that book in hand, try these strategies:

Log in the assignment the minute you get it. For each one, write down the date you get the assignment, what subject or class it's for, and when it's due.

Write down any special requirements such as length, format, use of ink or pencil, and so on. Make a "mind movie" of yourself doing each assignment; this mind-movie will help you anticipate problems or questions and get them cleared up in advance.

Read over the day's assignments every afternoon before you leave school so that you'll remember to take home whatever books or resources you'll need.

Look over the day's assignments again as you prepare to do your homework. Decide which ones can be done easily and which will need more effort. Plan the order for doing the assignments and how you'll divide your time. Will it be easier for you to do the hard ones first while you're more alert or work from the simplest to the most complex?

Use a marker or symbol to highlight long-range assignments, like studying for a test, writing a book report, or completing a research project. You'll want to break these assignments into smaller steps and complete them over a period of time.

Check off each assignment as you complete it.

Try a Monthly Planner

Instead of keeping an assignment book, you could use a month-by-month calendar. That way you can see at a glance what you've accomplished and what you still need to do each day. You can write short- and long-range plans right on the same page.

Make Each Minute Count!

Is this a familiar scene: Ida Lee is sitting at her desk, staring at an open book. She's been working on this assignment for two hours, and she's not even halfway done. What's the problem? Ida Lee thinks she's working hard, but she really only *appears* to be studying. Her mind has wandered off the subject at least ten times since she began. If you share Ida Lee's problem, don't despair. With practice, you can learn to concentrate better and get more work done in less time.

Need help making sense of informational texts? Learn some strategies for reading non-fiction. **See page 116.**

BRIGHT Ideas

FOR USING YOUR STUDY TIME EFFECTIVELY

Collect a penny for your thoughts. To make yourself aware of moments when your mind drifts away from your studies, put a penny in a dish each time you catch yourself daydreaming. Focus on improving your concentration; try to cut your costs and become a more efficient—and richer—learner.

Take a break. Set short-term goals (reading five pages of a chapter, drafting an answer to one essay question), and reward yourself with a few minutes off after completing each one. Stand up, stretch, eat a slice of fruit, and then get back to work. Taking a break will help you keep your mind fresh, and give ideas a chance to settle down. You might suddenly think of a better way to arrange your essay or solve a math problem.

Decide where, when, and how. Figure out when and where you do your best work. Do you need to be in your room at your desk with your poster on the wall? Or do you find a quiet library atmosphere helpful? Do you need lots of books and papers piled around? Or clear surfaces and sharp pencils? What's important is to learn what's most comfortable for you and stick to a routine—a regular place and time for studying.

HOMEWORK HOT-LINE

IF THIS SOUNDS LIKE YOU . . .	GET HOT-LINE ADVICE!
"I couldn't do my homework because I needed to use the encyclopedia at the library, and the library was closed when I got there."	When you're given an assignment, try to picture yourself doing it. Then you can take the necessary steps—such as finding out how late the library is open—to complete it.
"I knew the book report was due, but I didn't finish reading the book."	Here's where long-range planning can help. Break a big job into smaller parts, and set daily goals for those parts. You can get it done if you stick to a schedule.
"I did all the math problems in Section C, but I was supposed to do Section B."	You can eliminate mistakes like this if you write down each assignment in your notebook and refer to your notes before beginning each task.
"By the time I got home from soccer practice and finished my math homework, I was too tired to do the assigned science experiment."	Make a realistic schedule. If you know soccer practice always runs long on Tuesdays, schedule an extra study hour each Monday. Be sure to consider all your activities and then budget your time.

Reach Your Goal!

Pierre is trying to save enough money to buy a jacket. Midori is planning a surprise birthday party for a friend. Coach Saldanha is getting her team ready for the first game of the season. What do all three have in common? They are all setting goals.

Here are two basic things you can do to reach a goal: First, figure out what steps are needed to reach the goal. Second, set aside enough time to take each step. This is how one student planned to achieve her goal.

GOAL

Present an oral science report on February 8.

10 D-DAY! Feb. 8

9 Put oral and visual elements together and practise presentation Feb. 5–6.

8 Fine-tune artwork Feb. 3–4.

7 Begin to practise oral part of report Feb. 1–2.

6 Revise draft Jan. 25–30.

5 Write a first draft; gather visual display materials Jan. 18–22.

4 Make working outline by Jan. 16.

3 Collect information, one hour each day: Jan. 9, 11, 12, 13, 15.

2 Get topic approved by Mr. Ramos on Jan. 8.

1 Choose a topic; may need to do research at library Jan. 4–7.

P.S. Checking off each step after it's done can be a satisfying experience.

Memory Workout

Memory Workout
Strengthen Your Mental Muscles

These steps can help you remember information. First, have the desire to learn it. Second, separate what's essential from what's less important, and focus attention on what's essential. Finally, form associations: connect the new with the known.

Link It Up

You can connect items on a list by creating powerful, silly, or shocking mental images. Need to bring a ruler, a sheet of cardboard, and coloured pencils to art class? Picture the ruler with legs. Then imagine it riding the cardboard like a magic carpet, whooshing through a forest of coloured pencils. Recall that image a few times, and you'll arrive in art class prepared.

Use Letter Strategies

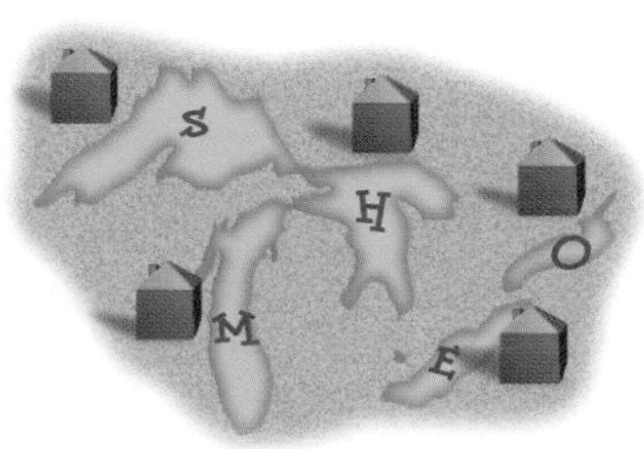
S
H
O
M
E

You can use letter strategies to help recall terms. Create acronyms—new words that use the first letters of the words you want to recall. For example, the acronym *HOMES* can represent the Great Lakes (**H**uron, **O**ntario, **M**ichigan, **E**rie, **S**uperior). Or create a sentence using words that begin with the first letters of the terms you're memorizing: *Someone Was Playing Badly* can help you recall the major sections of the orchestra (**s**trings, **w**oodwinds, **p**ercussion, **b**rass).

Rhymes and Rhythms

"Thirty days hath September, April, June, and November"—rhymes and rhythmical patterns are powerful memory aids. Try chanting, tapping, or making up songs to help you remember.

Use Categories

Twenty facts are hard to recall. But if you group facts into categories—by meaning, by size, by sound, or by any other grouping—you'll remember them more easily. Suppose you have to describe the work of twenty people. Put the names in small groups—for example, seven national leaders, four scientists, four explorers, and five writers.

Test-Taking Secrets

You're probably sick of hearing this: "Read the directions carefully." You'd be surprised how often people lower their test scores by not following that piece of advice. For some tests, following directions may not be easy. A test may be divided into many parts, with different directions applying to each part. And test directions come in many forms, too, including some tricky varieties. So it's important to remember the following steps:

inside INFO

People use test-taking skills throughout their lives. Many jobs require licences that can be obtained only by passing a test. Some promotions are based on test scores. People who move to new locations sometimes have to pass written tests to get a new driver's licence.

Take the time to read each set of directions as slowly as you need to.

Study any examples provided.

Proceed only when you are sure of what you are supposed to do.

Advice from the Zone

Dear Z:

Yesterday I took a test in French. When the teacher said, "Clear your desks," my brain cleared itself too! When she passed out the papers, I almost passed out. By the time I was ready to begin, the other kids were already halfway done. Things have gotten so bad that I can't even hear the word test without feeling butterflies in my stomach. Is there hope for me?

—Tense About Tests

Dear Tense:

Lots of people get nervous when it comes to taking tests. But it doesn't have to happen! You just need a little confidence. Here's a sure-fire way to get it: master the art of test taking. Knowing how to take a test—on any subject—is a skill that you can learn. Start with these basic rules:

- Know how the test will be scored. Some tests penalize you for guessing, while others don't.
- Look over the whole test first for length and general content.
- Decide on an order for answering the questions. Do the easy ones first.
- Don't get hung up on a question. If you can't think of the answer, move on and come back to it later.
- For multiple-choice questions, use the process of elimination. For questions that require longer answers, take the time to outline and draft your response.
- Prepare yourself well so that you walk in knowing you'll do well.

And say *adieu* to *les papillons* in your stomach. Stay cool.

Z.

What's Your Test-Ability?

1. What is the first thing you should do when you hear there's going to be a test next week? (Choose one answer.)
   A. Read the directions.
   B. Start laughing hysterically.
   (C) Find out what topics will be included.
   D. Plan to be absent.

2. What else should you do? (Choose at least one answer.)
   A. Start working yourself into a frenzy of panic.
   (B) Find out how long the test will be.
   (C) Find out what kinds of questions will be included.
   (D) Write down the names of any specific readings or materials the teacher says to review.

3. Define study schedule. Then, explain why a study schedule is important. study schedule: a plan for reviewing each topic at least twice before the test. A study schedule helps you review information in short sessions over time. You learn better using a schedule, and you are more alert during the test than if you cram the night before.

4. Studying with a partner or a small group can be useful. Tell why by writing *T* for true or *F* for false next to each item below.
   T You can share your understanding of a topic.
   F You can take lots of breaks to fool around and feel relaxed.
   T You can come up with the kinds of questions that might be asked and hear each other's answers.
   T You can ask each other to explain things that confuse you.

5. Name three good techniques for studying for a test.
   A) Read over your notes several times.
   B) Go over previous quizzes.
   C) Take notes on your notes by jotting down the most important terms and ideas.

6. How can you remember to bring the items you need (a No. 2 pencil, a ruler, a calculator) on the day of the test? (Choose one answer.)
   A. Ask someone to remind you.
   B. You can't.
   C. Just tell yourself to remember.
   (D) Post a reminder on your mirror to put necessary items into your school pack the night before the test.

7. What should you do before you answer the first question on the test? (Circle T if the statement is true. Circle F if the statement is false, and change the underlined words to make the statement true.)
   T (F) Look over the ~~beginning part of the~~ test. whole
   (T) F Read all the directions.

8. How should you plan to answer the questions? (For each item, choose the correct answer, and write it on the blank.)
   A. Start with the easiest questions.
   easiest *hardest* *bonus*
   B. Budget your time to draft and revise longer written answers.
   look up facts for *draft and revise* *select*

9. Describe an imaginary student using the *process of elimination* to answer a test question, and tell why the process is useful.
   Tess must answer the question, "Which country borders Venezuela?" The answer choices are a) Colombia, b) Argentina, c) Japan, and d) Cuba. Tess knows that Venezuela is in South America and Japan is in Asia, so she omits Japan. She also eliminates Cuba because it's an island. By eliminating two wrong answers, Tess improves her chances of getting the correct answer.

10. What steps should you follow while answering an essay question? (Complete each statement below by filling in the blanks.)
   A. First, read the directions carefully, and make sure you understand the question.
   B. Second, make a quick outline listing all the parts of the answer, and then write your answer.
   C. Third, review to make sure that you have stuck to the topic and answered all parts of the question completely.
   D. Fourth, proofread for correct spelling, punctuation, and usage.

Great! 100%

Handbook

Do you need to check your verbs for vigour? Tighten your sentences? Tune up your transitions? Check out this communications tool box!

Wor

together!

go

ds

Words go together like building blocks. Use your words to express yourself!

Contents

Words

Puzzling over which word to use? It's no wonder. You've got thousands to choose from. The following pages will help you know when and how to use words effectively. The first thing you'll discover is that words fall into eight different categories, called parts of speech.

Contents

Nouns

Nouns are namers. They name persons, places, things, and ideas so that you can identify them and talk about them. When you ask someone, "What's that?" the answer you get is usually a noun—"a hippopotamus," "Lake Winnipeg," "music," "an earthquake," "the band."

For more about nouns, read on!

DRAFT

"Life in a Rock Group"

by Priscilla Larsen

Most kids think being in a rock group is a real blast. But that's not what the Me2s told me when I interviewed them after their concert on tuesday.

Cap or no cap?

Lucas Labelle is the groups' drummer. He said, "Our lifes are nothin' like what peoples think. Mostly we gotta hang out in cold studioes and crummy dressing rooms."

-*'s* or -*s'*?

Plural check

Duchess Dee said the same thing. She's the key-board player. "A lot of the time we play in real dives, but when we hear the crowds applause, it all seems worth it."

Compound check

Plural or possessive?

Find out how to edit Priscilla's draft on page 278.

Noun Info

Types of Nouns

Nouns can be grouped in different ways, depending on what they name or how they're written.

Common Nouns

Common nouns name kinds of persons, places, things, or ideas.

Proper Nouns

Proper nouns give particular names of persons, places, things, or ideas.

Not capitalized → Always capitalized

Common Nouns	Proper Nouns
band	**Metal Heads**
province	**Alberta**
car	**Corvette**
month	**April**
magazine	***Teen Beat***

Compound Nouns

Compound nouns are made up of two or more words. Some are written as one word, some have a hyphen, and some are separate words.

One word:
keyboard
classroom
grandmother

Hyphen:
yo-yo
sister-in-law

Separate words:
Duchess Dee
folk song
high school

Check the dictionary to find out how to write a compound noun.

Collective Nouns

Collective nouns name groups of people, animals, or things that act together.

people
band
class
team
group
herd
family
audience

Making collective nouns agree with verbs can be tricky. See page 299 for more information.

Concrete Nouns

Concrete nouns name something or someone that can be seen or touched.

drum
guitarist
Lake Erie
aunt
smoke
window

Abstract Nouns

Abstract nouns name ideas, qualities, or feelings—things that can't be seen or touched.

freedom
beauty
love
courage
time
nation

Features of Nouns

Gender

Gender tells you whether a noun is referring to a male, a female, or a thing. A noun is masculine if it refers to a male and feminine if it refers to a female. All other nouns are neuter.

Pronouns, words that rename nouns, also show gender. **See Pronouns, page 282.**

*Does that **boy** know where his seat is?* . . . . . Masculine

***Sheryl** found her seat by herself.* . . . . . Feminine

*The **ticket** has the seat number on it.* . . . . . Neuter

Number

Number tells you how many persons or things there are. A noun is singular if it names one item and plural if it names more than one. Most nouns change their form in the plural.

*The **singer** had a terrific **voice.*** . . . . . Singular nouns

*The **singers** had terrific **voices.*** . . . . . Plural nouns

Here's How

To Form Noun Plurals

When you use a plural form, you are telling your listener or reader that you are talking about more than one thing.

For most nouns, you form the plural just by adding *-s.* Some nouns have special plurals, though. You have to memorize these or learn when to check your dictionary.

For most nouns, just add *-s.* .... **band + s = bands**

For nouns ending in *s, sh, ch, x, z,* add *-es.* .... **glass + es = glasses**

For nouns ending in *y:*

- **If a vowel comes before *y,* add *-s.*** .... **toy + s = toys**
- **If a consonant comes before *y,* change the *y* to *i* and add *-es.*** .... **sky + es = skies**

For nouns ending in *f* or *fe:* (Check your dictionary.)

- **For some nouns, change the *f* to *v* and add *-s* or *-es.*** .... **life + s = lives**
- **For other nouns, add *-s.*** .... **roof + s = roofs**

For nouns ending in *o:* (Check your dictionary.)

- **If a vowel comes before *o,* add *-s.*** .... **studio + s = studios**
- **If a consonant comes before *o,* add *-es* to most words.** .... **potato + es = potatoes**
- **If the noun is a musical term, add *-s.*** .... **piano + s = pianos**

Special Plurals

Some nouns have only plural forms.

jeans
scissors
pants
trousers
thanks

Some singular nouns end in *s* and have no plural forms.

news
mathematics
physics
economics
measles

Some nouns have special plural forms.

person—people
man—men
woman—women
child—children
mouse—mice
foot—feet
ox—oxen

For a compound noun written as one word, make the last part plural.

newspapers
bookshelves
grandchildren

Some nouns do not change forms in the plural.

sheep—sheep
deer—deer
salmon—salmon
moose—moose
Inuit—Inuit

For other compound nouns, make the most important word plural.

music boxes
rock bands
sisters-in-law

Endings

Some word endings are typical of nouns. Spot one of these endings or suffixes and you've probably found a noun. Learn more about noun endings in **Spelling, page 318,** and **Word Building, page 327.**

Base word		Ending		Noun
sing	+	er	=	singer

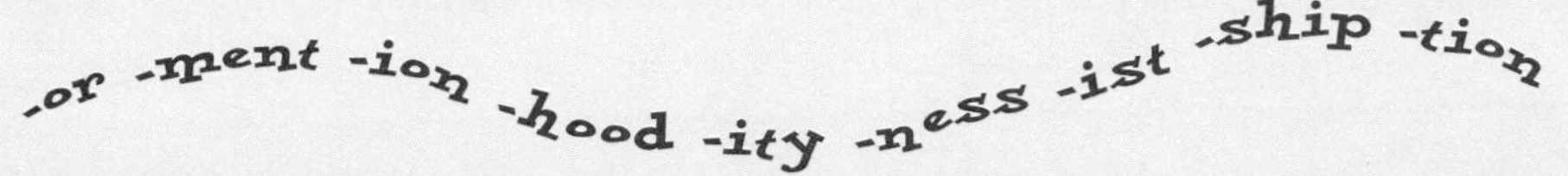

-or -ment -ion -hood -ity -ness -ist -ship -tion

Here are some more endings.

Case

Case tells you how a noun is used in a sentence. Nouns can be used as subjects, as objects, and as possessives. **For more about nouns in sentences, see pages 336 and 337.** Pronouns have different forms for the different cases. **See Pronouns, page 282.** But nouns have special forms only for the possessive case.

The possessive form shows that the noun owns or is closely related to the noun that follows it. Often a possessive noun is used instead of a phrase with *have* or *of.*

Subjective	
Noun as subject of sentence	***Lucas*** *is a member of the Me2s.*
Noun as subject complement	*He is an awesome* ***drummer.***
Objective	
Noun as object of verb	*Duchess plays* ***keyboard.***
Noun as object of preposition	*The band is going to* ***Winnipeg.***
Possessive	
Noun shows ownership	*Those are* ***Lucas's*** *drums.*
Noun shows close relationship	*Is Marta the* ***band's*** *manager?*

Here's How

To Form Possessive Nouns

For a singular noun, add an apostrophe plus -*s*.

voice of the singer = singer**'s** voice

voice of Lucas = Lucas'**s** voice

For a plural noun ending in *s*, add only an apostrophe.

The musicians have a schedule = musician**s'** schedule

For a plural noun not ending in *s*, add an apostrophe plus -*s*.

cheers of the people = people**'s** cheers

Things can get a little tricky when you're talking about two people owning something.

If two people own one thing, add an apostrophe plus -*s* to the last noun only.

Julie and Jim**'s** kitten

If two people own things separately, add an apostrophe plus -*s* to each noun.

Julie**'s** and Jim**'s** kittens

Edit It!

Here are the noun errors from Priscilla's draft. Find out why they're errors and how Priscilla can fix them. You'll do a better job of editing your own work.

Know when to cap and when not to cap.

DRAFT *. . . I interviewed them after their concert on* ***tuesday.*** . . . . . . Cap or no cap?

What's Wrong? *Tuesday* names a particular day. It's a proper noun and should begin with a capital letter.

Edit It! *. . . I interviewed them after their concert on* ***Tuesday.***

Know where the apostrophe goes.

DRAFT *Lucas Labelle is the* ***groups'*** *drummer.* . . . . . . *-'s* or *-s'*?

What's Wrong? To make a singular noun possessive, add *-'s*, not *-s'*.

Edit It! *Lucas Labelle is the* ***group's*** *drummer.*

Check plurals in a dictionary.

DRAFT *He said "Our* ***lifes*** *are nothin' like what* ***peoples think.****"* . . . . . Plural check

What's Wrong? The *f* in *life* changes to *v* in the plural. *People* is already a plural form and doesn't need *-s* added.

Edit It! *He said, "Our* ***lives*** *are nothin' like what* ***people*** *think."*

DRAFT *"Mostly we gotta hang out in cold* ***studioes*** *and crummy dressing rooms."*

What's Wrong? *Studio* ends in a vowel plus *o* and therefore forms the plural with *-s*, not *-es*.

Edit It! *"Mostly we gotta hang out in cold* ***studios*** *and crummy dressing rooms."*

Check compound nouns in a dictionary.

DRAFT *She's the* ***key-board*** *player.* . . . . . . Compound check

What's Wrong? *Keyboard* is listed as a single word in the dictionary.

Edit It! *She's the* ***keyboard*** *player.*

Know the difference between a plural and a possessive.

DRAFT *". . . when we hear the* ***crowds*** *applause, it all seems worth it."* . . . . . Plural or possessive?

What's Wrong? *The crowds applause* stands for *the applause of the crowd. Crowds* is not a plural here but a possessive. Change *-s* to *-'s* for the possessive form.

Edit It! *". . . when we hear the* ***crowd's*** *applause, it all seems worth it."*

Pronouns

Pronouns are **replacers** or "stand-ins" for nouns or other pronouns. They keep nouns from being overworked.

An **antecedent** is the word that the pronoun stands for. It can be a noun or a pronoun. It usually comes before the pronoun that refers to it.

For more about pronouns, read on!

DRAFT

"How I Spent Saturday"

by Toby Brown

Me and my family went to the cinema Saturday afternoon. Us Browns really like scary films, so naturally we couldn't miss the double feature they were showing. I like horror shows because you can actually feel the suspense. Nobody (not even my little brother) was scared by the first film, *Chilly Billy,* but everybody screamed their lungs out during *Lizard Lips.* Your going to love that one when you see it!

Subject or object pronouns?

Who is meant by *they*?

Stick to one person.

Match the antecedent.

Pronoun or contraction?

Find out how to edit Toby's draft on page 285.

Pronoun Info

Types of Pronouns

There are several different kinds of pronouns, and each has a different job to do.

Personal Pronouns

These pronouns stand for persons or things. They are the pronouns you use most.

I
me
my
mine
we
us
our
ours
you
your
yours
he
him
his
she
her
hers
it
its
they
them
their
theirs

Reflexive and Intensive Pronouns

These are the pronouns that end in *-self* or *-selves.* They never stand alone. They always have antecedents in the same sentence.

myself
ourselves
yourself
yourselves
himself
herself
itself
themselves

Relative Pronouns

These pronouns begin subordinate clauses and connect them to independent clauses. **For more on clauses, see page 340.** All of the relative pronouns except *that* can also work as interrogative pronouns.

Refer to people: **who**, **whom**, **whose**

which — Refers to things

that — Refers to people or things

Demonstrative Pronouns

These pronouns point out specific people, places, or things. The antecedent usually comes after a demonstrative pronoun.

Use *this* and *these* to point out people or things nearby.

this
these
that
those

Use *that* and *those* to point out people or things not nearby.

Interrogative Pronouns

These pronouns ask questions. They do not always have specific antecedents.

what
which
who
whom
whose

Indefinite Pronouns

These pronouns refer to people, places, or things, often in a general, unspecific way. They usually don't need antecedents.

Singular

another
anybody
anyone
anything
each
either
everybody
everyone
everything
little
much
neither
nobody
no one
nothing
one
other
somebody
someone
something

Plural

both
few
many
others
several

Either

all
any
more
most
none
some

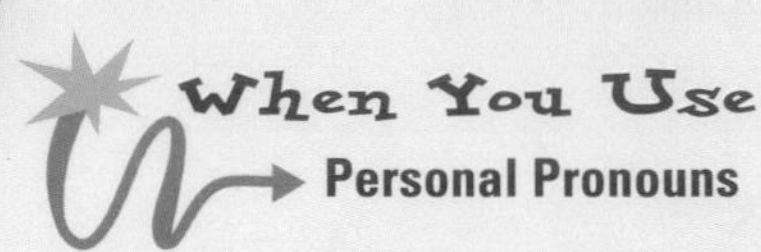
When You Use
Personal Pronouns

Know the different features of personal pronouns.

Personal pronouns show the features of case, person, gender, and number.

Case: Case tells you how a pronoun is used in a sentence.

Person: Person tells you who is speaking (first), being spoken to (second), or being spoken about (third).

Gender: Gender tells you whether a third-person singular pronoun is referring to a male, a female, or a thing.

Number: Number tells you how many persons or things there are.

Case	Person	Gender	Singular	Plural
Subject pronouns	**first**		I	we
	second		you	you
	third	masculine	he	they
		feminine	she	
		neuter	it	
Object pronouns	**first**		me	us
	second		you	you
	third	masculine	him	them
		feminine	her	
		neuter	it	
Possessive pronouns	**first**		my, mine	our, ours
	second		your, yours	your, yours
	third	masculine	his	their, theirs
		feminine	her, hers	
		neuter	its	

Make the personal pronoun agree with its antecedent.

A pronoun should have the same features as the noun or pronoun it stands for. Make a pronoun agree with its antecedent in person, number, and gender.

antecedent pronoun

*Does your **sister** have **her** ticket?* . . . . . Third person, singular, feminine

Make sure the antecedent is clear.

Don't confuse your reader with an unclear pronoun reference. You may need to name a noun again or rewrite the sentence so that your meaning is clear.

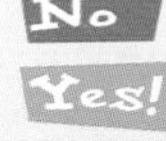
No
Yes!

*Toby told Alex **he** had won a box of candy.* . . . . . Unclear

Toby told Alex that Alex had won a box of candy. . . . . . Clear

"Alex, you won a box of candy!" exclaimed Toby. . . . . . Clear

Use the right case.

Use a subject pronoun when the pronoun is a single or compound subject, or a subject complement. **See page 336 for more about subjects.**

Subject	***She** went to the cinema with the Browns.*
Compound subject	***He** and **I** thought* Chilly Billy *was silly.*
Subject complement	***It** is I.*

Use an object pronoun when the pronoun is a single or compound direct object, an indirect object, or an object of a preposition. **See page 337 for more about objects.**

Direct object	*My parents drove **us** to the cinema.*
Compound direct object	*My parents drove **him** and **me** to the cinema.*
Indirect object	*Did Toby tell **her** about that scary film?*
Object of a preposition	*She gave it to Lee and **me**.*

Use a possessive pronoun to show ownership or a close relationship. Some possessive pronouns are used before nouns; others are used alone.

Possessive used with a noun	*Is that **your** jacket on the seat?*
Possessive used alone	*Is that **yours**?*

Leave out the apostrophe.

Possessive pronouns often get confused with contractions. A contraction gets an apostrophe because it's an abbreviation for two words. A possessive pronoun is just one word and doesn't need an apostrophe.

Possessive Pronouns	Contractions
its	it's = it is
their	they're = they are
your	you're = you are
whose	who's = who is

Don't shift person needlessly.

Stick to the same person—first, second, or third—unless you have a reason to change.

No

***We** like horror films because **you** can feel **your** heart pound.* . . . . . Needless shift

Yes!

***We** like horror films because **we** can feel **our** hearts pound.* . . . . . No shift

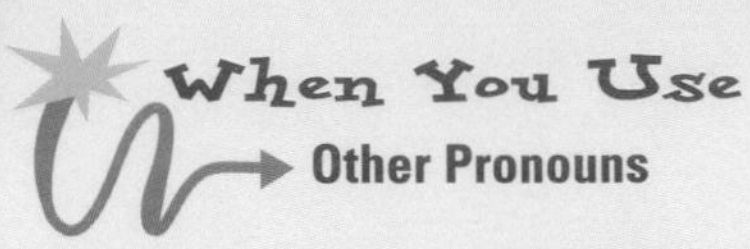
When You Use
Other Pronouns

Know the difference between reflexive and intensive pronouns.

A reflexive pronoun adds information to a sentence. An intensive pronoun emphasizes its antecedent and can be left out without changing the meaning of a sentence.

Reflexive pronoun *Toby brought **himself** a box of popcorn.*

Intensive pronoun *I **myself** would never talk during a film.*

Don't use a *-self* pronoun by itself.

Watch out for a *-self* pronoun used alone. It should always have an antecedent in the same sentence.

 *Alex and **myself** loved watching* Lizard Lips. . . . . . Reflexive alone

Yes! *Alex and **I** loved watching* Lizard Lips. . . . . . Use personal pronoun

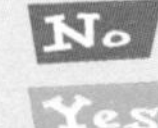 *I found **myself** terrified by* Lizard Lips.

Don't add *here* or *there* to demonstrative pronouns.

Avoid using the expressions *this here* and *that there.* The demonstrative pronoun *this* already means "here," and *that* already means "there."

No *This **here** is my seat, isn't it?*

Yes! *This is my seat, isn't it?*

Know the difference between *who's* and the interrogative pronoun *whose.*

Who's is the contraction for *who is;* it is not an interrogative pronoun.

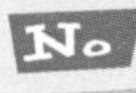 ***Who's** are these ticket stubs?* . . . . . Contraction

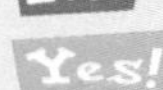 ***Whose** are these ticket stubs?* . . . . . Interrogative pronoun

Make personal pronouns agree with indefinite pronouns.

Indefinite pronouns can be antecedents of personal pronouns. Make the personal pronoun agree in number and gender with the indefinite pronoun to which it refers.

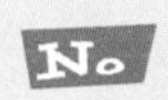 (singular / plural) ***Everyone** on the girls' team has **their** uniform.*

 (singular / singular) ***Everyone** on the girls' team has **her** uniform.*

Think about the gender of indefinite pronouns.

In the past, the pronouns *he, him,* or *his* were used to refer to both males and females as a group. Today, most people avoid using a masculine pronoun to refer to people in general, unless the group is specifically male.

 *Every **person** must find **his** own way in life.*

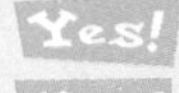 ***Everyone** must find **his** or **her** own seat.*

 ***All** must find **their** own seats.*

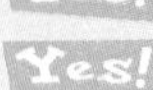 *Everyone on the **boys'** hockey team had **his** own locker.*

Edit It!

Here are the pronoun mistakes from Toby's draft. Read about why they are errors and how Toby can correct them, and you'll be able to fix your own pronoun errors.

Keep an eye on the case of personal pronouns.

DRAFT ***Me and my family*** *went to the cinema Saturday afternoon.* . . . . . Subject or object pronouns?

What's Wrong? *Me and my family* is the subject, but *me* is an object pronoun. Use the subject pronoun *I*. Also, *I* is part of a compound; it should always come last.

Edit It! ***My family and I*** *went to the cinema Saturday afternoon.*

DRAFT ***Us Browns*** *really like scary films, . . .*

What's Wrong? *Us* is an object pronoun, but it is used along with *Browns* as the subject of the sentence. Use the subject pronoun *we*.

Edit It! ***We Browns*** *really like scary films, . . .*

Make sure your pronouns have clear antecedents.

DRAFT *. . . so naturally we couldn't miss the double feature* ***they*** *were showing.* . . . . . Who is meant by *they*?

What's Wrong? The reader can't tell who *they* refers to. Don't give your readers an unclear or vague pronoun reference. Use a noun.

Edit It! *. . . so naturally we couldn't miss the double feature* ***the cinema*** *was showing.*

Don't switch the pronoun to *you* unless there's a reason.

DRAFT *I like horror shows because* ***you*** *can actually feel the suspense.* . . . . . Stick to one person.

What's Wrong? Why did Toby change from *I* to *you*? No reason. Stick with the same personal pronoun unless you actually change person.

Edit It! *I like horror shows because* ***I*** *can actually feel the suspense.*

Make a pronoun match or agree with its antecedent.

DRAFT *. . .* ***everybody*** *screamed* ***their*** *lungs out during* Lizard Lips. . . . . . Match the antecedent.

What's Wrong? *Their* refers to *everybody*, but *everybody* is singular and *their* is plural. When you're referring to a group that includes males and females, use *his or her*, or, even better, make the antecedent plural.

Edit It! *. . .* ***all the viewers*** *screamed* ***their*** *lungs out during* Lizard Lips.

Know the difference between possessive pronouns and contractions.

DRAFT ***Your*** *going to love that one when you see it!* . . . . . Pronoun or contraction?

What's Wrong? *Your* should be a contraction of *you are*, not a possessive pronoun. Use an apostrophe.

Edit It! ***You're*** *going to love that one when you see it!*

Adjectives

Adjectives describe. They tell what the things named by nouns and pronouns are like. Adjectives can show which or what kind of thing you're talking about—the *tiny* one, the *awesome* one, *that* one, or *no* one.

For more about **adjectives**, read on!

DRAFT

"A Gift for Aunt Daphne"

by Neil Hamilton

When Aunt Daphne visits us, I don't know who's happiest, Mom or me. My scottish aunt is the greatest. When she visits, it's like a holiday around our house. Last time she brought me a orange kite with blue stripes. It's really neat.

But this time was different. Aunt Daphne seemed more sad than usual. She brought us less presents, too. When we found out what was wrong, it was worser than we thought. So Mom and I asked Aunt Daphne to stay with us for a while. Finally we got a chance to do something nice for her.

How many compared?

Cap or no cap?

A or *an*?

-er/-est or *more/most*?

Fewer or *less*?

Irregular adjectives

Find out how to edit Neil's draft on page 290.

Adjective Info

Types of Adjectives

Adjectives fall into different groups, depending on what job they perform and how they're written.

Descriptive Adjectives

These adjectives add details. They answer these questions: **What kind? What's it like?**

EXAMPLES

long
red
squishy
strong
hilarious
rainy
round
box-shaped
faithful
Canadian

Compound Adjectives

Compound adjectives are made up of more than one word. They can be written as one word, as hyphenated words, or as separate words. Check your dictionary to find the correct form.

EXAMPLES

lightweight jacket
wide-eyed fans
Nova Scotia salmon
hair-raising stories

Find out more about hyphenating compound adjectives on page 353.

Proper Adjectives

These adjectives are formed from proper nouns and begin with a capital letter. Sometimes proper adjectives look just like proper nouns. At other times they have special forms.

EXAMPLES

Same as noun **Newfoundland** coast
Special form **Vietnamese** culture

Turn to page 324 to learn more about capitalizing proper adjectives.

Articles

Articles are special adjectives that help you introduce nouns.

Definite **the** — Points out one of a certain group

Indefinite **a** / **an** — Refers to any one of a certain group

Limiting Adjectives

These adjectives make nouns and pronouns more specific. They answer these questions: **Which one? How many? How much?**

EXAMPLES

this
that
these
those
my
our
your
his
her
its
their
first
last
right
left
one
thirteen
ninety-six
many
few
some
both
no
most
more
less
which
whose
what

Features of Adjectives

Placement

Most of the time, adjectives go before the nouns they describe. You can also put them after a noun and after a linking verb.

Before a noun	*My **orange** kite flies wonderfully.*
After a noun	*My kite, **orange** as a pumpkin, flies wonderfully.*
After a linking verb	*My kite is **orange** and flies wonderfully.*

Endings

Add one of the endings listed to a word root or word, and what do you get? An adjective. Learn more about adjective endings in **Spelling, page 318** and **Word Building, page 327.**

Base word		Ending		Adjective
move	+	able	=	movable

-ful -ic -ish -less -like -ous

Here are some more endings.

Comparisons

Adjectives have three different forms for making comparisons. Which form you use depends on how many things you're comparing, how many syllables the word has, and whether the adjective is regular or irregular.

Positive Form	Comparative Form	Superlative Form
When there's no comparison	When two things are compared	When three or more things are compared

Regular Adjectives

You can form most comparisons by adding either *-er* or *-est* to the adjective or by using *more* or *most* with it. For one-syllable words, add *-er* or *-est.* For some two-syllable words, add *-er* or *-est;* others require *more* or *most.* For three-syllable or longer words, use *more* or *most.*

clear	clearer	clearest	One syllable
pretty	prettier	prettiest	Two syllables
careful	more careful	most careful	
difficult	more difficult	most difficult	Three syllables

Irregular Adjectives

Some adjectives that you use often have irregular forms. They don't follow the rules above, so you just have to learn them.

good	better	best
bad	worse	worst
little	less	least
much, many	more	most

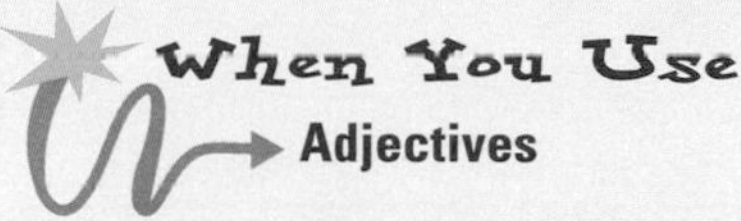
When You Use
Adjectives

Know when to use *a* or *an*.

Use the article *a* before a word beginning with a consonant sound. Use *an* before a word beginning with a vowel sound.

Beginning consonant	*a **t**ruck*	Use *a*
Beginning vowel	*an **a**utomobile*	Use *an*

Know which form of comparison to use.

If you're not sure which form to use for a two-syllable adjective, just look in the dictionary. It will list *-er* and *-est* forms. If no forms are given, use *more* or *most.*

No: *Nobody felt **cheerfuler** than I did.*

Yes! *Nobody felt **more cheerful** than I did.*

Avoid double comparisons.

Use an ending (*-er* or *-est*) or use a word (*more* or *most*). Don't use both.

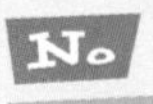
No: *My new kite is **more stronger** than my old one.*

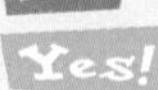
Yes! *My new kite is **stronger** than my old one.*

No: *It's the **most beautifulest** kite I've ever had.*

Yes! *It's the **most beautiful** kite I've ever had.*

Know how to use *less* and *least*.

Sometimes a comparison has to do with less of something, not more. Then, instead of *more* or *most,* you use *less* or *least,* no matter how many syllables the adjective has.

One Syllable	*That hill is **steep.***	Positive
	*That hill is **less steep** than this one.*	Comparative
	*That hill is the **least steep** of all.*	Superlative
Three Syllables	*My sister was **excited.***	Positive
	*My sister was **less excited** than I was.*	Comparative
	*She was the **least excited** family member.*	Superlative

Know the difference between *fewer* and *less*.

The adjectives *fewer* and *less* mean just about the same thing, but *fewer* counts separate items, and *less* measures the amount of a substance. Use *fewer* with plural nouns. Use *less* with singular nouns.

Plural	*Which bread has **fewer calories**?*
Singular	*Which bread has **less sugar**?*

Edit It!

Here are the adjective errors from Neil's draft. Read about why they're errors and how Neil can fix them, and you'll do a better job of editing your own work.

Count the things compared.

DRAFT . . . *I don't know who's* ***happiest,*** *Mom or me.* . . . . . . How many compared?

What's Wrong? Only two people are being compared—*Mom* and *me.* The comparative form is needed, not the superlative.

Edit It! . . . *I don't know who's* ***happier,*** *Mom or me.*

Put a cap on proper adjectives.

DRAFT *My* ***scottish*** *aunt is the greatest.* . . . . . . Cap or no cap?

What's Wrong? *Scottish* comes from the proper noun *Scotland,* so it needs a capital letter.

Edit It! *My* ***Scottish*** *aunt is the greatest.*

Know the difference between *a* and *an.*

DRAFT *Last time she brought me* ***a*** *orange kite with blue stripes.* . . . . . . *A* or *an*?

What's Wrong? *Orange* begins with a vowel sound, so the article before it should be *an,* not *a.*

Edit It! *Last time she brought me* ***an*** *orange kite with blue stripes.*

Know whether to use *-er/-est* or *more/most.*

DRAFT *Aunt Daphne seemed* ***more sad*** *than usual.* . . . . . . *-er/-est* or *more/most*?

What's Wrong? *Sad* has only one syllable, so it forms the comparative with *-er,* not *more.*

Edit It! *Aunt Daphne seemed* ***sadder*** *than usual.*

Fewer and *less* go with different nouns.

DRAFT *She brought us* ***less*** *presents, too.* . . . . . . *Fewer* or *less*?

What's Wrong? *Less* is used with singular nouns, but *presents* is plural. Use *fewer* with plural nouns.

Edit It! *She brought us* ***fewer*** *presents, too.*

Know the irregular forms for comparing.

DRAFT . . . *it was* ***worser*** *than we thought.* . . . . . . Irregular adjectives

What's Wrong? The comparative form of *bad* is *worse,* not *worser.*

Edit It! . . . *it was* ***worse*** *than we thought.*

Verbs

Verbs make other words move. Without them, there wouldn't be any action in your sentences. Nothing would dance or laugh or worry or roar. You need verbs to tell what nouns or pronouns can do, be, and feel.

For more about *verbs*, read on!

"Missed Adventure"

by Jan Susskit

Kevin is laying on the grass outside the cave. His ankle is killing him. He sure hopes he hasn't breaked it. What a dope! Now everybody else are off exploring the cave.

Before long it begins to get dark. Where are the other kids? Leo and Ben is supposed to come back to keep him company. And Tina should of gotten help by now.

Kevin checked his watch. Four thirty-five. He doesn't know what to do. What would you do if you were Kevin?

Confusing verb pairs

Irregular verbs

Agreement with pronouns

Agreement with compounds

Have or *of*?

Stick with one tense

Find out how to edit Jan's draft on page 301.

Verb Info

Types of Verbs

There are three types of verbs. Action and linking verbs work with nouns and pronouns. Helping verbs work with other verbs.

Action Verbs

An **action verb** tells what someone or something does. An action isn't always physical. An action can be mental, too.

EXAMPLES

- cook
- compose
- hop
- paint
- run
- realize
- think
- type
- write
- point
- draw
- sing
- catch
- take
- make
- create
- dream
- skip

Linking Verbs

A **linking verb** links, or joins, a noun or pronoun to another word that tells something about the noun or pronoun. A linking verb expresses a state of being.

Forms of the verb *to be* are the most common linking verbs.

- be
- being
- been
- am
- are
- is
- was
- were
- appear
- become
- feel
- grow
- look
- remain
- seem
- smell
- sound
- stay
- taste

Helping Verbs

A **helping verb** does just what its name says. It helps another verb, the **main verb,** do its job. Together the helping verb and the main verb make a **verb phrase.**

- be
- being
- been
- am
- are
- is
- was
- were
- has
- have
- had
- does
- do
- did
- can
- could
- will
- would
- shall
- should
- may
- might
- must

When You Use
Action, Linking, and Helping Verbs

Know the difference between transitive and intransitive verbs.

A **transitive verb** directs its action to another word, the direct object. An **intransitive verb** doesn't need a direct object to complete its meaning. **For more on direct objects, see page 337.**

Transitive	*Tina **found** the **cave.*** . . . . . Direct object
Intransitive	*They all **rested.***

Some verbs can be used as both transitive and intransitive verbs.

Transitive	*Kevin is afraid they **forgot him.*** . . . . . Direct object
Intransitive	*Oh, no! They **forgot.***

Know the difference between the active and the passive voice.

Action verbs tell whether the subject of the sentence carries out the action or receives it.

Active voice	***Tina found** the cave.* . . . . . Subject acts.
Passive voice	*The **cave was found** by Tina.* . . . . . Subject receives.

Watch out for verbs that can be used as both linking and action verbs.

A verb is a linking verb if a form of *to be* can be substituted for the verb. A verb is an action verb if it is followed by a direct object.

Linking verb	*The cave **smelled** musty. = The cave **is** musty.*
Action verb	*Ben **smelled** the **flower.*** . . . . . Direct object

Remember that other words can come between helping verbs and the main verb.

Two or more verbs can combine to help a main verb. Other words can come between the parts of the verb phrase, especially when you form questions.

Verb phrase together	*Kevin **will be rescued** by someone.*
Verb phrase separated	***Will** Kevin **be rescued** by someone?*

Don't forget the apostrophe in a contraction.

Helping verbs can hide in contractions. Use an apostrophe to replace left-out letters in contractions.

Helping verbs	*He **is** going.*	*He **will** go.*
Contractions	***He's** going.*	***He'll** go.*

The contraction *n't* is different. It means "not" and isn't part of the verb. **See adverbs, page 303.**

Helping verb	*I **do** not know.*
Contraction	*I **don't** know.*

Know the difference between *have* and *of*.

When you say *could have gone,* you're using *could* and *have* as helping verbs for *gone.* Don't use *of* instead of the helping verb *have.*

No	*could of*	*would of*	*should of*
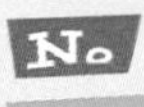	*could have*	*would have*	*should have*

Features of Verbs

Tense

Want to know **when** something happened? Ask the verb. Verbs are time tellers. They have different forms, called **tenses.** There are six tenses in English—three **simple tenses** and three **perfect tenses**—that help you place an event in time. The six tenses are formed by using the helping verbs *has, had,* and *will,* plus verb forms called **principal parts.**

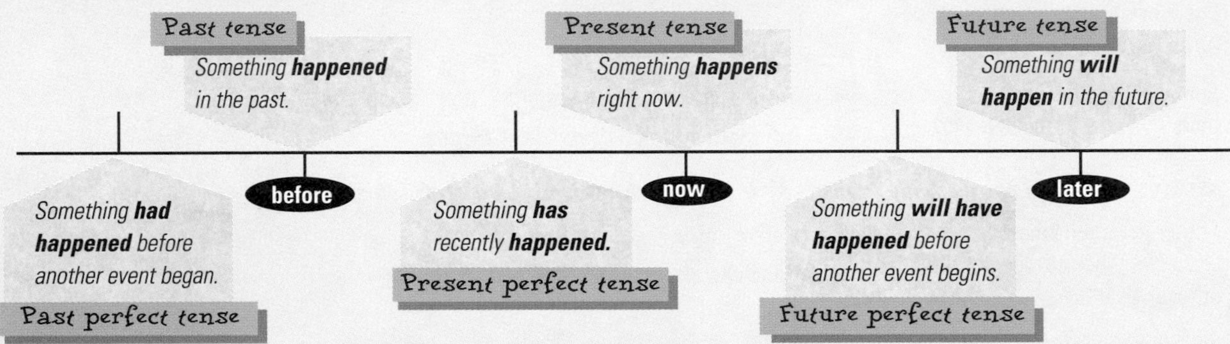

Past tense
Something happened in the past.
Present tense
Something happens right now.
Future tense
Something will happen in the future.
before
now
later
Something had happened before another event began.
Past perfect tense
Something has recently happened.
Present perfect tense
Something will have happened before another event begins.
Future perfect tense

Principal Parts of Verbs

Every verb has four forms called **principal parts.** Present and past participles are made with helping verbs. (Participles can also work as adjectives and nouns. **To learn more about participles, see page 339.**)

	Present	**Present participle**	**Past**	**Past participle**
	Basic form of the verb	Basic form + *-ing* Used with forms of *to be*	Basic form + *-ed*	Basic form + *-ed* Used with forms of *to have*
Regular Verbs These verbs form the past and past participle by adding *-ed* or *-d.* Most verbs follow this pattern.	walk	is walking	walked	has walked
Irregular Verbs These verbs form the past and past participle in different ways. You can either memorize the different parts or look them up in the dictionary in the entry for the main verb. **See Dictionary, page 328.** Here are some of the patterns of irregular verbs.	hurt	is hurting	hurt	has hurt
	bring	is bringing	brought	has brought
	become	is becoming	became	has become
	break	is breaking	broke	has broken
	eat	is eating	ate	has eaten
	begin	is beginning	began	has begun
	lie	is lying	lay	has lain
	be	is being	was, were	has been

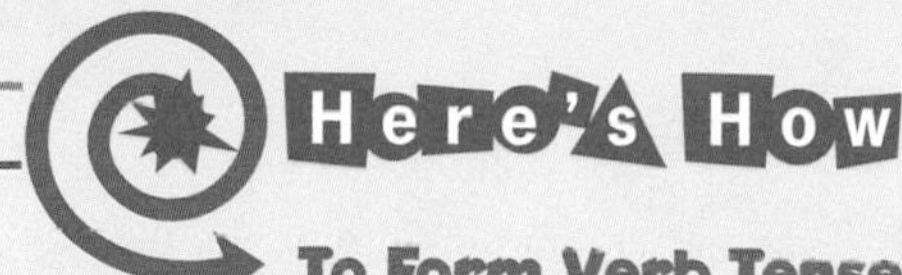
Here's How

To Form Verb Tenses

Here are the correct ways to form all six tenses of the verb *to check*.

For the simple present, use the basic verb form.	*I* ***check*** *my watch.*
For the simple past, use the past form.	*I* ***checked*** *my watch.*
For the simple future, use *will* + the basic verb form.	*I* ***will check*** *my watch.*
For the present perfect, use *have* or *has* + the past participle.	*I* ***have checked*** *my watch.* *Tina* ***has checked*** *her watch.*
For the past perfect, use *had* + the past participle.	*I* ***had checked*** *my watch.*
For the future perfect, use *will have* + the past participle.	*I* ***will have checked*** *my watch fifty times by sunset.*

When You Use

Verb Tenses

Use progressive verb forms to show continuing action.

The six tenses let you talk about actions that begin and end. To talk about actions that keep going, use **progressive verb forms.** There's a progressive form for each of the six tenses. Make the progressive by adding a form of the verb *to be* to the present participle.

Kevin ***is waiting*** *for you.* . . . . . Present progressive

Kevin ***was waiting*** *for you.* . . . . . Past progressive

Kevin ***will be waiting*** *for you.* . . . . . Future progressive

Kevin ***has been waiting*** *for you.* . . . . . Present perfect progressive

Kevin ***had been waiting*** *for you, but then he left.* . . Past perfect progressive

By noon, Kevin ***will have been waiting*** *for you for two hours.* . . . . . Future perfect progressive

Stay with a tense.

Don't jump from one tense to another unless there's a good reason to do so. You'll confuse your reader about when the action happened.

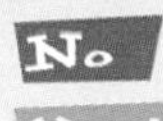
No *It was getting dark. Kevin doesn't know what to do.* Different tenses

Yes! *It was getting dark. Kevin didn't know what to do.* . . . . Same tense

Yes! *It is getting dark. Kevin doesn't know what to do.* . . . . Same tense

Change tense only when the time changes.

When you're talking about two events in the past, use the past perfect tense for the first event and the past tense for the second.

Tina ***had returned*** (past perfect) *by the time the rescuers* ***arrived.*** (past)

When you're talking about two events in the future, use the future perfect tense for the first event and the present tense for the second.

Tina ***will have returned*** (future perfect) *by the time the rescuers* ***arrive.*** (present)

Number

The number of a verb depends on the number of its subject—the noun or pronoun that performs the action. A singular noun takes a singular verb, and a plural noun takes a plural verb.

Present tense

Singular	*The tree **looks** like an oak.*	Add *-s* to the verb.
Plural	*The trees **look** like oaks.*	Don't add *-s* to the verb.

Present perfect tense

Singular	*The tree **has lost** its leaves.*	Use *has* with the verb.
Plural	*The trees **have lost** their leaves.*	Use *have* with the verb.

Verb Conjugation

A **verb conjugation** shows all the forms of a verb. Here are the conjugations of the regular verb *to wait,* and the irregular verb *to be.* These charts show verbs with pronoun subjects only; if you're using a noun subject, just substitute it for a third person singular or third person plural pronoun.

Conjugation of the Regular Verb *to Wait*

Tense	Person	Number: Singular	Number: Plural
Present tense	*first person*	I wait	we wait
	second person	you wait	you wait
	third person	he, she, it waits	they wait
Past tense	*first person*	I waited	we waited
	second person	you waited	you waited
	third person	he, she, it waited	they waited
Future tense	*first person*	I will wait	we will wait
	second person	you will wait	you will wait
	third person	he, she, it will wait	they will wait
Present perfect tense	*first person*	I have waited	we have waited
	second person	you have waited	you have waited
	third person	he, she, it has waited	they have waited
Past perfect tense	*first person*	I had waited	we had waited
	second person	you had waited	you had waited
	third person	he, she, it had waited	they had waited
Future perfect tense	*first person*	I will have waited	we will have waited
	second person	you will have waited	you will have waited
	third person	he, she, it will have waited	they will have waited

Person

Pronouns have different forms to show person. The form of a verb sometimes depends on the person of its subject, especially in the third person singular. **See page 282 for more about person and pronouns.**

Person	**Singular**	**Plural**
first person	I learn	we learn
second person	you learn	you learn
third person	he, she, it learns	they learn
	a student learns	students learn

Conjugation of the Irregular Verb *to Be*

Tense	Person	Number: Singular	Number: Plural
Present tense	*first person*	I am	we are
	second person	you are	you are
	third person	he, she, it is	they are
Past tense	*first person*	I was	we were
	second person	you were	you were
	third person	he, she, it was	they were
Future tense	*first person*	I will be	we will be
	second person	you will be	you will be
	third person	he, she, it will be	they will be
Present perfect tense	*first person*	I have been	we have been
	second person	you have been	you have been
	third person	he, she, it has been	they have been
Past perfect tense	*first person*	I had been	we had been
	second person	you had been	you had been
	third person	he, she, it had been	they had been
Future perfect tense	*first person*	I will have been	we will have been
	second person	you will have been	you will have been
	third person	he, she, it will have been	they will have been

Verb Know-how

There's a lot to know about how verbs work. These reminders can make using verbs a little easier.

Remember to make a verb agree with its subject.

A singular subject requires a singular verb just as a plural subject needs a plural verb. Think about this, especially when you use the present and present perfect tenses and their progressive forms. Tip: If a sentence has one or more helping verbs, it's the first helping verb that must agree with the subject.

Singular	*A smart hiker **rests** every hour.*	Present
Plural	*Smart hikers **rest** every hour.*	Present
Singular	*The hiker **has rested.***	Present perfect
Plural	*The hikers **have rested.***	Present perfect
Singular	*The hiker **has been resting.***	Present perfect progressive
Plural	*The hikers **have been resting.***	Present perfect progressive

Make the verb agree with its subject, not with a noun that comes between them.

The subject of a verb doesn't always come right before it. Sometimes other words can intervene. Be sure the verb agrees with its subject, not just the nearest noun.

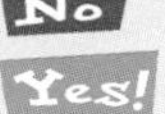

No — *The smell of the pine **trees are** wonderful.*

Yes! — *The **smell** of the pine trees **is** wonderful.*

Make verbs agree with indefinite pronouns.

Some indefinite pronouns are always singular, some are always plural, and some can be either singular or plural, depending on the words they refer to. **For more on indefinite pronouns, see page 281.**

Singular	***Everybody is** here at last.*
Plural	*Only a **few have** left.*
Either	***All** of the **water has** been drunk.*
	***All** of the **peanuts have** been eaten.*

Make a linking verb agree with its subject.

Don't let a noun that follows a linking verb confuse you. The verb always agrees with its subject, not with any other noun.

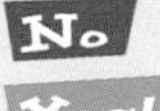

No — *Our only weapon **were cans** of bug spray.*

Yes! — *Our only **weapon was** cans of bug spray.*

Remember, the subject doesn't always come first.

Some sentences are **inverted.** The subject comes **after** the verb, not before it. Find the subject and make the verb agree with it. **See Word Order, page 343.**

Verb + subject	*Where **does** that **trail** take us?*
Verb + subject	*There **are bats** in that cave.*
Verb + subject	*Here **comes one** of the hikers.*

Watch out for compound subjects.

A **compound subject** has two or more parts. When the parts are joined by *and,* the subject is plural and takes a plural verb.

Plural *Tina **and** Leo **have** just come out of the cave.*

When the parts are joined by *or*, the verb agrees with the last part.

Singular *Tina **or** the other **hikers** have dropped a flashlight.*

Plural *The other hikers **or** Tina **has** dropped a flashlight.*

When *each* or *every* is part of a compound, the subject is singular.

Singular ***Each** boy and girl **has** a backpack.*

Some compounds are used together so much they're thought of as one thing. They even take singular verbs.

Singular *Bread and butter **was** served for breakfast.*

*Rock-and-roll **is** my favourite music.*

Recognize collective nouns.

A collective noun names a group—*class, team, club.* **See nouns, page 274.** It's considered singular when it refers to the group as a whole, but it's considered plural when it refers to the members as individuals.

Singular *The group **is arriving** at ten o'clock.*

Plural *The group **are signing** their permission forms now.*

Watch out for singular nouns that end in *-s.*

Usually a noun that ends in *-s* is plural—but not always! Be sure to use a singular verb with nouns such as *news, economics, physics, mathematics, measles,* and *mumps.*

No *The **news were** good today.*

Yes! *The **news was** good today.*

Don't be fooled by titles.

Titles of things are always singular, even when they look plural.

No Great Expectations ***are** a famous novel by Charles Dickens.*

Yes! Great Expectations ***is** a famous novel by Charles Dickens.*

Look out for amounts.

Amounts, time, and measurements are singular when they're considered as a single unit. Otherwise, they are considered plural.

Singular *Ten dollars **is** too much for that.* . . . . . Single amount

Plural *Ten dollars **were** scattered on the ground.* . . . . . Individual bills

Verb Know-how (cont.)

Use the active voice most of the time.

The active voice is just what the name says—active. It's stronger and more direct than the passive voice, which can be weak and clumsy.

Passive *The sandwiches for the hikers were made by Kevin's dad.*

Active *Kevin's dad made sandwiches for the hikers.*

Know the difference between these commonly confused verbs.

You **bring** things to someone or someplace. You **take** things away from someone or someplace.

Bring *Please **bring** that flashlight here.*

Take *Please **take** those matches from the child.*

To lay means "to put or set something down." It is followed by a direct object. *To lie* means "to rest or recline." It is not followed by a direct object.

Lay ***Lay** the **flashlight** next to you.* . . . . . Direct object

Lie ***Lie** on the grass and rest for a while.*

To learn means "to get knowledge from." *To teach* means "to give knowledge to."

Learn *My sister will **learn** how to drive next year.*

Teach *Dad will **teach** her how to drive.*

To lend means "to give something with the understanding that it will be returned." *To borrow* means "to take something with the understanding that it must be returned."

Lend *Kevin won't **lend** Tina his flashlight.*

Borrow *May she **borrow** Ben's flashlight instead?*

To raise means "to lift up." It is usually followed by a direct object. *To rise* means "to move upward." It is not followed by a direct object.

Raise *Please **raise** your **hand** if you're going.* . . . . . Direct object

Rise *The sun will **rise** at 6:00 A.M., so we will leave at 6:30.*

To set means "to put or place." It is usually followed by a direct object. *To sit* means "to rest in a seated position." It is not followed by a direct object.

Set *We can **set** the **sleeping bags** down right here.* . . Direct object

Sit *Don't **sit** on the wet grass.*

Edit It!

Keep a special eye on verbs when you edit. Here are the verb problems from Jan Susskit's draft. Find out why they are problems and how Jan can fix them.

Remember the difference between *lie* and *lay.*

DRAFT *Kevin is **laying** on the grass outside the cave.* . . . . . Confusing verb pairs

What's Wrong? *To lay* means "to put or set down." It's *to lie* that means "to rest or recline."

Edit It! *Kevin is **lying** on the grass outside the cave.*

Know which verb forms don't follow the regular rules.

DRAFT *He sure hopes he hasn't **breaked** it.* . . . . . Irregular verbs

What's Wrong? The forms of *to break* are irregular.

Edit It! *He sure hopes he hasn't **broken** it.*

Make verbs agree with indefinite pronouns.

DRAFT *Now everybody else **are** off exploring the cave.* . . . . . Agreement with pronouns

What's Wrong? *Everybody* is the subject and it's singular, but *are* is plural. Use *is,* the singular form.

Edit It! *Now everybody else **is** off exploring the cave.*

Use the plural for subjects with *and.*

DRAFT *Leo and Ben **is** supposed to come back to keep him company.* . . . . . Agreement with compounds

What's Wrong? Subjects joined with *and* are plural, but *is* is singular. Use *are,* the plural form.

Edit It! *Leo and Ben **are** supposed to come back to keep him company.*

Use *have,* not *of.*

DRAFT *And Tina should **of** gotten help by now.* . . . . . *Have* or *of*?

What's Wrong? The main verb *gotten* needs the helping verb *have. Of* isn't a helping verb.

Edit It! *And Tina should **have** gotten help by now.*

Don't switch the tense unless there's a reason.

DRAFT *Kevin **checked** his watch.* . . . . . Stick with one tense.

What's Wrong? *Checked* is past tense, but the rest of the paragraph is in the present tense. Use *checks.*

Edit It! *Kevin **checks** his watch.*

Adverbs

Adverbs describe and modify or change other words, just as adjectives do. But instead of describing things, they describe actions and qualities. Rather than modifying nouns and pronouns, adverbs qualify the meanings of verbs, adjectives, and other adverbs. How did the runner run? How deep was the snow? How well did the singer sing? Adverbs will tell you.

For more about adverbs, read on!

DRAFT

"Get a Light . . . Now!"

by Ricky Lee and Chad Metz

Adjective or adverb?

We feel badly about the bike accident at Judge's Corner, just two blocks from Harrison Junior High. But we aren't really surprised. Cars speed around that corner way too fast, and it's getting worse all the time.

Just one negative

How many items compared?

Our question is this. Why don't we have a traffic light there? Everybody complains, but nobody does nothing about it. We students should talk to the school board. They need to work faster. Maybe the mayor could do things fastest. We should talk to her too. How many more accidents have to happen before we get a light at Judge's Corner?

Find out how to edit Ricky and Chad's draft on page 305.

Adverb Info

Types of Adverbs

Adverbs describe or modify verbs, adjectives, and other adverbs. The four types of adverbs answer different questions about the words they modify.

Adverbs of Manner

These adverbs tell how an action was performed.

EXAMPLES

badly
carefully
cheerfully
easily
fast
innocently
loudly
quickly
quietly
well
wildly

Adverbs of Place

These adverbs tell where an action took place.

EXAMPLES

anywhere
down
everywhere
far
here
inside
near
nowhere
outside
there
up

Adverbs of Time

These adverbs tell when or how often an action was done.

EXAMPLES

always
anytime
early
immediately
later
never
now
often
sometimes
soon
yesterday

Adverbs of Degree

These adverbs tell to what extent—how much or how little—an action was performed.

EXAMPLES

almost
extremely
hardly
less
more
nearly
not
really
too
very

Intensifiers

Some adverbs of degree are called intensifiers because they make the meaning of an adjective or adverb more intense.

deep
very deep ← More intense
small
too small ← More intense

Negatives

Some adverbs are called negatives because they counter the meaning of the words they modify. The word *not* and the contraction *-n't* that you attach to the ends of verbs are adverbs. There are other negative words that are adverbs, too.

not
-n't
nowhere
never
hardly
scarcely

Features of Adverbs

Knowing what an adverb looks like, what it can modify, and where it goes in a sentence will help you recognize an adverb when you see one.

-ly Ending

Many adverbs are formed by adding *-ly* to an adjective. Be careful, though. The *-ly* ending doesn't guarantee that a word is an adverb. *Love**ly*** and *ug**ly*** are adjectives.

Adjective		-ly Ending		Adverb
quiet	+	ly	=	quietly

sadly happily briefly easily truly

Here are some more adverbs.

Adverbs Modify

When you use an adverb, you modify or change the meaning of a verb, an adjective, or another adverb.

Modify verb *Good drivers turn that corner **slowly.***

Modify adjective ***Really** good drivers turn that corner slowly.*

Modify adverb *Good drivers turn that corner **very** slowly.*

Placement

Adverbs that modify verbs can usually be moved around in a sentence without changing the meaning.

Before verb *The car **immediately** stopped.*

After verb *The car stopped **immediately.***

Adverbs that modify adjectives or other adverbs belong right in front of the words they modify.

Before adjective *That's an **extremely** dangerous corner for bicycle riders.*

Before adverb *The car turned the corner **really** fast.*

Comparisons

Adverbs, like adjectives, have positive, comparative, and superlative forms that let you make comparisons. Which form you use depends on how many things you're comparing and how many syllables the adverb has. It also depends on whether the adverb is regular or irregular. **See page 288 for more about regular and irregular comparisons.**

	Positive	Comparative	Superlative	
Regular adverbs	*fast*	*faster*	*fastest*	One syllable
	early	*earlier*	*earliest*	Two syllables
	quickly	*more quickly*	*most quickly*	
	easily	*more easily*	*most easily*	Three syllables
Irregular adverbs	*badly*	*worse*	*worst*	
	far	*farther*	*farthest*	
	well	*better*	*best*	

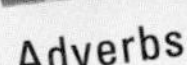

When You Use Adverbs

One *no* is enough.

Don't use a double negative— two negative words for one negative idea. Two negatives cancel each other out.

No: *There* ***isn't no*** *traffic light on the corner yet.* . . . . . . Two negatives

Yes! *There* ***isn't*** *a traffic light on the corner yet.* . . . . . . One negative

Know the difference between adverbs and adjectives.

If you keep these differences between adverbs and adjectives in mind, you'll be able to tell them apart more easily.

Adverbs	Adverbs modify action verbs, adjectives, or other adverbs. They tell **how, where, when,** or **to what extent.**
Adjectives	Adjectives modify nouns or pronouns, or follow linking verbs. They tell **what kind, which one, how much,** or **how many.**

Watch out for these confusing adverb-adjective pairs.

Get these adverb-adjective pairs straight so you can get them right.

Adverb	*well*	*badly*	*really*	*surely*
Adjective	*good*	*bad*	*real*	*sure*

Avoid double comparisons.

To make a comparison with an adverb, use an ending (*-er* or *est*) or a word (*more* or *most*). Never use both.

No: *My father drives* ***more better*** *in the daylight.*

Yes! *My father drives* ***better*** *in the daylight.*

Edit It!

Ricky and Chad made some adverb errors in the draft of their letter. Here you'll find out why they are problems and how Ricky and Chad can fix them.

Know the difference between adjectives and adverbs.

DRAFT *We feel* ***badly*** *about the bike accident at Judge's Corner. . .* . . . . . . Adjective or adverb?

What's Wrong? *Feel* is used as a linking verb. Use the adjective *bad,* not the adverb *badly.*

Edit It! *We feel* ***bad*** *about the bike accident at Judge's Corner. . .*

Use only one negative word for each negative idea.

DRAFT *Everybody complains, but* ***nobody*** *does* ***nothing*** *about it.* . . . . . . Just one negative

What's Wrong? *Nobody* and *nothing* are both negative words. Only one is needed.

Edit It! *Everybody complains, but* ***nobody*** *does* ***anything*** *about it.*

Count the things compared.

DRAFT *Maybe the mayor could do things* ***fastest.*** . . . . . . How many items compared?

What's Wrong? The mayor is compared with the school board. Use *-er,* not *-est,* when comparing two things.

Edit It! *Maybe the mayor could do things* ***faster.***

Prepositions

Prepositions show relationships between things. Consider the relationship between a cat and a mouse, for instance. The mouse might be near the cat, behind the cat, in front of the cat, beside the cat, or even inside the cat. All the little words above that show the different relationships are prepositions.

For more about prepositions, read on!

DRAFT

"What's for Dinner?"

by Mitzy the Cat (as told to Natalie Padia)

Meow . . . it's dinnertime again at the Padia house, but where is everybody at? Isn't anybody hungry beside me? Nobody's in the room, so I think I'll just hop on this chair and take a peek. Mmmm. Two platters of fried chicken! And what's in the bowl among the two platters? Chopped liver! My favourite!

Oops! Here's Mrs. Padia with another dish of food. I'd better jump off of this chair or she'll . . . Thump! Oh, well, maybe I'll hang out under the table until somebody gets the hint and FEEDS ME!

No extra prepositions

Beside or *besides*?

Among or *between*?

No extra prepositions

Find out how to edit Natalie's draft on page 308.

Preposition Info

Types of Prepositions

Prepositions show the relationship of a noun or a pronoun to some other word in the sentence. They also introducc phrases. **For more about phrases, see page 338.** Here are some common prepositions:

Single-Word Prepositions

These prepositions consist of one word.

EXAMPLES

about	**beneath**	**like**
above	**beside**	**near**
across	**besides**	**of**
after	**between**	**off**
against	**beyond**	**outside**
along	**by**	**through**
among	**down**	**to**
around	**except**	**toward**
as	**for**	**under**
at	**from**	**until**
before	**in**	**up**
behind	**inside**	**with**
below	**into**	**without**

Multiple-Word Prepositions

These prepositions are compound. They are made up of more than one word.

EXAMPLES

according to
along with
because of
in addition to
in back of
in front of
in regard to
in spite of
in view of
instead of
next to
on account of
prior to

When You Use Prepositions

Identify the object of the preposition.

If you look at the first few words that follow a preposition, you'll always find a noun or a pronoun. This noun or pronoun is called the **object of the preposition.** The preposition's job is to relate its object to another word in the sentence.

*Rachel sat **near** her **friend.*** . . . . . Object of the preposition

Preposition

Don't add extra prepositions to your sentences.

Sentences can get wordy when they're filled with prepositions that aren't necessary. Get to your point more quickly by substituting different words for some prepositions. Or, try leaving out extra prepositions and prepositional phrases.

Wordy *The dinner of the Padia family was of a delicious nature.*

To the point *The Padias' dinner was delicious.*

No *Where did Mrs. Padia put the chopped liver at?*

Yes! *Where did Mrs. Padia put the chopped liver?*

Know which preposition is which.

Use *between* when you talk about two things, and use *among* for three or more.

Mitzy passed silently ***between*** *two chairs.* . . . . . Two things

We split the dishwashing ***among*** *the three of us.* . . . . . Three things

Beside means "next to." *Besides* means "in addition to."

Besides *Mr. Padia, who else sat* ***beside*** *Natalie?*

In means "inside." *Into* means "moving from the outside in."

Mitzy crept ***into*** *the kitchen once the food was* ***in*** *there.*

Edit It!

Here are the preposition errors from Natalie's draft. Find out why they are errors and how she can fix them, and you'll do a better job of editing your own work.

Don't add prepositions that aren't needed.

DRAFT *. . . where is everybody* ***at****?* . . . . . No extra prepositions

What's Wrong? The preposition *at* doesn't make the sentence any clearer. It does, however, make the sentence wordier. Leave it out.

Edit It! *. . . where is everybody?*

DRAFT *I'd better jump off* ***of*** *this chair.* . . . . No extra prepositions

What's Wrong? *Off* should be used by itself as a preposition. Delete *of.*

Edit It! *I'd better jump off this chair. . . .*

Know which preposition is which.

DRAFT *Isn't anybody hungry* ***beside*** *me?* . . . . . *Beside* or *besides?*

What's Wrong? *Beside* means "next to," **not** "in addition to." Change *beside* to *besides.*

Edit It! *Isn't anybody hungry* ***besides*** *me?*

DRAFT *And what's in the bowl* ***among*** *the two platters?* . . . . . *Among* or *between*?

What's Wrong? With two things, use *between.* Change *among* to *between.*

Edit It! *And what's in the bowl* ***between*** *the two platters?*

Conjunctions

Conjunctions connect words and groups of words. They don't hook up just any old words and phrases, though. They join parts of a sentence—words, phrases, and clauses—that function in the same way or in a closely related way.

For more about *conjunctions*, read on!

DRAFT

A Book Report on *Harriet's Daughter*

by Keesha Mondesir

Harriet's Daughter by Marlene Nourbese Philip is a great book. I liked not only the story, but I also liked the characters. Margaret is my favourite character. Margaret is strong. Margaret always does what she thinks is right. Margaret's father loves her, although he complains that she's rude. He often threatens to send her to the West Indies to learn discipline, manners, proper respect. For fun Margaret thinks up the Underground Railroad game, which is based on the life of Black leader Harriet Tubman. Neither Margaret or Harriet could be stopped from doing what they thought was right.

Equal parts

Combine sentences.

Connect a series.

Two parts of a unit

Find out how to edit Keesha's draft on page 311.

Conjunction Info

Types of Conjunctions

There are three different kinds of conjunctions, and each has a different connecting job to do.

Co-ordinating Conjunctions

These conjunctions connect words or groups of words used in the same way. They can link a subject with another subject, a verb with another verb, or an independent clause with another independent clause. **Learn about verb agreement with co-ordinating conjunctions on page 299.**

*Margaret **and** Zulma were friends.*

and
but
for
or
so
yet

Subordinating Conjunctions

These conjunctions connect two clauses, making one dependent on the other. **For more about clauses, see page 341.**

*Zulma moved to Toronto **because** her mother lived there.*

EXAMPLES

after
although
as
because
before
if
since
than
unless
until
when
whenever
where
while

Correlative Conjunctions

These conjunctions work in pairs to connect words or groups of words used in the same way.

***Neither** Zulma's mother **nor** her stepfather understood her feelings.*

both—and
either—or
neither—nor
not only—but also

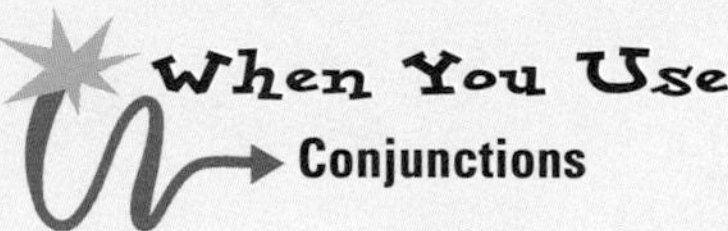
When You Use
Conjunctions

Connect things in a series.

When three or more words or word groups go together, you can use a co-ordinating conjunction to link the last two.

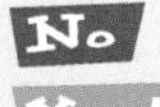
No
Zulma got dressed, braided her hair, dashed out the door.

Yes!
*Zulma got dressed, braided her hair, **and** dashed out the door.*

Join equal parts.

Co-ordinating and correlative conjunctions connect matching parts. Correlatives can be tricky because they have two parts themselves.

No
Margaret both respected and she admired Harriet Tubman.

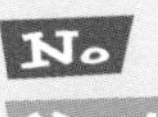
Yes!
*Margaret **both** respected **and** admired Harriet Tubman.*

Use conjunctions to combine sentences.

Look for sentences that belong together, and combine them with conjunctions. That way you show your reader just how your ideas are related. **Find out how to punctuate conjunctions on page 349.**

Two sentences	*Margaret wanted to watch TV. Zulma wanted to go to the park.*
Combined sentence	*Margaret wanted to watch TV,* ***but*** *Zulma wanted to go to the park.*

Edit It!

See how Keesha Mondesir improved the conjunctions in her book report draft, and you can learn to improve your own writing.

Make sure the joined parts match.

DRAFT *I liked not only the story, but I also liked the characters.* . . . . . Equal parts

What's Wrong? *Not only . . . but also* join unequal parts. Change the second part of the sentence to a noun, to match the first part.

Edit It! *I liked not only the* ***story but also the characters.***

Combine sentences that belong together.

DRAFT *Margaret is my favourite character. Margaret is strong. Margaret always does what she thinks is right.* . . . . . Combine sentences

What's Wrong? The connection between the sentences isn't clear, and repeating Margaret's name is awkward. Combine the ideas with conjunctions.

Edit It! *Margaret is my favourite character* ***because*** *she is strong* ***and*** *always does what she thinks is right.*

Connect a series with a conjunction.

DRAFT

He often threatens to send her to the West Indies to learn discipline, manners, proper respect. . . . . . Connect a series

What's Wrong? More than two joined items need a conjunction. Add *and.*

Edit It! *He often threatens to send her to the West Indies to learn discipline, manners,* ***and*** *proper respect.*

Be sure the parts of the correlative conjunction go together.

DRAFT ***Neither*** *Margaret* ***or*** *Harriet could be stopped from doing what they thought was right.* . . . . . Two parts of a unit

What's Wrong? *Neither* should be paired with *nor,* not *or.*

Edit It! ***Neither*** *Margaret* ***nor*** *Harriet could be stopped from doing what they thought was right.*

Interjections

Interjections

Interjections are exclamations or brief remarks. Often they appear at the beginning of sentences to get attention or to show strong feeling. An interjection can also make a statement all by itself. Everyday conversation is full of interjections.

For more about ***interjections***, read on!

EXAMPLES

Ah ha!
All right!
Hey!
Hurrah!
Mmmm!
Oh!
Oh boy!
O.K.!
Oops!
Ouch!
Phew!
Ugh!
Well!
Whew!
Wow!

DRAFT

"School Bus Rap"
by Max LaRoche

Bus driver: Hey you kids pipe down back there.

Set off interjections.

Pamela (howling, holding two CDs): Ouch Jeff, get off my foot, would ya?

Set off interjections.

Jeff (coolly): Awesome, check out those CD covers.

Jenny (holding her nose): Whew! What's that awful smell?

Hank (yelling, holding up a rumpled lunch bag): Yuck whose lunch?

Set off interjections.

Bus driver: Hey! Be quiet!

Find out how to edit Max's draft on the next page.

Interjection Info

Interjections usually appear at the beginning of the sentence and are followed by either a comma or an exclamation mark. They may also stand alone—unattached to a sentence. Either way, interjections need to be accompanied by punctuation.

When You Use Interjections

Separate an interjection from the rest of the sentence.

Use an **exclamation point** if the interjection is really strong. Capitalize the word that follows.

*Ugh! **I** hate that song.* . . . . . Capitalize.

*Great! **W**e're getting a new driver!*

*Phew! **T**hat was a close call.*

Use a **comma** if the interjection is not very strong. Don't capitalize the word that follows.

*Uh oh, **h**ere comes trouble.* . . . . . Don't capitalize.

*O.K., **t**hat's enough for now.*

*Oh, **h**e must be the new kid.*

Edit It!

Here are some problems Max LaRoche had with interjections in his script draft. Find out how Max can fix his errors, and you'll learn how to fix your own.

Use punctuation to set off interjections.

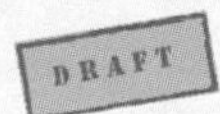

DRAFT ***Hey you** kids pipe down back there.* . . . . . Set off interjections.

What's Wrong? Interjections should be set off from the sentence. Either add a comma after the interjection, or add an exclamation point and capitalize the next word.

Edit It! ***Hey, you** kids pipe down back there.*

Or

Edit It! ***Hey! You** kids pipe down back there.*

DRAFT ***Ouch Jeff**, get off my foot, would ya?*

Edit It! ***Ouch! Jeff**, get off my foot, would ya?*

DRAFT ***Yuck whose** lunch?*

Edit It! ***Yuck, whose** lunch?*

Or

Edit It! ***Yuck! Whose** lunch?*

Spelling

A few centuries ago, you could spell words almost any way you liked. In those days, few people could read, and there weren't many books available anyway. It was only after printing presses came along in the late 1400s that reading and writing became widespread. Spelling started to become standardized when people began to write dictionaries. With printed words popping up everywhere, words had to be instantly recognizable. As a result, most people expect words to be spelled a certain way. So if you want your words to look correct, you have to spell them the standard way.

For more about spelling, read on!

DRAFT

"Beyond Planet Xabatron"

by Susan Nguyen

"I can't beleive it!" said Chief Keef. "There's that deserted spaceship again!" Later he joted in his diary, "I tried to make contact with the ship. There was no sine of life. I wish I new why it keeps chasing us. It seems impossable for a deserted ship to do that." Keef was in for a big surprize.

Vowel pairs

Double consonant or not?

Related words

Words that sound alike

Endings

Same sound, different letter

Find out how to correct the spellings on Susan's draft on page 321.

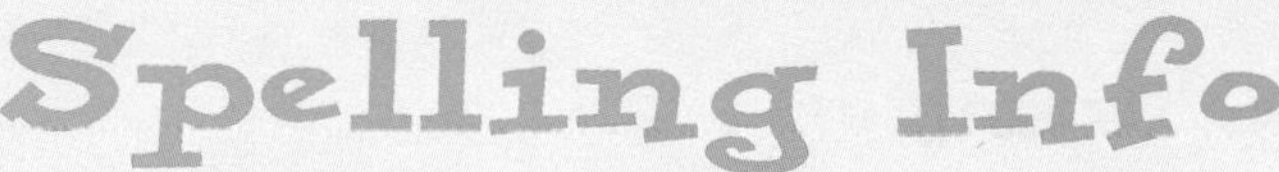

Spelling Info

Ooh, here's one vowel sound that's spelled ten different ways: b**oo**t, bl**ue,** r**u**by, thr**ew,** wh**o,** thr**ough,** s**ou**p, fr**ui**t, sh**oe,** n**eu**tral. No wonder people have such trouble spelling, right? Sound and spelling don't always match in English. If you look beyond the sound to language history and word meanings, though, you'll find that English spelling will make more sense. To become a good speller, all you need is some language know-how and a few smart strategies.

Language Know-how

You write words, not sounds. Think about the words—their parts, meanings, and history as well as their sounds—and you're more likely to spell them right.

☛ Think about the whole word.

Don't try to spell a word by breaking it into individual sounds. It probably won't work. Instead, look at the pattern of the word as a whole.

- A final *e* doesn't add an *e* sound. It changes the sound of the earlier vowel.

No *e*	*bit*	*cut*	*not*	*rat*
Final *e*	*bite*	*cute*	*note*	*rate*

- The letters *gh* sound one way at the beginning of a word and another at the end.

Beginning	***gh**ost*
End	*rou**gh***

☛ Think about meaning.

Words or word parts with the same meaning are likely to be spelled the same way.

bear	=	animal	*polar **bear***	***bear**skin*
bare	=	naked	***bare**foot*	*thread**bare***

☛ Think about related words.

Many words are parts of families—they're related to other words with the same root. Related words can give you hints about spelling. In a related word, a vowel sound might be pronounced differently, or a silent letter might be pronounced.

definition/define	*opposite/oppose*
similar/similarity	*autumn/autumnal*
sign/signal	*muscle/muscular*

Tricky Spellings

accept, except
accidentally
ache
address
advice, advise
affect, effect
aisle, I'll, isle
allowed, aloud
all ready, already
all right
although
answer
appearance
appreciate
argument
athlete
awful
awhile
balloon
beginning
believe
bibliography
biography
bought
brake, break
business
busy
buy, by, bye

Tricky Spellings

calendar
careful
ceiling
cent, scent, sent
centre
cereal, serial
chews, choose
close, clothes
committee
cough
council, counsel
country
cousin
decide
decision
definitely
desert, dessert
doctor
early
effect, affect
embarrass
emigrate, immigrate
enough
environment
excellent
except, accept
exercise

Spelling Strategies

Combine your language know-how with some smart strategies, and watch your spelling improve.

☛ Create a personal speller.

In your notebook or a separate booklet, keep a list of words that you tend to misspell. Circle the troublesome letters, and next to the word jot down any helpful hints. Study your list, and use it when you proofread.

February	*Remember that first* **r***!*
misspell	*You* ***miss*** *when you misspell.*

☛ Use the dictionary.

Give the dictionary a chance. Even though it isn't always easy to find the word you need, just the process of looking for it can help you remember how to spell it. **See page 328 for more information about how to use the dictionary.**

☛ Know the pros and cons of spell checkers.

A spell checker in a word-processing program will highlight a misspelled word and let you use the built-in dictionary to correct it. Spell checkers are great at finding words that you **spell** incorrectly, but they won't find words that you **use** incorrectly.

Will find	***thers*** *instead of* ***theirs***
Will not find	***bear*** *instead of* ***bare*** or ***too*** *instead of* ***two***

☛ Use memory helps.

A memory help can be a rhyme, a phrase, a statement, or anything else you can think of. Jot these memory helps and others you invent in your personal speller.

Rhyme	*A fri**end** to the **end***
	Use **i** *before* **e** *except after* **c.**
Phrase	*A **pie**ce of **pie***
Statement	*Station**e**ry is for l**e**tt**e**rs.*
	*A cell**ar** is d**ar**k.*
	*Se**par**ate the word into **par**ts.*

☛ Pronounce right to spell right.

If you don't pronounce carefully, you can end up adding letters that shouldn't be there or omitting letters that should be there.

No	*athaletic*	*suprise*
Yes!	*athletic*	*surprise*

☛ Study hard-to-spell words.

The words listed in the margins are words people find hard to spell. Look at them, study them, and learn them.

Here's How

To Study Hard-to-Spell Words

1. Look at the word. Say it. Spell it out loud.
2. Shut your eyes and picture the word. Spell it out loud.
3. Check the spelling. Not right? Try again.
4. If you spelled the word correctly, try writing it in a sentence.
5. If you wrote the word correctly, good for you. Check it again tomorrow.

☛ Have a proofreading plan.

Proofreading means looking at every letter of every word. Pay special attention to words that have these features.

Double letters	*mi**ss**pell, sto**pp**ed, ba**rr**el*	
Vowel pairs	*bel**ie**ve, c**ei**ling*	
Letters that sound alike	***c**ane, **k**ey*	*ca**s**e, ra**c**e*
Words that sound alike	*to, too, two*	*pair, pear, pare*
Tricky endings	*poss**i**ble, cap**a**ble*	
Silent letters	*bom**b**, bus**i**ness, strai**gh**t*	

exhibit
explanation
favourite
February
forth, fourth
forty
friend
government
grammar
guarantee
guess
half, have
hear, here
heard, herd
height
here, hear
hoarse, horse
hole, whole
horse, hoarse
hospital
hour, our
I'll, aisle, isle
immediately
immigrate, emigrate
impossible
incredible
interesting
isle, aisle, I'll
it's, its

Tricky Spellings

knew, new
loose, lose
machine
maybe
meant
minute
necessary
neither
new, knew
occasionally
occur
o'clock
often
opportunity
our, hour
parallel
passed, past
peace, piece
pleasant
possess
possible
practice, practise
principal, principle
privilege
probably
procedure
quarter
raise, rays, raze

Make Your Spelling Life Easier

Learn the guidelines that describe spelling patterns. Then follow them from the beginning to the end of each word as you proofread.

Word Beginnings

Know how to attach prefixes.

Prefixes don't change the spelling of the words or roots they're added to. Sometimes, though, the prefix itself changes to match the word. **See page 326 for more information on prefixes.**

No change	mis + lead = mislead	mis + spell = misspell
Prefix changes	in + logical = illogical	in + mature = immature

Word Middles

Know the difference between *ei* and *ie.*

Here's a memory aid that will help: If the vowel sound is long *e,* put *i* before *e* except after *c.* Go the other way if the vowel sound is long *a,* as in *neighbour* or *weigh.* Watch out for a few exceptions.

Long *e*	*niece, field, chief, relief, thief, piece, shield*
Long *a*	*neighbour, weight, reign, vein, sleigh, veil*
Exceptions	*seize, height, either, neither, weird, science*

Word Endings

Know how to attach endings and suffixes.

Endings include **inflected endings,** which change the number, tense, or comparative form of a word, and **suffixes,** which change the meaning or the part of speech of a word. **See page 327 for more information on suffixes.**

Inflected endings	*-s, -es, -ed, -ing, -er*
Suffixes	*-ful, -ly, -ment, -ness, -y*

Most of the time, just add the ending to the base word.

-s	play + s = play**s**	***-ly***	sincere + ly = sincere**ly**
-ed	happen + ed = happen**ed**	***-ness***	sudden + ness = sudden**ness**
-ing	repeat + ing = repeat**ing**	***-y***	rain + y = rain**y**

Double the consonant.

If the word has one syllable, one vowel, and one final consonant, **double** the consonant before an ending that begins with a vowel. Don't double the consonant, however, when the word ends in *x*.

Double	grab + ing = gra**bb**ing	fit + est = fi**tt**est
	shop + ed = sho**pp**ed	sun + y = su**nn**y
Don't double	wax + y = waxy	fix + ing = fixing

If the final syllable is stressed and has one vowel and one final consonant, **double** the consonant before an ending that begins with a vowel. If the stress is not on the last syllable, do not double the final consonant. Exception: For words that end in a single vowel and the letter *l*, double the *l* before a suffix that begins with a vowel.

Double	begin + ing = begi**nn**ing	control + er = contro**ll**er
	occur + ence = occu**rr**ence	permit + ed = permi**tt**ed
Don't double	benefit + ed = benefited	open + ing = opening
Exceptions	level + ing = leve**ll**ing	travel + er = trave**ll**er

Drop the silent *e*.

If the base word ends with a silent *e*, drop the *e* before any ending that begins with a vowel. The *e* is also dropped in certain words before endings that begin with a consonant.

Before a vowel	nerve + ous = nervous	value + able = valuable
Before some consonants	true + ly = truly	argue + ment = argument

Keep the silent *e*.

In words that end with *ce* or *ge*, the *e* stays before *-able* or *-ous*.

Before *-able*	change + able = chang**e**able
Before *-ous*	courage + ous = courag**e**ous

Change *y* to *i*.

If the base word ends with the consonant *y*, change the *y* to an *i* before endings except those that begin with *i*. Watch out for a few exceptions.

Change	penny + es = pennies	try + ed = tried
	pity + ful = pitiful	lazy + ly = lazily
Don't change	fly + ing = flying	
Exceptions	shy + ness = shyness	sly + ly = slyly

Drop the *le* at the end.

If the base word ends in a consonant that is followed by *le*, drop the *le* before the *-ly* ending.

simple + ly = simply   gentle + ly = gently

receive
recommend
remember
restaurant
rhythm
ridiculous
right, rite, write
root, route
sandwich
scent, cent, sent
separate
serial, cereal
several
similar
sincerely
souvenir
stationary, stationery
straight, strait
succeed
sugar
suppose
surprise
surrounded
syllable
terrible
their, there, they're
thorough
though

Tricky Spellings

thought
threw, through
tomorrow
tonight
truly
Tuesday
until
usually
vacation
vacuum
waist, waste
wait, weight
waste, waist
way, weigh
weather, whether
Wednesday
weigh, way
weight, wait
weird
whether, weather
which, witch
whole, hole
who's, whose
witch, which
withhold
women
write, right, rite
yore, your, you're

Watch out for these tricky endings.

Is it *-able* or *-ible*? In general, add *-able* to words that can stand alone and *-ible* to word parts that cannot. When in doubt, you can choose *-able,* because it's more common.

Can stand alone	**drink** + able = drink**able**
Cannot stand alone	**incred** + ible = incred**ible**

Is it *-ance* or *-ence*? You just have to memorize words with these endings or remember to check in the dictionary.

-ance	*assist**ance***	*guid**ance***	*perform**ance***
-ence	*abs**ence***	*differ**ence***	*occurr**ence***

Is it *-cede, -ceed,* or *-sede*? These are a cinch to memorize.

Only one word ends in *-sede.*	*super**sede***
Three words end in *-ceed.*	*ex**ceed,** pro**ceed,** suc**ceed***
All others end in *-cede.*	*con**cede,** pre**cede,** re**cede***

Make most nouns plural by adding *-s* or *-es.*

Most nouns form their plurals in regular ways, but the few that don't can give you trouble. Learn the rules and use them. **See page 275 for more information on noun plurals.**

Beware of compound words.

A **compound word** is made up of two or more words written with no space between them, connected with hyphens, or written as separate words. Compound spellings are always changing, so check a recent dictionary. **See page 274 for more information on compound words.**

Know the difference between easily confused words.

Do you eat a *desert* or ride a camel through it? *Desert* and *dessert* can be easily confused. Here are some other words you need to keep *strait*—oops, *straight.*

advice—opinion or suggestion
advise—to suggest

affect—to influence
effect—result

all ready—fully ready
already—by this time

desert—dry land
desert—to abandon
dessert—last course of a meal

knew—was familiar with
new—not old

stationary—not moving
stationery—writing paper

straight—not curved
strait—narrow passage of water

their—belonging to them
there—at that place
they're—they are

Spell It Right!

Susan found and fixed these spelling errors when she proofread her draft. Watch for errors like these in your work, too.

Know the difference between *ei* and *ie*.

DRAFT *"I can't **beleive** it!" said Chief Keef.* . . . . . Vowel pairs

What's Wrong? The vowel letters ***e*** and *i* are reversed.

Edit It! *"I can't **believe** it!" said Chief Keef.*

Know when to double a final consonant.

DRAFT *Later he **joted** in his diary,* . . . . Double consonant or not?

What's Wrong? *Jot* is a one-syllable word ending in a consonant, so the final *t* should be doubled before *-ed*.

Edit It! *Later he **jotted** in his diary, . . .*

Think about related words.

DRAFT *There was no **sine** of life.* . . . . . . Related words

What's Wrong? The word that Susan intends, *sign,* has a silent *g,* which can be heard in the related word *signal.*

Edit It! *There was no **sign** of life.*

Know the difference between easily confused words.

DRAFT *"I wish I **new** why it keeps chasing us."* . . . . . Words that sound alike

What's Wrong? *New* means "not old." The word needed here is *knew,* the past tense of *know.*

Edit It! *"I wish I **knew** why it keeps chasing us."*

Watch out for tricky endings.

DRAFT *"It seems **impossable** for a deserted ship to do that."* . . . . . Endings

What's Wrong? The ending should be *-ible,* not *-able.*

Edit It! *"It seems **impossible** for a deserted ship to do that."*

Remember that different letters can sound alike.

DRAFT *Keef was in for a big **surprize.*** . . . . . Same sound, different letter

What's Wrong? The sound *z* is spelled *s* here, not *z.*

Edit It! *Keef was in for a big **surprise.***

Capitalization

What's the difference between *red cross* and *Red Cross*? Just some capital letters. But those capitals are important signals. They tell you that the words name something specific. Without them, you wouldn't be able to tell the difference between a cross that happens to be red and the worldwide organization called the Red Cross.

Like most language rules, capitalization rules have a purpose. They make meanings clearer for the reader. So, do your reader a favour. Use this section to put capital letters in their right places.

Capitalization Know-how

There's a lot to know about capitalization. Follow these guidelines so that you will know when to capitalize and when not to capitalize.

The Pronoun "I"

Capitalize the pronoun *I*.

I *have no idea where* ***I****'m going!*

First Word in a Sentence

Capitalize the first word in a sentence, in a line of certain forms of poetry, and in a direct quotation.

Sentence ***W****ho wrote this limerick?*

Poetry ***T****here was an old man with a beard,*
W*ho said, "It is just as I feared!"*

Quotation *Who said, "****W****e have nothing to fear but fear itself"?*

You do **not** need to capitalize the continuation of a quotation unless it begins a new sentence.

Continuation *"Every day," he replied, "****she*** *walks two kilometres."*

New sentence *"That's true," Eva agreed. "****She*** *walks the dog."*

Proper Nouns

Capitalize the names and initials of people and animals.

M*ichael* ***J. F****ox*   ***L****aura* ***S****ecord*   ***S****noopy*

Capitalize titles used with names, including titles that are abbreviated.

P*remier* ***J****oe* ***G****hiz*
M*r.* ***I****ra* ***R****oss,* ***J****r.*
C*ol.* ***Q****uigley*
D*r.* ***M****ohammed*
M*ayor* ***J****une* ***R****owlands*
M*s.* ***R****osa* ***Q****uintero*

Capitalize family titles when used as names or parts of names.

*Where are you going, **M**om?*

*Here comes **U**ncle Ezra now.*

You do **not** need to capitalize a family title if it comes after a possessive pronoun or article.

No — *My Mom works in a bank.*

Yes! — *My **mom** works in a bank.*

Capitalize the names of specific places.

Planets	***M**ars, **E**arth, **P**luto*
Heavenly bodies	***M**ilky **W**ay, **N**orth **S**tar*
Continents	***A**frica, **S**outh **A**merica, **E**urope*
Countries	***J**amaica, **B**elgium, **E**l **S**alvador, **I**ran*
Regions	*the **M**aritimes, the **P**rairies, the **M**iddle **E**ast*
Provinces	***A**lberta, **O**ntario, **Q**uebec, **N**ova **S**cotia*
U.S. states	***N**ew **M**exico, **M**innesota, **F**lorida*
Cities and towns	***N**ew **D**elhi, **S**t. Louis, **V**ancouver, **L**a **P**az*
Bodies of water	***P**acific **O**cean, **L**ake **W**innipeg, **H**udson **B**ay, **F**raser **R**iver*
Mountains	***M**ount **R**obson, **C**anadian **R**ockies*
Deserts	***G**obi **D**esert, **S**ahara **D**esert*
Parks	***B**anff **N**ational **P**ark, **W**ood **B**uffalo **N**ational **P**ark*
Forests	***S**herwood **F**orest, **B**lack **F**orest*
Buildings and monuments	***P**eace **T**ower, **S**addledome, **B**ellevue **H**ouse*
Streets	***T**rans-**C**anada **H**ighway, **R**oute 1A, **R**obson **S**treet*

You do **not** need to capitalize words like *city, desert, park,* and *street* unless they are part of a name.

No — *The City of Rome is ancient.*

Yes! — *The **city** of Rome is ancient.*

You do **not** need to capitalize directions unless they name specific regions.

No — ***D**o you prefer living **E**ast or **N**orth of the city?*

Yes! — ***D**o you prefer living **east** or **north** of the city?*

Yes! — *I lived in the **W**est before I moved to the **N**orth.*

Capitalize the names of ships, trains, planes, and spacecraft.

***B**luenose*	***O**rient **E**xpress*
***C**oncorde*	***V**oyager*

Alberta, British Columbia, Manitoba, New Brunswick, ...

Capitalize languages, nationalities, and religions.

Languages	*Hindi, French, Vietnamese, Arabic, Cree*
Nationalities	*a Spaniard, an Israeli, a Canadian*
Religions	*Roman Catholicism, Islam, Judaism, Hinduism*

Capitalize the names of specific groups and businesses.

Organizations	*Math Club, National Hockey League*
Institutions	*Queens General Hospital, Concord High School*
Government bodies	*Canadian Senate, British Parliament*
Businesses	*Ford Motor Company, McCain's*

Capitalize the names of historical events, periods, and documents.

Events	*World War II, Industrial Revolution*
Periods	*Middle Ages, Renaissance, Eighteenth Dynasty*
Documents	*Canadian Charter of Rights and Freedoms*

Capitalize the names of special events, days, months, and holidays.

Special events	*Stanley Cup, World Series, Senior Prom*
Days	*Monday, Saturday*
Months	*January, November*
Holidays	*Victoria Day, New Year's Day, Canada Day*

You do **not** need to capitalize the names of the seasons.

No *Uncle Jon visits Montréal every Summer.*

Yes! *Uncle Jon visits Montréal every* ***summer****.*

Capitalize names of brands, awards, language courses, and numbered courses.

You do **not** need to capitalize the noun that follows a brand name.

Brands	*Bata shoes, Macintosh computers, Wheaties cereal*
Awards	*Grammy, Governor General's Award, Genie Award*
Courses	*French, English, History 2, Woodworking 101*

. . . . Newfoundland, Nova Scotia, Ontario, Prince Edward Island, ...

Proper Adjectives

Capitalize adjectives formed from proper nouns.

Proper noun	*Italy*	*Shakespeare*
Proper adjective	*Italian bread*	*Shakespearean plays*

Titles of Works

Capitalize the first word, last word, and all other important words in titles.

You do **not** need to capitalize articles, conjunctions, or short prepositions unless they're the first or last words in a title. You may, however, capitalize these parts of speech if they contain four or more characters. Remember, when *copying* titles of works, you should capitalize the words as they appear in the titles.

Books	The Outsiders
Magazines	Maclean's, Time
Newspapers	The Globe and Mail
Short stories	"To Build a Fire"
Films	Star Wars
Plays	You Can't Take It with You
TV series	Road to Avonlea, Fresh Prince of Bel Air
Musical works	the opera Madama Butterfly
	the song "Beauty and the Beast"
Works of art	the painting "The Habitant Farm"

Letters

Capitalize the words in the greeting of a letter.

Dear Ms. Chang: *Dear Sir or Madam:*

Dear Jacob, *Dear Dad,*

Capitalize only the first word in the closing.

Sincerely yours, *Yours truly,* *Your friend,*

. . . . . Quebec, Saskatchewan—provinces of any size are capitalized!

Word Building

Words are your basic language tools. If you know where they come from and how they're put together, you're better able to work with them, play with them, and maybe even make up some of your own. In a language that's alive and well, words are always coming, going, and changing.

Words can be built from separate parts. The word *returnable,* for example, is made up of *re* + *turn* + *able*. The **root,** or base, of a word carries the main meaning. A **prefix** added at the beginning or a **suffix** added at the end can alter the meaning and form a new word.

Prefixes

A prefix is one or more syllables that can be added at the beginning of a word or word part to form a new word.

ad-	to; toward	**ad**join
anti-	opposed to	**anti**social
bi-	two	**bi**cycle
com-	together; with	**com**press
con-	together; with	**con**form
de-	opposite of	**de**forest
dis-	opposite of	**dis**agree
ex-	out of	**ex**port
im-	not; opposite of	**im**possible
in-	not; opposite of	**in**active
inter-	between	**inter**national
mis-	wrong	**mis**spell
post-	after	**post**date
pre-	before	**pre**school
re-	again	**re**read
sub-	under; below	**sub**marine
super-	over; more than	**super**human
trans-	across	**trans**mit
un-	not; opposite of	**un**load

Word Origins

The history of a word is called its **etymology.** **See Dictionary, page 329.** It can tell you something about the history of the people who use it. We know, for instance, that the Romans first brought Latin to Britain in A.D. 43. Then Germanic tribes, the Angles, Jutes, and Saxons, came to Britain and introduced a language that is now known as Old English. This early version of English contained familiar words such as *and, eat, go,* and *the*. More Latin words, such as *candle,* were added to the English language with

Roots

A root, or base, is a word part to which prefixes and suffixes can be added to form new words, or derivatives.

Root	Meaning	Derivatives
-bio-	life	**bio**graphy **bio**logy micro**bio**logy
-lab-	to work	e**lab**orate **lab**our **lab**oratory **lab**orious

the spread of Christianity throughout the Roman Empire. Later, Viking settlers who spoke Old Norse contributed words such as *skin* and *sky*. Norman conquerors who spoke French added words like *art* and *beauty*. Since then, travel and immigration have introduced words from around the world into the English language. New words are still coming from technological advances, changes in the way people live, and the natural wear and tear of language use. **For more about word origins, see page 370.**

Root	Meaning	Derivatives
-phone-	sound; voice	micro**phone** **phono**graph tele**phone**
-port-	to carry	im**port** ex**port** **port**able trans**port**ation

Suffixes

A suffix is one or more syllables that can be added at the end of a word or word part to form a new word.

Adjective Suffixes

-able	capable of	port**able**
-ful	characterized by	beauti**ful**
-less	without	speech**less**
-ous	full of	envi**ous**

Noun Suffixes

-er, -or	one who does	paint**er**
-hood	condition or quality of	child**hood**
-ment	product of	enjoy**ment**
-ness	state of being	silli**ness**
-ship	quality or state of	friend**ship**
-tion	act of	construc**tion**
-ty	state of being	varie**ty**

Verb Suffixes

-ate	to make	alien**ate**
-en	to cause to be	fright**en**
-fy	to make	simpli**fy**
-ize	to cause to be	vapor**ize**

Adverb Suffix

-ly	in a certain way	proud**ly**

dic•tion•ar•y

A **dictionary** is a reference book or software program that lists words in alphabetical order. It gives information about the meaning, pronunciation, and history of each entry word. You can use it to learn more about the words you already know and about words you have yet to discover.

Guide words ········ **book learning** **131** **boot**

Pronunciation key ······ hat, āge, fär; let, ēqual, tėrm; it, īce
hot, ōpen, ôrder; oil, out; cup, pu̇t, rüle,
əbove, takən, pencəl, lemən, circəs

ch, child; ng, long; sh, ship
th, thin; ᴛʜ, then; zh, measure

Entry word · Definitions · Part-of-speech label · Example phrase · Etymology · Respelling · Inflected forms · Restrictive label

boon[1] (bün) *n.* **1** a blessing; great benefit. **2** *Archaic.* something asked or granted as a favor. [ME < ON *bón* petition]

boon[2] (bün) *adj.* **1** jolly; merry: *a boon companion.* **2** *Poetic.* kindly; pleasant. [ME < OF *bon* good < L *bonus*]

boon•docks (bün′doks) *n.pl. Slang.* rough backwoods; bush country. [< Tagalog *bundók* mountain]

boon•dog•gle (bün′dog′əl) *v.* **-gled, -gling;** *n.* —*v. Informal.* do trivial, unnecessary, or pointless work. —*n.* **1** *Informal.* trivial, unnecessary, or pointless work or its product. **2** *Cdn.* a device used to take up the slack in a chin strap, such as a large wooden bead. [origin uncertain] —**boon′dog′gler,** *n.*

From *Gage Canadian Dictionary,* 1983

Here's How

To Find a Word You Don't Know How to Spell

1. **Think about the beginning sounds of the word.** Decide what the likely spellings are for those sounds. There may be more than one possibility. For example, the *far* sound could be spelled *far,* as in *farmer,* or *phar,* as in *pharmacist.* **See page 314 to learn more about spelling.**
2. **Open the dictionary to words beginning with the likely letters.** Run your finger down the entries. You may need to do this for several pages.
3. **Find the word.** Then check the pronunciation and meaning to make sure it's the word you want.
4. **Copy down the word for future reference.**

(dik′shən er′ē)

Guide words .... The guide words name the first and last entries on the page. Compare the word you're looking up with the guide words to see if you're on the right page.

Pronunciation key .... The pronunciation key shows how to pronounce the sounds indicated in the respelling. A short pronunciation key can be found at the top or bottom of each right-hand page. A full pronunciation key is often on the inside front and back covers of the dictionary.

Entry word .... The entry word shows the spelling of the word. If the word is longer than one syllable, it is divided into syllables, as in *boondocks* or *boondoggle.* Dots are placed where the word may be hyphenated. **boon • docks**

Part-of-speech label .... The part-of-speech label shows how the word can be used in a sentence: ***n.*** = noun, ***pron.*** = pronoun, ***adj.*** = adjective, ***v.i.*** = intransitive verb, ***v.t.*** = transitive verb, ***adv.*** = adverb, ***prep.*** = preposition, ***conj.*** = conjunction, ***interj.*** = interjection.

Respelling .... The respelling of the word shows how it is pronounced. The letters and symbols in the respelling indicate specific sounds. Look at the pronunciation key to find out what the letters and symbols sound like.

Inflected forms .... The inflected forms include the principal parts of verbs **(see page 294),** the plurals of nouns **(see page 275),** and the comparatives and superlatives of adjectives and adverbs **(see pages 288 and 305).**

Definitions .... The definitions, or meanings, of the word are grouped by part of speech. Definitions are numbered, showing the most common meaning first.

Example phrase .... An example phrase or sentence in italic type shows how the word can be used in speech or writing.

Etymology .... The etymology is the origin and historical development of the word. Here are some of the symbols and abbreviations you may find in etymologies: The arrow sign (<) means "from" or "taken from." F–French, Sp–Spanish, L–Latin, LL–Late Latin, OE–Old English, ME–Middle English, Gk–Greek, OF–Old French, ON–Old Norse, ult.–ultimately. You can read, for example, the etymology of the adjective *boon* like this: *Boon* is a Middle English word, which was taken from the Old French word *bon,* which means "good," which came from the Latin word *bonus.*

Restrictive label .... A restrictive label identifies a word or particular meaning as being special or different from typical usage. It usually appears in italic type before the definition to which it applies. For example, the abbreviation ***Cdn.*** indicates that the meaning is Canadian in origin or usage.

the•sau•rus

A **thesaurus** is a reference book or software program that you can use to find new and more lively words that have similar meanings to the words you use all the time. A thesaurus can help you broaden your vocabulary and make your writing more interesting.

Thesauri come in different forms. Some thesauri list entries alphabetically while others list them by category or key word. Still others, like the one below, use a format that lists categories of words alphabetically. Most thesauri contain indexes to help you quickly locate the word you want.

Entry or key word — Part-of-speech label

great *adjective*

Definition — very good or fine. When **great** is used this way it is more suited to everyday language. *We had a* ***great*** *time at the party.*

Example sentence

Related words:

splendid	**Splendid** means extremely good. *The orchestra gave a splendid performance.*
superb	**Superb** is so similar to **splendid** that you can usually use either. *The meal was superb.*
super	**Super** means extremely good or pleasing. It is more suited to everyday language. *We had a super holiday at the beach.*
first-rate	**First-rate** means very good or outstanding. It is more suited to everyday language. *She got a high mark for her first-rate work.*

Synonyms — similar words: **good, excellent, best, superior**

Antonyms — contrasting words: **bad, nasty**

From *Young Canada Thesaurus,* 1988

(thi sôʹrəs)

Entry or key word .... The entry or key word is the word you look for if you want to find other words that express the same idea.

Part-of-speech label .... The part-of-speech label tells you how the word can be used in a sentence: as a noun, pronoun, adjective, verb, adverb, preposition, conjunction, or interjection.

Definition .... The definition shows what the word means. It can help you choose a word that conveys precisely the meaning you want.

Example sentence .... An example sentence shows how a word is used in speech or writing.

Related words .... These are the synonyms or words that are related in meaning to the entry word.

Synonyms .... Synonyms are words that mean the same or nearly the same as the entry word.

Antonyms .... Antonyms are words that have the opposite meaning of the entry word.

Here's How

To Find the Word You Want in a Thesaurus

1. Look in the index for the word you would like to replace. There are guide words to help you locate the word quickly. The index listing for *great* might look like this:

   great *adjective* 182

   great *adjective* **important** 205

   The bold, or dark, type tells you that *great* is the key word for a group of words with the overall meaning "great." The second listing, in normal type, indicates that *great* is also listed in a group of words meaning "important."
2. Take note of the page number following the meaning closest to the one you want.
3. Go to that page in the body of the thesaurus and read through the entry for word suggestions.
4. Double-check the new word in the dictionary to make sure it really means what you think it does.

Sentences

How are sentences made? You put them together, word by word. There are only a few basic patterns, but by placing different words in different combinations, you can go on creating new sentences forever.

together!

Words
go

Contents

Constructing Sentences

A sentence is a group of words that expresses a complete thought. You mark a sentence with a capital letter at the beginning and a closing punctuation mark at the end.

For more about *sentences*, read on!

DRAFT

"A Real Dragon" by Lara Haddad

You may think dragons don't exist, they do. There is a real-life dragon. It lives on an island. The island is called Komodo. It is in Indonesia. The dragon of Komodo is a huge lizard The biggest lizard in the world, in fact.

This is what the dragon looks like. It can grow to be three metres long and is covered with scales. It has a powerful body and a long, flat head with a mighty tail. A forked tongue shoots out of its mouth, which is lined with rows of sharp teeth. The only thing missing is that this dragon doesn't breathe fire.

Avoid run-ons.

Combine sentences.

Avoid fragments.

Sentence types

Modifier placement

Find out how to edit Lara's draft on page 347.

Sentence Info

Types of Sentences

Sentences are grouped or classified according to their content. Statements of fact have a different form and meaning than questions, and questions have a different form and meaning than commands or exclamations. What do you want to say? The four different kinds of sentences—declarative, interrogative, imperative, and exclamatory—will help you say it.

Declarative Sentences

These sentences state facts or ideas and usually end with a period.

Apollo was a figure in ancient myths.

Any declarative, interrogative, or imperative sentence spoken with strong emotion can be followed by an exclamation point.

Interrogative Sentences

These sentences ask questions. They end with a question mark.

Didn't he battle the dragon Python?

Imperative Sentences

These sentences make commands or requests. They usually end with a period but can also end with an exclamation point when the command is really strong.

Tell me more, please.
Please hurry!

Exclamatory Sentences

These sentences express strong feeling and end with an exclamation point.

What an amazing story that was!
I loved that story!

Sentence Structures

Sentences are also classified according to their structures. You can learn about the four basic sentence structures below.

Simple Sentences

A simple sentence is made up of one independent clause, which may have compound parts and added phrases. **See Independent Clauses, page 340.**

Apollo slew a dragon.

Apollo and Hercules, two figures in mythology, fought with dragons and won.

Compound Sentences

A compound sentence is made up of two or more independent clauses joined by a co-ordinating conjunction: *and, but, for, or, so, yet.*

Some dragons had many heads, but most had only one.

Complex Sentences

A complex sentence is made up of one independent clause and one or more subordinate clauses. **See Subordinate Clauses, page 341.**

Although some dragons had many heads, most had only one.

As you can see, artists who draw dragons can be very creative.

Compound-Complex Sentences

A compound-complex sentence is made up of two or more independent clauses and one or more subordinate clauses.

Some dragons guarded treasures, and anyone who slew the beast won the treasure.

Parts of the Sentence

Tripped over a dragon lying in its cave isn't a sentence, but *I tripped* is. A sentence doesn't have to have a lot of words. What does it have to have? Most sentences have two basic parts, a **subject** and a **predicate.** Each part can be expanded. Some sentences also have **objects** and **complements** that complete the meaning of the verb or the subject.

Subject

The subject names what the sentence is about. The **complete subject** is all the words that tell what the sentence is about. It always contains the **simple subject**—a noun or pronoun that actually names the subject.

Predicate

The predicate tells about the subject. The **complete predicate** is all the words that tell what the subject is or does. Its key part is always a verb, called the **simple predicate.**

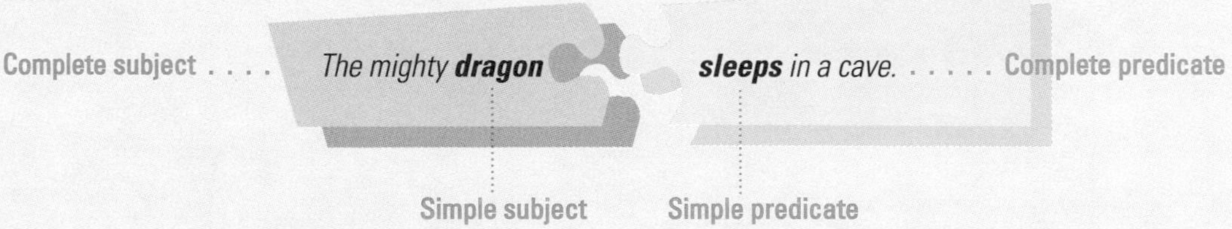

Complete subject . . . . *The mighty* ***dragon*** ***sleeps*** *in a cave.* . . . . . Complete predicate

Simple subject Simple predicate

Compound Subject

A compound subject is made of two or more simple subjects that are joined by a conjunction and share the same predicate.

Compound Predicate

A compound predicate is made of two or more verbs that are joined by a conjunction and share the same subject.

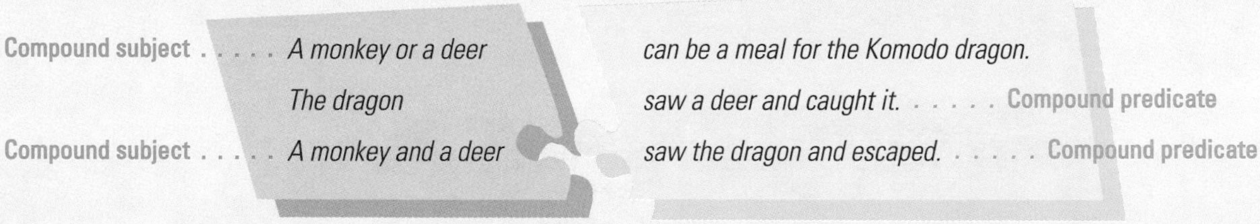

Compound subject . . . . . *A monkey or a deer* *can be a meal for the Komodo dragon.*

The dragon *saw a deer and caught it.* . . . . . Compound predicate

Compound subject . . . . . *A monkey and a deer* *saw the dragon and escaped.* . . . . . Compound predicate

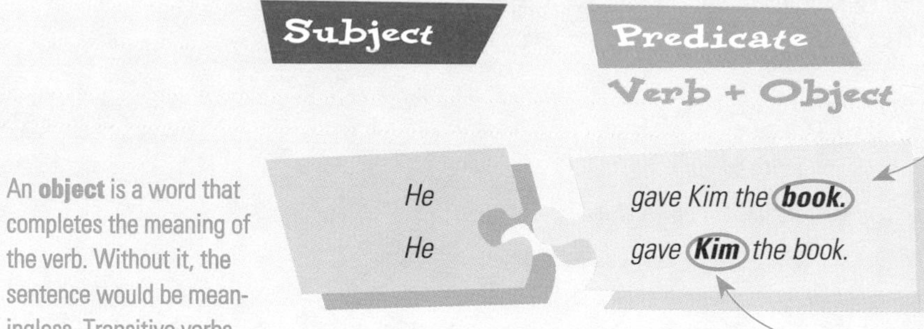
Subject
Predicate
Verb + Object
He
He
gave Kim the book.
gave Kim the book.

An **object** is a word that completes the meaning of the verb. Without it, the sentence would be meaningless. Transitive verbs always require an object.

The noun or pronoun that receives the action of the verb is called the **direct object.** To find the direct object, locate the verb. Then ask *what* or *whom* about it.

The **indirect object** is a noun or pronoun that answers the questions "To whom or for whom?" or "To what or for what?" about the verb. The words *to* and *for* are often implied.

Subject

Predicate

Verb + Subject Complement

Objects are used with action verbs. **Subject complements** are used with linking verbs. A subject complement can be a noun, a pronoun, or an adjective. It comes after a linking verb and says something about the subject.

Dragon Tales	***is*** *a fascinating book.*	Predicate noun
That	***must be*** *it.*	Predicate pronoun
The pictures	***look*** *real.*	Predicate adjective

Adding to the Basic Sentence Parts

All a sentence usually needs is a subject and a predicate, as in *Dragons fly.* But such plain sentences can be awfully boring. And what's more important, they don't say much. Fortunately, sentence-making can be a lot more creative. You can take the basic sentence and keep adding parts—words, phrases, and clauses—to it.

Basic sentence	*Dragons fly.*
Added parts	***Some of the fire-breathing*** *dragons* ***that we read about in myths and legends*** *fly* ***through the air on huge, batlike wings.***

Phrases

A phrase is a group of words, but not just any group. A phrase acts as a single word and doesn't have a subject and verb. You can liven up a basic sentence by adding a phrase to it.

Basic sentence	*Earl drew a dragon.*
Phrase added	*Earl drew a dragon* ***with wings.***
Phrase added	*Earl drew a dragon* ***flying through the air.***

Prepositional Phrases

A prepositional phrase begins with a preposition and ends with a noun or pronoun. The noun or pronoun is called the **object of the preposition.**

A prepositional phrase is usually one or two words long, though it can be longer. If there are any words modifying the noun or pronoun, they're part of the phrase too.

Earl drew a dragon ***with wings.*** — Object of preposition: *wings*; Preposition: *with*

It was a dragon ***with huge, batlike wings.*** — Object of preposition: *wings*; Preposition: *with*

A preposition can have more than one object in a phrase.

The dragon flew over ***land*** *and* ***sea.***

One sentence can have lots of prepositional phrases.

According to some legends, *dragons* ***with huge wings*** *would fly* ***over ships on the sea.***

A prepositional phrase can be used as an adjective or an adverb.

Most dragons have bodies ***like serpents.*** . . . . . Used as an adjective

Many ***of them*** *have wings too.*

Ancient people talked ***about dragons.*** . . . . . Used as an adverb

They were afraid ***of dragons.***

See page 307 for a list of commonly used prepositions.

Appositives and Appositive Phrases

An appositive is a noun or pronoun that goes next to another noun or pronoun to identify or explain it. If it has any modifying words, the appositive becomes an appositive phrase.

The appositive *Hercules* identifies the noun *hero.* No commas are necessary because Hercules is one of many heroes.

The hero ***Hercules*** *killed a dragon.*

The appositive phrase explains the noun *Hercules.* Commas are necessary to set off the phrase from the rest of the sentence.

Hercules, ***a hero of Greek myths,*** *killed a dragon.*

For more about punctuating appositives and appositive phrases, **see page 351.**

Verbals and Verbal Phrases

A verbal is a verb form that's used as a noun, an adverb, or an adjective. Add a modifier or object to the verbal, and it becomes a verbal phrase.

Verb	*The dragon* ***was roaring*** *like thunder.*
Verbal	*The* ***roaring*** *dragon crashed out of its cave.*
Verbal phrase	***Roaring like thunder,*** *the dragon crashed out of its cave.*

Participles and Participial Phrases

A participle is an *-ing* or *-ed* verb form that is used as an adjective. **See verbs on page 294.** It becomes a participial phrase when you add modifying words. A participial phrase can be used as an adjective to modify a noun or pronoun.

Present participle	*a* ***sleeping*** *dragon*
Past participle	*an* ***excited*** *dragon*
Participial phrase	*Is that a dragon* ***sleeping in the sun?***
Participial phrase	***Excited by the noise,*** *the dragon swished its mighty tail.*

Gerunds and Gerund Phrases

A gerund is an *-ing* verb form that is used as a noun. It becomes a gerund phrase when you add modifying words.

Verb	*Some dragons* ***fly*** *easily.*	
Gerund	***Flying*** *was easy for some dragons.*	
Gerund phrase	***Breathing fire*** *was another dragon pastime.*	Subject
Gerund phrase	*Dragons enjoyed* ***frightening people.***	Direct object
Gerund phrase	*They did not excel at* ***being affectionate.***	Indirect object
Gerund phrase	*They scared people by* ***breathing fire.***	Object of preposition
Gerund phrase	*A favourite hobby was* ***battling knights.***	Predicate noun
Gerund phrase	*Dragons loved one thing,* ***battling knights.***	Appositive

Infinitives and Infinitive Phrases

An infinitive is a verb form (*to* + basic form of verb) that is used as a noun, an adjective, or an adverb. Add words to an infinitive to make an infinitive phrase.

Verb	*Dragons usually liked* ***to roar.***	
Infinitive phrase	***To breathe fire*** *was easy for them.*	Noun/Subject
Infinitive phrase	*Dragons liked* ***to destroy things.***	Noun/Direct object
Infinitive phrase	*Now is the time* ***to read about dragons.***	Adjective
Infinitive phrase	*Some dragons were able* ***to fly.***	Adverb

Clauses

A clause, like a phrase, is a group of words. Unlike a phrase, however, a clause has both a subject and a verb.

Independent Clauses

An independent clause can stand alone. It can be a sentence itself, or it can work with other clauses.

As a complete sentence	*The dragon lashed its tail.*
With a subordinate clause	*The dragon lashed its tail because it was angry.*
Two independent clauses	*The dragon lashed its tail, and everyone trembled.*

Subordinate Clauses

A subordinate clause, also called a dependent clause, can't stand alone. It always needs to be connected to an independent clause. A subordinate clause begins with a word—such as *because* or *although*—that connects it to the independent clause. There are three types of subordinate clauses: adjective, adverb, and noun.

Adjective Clause

An adjective clause is used as an adjective to modify a noun or pronoun in the independent clause. It usually begins with a relative pronoun. **See Types of Pronouns, page 280.**

The dragon, ***which was angry,*** *lashed its tail.* . . . . . Modifies noun *dragon*

There once were many people ***who believed in dragons.*** . . . . . Modifies noun *people*

A dragon ***that is angry*** *may lash its tail.* . . . . . Modifies noun *dragon*

Adverb Clause

An adverb clause is used as an adverb to modify a verb, adjective, or adverb in the independent clause. It begins with a subordinating conjunction. **See Types of Conjunctions, page 310.**

Dragon stories were told ***before people could write.*** . . . . . Modifies verb *were told*

People grew frightened ***when they heard the tales.*** . . . . . Modifies adjective *frightened*

Made-up things can scare people more ***than real things do.*** . . . . . Modifies adverb *more*

Noun Clause

A noun clause is used as a noun within an independent clause. It can act in the same way as a noun in a sentence.

How legends begin *is an interesting topic.* . . . . . Subject

Did you know ***that dragons never existed?*** . . . . .Direct object

Give ***whoever asks*** *the book about dragons.* . . . . . Indirect object

Information about dragons is ***what they want.*** . . . . . Predicate noun

Sentence Know-how

There's a lot to know about how sentences work. This section will help you sort a sentence fragment from a run-on and natural word order from inverted word order. You'll also learn about combining sentences, adding variety to sentences, and fixing modifiers that aren't quite right.

Sentence Fragments

You can't take a bunch of words, add a capital letter and a period, and say it's a sentence. A sentence has to express a complete thought. A sentence fragment only expresses part of a thought. Something's missing, perhaps a subject, a verb, or both.

No subject	*Never saw a dragon.* . . . . . Fragment
Add subject	***Ancient people*** *never saw a dragon.* . . . . . Sentence
No verb	*Dragons like Puff the Magic Dragon.* . . . . . Fragment
Add verb	*Dragons like Puff the Magic Dragon* ***exist*** *in songs.* . . . . . Sentence
No subject or verb	*In art too.* . . . . . Fragment
Add subject and verb	***Dragons appear*** *in art too.* . . . . . Sentence
No independent clause	*Whenever Alma goes to the library.* . . . . . Fragment
Add independent clause	*Whenever Alma goes to the library,* ***she looks for books about dragons.*** . . . . . Sentence

Here's How

To Form Complete Sentences

- Add the missing words or phrases that will make the sentence a complete thought.

  Fragment *The dragon, which is fun to draw.*

  Sentence *The dragon, which is fun to draw, can be found in lots of storybooks.*

- Attach the fragment to a sentence that comes before or after it.

  Sentence + Fragment *Mia loves books. About dragons.*

  Sentence *Mia loves books about dragons.*

Many published works—novels, articles, essays—are full of fragments. Even this book has some. Many writers use fragments for special effect, especially in dialogue. For most formal writing, though, it's better to use complete sentences. Your writing will be taken more seriously if you do.

Run-on Sentences

While a sentence fragment expresses too little, a run-on tries to express too much. A run-on sentence consists of two or more complete thoughts written as one sentence. The thoughts are connected without showing where one ends and the other begins.

Sometimes two independent clauses—two complete thoughts—are run together with all the punctuation missing except the period at the end. Or, a comma is stuck in the middle even though it doesn't really belong there.

No punctuation	*Our library is great we go there a lot.*	Run-on
Comma fault	*Our library is great, we go there a lot.*	Run-on

Earl drew a dragon with huge, batlike wings, but the dragon was so big it didn't all fit on one page so Earl taped two pieces of paper together but he still needed more paper, by the time he was done drawing he'd used six pieces of paper!

Here's How

To Fix a Run-on Sentence

- Separate the run-on into two sentences.
  Our library is great. ***We*** *go there a lot.*
- Connect the sentences in a run-on with a comma and a co-ordinating conjunction.
  Our library is great, ***and*** *we go there a lot.*
- Connect the sentences in a run-on with a semicolon.
  Our library is great; we go there a lot.
- Add a subordinating conjunction to make one of the clauses dependent on the other.
  Because *our library is great, we go there a lot.*

Word Order

The word order of a sentence is determined by the position of the subject and the verb in that sentence. There are two kinds of word order in English: natural and inverted.

Natural Word Order

Sentences that name their subject and then say something about it are in natural word order. Most statements follow this pattern. Even commands where the subject is unstated are in natural word order.

Subject + verb

Indonesia is in Asia. . . . . . Statement

I've seen that book before. . . . . . Statement

The creature is very big. . . . . . Statement

(You) Watch out for that dragon! . . . . . Command

(You) Lend me your book about dragons. . . . . . Command

Inverted Word Order

Sometimes the complete predicate, or part of it, comes first. Then the word order is inverted, or turned around, so that the verb is followed by its subject. Most questions and most sentences that start with *here* or *there* follow this pattern.

Verb + subject

Is Indonesia in Asia? . . . . . Question

Have you ever seen this book? . . . . . Question

How big is the creature? . . . . . Question

Here is a book of dragon myths. . . . . . Here

There are many stories about dragons. . . . . . There

Here's How

To Find the Subject in an Inverted Sentence

Finding the subject in an inverted sentence can be tricky. Does it matter where the subject is? It sure does. You have to find the subject so you can make the verb agree with it. **For more on verb agreement, see page 298.**

- First find the verb or verb phrase.

  Through the forest ***raced*** *a Komodo dragon.*

  Is *the creature* ***coming*** *toward us?*

  There ***are*** *people on the island.* . . . . . Don't be fooled by *here* or *there.* They are never the subject.

- Then ask *who* or *what* about the verb. The answer will be the subject of the sentence.

  What ***raced*** *through the forest?* . . . . . a Komodo dragon

  What ***is coming*** *toward us?* . . . . . the creature

  Who ***are*** *on the island?* . . . . . people

- Double-check your answer by putting the sentence in natural word order: subject + verb.

  A ***Komodo dragon raced*** *through the forest.*

  The ***creature is coming*** *toward us.*

  People are *on the island.*

Combining Sentences

How do you get rid of short, choppy, rat-a-tat sentences? Combine separate sentences that have related content into longer, smoother ones. There are lots of possible combinations. Let your ear help you choose one.

Choppy *Dragons had snake bodies. They had bat wings too. They also had lion claws.* . . . . . Separate

Smooth *Dragons had snake bodies,* ***bat wings, and lion claws.*** . . . . . Combined

Combine related sentences with co-ordinating conjunctions.

Separate *Ancient Egypt had dragon stories. So did Greece.*

Combined *Ancient Egypt* ***and*** *Greece had dragon stories.* . . . . . Use *and.*

Separate *The stories were not real. People believed them.*

Combined *The stories were not real,* ***but*** *people believed them anyway.* . . . . . Use *but.*

Separate *In stories people fought dragons. Others ran away.*

Combined *In stories people fought dragons* ***or*** *ran away.* . . . . . Use *or.*

Combine sentences that have related content with phrases.

Separate *St. George slew a dragon. He did it with a lance.*

Combined ***With a lance,*** *St. George slew a dragon.* . . . . . Prepositional phrase

Separate *St. George slew a dragon. He used a lance.*

Combined ***Using a lance,*** *St. George slew a dragon.* . . . . . Verbal phrase

Separate *Artists like to paint St. George. He is the patron saint of England.*

Combined *Artists like to paint St. George,* ***the patron saint of England.*** . . . . . Appositive phrase

Combine related sentences with subordinate clauses.

Separate *European dragons are fierce. Asian dragons are friendly.*

Combined ***Although European dragons are fierce,*** *Asian dragons are friendly.* . . . . . Subordinate clause

Separate *Dragons are a symbol of good luck. Many Asian cultures believe that.*

Combined *Many Asian cultures believe* ***that dragons are a symbol of good luck.*** . . . . . Subordinate clause

Sentence Variety

You can vary the rhythm of your sentences by moving certain parts around—as long as you're careful where you place them. You don't need to arrange every sentence in the same way. Keep your reader engaged and interested in your writing by using a variety of sentence types and structures, phrases and clauses, and word orders.

You can use a variety of sentence types.

Many people parade as dragons on the Chinese New Year. . . . . . Declarative sentence

Did you know that many people parade as dragons on the Chinese New Year? . . . . . Interrogative sentence

Let me tell you about the people who parade as dragons on the Chinese New Year. . . . . . Imperative sentence

What a tremendous sight it was to see people parading as dragons on the Chinese New Year! . . . . . Exclamatory sentence

Be sure to use a variety of sentence structures.

Many people parade as dragons on the Chinese New Year. . . . . . Simple sentence

Many people parade as dragons on the Chinese New Year, but I could only see a few of them from where I stood. . . . . . Compound sentence

Because so many people parade as dragons on the Chinese New Year, I think that the dragon could be an important symbol. . . . . . Complex sentence

The parade that I watched was on the Chinese New Year, and many people were dressed up as dragons. . . . . . Compound-complex sentence

Experiment with different kinds of phrases and clauses.

On the Chinese New Year, many people parade as dragons. . . . . . Prepositional phrase

When the Chinese New Year comes, many people parade as dragons. . . . . . Adverb clause

You can rearrange the word order of some of your sentences.

Many people parade as dragons on the Chinese New Year. . . . . . Natural word order

There are many people who parade as dragons on the Chinese New Year. . . . . . Inverted word order

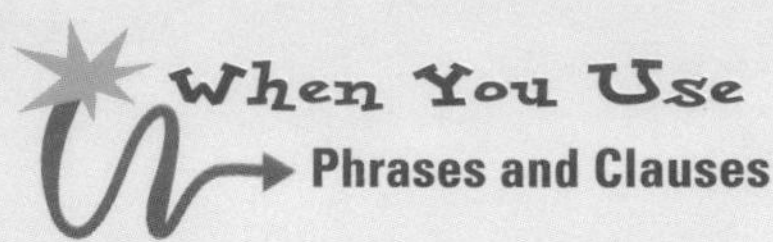

When You Use Phrases and Clauses

You already know how to use phrases and clauses because you use them all the time when you write and talk. There are a few tips you can follow, though, when you want to make your writing clear.

Watch out for misplaced and dangling modifiers.

A modifying phrase should go with the word that it modifies. Be sure to double-check the modifiers in your sentences so you don't say something that sounds strange.

Basic sentence *People wind through the streets.*
Modifying phrase *wearing dragon costumes*

Basic sentence *The streets are crowded.*
Modifying phrase *making lots of noise.*

A modifier is called "misplaced" when it's put next to the wrong word in a sentence. Do the streets wear dragon costumes or do people? The phrase *wearing dragon costumes* is in the wrong place.

No *People wind through the streets wearing dragon costumes.*
Yes! *People wearing dragon costumes wind through the streets.*

A modifier is called "dangling" when it doesn't have a word to modify in the sentence. The phrase *making lots of noise* is dangling because there's no noun for it to modify. Streets can't make noise, people can.

No *Making lots of noise, the streets are crowded.*
Yes! *Making lots of noise, people crowd the streets.*

Know the difference between *who* and *whom.*

You can use *who* if it is the subject of its own clause. You can use *whom* if it is the object in its own clause. Look at the clause by itself to find its subject, verb, and object.

No *I wonder whom wrote it.*
Yes! *I wonder* ***who*** *wrote it.* . . . . . Subject of clause
No *I wonder who I can ask.*
Yes! *I wonder* ***whom*** *I can ask.* . . . . . Object in clause

Know the difference between an essential clause and a non-essential clause.

Is the clause needed to identify the noun, or does it just add extra information? A clause that identifies a noun is considered **essential** to the sentence. It isn't set off with commas. A clause that provides extra information is considered **non-essential** and does need to be set off with commas.

Essential *Dragons that breathe fire are common in ancient legends.* . . . . . No commas

Non-essential *Dragons, which often breathe fire, are imaginary monsters.* . . . . . Use commas

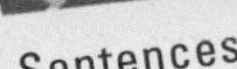

Edit It!

Lara Haddad had some sentence problems in her report draft. Read about how she changed them, and you'll learn how to revise your sentences.

Don't let your sentences run on.

DRAFT *You may think dragons don't exist, they do.* . . . . . Avoid run-ons

What's Wrong? Two complete thoughts, or independent clauses, need to be separated by more than just a comma. Add *but* after the comma.

Edit It! *You may think dragons don't exist,* ***but*** *they do.*

Combine sentences that can go together.

DRAFT *There is a real-life dragon. It lives on an island. The island is called Komodo. It is in Indonesia.* . . . . . Combine sentences

What's Wrong? Many short sentences in a row can sound choppy and immature. Combine them by using a subordinate clause or a participial phrase.

Edit It! *There is a real-life dragon* ***that lives on the island of Komodo in Indonesia.*** . . Subordinate clause

Or

Edit It! *There is a real-life dragon* ***living on the island of Komodo in Indonesia.*** . . . . . Participial phrase

Write complete thoughts.

DRAFT *The biggest lizard in the world, in fact.* . . . . . Avoid fragments

What's Wrong? It's only a fragment; it has no subject or verb. Add *It is* as subject and verb.

Edit It! ***It is*** *the biggest lizard in the world, in fact.*

Use different kinds of sentences.

DRAFT *This is what the dragon looks like.* . . . . . Sentence types

What's Wrong? Declarative sentences are the sentences that we use the most. For variety, try sprinkling different kinds of sentences—interrogative, imperative, and exclamatory—throughout your writing.

Edit It! ***What amazing features belong to the Komodo dragon!***

Watch out for misplaced modifiers.

DRAFT *It has a powerful body and a long, flat head with a mighty tail.* . . . . . Modifier placement

What's Wrong? It's not the head that has a mighty tail. Move the phrase next to the word *body,* which it modifies.

Edit It! *It has a powerful body* ***with a mighty tail and a long, flat head.***

Punctuation

Punctuation marks are standard symbols used in writing. They help the reader by showing where sentences end and where pauses occur. Your writing will be clearer and more polished if you know what the marks of punctuation mean and how to use them.

Punctuation Know-how

There's a lot to know about the various punctuation marks. Follow these guidelines and your writing will be clearer and more accurate.

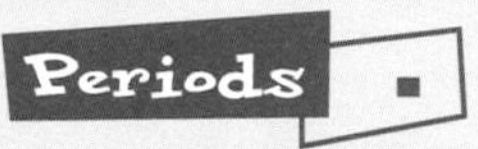
Periods

A period signals that a statement, a mild command, an indirect question, or a polite request has ended.

Statement	*Nadia is in grade eight this year.*
Mild command	*Remember to shut the door after you leave.*
Indirect question	*I asked if I could go to the library.*
Polite request	*Will you please send me your latest catalogue.*

A period after initials and many abbreviations shows that letters have been left out.

Initials	*T. S. Eliot*		*L. M. Montgomery*		
Abbreviations					
Titles of people	*Mr.*	*Ms.*	*M.D.*	*R.N.*	*Prof.*
Geographic locations	*Rd.*	*St.*	*Ont.*	*Man.*	*Que.*
Time references	*A.M.*	*P.M.*	*B.C.*	*Thurs.*	*Feb.*

If a sentence ends in an abbreviation, use only one period. But if the sentence needs a question mark or exclamation point, use the abbreviation period plus the other mark.

The show begins at 7:00 P.M.
*Will it be over by 9:00 P.M.**?***

Some abbreviations do **not** require periods.

Acronyms, words formed from the initial letters of a series of words, are often written without periods.

CBC	*(**C**anadian **B**roadcasting **C**orporation)*
km	*(**k**ilometres)*
radar	*(stands for **ra**dio **d**etecting **a**nd **r**anging)*
DOS	*(stands for **d**isk **o**perating **s**ystem)*
UNICEF	*(stands for **U**nited **N**ations **I**nternational **C**hildren's **E**mergency **F**und)*

Question Marks ?

A question mark signals that a direct question, an incomplete question, or a statement intended as a question has been completed.

Question	*Where did Kim Wan-soo get her cats?*
Incomplete questions	*When? How many? What kind?*
Intended question	*Kim has four cats?*

Exclamation Points !

An exclamation point shows that an exclamatory statement, a strong command, or an interjection expressing strong emotion has ended.

Exclamatory statement	*What a wonderful surprise!*
Strong command	*Get out of that street!*
Interjections	*Hey! Phew! Unbelievable! Wow!*

Sometimes an interjection can appear before a short exclamatory sentence or a question. You can use either a comma or an exclamation point after the interjection.

With comma	*Phew, whose socks are these?*
With exclamation point	*Phew! Whose socks are these?*

Commas ,

Commas separate items in a series.

A series consists of three or more items of the same kind: words, phrases, clauses, or numbers.

Words	*My morning classes are art, English, and science.*
Phrases	*Run over the bridge, around the tree, and up the hill.*
Clauses	*I saw a green T-shirt, I liked it, and I bought it.*
Numbers	*The answers in order are 3, 119, and 647.*

You do **not** use commas if *and* or if *or* connects all the items in a series.

No *Omar worked, and saved, and then bought a new bicycle.*

Yes! *Omar worked and saved and then bought a new bicycle.*

Words that work as a unit do **not** need to be separated by a comma.

No *We ate bacon, and eggs, toast, and cereal for breakfast.*

Yes! *We ate* ***bacon and eggs,*** *toast, and cereal for breakfast.*

Commas separate adjectives that come before a noun.

Try saying the word *and* between the adjectives. If *and* makes sense, then the words should be separated with a comma.

We live in a small cozy house.

We live in a small and cozy house.

We live in a small, cozy house.

A comma isn't necessary if the word *and* doesn't make sense when it's inserted between the adjectives.

No *Anna caught a huge and red snapper.*

Yes! *Anna caught a huge red snapper.*

A comma separates clauses in a compound sentence.

Put a comma before the joining word, or conjunction.

*I received ice skates three years ago**, and** they still fit.*

A comma isn't necessary if two verbs share one subject.

No *I own ice skates, and use them almost daily.*

Yes! *I own ice skates and use them almost daily.*

A comma is optional when the clauses in a compound sentence are very short. **See page 335 for more about compound sentences.**

O.K. *Ben drove, and I gave directions.*

O.K. *Ben drove and I gave directions.*

A comma sets off a word, phrase, or clause that introduces a sentence.

Word	***Actually,*** *the first automobile was funny looking.*
Phrase	***Instead of a steering wheel,*** *it had a stick.*
Clause	***Although it is about a hundred years old,*** *the car still runs.*

You do **not** need to use a comma when the opening phrase is short. Use a comma, however, when the opening phrase is long.

Short phrase	***At first*** *I couldn't see what was ahead of me.*	No comma
Long phrase	***As my eyes adjusted to the dimness,*** *I began to make out shapes.*	Use comma

A comma sets off an interrupter.

An interrupter is a word or phrase that breaks into the main thought of a sentence. It supplies extra information and can be put almost anywhere in the sentence.

The fishermen, ***incidentally,*** *came ashore to dry their fish.*

Incidentally, *the fishermen came ashore to dry their fish.*

The fishermen came ashore, ***incidentally,*** *to dry their fish.*

Common Interrupters

EXAMPLES

after all	**by the way**	**for example**
furthermore	**however**	**in fact**
in my opinion	**incidentally**	**nevertheless**
of course	**on the other hand**	**therefore**

A comma sets off a noun of direct address.

When you speak or write to someone directly, you set off that person's name with a comma.

Your report was interesting, ***Nura.***

Another report, ***class,*** *will be due in two weeks.*

Guy, *how would you like to write about the fur trade?*

A comma sets off the speaker from a quotation.

The comma falls inside the quotation marks when it comes at the end of the quotation.

Sara said, "I can't type."

"I'll type it for you," Eva replied.

Commas can set off words, phrases, and clauses that are not necessary to the basic idea of the sentence.

A word, phrase, or clause is not necessary if it adds information that can be left out without changing the main idea of the sentence.

Main sentence	*Canada's coastline is one of the longest.*
Added information	*Canada's coastline,* ***which stretches for more than 243 797 kilometres,*** *is one of the longest.*

You do **not** use commas with words, phrases, and clauses that **are** necessary to the basic idea of the sentence. A word, phrase, or clause is necessary if it clarifies or identifies a noun.

Noun unidentified	*My sister plays on the hockey team.*
Noun identified	*My sister* ***Miranda*** *plays on the hockey team.*

If the speaker has only one sister, set off the name with commas.

My sister, ***Miranda,*** *plays on the hockey team.*

Use commas to set off dates, places, addresses, and titles.

Dates	*On Friday, March 3, 1993, Ms. Lee bought a boat.*
Places	*Jane was born in Vancouver, British Columbia.*
Addresses	*We live at 12 Gary Road West, Sudbury, Ontario.*
Titles	*My father's name is Alan Oates, Esquire.*

You do **not** need to use a comma between month and year.

No	*We drove to Thunder Bay in January, 1993.*
Yes!	*We drove to Thunder Bay in January 1993.*

You do **not** need a comma before a postal code.

No	*Coquitlam, B.C., V3K 3H8*
Yes!	*Coquitlam, B.C. V3K 3H8*

Use a comma after the salutation of a friendly letter and after all letter closings.

Salutations	*Dear Goldie,*	*Dear Dad,*
Closings	*Your friend,*	*Sincerely yours,*

Semicolons

A semicolon joins independent clauses in a compound sentence when the words *and, but,* or *or* are not used.

New Brunswick joined Confederation in 1867; Newfoundland didn't join Confederation until 1949.

Semicolons are used in a series to separate items that already contain commas.

On our last vacation, we stopped at Vancouver, British Columbia; Banff, Alberta; Regina, Saskatchewan; and Winnipeg, Manitoba.

Use a semicolon between independent clauses connected by transition words.

Our vacation was terrific; however, I was glad to get home after being on the road for two weeks.

Transition Words

EXAMPLES

consequently	**furthermore**	**however**
instead	**moreover**	**nevertheless**
otherwise	**therefore**	**thus**

Colons

A colon can introduce a list, especially after words like *the following* or *these.*

My favourite fish include ***the following:*** *sockeye salmon, halibut, and red snapper.*

These *are my favourite fish: sockeye salmon, halibut, and red snapper.*

You do **not** need a colon after a verb or a preposition.

Verb *My favourite fish* ***are*** *sockeye salmon, halibut, and red snapper.*

Preposition *This salmon was caught* ***by*** *my Uncle Lei.*

A colon can introduce a long or formal quotation.

As Shakespeare said in As You Like It: *"All the world's a stage, / And all the men and women merely players."*

You can use a colon after the introductory salutation in a formal letter.

Dear Ms. Feld: *Dear Sir or Madam:*

You can use a colon between numbers showing hours and minutes.

7:18 P.M. *12:01* A.M.

Dashes
—

A dash is a long horizontal mark that sets off words that break into the main idea.

Large numbers of immigrants from Great Britain—England, Ireland, Scotland and Wales—came to Canada after the War of 1812.

Dashes can be used to show an abrupt change in thought.

Dashes can also show a hesitation, an interruption, or a change in tone.

Here comes the bus—oh, no, where's my homework?

"Do you think we—" Gina began, but she was interrupted by Frank .

Dashes can introduce a summary or development of what has come before.

Aerobic exercise can raise your heart rate, enlarge your heart muscle, and increase your endurance—in other words, it's good for you.

Parentheses
( )

You can use parentheses to set off added information.

Punctuation that belongs to the parenthetical material goes **inside** the parentheses. Punctuation that belongs to the whole sentence goes **outside** the parentheses.

Inside	*Jared drove us to the store (Uncle Pete had said, "I can't drive") and then took us home.*
Outside	*Coast-to-coast rail service was provided in 1886 by the Canadian Pacific Railway (now CP Rail).*

Hyphens -

A hyphen is a short horizontal mark that is used in some compound nouns and with certain prefixes and suffixes.

Most compound nouns are **not** connected by hyphens, however. Check your dictionary to be sure.

sister-in-law *ex-mayor* *self-control* *all-star* *non-fiction*

A hyphen connects compound adjectives that precede nouns.

You do **not** need to use hyphens in most compound adjectives that follow nouns or with adverbs ending in *-ly*.

Hyphen	*It is a* ***25-year-old*** *house.*
No hyphen	*The house is 25 years old.*
No hyphen	*It's a carefully constructed house.*

You use hyphens when spelling out numbers from twenty-one through ninety-nine.

twenty-three *eighty-seven* *ninety-two*

You can use a hyphen to break a word at the end of a line.

Use your dictionary to double-check where a word may be hyphenated.

No
pun-ctu-ate

Yes!
punc-tu-ate

Apostrophes

You can use an apostrophe and *s* to form possessive nouns.

See page 277 for more about possessive nouns.

Keiko's first date *driver's seat* *Mr. Jones's book*

You can use an apostrophe and *s* to form the possessive of indefinite pronouns.

anyone's *somebody's* *everybody's*

You can use an apostrophe and *s* to form the plural of a letter, a number, a symbol, or a word used as a word.

several A*'s* *some 9's* *no #'s* *too many* the*'s*

An apostrophe stands for the missing letters in a contraction.

don't = do n**o**t he'll = he **wi**ll it's = it **i**s

Underlining and Italics

Underline or italicize the titles of long works.

Use underlining if you're writing by hand or using a typewriter. Use italics if you're using a word processor. Long works include books, plays, long poems, newspapers, magazines, films, radio and TV series, operas, record albums and CDs, and the names of ships, spacecraft, and trains.

Find out how to capitalize titles on page 325.

Book	<u>All Creatures Great and Small</u> or *All Creatures Great and Small*
Magazine	<u>Seventeen</u> magazine or *Seventeen* magazine
Film	<u>Aladdin</u> or *Aladdin*
TV series	<u>Road to Avonlea</u> or *Road to Avonlea*
CD	<u>The Joshua Tree</u> or *The Joshua Tree*
Ship	<u>Titanic</u> or *Titanic*

Underline or italicize letters used as letters, words used as words, and words from languages other than English.

Letters as letters	Is that a <u>T</u> or an <u>F</u>?
	Is that a *T* or an *F*?
Words as words	Your report overuses <u>therefore</u>.
	Your report overuses *therefore*.
Non-English words	<u>Noche</u> means "night" in Spanish.
	Noche means "night" in Spanish.

Quotation Marks " " and ' '

Quotation marks can set off a person's exact words.

Quotation marks indicate where a speaker's exact words begin and end.

Meera said, "Pollution is ruining our planet."

You do **not** need to set off words that aren't the speaker's exact words.

No *Roy said that "Electricity changed life for the better."*

Yes! *Roy said that electricity changed life for the better.*

A quotation within another quotation requires single quotation marks.

Frank asked, "Who wrote, 'Life is a fragile dew-drop'?"

Here's How

To Punctuate with Quotation Marks

Find out how to use capitalization with quotations on page 322.

- Always put commas inside quotation marks.
  "Cars are a mixed blessing," said Moira. . . . . . **Inside quotation marks**
- When a quotation mark ends a sentence, the period falls inside of the quotation marks.
  Moira said, "Cars are a mixed blessing." . . . . . **Inside quotation marks**
- Exclamation points and question marks fall inside only if they are part of the quotation.
  Zhura asked, "Is that what you think?" . . . . . **Inside quotation marks**
  Did Moira say, "Cars are a mixed blessing"? . . . . . **Outside quotation marks**
- Colons and semicolons go outside the quotation marks unless they are part of the quotation.
  Zhura said, "I agree"; however, he changed his mind later. . . . . . **Outside quotation marks**
- Remember to begin a new paragraph for each new speaker's words.
  "I believe," said Moira, "that cars are a mixed blessing."
  "I disagree," offered Zhura.
  "What?" Moira asked sharply. "Look at what they've done to the environment."

Quotation marks enclose titles of short works.

A work is generally considered to be short when it is part of a longer work, such as a book, an audiotape, or a television series. Short works include short stories, articles, poems, songs, and radio or TV episodes.

Short story	"A Mother in Manville"
Magazine article	"Today's Hottest T-shirts"
Poem	"The Road Not Taken"
Song	"Over the Rainbow"

Paragraphs

You've found some exciting words and put them together to make terrific sentences. Now all you have to do is put the sentences together, and you'll have a good paragraph, right? Not quite. These parts have to fit together to create the effect you want.

Words go together like building blocks. Use your words to express yourself!

Contents

Constructing Paragraphs

A paragraph is a group of sentences that develops a main idea. The beginning of a new paragraph signals that a new idea will be introduced, a new voice will speak, or the main idea of the previous paragraph will be expanded and developed.

For more about paragraphs, read on!

DRAFT

"Trying Out for Track and Field"

by Bryant Lawlor

Effective topic sentence?

Some people want to be part of a team and aren't good at team play. Why don't you try out for track and field? If you're a good runner, there are lots of events to choose from. Javelin and discus throwers develop strong arms. Sprinters develop strong legs. Find out what you're good at. I'm sure there's a track or field event that you could enter and have fun at.

Coherent?

Enough supporting details?

Well organized?

Satisfying closing sentence?

Find out how to edit Bryant's draft on page 367.

Paragraph Info

Parts of a Paragraph

In non-fiction writing, good paragraphs have three main parts: a main idea that is expressed in a topic sentence or implied indirectly, one or more supporting sentences, and a closing sentence that lets readers know you've completed your thought.

Main Idea

The main idea of a paragraph can be clearly expressed in a topic sentence, which can appear anywhere in the paragraph. A main idea can also be implied, or suggested, although it is not spelled out in one sentence. Descriptive paragraphs and dialogue often express a main idea in this way.

Supporting Sentences

Supporting sentences explain the main idea of a paragraph. They develop your idea with logically related details, facts, reasons, and examples. You link your sentences one to another so that each new sentence clearly shows its relationship to those already written.

Closing Sentence

A good closing sentence reinforces the main idea, adds something new, and leaves the reader with a manageable chunk of information to think about.

Walking is probably the best all-around exercise for you, whether you're age nine or ninety! It can strengthen your heart and lungs without overworking them. It can give your whole body a good workout without straining any part of it. Better still, expensive equipment and flashy outfits aren't required. You need a comfortable pair of shoes or sneakers and your everyday clothes. You don't have to find a special stadium, court, or track. No matter where you live, it should be possible to find a safe place to walk. At the end of a good walk, you'll find yourself refreshed and cheery, rather than exhausted and dripping with sweat. Walking has all of these advantages and, best of all, it's fun.

Features of a Paragraph

Besides the three basic parts, a good paragraph has other important features: organization, unity, and coherence. Organization allows for an orderly development of the main idea. Unity means that all the sentences are focussed on the main idea. Coherence provides smooth connections between the sentences, like the links that form a chain.

Organization

The way you build a paragraph around your main idea gives the paragraph shape. The way you arrange your support material gives order to your paragraph. It will be easier for you to develop your thoughts fully and clearly in a paragraph if you have a sense of its shape and order.

Shape

The information in your paragraph can be organized to follow a variety of "shapes." These shapes are **not** literal visual images, but ways to describe the flow of information in a paragraph.

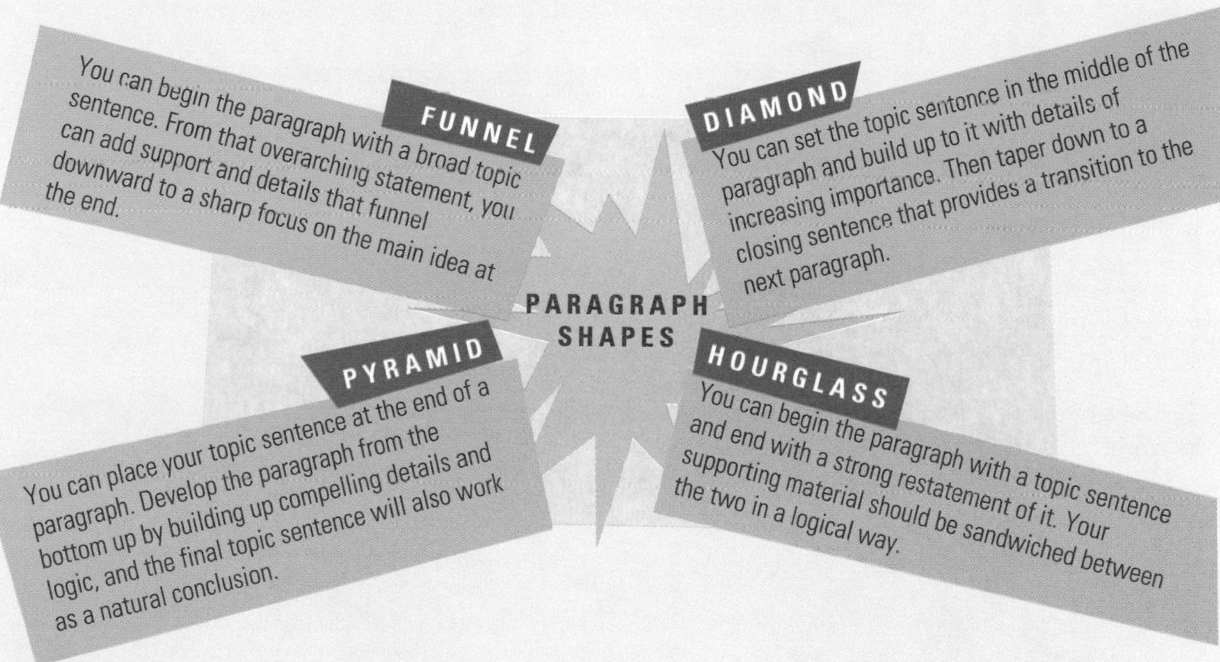
PARAGRAPH SHAPES
FUNNEL
You can begin the paragraph with a broad topic sentence. From that overarching statement, you can add support and details that funnel downward to a sharp focus on the main idea at the end.
DIAMOND
You can set the topic sentence in the middle of the paragraph and build up to it with details of increasing importance. Then taper down to a closing sentence that provides a transition to the next paragraph.
PYRAMID
You can place your topic sentence at the end of a paragraph. Develop the paragraph from the bottom up by building up compelling details and logic, and the final topic sentence will also work as a natural conclusion.
HOURGLASS
You can begin the paragraph with a topic sentence and end with a strong restatement of it. Your supporting material should be sandwiched between the two in a logical way.

Order

The information in your paragraph can be organized to follow a variety of "orders." With these orders you can argue a specific point, narrate a sequence of events, or describe a particular place.

Logical Order

Organizing a paragraph in logical order means arranging its details and information in a way that makes sense. Logical order can help you position your ideas for a persuasive letter or a research report so that they are clear and easy to follow.

Types of Logical Order

Most important to least important
I had run the race of my life. The crowd cheered.

Least important to most important
The crowd cheered. I had run the race of my life.

General to specific
It was a beautiful day, but I felt sad that summer was almost over.

Specific to general
I felt sad that summer was almost over, but it was a beautiful day!

Most familiar to least familiar
I glanced at Spot. Then I faced the snarling bear.

Least familiar to most familiar
I faced the snarling bear. Then I glanced at Spot.

Simplest to most complex
That single drop of rain grew into a mighty storm.

Most complex to simplest
That mighty storm began with a single drop of rain.

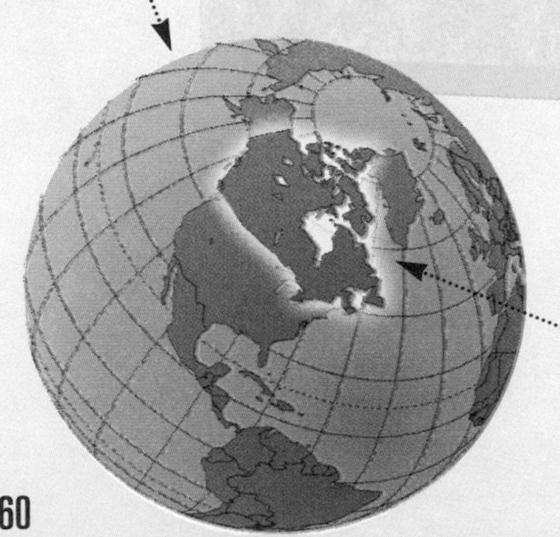
General
the World
Specific
Canada

Time Order

This organizing method focusses on the order in which events take place in time. Time order ensures that events in a story or a personal narrative unfold in the proper sequence. Whether moving from past to present, present to future, or both, time order helps the reader sort out what happened when.

Time Expressions

- **within minutes**
- **now**
- **then**
- **before**
- **later**
- **as time passed**
- **eventually**
- **immediately**
- **soon**
- **previously**

__From the moment__ I was out of the starting block, I tried to keep my mind on just one lap at a time. __First__ I pulled my thoughts away from the poor start I'd made. __Then__ I focussed on the goal ahead. __Before__ I knew it, I had reached the finish line and everybody was clapping.

Past
Present
Future

Spatial Order

This organizing method focusses on where things stand physically in space. Descriptive details are arranged in relation to one another with the help of expressions such as *down*, *between*, or *next to*. Spatial order can help you describe your settings and characters in ways that your readers will "see."

Spatial Expressions

- **across**
- **down**
- **between**
- **beyond**
- **over**
- **next to**
- **distant**
- **nearby**
- **adjacent**

The ballpark was quiet and empty. I pushed my cap __back__ on my head and looked __down__ at Daisy, my dog. She was walking __between__ me and Kate as we crossed centre field and moved __toward__ home plate. The game was over. We had lost, but there would be other games.

Types of order:

top
to
bottom

side to side

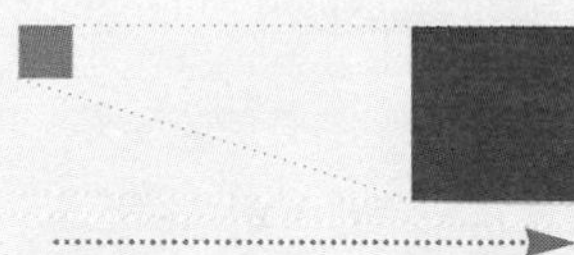
farther point to closer point

Unity

Your paragraph has unity when every sentence is focussed on the main idea. All the pieces fit together. Not one sentence takes off in pursuit of a different point.

Unifying Expressions

in addition to
furthermore
in the same way
all together
also
but

Weak

Some people, like Wayne Gretzky, are natural athletes. My sister is a great runner. One day last month, I tripped over the curb and broke my arm.

Better!

Some people, like Wayne Gretzky, are natural athletes. ***In the same way,*** *my sister has always been a great runner. I* ***also*** *dream of having natural grace and agility,* ***but*** *since the day I tripped over the curb and broke my arm, I have had my doubts.*

Coherence

Even if every sentence is hard at work developing the main idea of your paragraph, your writing may still be difficult to follow. If you make your sentences flow together and build on one another, your paragraph will make sense!

Transitional Expressions

first
next
then
finally
but
even though
because
however
therefore
for example
meanwhile

Weak

This spring I decided to try the low hurdles. I didn't know how I'd do. I hoped I wouldn't fall flat on my face. I got into the starting block. I took off. I knocked down the first hurdle. Sailing over the second and third hurdles, I had room to spare. The fourth hurdle came up. I felt like I'd learned to fly.

Better!

This spring I decided to try the low hurdles. I didn't know how I'd do, ***but*** *I hoped I wouldn't fall flat on my face.* ***First*** *I got into the starting block.* ***Next*** *I heard the coach blow the whistle.* ***Then*** *I took off.* ***Even though*** *I knocked down the first hurdle, I sailed over the second and third hurdles with room to spare.* ***By*** *the fourth hurdle, I felt like I'd learned to fly.*

Types of Paragraphs

There are different types of paragraphs for different kinds of writing. A descriptive paragraph has a particular function. Narrative paragraphs and paragraphs of explanation have entirely different functions. Your choice of paragraph depends on your purpose in writing. Sometimes different types of paragraphs may need to be combined. For example, an explanatory paragraph may include description or persuasion.

Descriptive Paragraphs

This kind of paragraph describes a person, place, or thing as vividly as possible. It makes the reader see, hear, and sense everything that will bring the subject to life.

I was within twenty yards of the Elkington lion before I saw him. He lay sprawled in the morning sun, huge, black-maned, and gleaming with life. His tail moved slowly, stroking the rough grass like a knotted rope end. His body was sleek and easy, making a mould where he lay, a cool mould, that would be there when he had gone. He was not asleep; he was only idle. He was rusty-red, and soft, like a strokable cat.

From *West with the Night* by Beryl Markham

When You Write

Descriptive Paragraphs

1. Create an overall impression of the person, place, or thing you are describing.
2. You can use sensory details of sight, sound, taste, smell, colour, and touch as well as details of time, space, and motion.
3. Similes and metaphors can make your description more interesting. **For an explanation of these writing tools, see page 43.**
4. Use exact words whenever possible.

Narrative Paragraphs

A narrative paragraph tells a story or relates an event. You can use this type of paragraph not only in a formal narrative, but also in any form of writing whenever you want to tell a story.

It was Tuesday, July 14, 1987. Lydia Marie Barragan, 24, felt exhilarated. About a month earlier, she and her fiancé, Jean-Jacques LeFrancq, 28, both from France, had arrived at their Northwest Territories camp, 120 kilometres above the Arctic Circle, for a year-long study of caribou. Now, with a supply of fish stored in a pit beneath the tundra, they were almost ready for winter and the first migrating herds.

From "Terror Above the Arctic Circle" by Sheldon Kelly

When You Write

Narrative Paragraphs

1. Establish the point of view from which you are writing: first person, second person, or third person.
2. Set the scene with your opening sentence.
3. Organize the events of your paragraph in time order.

Explanatory Paragraphs

Explanatory paragraphs explain a circumstance, event, or experience. They answer the questions *who, what, when, why, where,* and *how.* Use description, comparison and contrast, or cause-and-effect relationships to make your explanation clear.

Wheelchair racers are incredibly fast. The world record in the marathon for a wheelchair is almost an hour faster than the record for a racer on foot. The wheelchair athletes' immense arm and upper-body strength enables them to propel themselves forward at great speed.

From "Pacesetting Athletes" by Nancy Nienhuis

When You Write

Explanatory Paragraphs

1. Clearly state the topic that needs explanation.
2. Support your topic sentence with detailed information.
3. Be sure to research your topic to make your explanation accurate and complete.

Instructive Paragraphs

An instructive paragraph gives detailed, or step-by-step, instructions. You may need to use explanation, description, comparison and contrast, or cause-and-effect relationships to make your instructions clear.

Try this experiment: take a piece of paper and outline all seven continents. Then cut out each continent separately and lay all the pieces on a table, positioning them to resemble the earth's surface. Now push the continents together and try to fit them into one big land mass. . . . it's easy to imagine that they once were part of the same continent—which, in fact, they were. It's all a matter of plate tectonics.

From "Travelling Turf" by Neal Shusterman

When You Write

Instructive Paragraphs

1. State your main idea clearly.
2. You can organize your instructions step by step in logical order.
3. Be sure to warn the reader of possible difficulties in the procedure you're describing.
4. Remember to use explanation, description, comparison and contrast, or cause-and-effect relationships whenever they may be helpful.

Summary Paragraphs

This kind of paragraph summarizes, in one or more stand-alone sentences, the information or events from a longer piece of writing. You can use it as the closing paragraph of an essay or report, or by itself as a brief review.

Today Lydia lives quietly in the Pyrenees Mountains near her close-knit family. Memories of her Arctic ordeal stay fresh. It was there she learned of human courage and resilience and the fragile preciousness of life. Her determination to survive stands as an inspiration to others—just as Jean-Jacques was to her.

From "Terror Above the Arctic Circle" by Sheldon Kelly

When You Write

Summary Paragraphs

1. Briefly restate the main points or events that have been outlined.
2. You can summarize the conclusions that may be drawn from these points.

Comparison and Contrast Paragraphs

This kind of paragraph either compares the ways in which two things are alike or contrasts the ways in which they are different. Sometimes it both compares and contrasts. Comparison and contrast are useful when writing to explain, to inform, or to persuade.

Sports shoes used to be simple, inexpensive affairs made to be worn on gym floors or tennis courts. They were very different from the high-tech, big-bucks sports shoes of today, but kids loved them even then. Those early canvas shoes, known as "tennis shoes," were rumoured to cause flat feet, and kids were discouraged from wearing them outside of gym class. However, by the time sports shoes became a craze in the 1950s, canvas shoes were being produced with good arch support and rubber soles. Today, sports shoes are approved footwear and often cost far more than leather shoes.

When You Write

Comparison and Contrast Paragraphs

1. Choose clear-cut similarities and differences for your comparisons and contrasts.
2. Use exact descriptive words to make similarities and differences as vivid as possible.
3. You can clarify your arguments by using expressions such as these:

   Comparison: *even then, similarly, both . . . and*

   Contrast: *but, on the other hand, whereas*

Cause-and-Effect Paragraphs

A cause-and-effect paragraph answers the question *why*. It shows how one event brought about another. Cause-and-effect relationships are useful in writing that is meant to inform, to explain, or to persuade.

Imagine the world before television. Now imagine the power of the radio in such a world. It couldn't broadcast pictures, but it played music, announced the news, delivered jokes, told stories, and more. It transformed the car into a juke box on wheels and brought families together for an hour or two each evening, hungry for news or a favourite program. For many North Americans in the 1930s, a good radio play was the finest kind of entertainment. They would sit quietly by their radios, their imaginations primed, while unseen dramas slowly unfolded right before their ears.

From "The Martians Are Coming!" by Lauren E. Wolk

When You Write

Cause-and-Effect Paragraphs

1. State both cause and effect as clearly as you can.
2. Be sure to show how the cause and the effect are related.
3. You can use words that express cause and effect, such as *why, when, because, as a result, so,* and *therefore.*

Persuasive Paragraphs

A persuasive paragraph uses reasons and examples to convince readers that a particular opinion is valid. A persuasive paragraph may be one part of a longer piece of writing, such as a persuasive essay or letter.

If you doubt that you could be fooled today in the way so many were fooled in 1938, turn on the radio and listen closely to the news. You'll probably hear some remarkable things, some of them strange enough to make your blood run cold. But you'll believe them because the radio announcer is insisting that they're true. If the announcer were suddenly to introduce an out-of-this-world news flash, you might be sceptical, but your imagination would also be activated, blurring the border between fact and fiction. "What if it's really true? And why wouldn't it be?" you might ask yourself. "After all, I heard it on the radio."

From "The Martians Are Coming!" by Lauren E. Wolk

When You Write

Persuasive Paragraphs

1. State your opinion as clearly as you can.
2. You can support your opinion with logical reasons and solid information. Avoid angry or inflammatory words and cheap appeals to emotions or prejudices.
3. If there is something fair to say in favour of an opponent's position, state it. Try to show, however, how your position is the better one.

Edit It!

Here is Byrant's draft. Find out how he can edit it so that you can learn how to improve your own paragraphs.

Effective topic sentence?

This draft has a weak beginning. Combining the first two sentences into a strong topic sentence will express the main idea more effectively .

Well organized?

The paragraph moves from the topic of running, to throwing, and back again. Stick to one organizational plan, such as running first and then throwing.

Satisfying closing sentence?

This closing could be more effective if it had a stronger link to the sentences before it.

DRAFT

Some people want to be part of a team and aren't good at team play. Why don't you try out for track and field? If you're a good runner, there are lots of events to choose from. Javelin and discus throwers develop strong arms. Sprinters develop strong legs. Find out what you're good at. I'm sure there's a track or field event that you could enter and have fun at.

Enough supporting details?

Try comparing and contrasting events for athletes who like to run with events for athletes with strong arms. Use more detail about running events. What about the high jump or other jumping events? Give as many examples as you can to make your argument complete.

Coherent?

This paragraph is choppy and unclear in spots because the sentences do not build on one another. Make each sentence flow smoothly to the next one by using effective transitions.

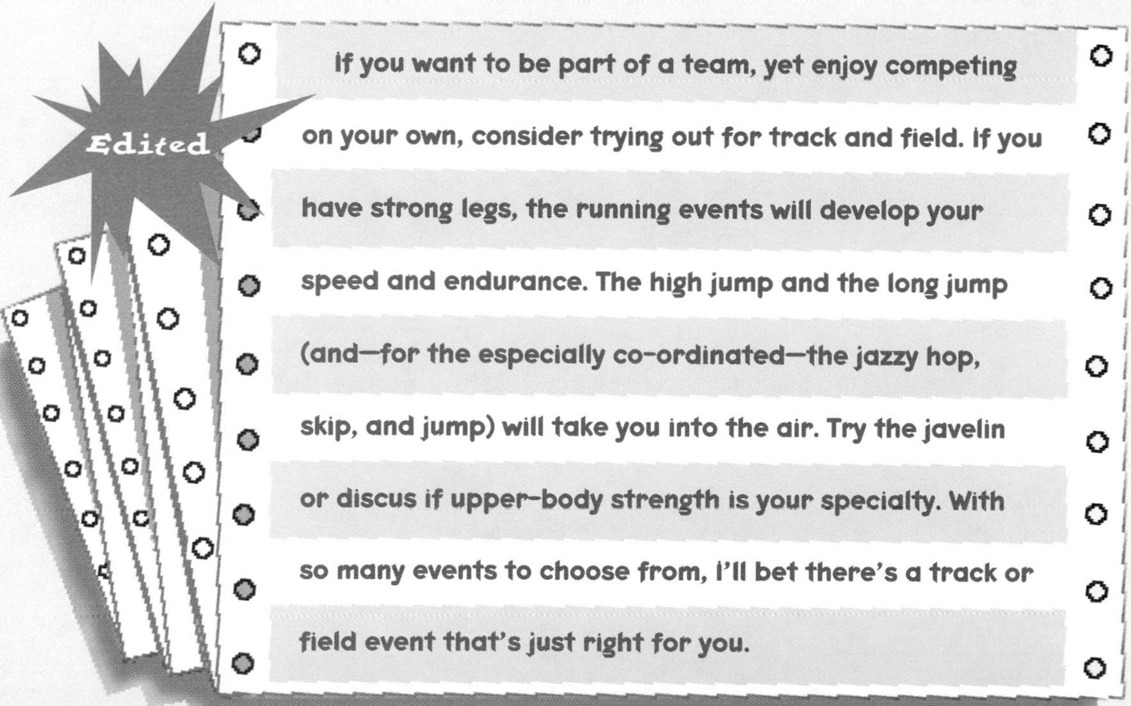
Edited
If you want to be part of a team, yet enjoy competing on your own, consider trying out for track and field. If you have strong legs, the running events will develop your speed and endurance. The high jump and the long jump (and—for the especially co-ordinated—the jazzy hop, skip, and jump) will take you into the air. Try the javelin or discus if upper-body strength is your specialty. With so many events to choose from, I'll bet there's a track or field event that's just right for you.

FACT FILE

Alphabets

Before alphabets were invented, writing was no easy task. Writers had to memorize a different picture or symbol for every single word and idea. Alphabets, which came into use in about 1600 B.C., were a big improvement because their letters represent the shortest sounds in words. This smaller group of symbols is much easier on the memory.

Words can also be spelled using any of the alphabets on these pages, which are based on the alphabet you use every day.

Morse Code

Samuel F. B. Morse invented the first version of this alphabet of dots and dashes in the 1830s so he could send messages instantly, without waiting for the mail. Signals can be made with light, sound, or electrical pulses.

A •–	**J** •–––	**S** •••
B –•••	**K** –•–	**T** –
C –•–•	**L** •–••	**U** ••–
D –••	**M** ––	**V** •••–
E •	**N** –•	**W** •––
F ••–•	**O** –––	**X** –••–
G ––•	**P** •––•	**Y** –•––
H ••••	**Q** ––•–	**Z** ––••
I ••	**R** •–•	

Using a Keyboard

The keyboard alphabet is still arranged as it was on the original 1874 typewriter. This QWERTY arrangement, named for the first six letters on the keyboard, forced people to type slowly enough to keep mechanical parts from getting tangled. Several better layouts have been proposed through the decades—layouts that are easier to learn, allow faster typing, and strain the hands less. But people refuse to let go of the familiar method.

The quickest way to type is to let your fingers rest on the home keys and to assign each finger to a certain keyboard area, as suggested in this diagram. Each colour represents a finger.

Pushing these keys allows other keys to perform additional functions, according to the computer program you're using.

esc
! 1
@ 2
# 3
$ 4
% 5
^ 6
tab
Q
W
E
R
T
caps lock
A
S
D
F
G
shift
Z
X
C
V
B
control
alt option
⌘
~ `

Braille

This alphabet is used by people who can't see words printed on a page; they use their fingers to feel the patterns of bumps instead. It was first developed in 1824 by a fifteen-year-old blind boy named Louis Braille.

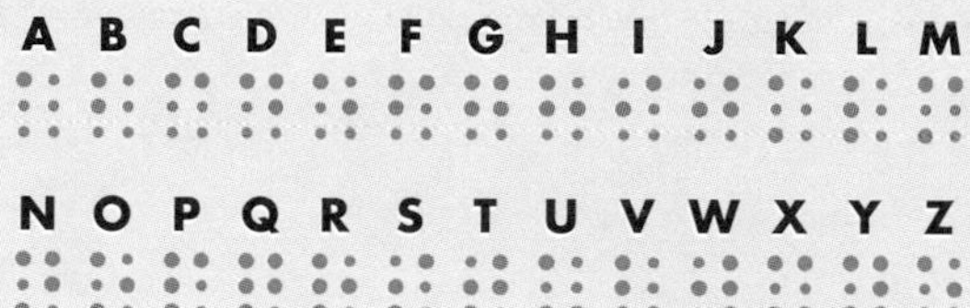
A B C D E F G H I J K L M
N O P Q R S T U V W X Y Z

Manual Alphabet

This alphabet allows people to use their hands to spell out words. Because many deaf people use a sign language that communicates entire words, they need to finger-spell only occasionally, for things like names and places.

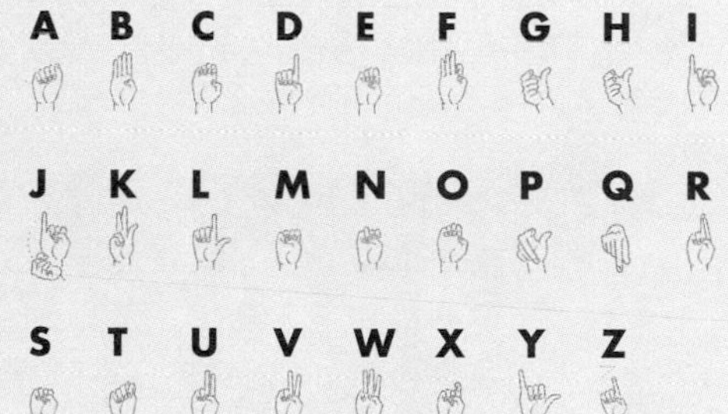
A B C D E F G H I
J K L M N O P Q R
S T U V W X Y Z

Match your fingers to the colours shown below:

Left hand Pinky Ring Middle Index Thumb

Right hand Thumb Index Middle Ring Pinky

Home keys

Home keys are where your fingers rest between keystrokes. They are shown outlined in pink.

& 7 | * 8 | (9 |) 0 | _ - | + = | delete

Y U I O P { [}]

H J K L : ; " ' return

N M < , > . ? / shift

/ \ ← → ↓ ↑

Directional keys allow you to move the cursor around the computer screen.

FACT FILE

Words from Around the World

The English you speak today uses thousands of words borrowed from other languages. English came from England, where over the centuries invaders and visitors had enriched the language. Many of them spoke languages based on Latin, which in turn had borrowed words from Greek.

English came to North America and kept on changing. We continue to add new words and expressions to this day.

Borrowed Roots

Greek Roots	English Words
bio (life)	biography, antibiotics, bionics
geo (earth)	geology, geometry, geography
graph (write)	biography, autograph, graphite
logy (the study of)	theology, biology, ecology
micro (small)	microwave, microscope, microfilm
phone (sound, voice)	saxophone, phonetic, telephone
photo (light)	photograph, photocopy, telephoto
tele (distant)	telescope, telephoto, telecast

Latin Roots	English Words
dict (say)	dictate, predict, contradict
lab (work)	labour, laboratory, elaborate
mot (move)	motion, promote, motorcycle
ped (foot)	pedal, pedestrian, stampede
rupt (break)	interrupt, rupture, bankrupt
struct (build)	instruct, structure, destruction
term (end)	determine, exterminate, intermittent
ven (come)	adventure, avenue, prevent
vid (see)	evidence, video, vivid

Borrowed Words

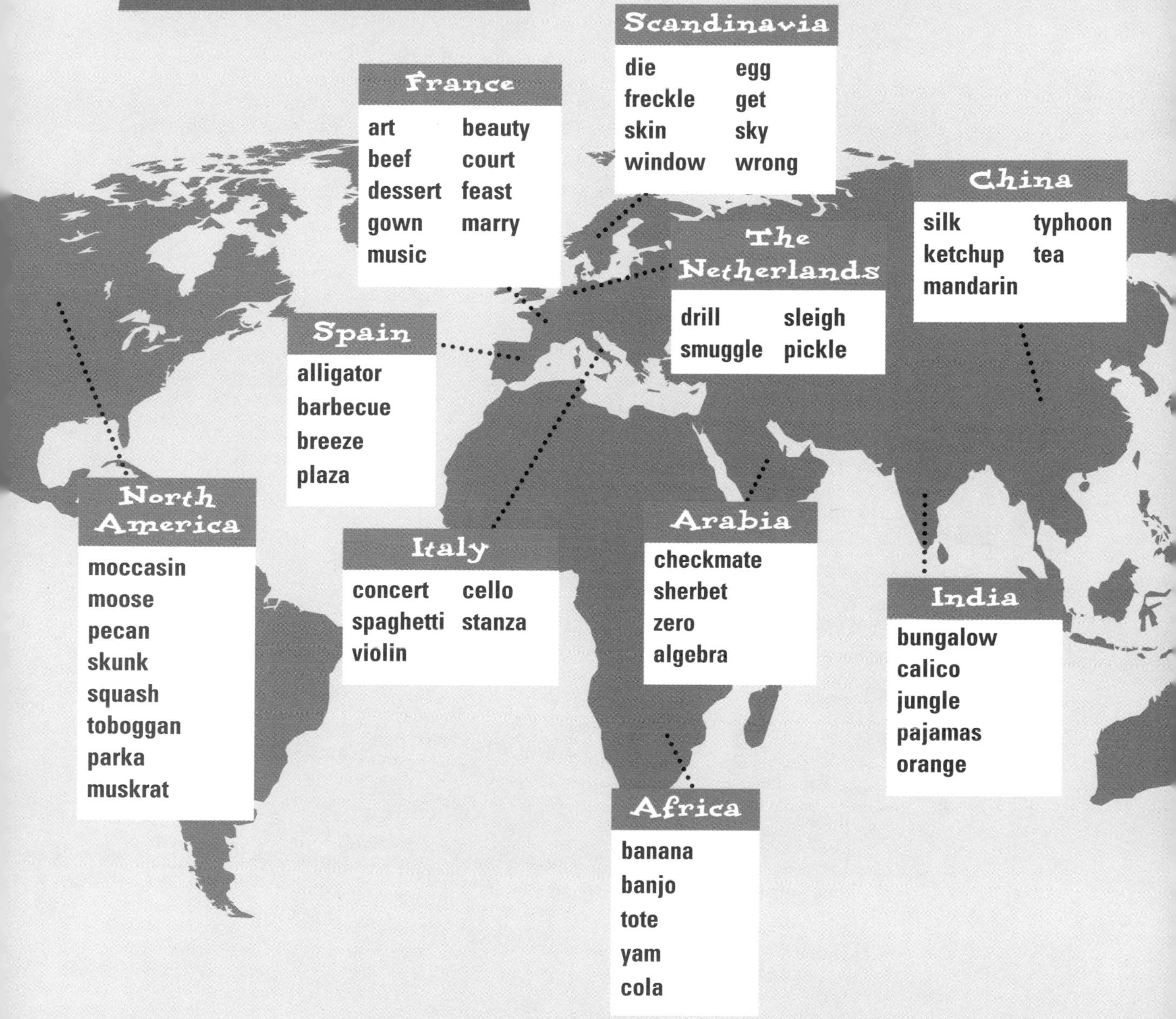

Scandinavia
die, egg, freckle, get, skin, sky, window, wrong

France
art, beauty, beef, court, dessert, feast, gown, marry, music

China
silk, typhoon, ketchup, tea, mandarin

The Netherlands
drill, sleigh, smuggle, pickle

Spain
alligator, barbecue, breeze, plaza

North America
moccasin, moose, pecan, skunk, squash, toboggan, parka, muskrat

Italy
concert, cello, spaghetti, stanza, violin

Arabia
checkmate, sherbet, zero, algebra

India
bungalow, calico, jungle, pajamas, orange

Africa
banana, banjo, tote, yam, cola

To read more about the origins of English, see page 326.

FACT FILE

Writing a Business Letter

Business letters may seem a bit formal, but they show your reader that you care enough about a letter to give it some professional polish. They also tell the reader when the letter was written and how to reach you, the writer.

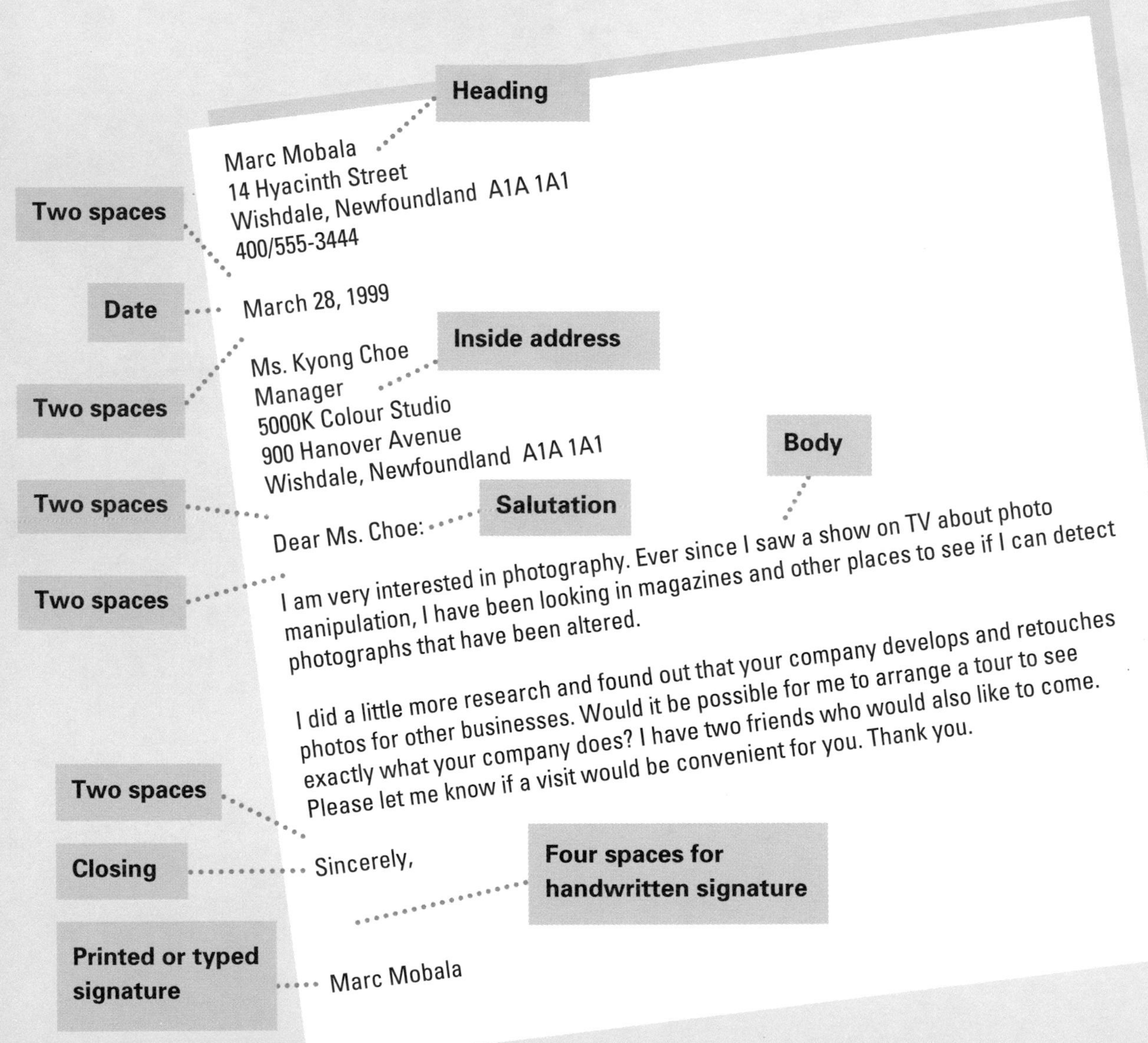
Heading
Marc Mobala
14 Hyacinth Street
Wishdale, Newfoundland A1A 1A1
400/555-3444
Two spaces
Date
March 28, 1999
Two spaces
Inside address
Ms. Kyong Choe
Manager
5000K Colour Studio
900 Hanover Avenue
Wishdale, Newfoundland A1A 1A1
Two spaces
Salutation
Dear Ms. Choe:
Body
Two spaces
I am very interested in photography. Ever since I saw a show on TV about photo manipulation, I have been looking in magazines and other places to see if I can detect photographs that have been altered.
I did a little more research and found out that your company develops and retouches photos for other businesses. Would it be possible for me to arrange a tour to see exactly what your company does? I have two friends who would also like to come. Please let me know if a visit would be convenient for you. Thank you.
Two spaces
Closing
Sincerely,
Four spaces for handwritten signature
Printed or typed signature
Marc Mobala

FACT FILE

Essay and Report Topics

"I can't think of anything to write about!" Let this problem plague you no more. Browse through the list below, and see if any ideas catch your eye or inspire your own intriguing ideas.

- bee stings
- favourite TV show
- hummingbirds
- what bothers me most
- giants
- TV commercials
- pets
- if I had a time machine
- cartoonists
- advice
- the best or worst day of my life

- privacy
- dancing
- cliques
- the best quality a person can have
- police
- popularity
- Australia
- forgiveness
- what I would change about ____
- computers
- crying
- wetlands

- food around the world
- trust
- fairy tales
- the media
- vegetarianism
- what I hope to do in my lifetime
- reading
- nuclear power
- slang
- my family
- Marie Curie
- what life will be like in 100 years

Here are some topics—now you think of a slant!

Proofreader's Marks

Use these marks when revising and editing your work. They will make your corrections easy to read when it's time to make your final copy.

Changes needed	Marks to use
• Delete (take out).	What's the the problem?
• Insert at caret.	What's the p^blem? (r)
• Capitalize.	what's the problem?
• Make a capital letter lower-case.	What's the Problem?
• Transpose (reverse the order).	Whats' the problem?
• Add a space.	What'sthe problem? (#)
• Make a new paragraph.	"What's the problem?" ¶ "Oh! So you want to know what the problem is!"
• Insert a period.	The problem began yesterday⊙

FACT FILE

Mastering the Metric System

It began during the French Revolution. The many measuring systems used in France were causing too much confusion—so the people decided to settle on one system for good. Scientists wanted to base their new system on a naturally occurring distance that wasn't changeable. They named their new unit the *metre,* and this is what it measured: one ten-millionth of a line extending from the North Pole to the equator, passing through Paris on the way!

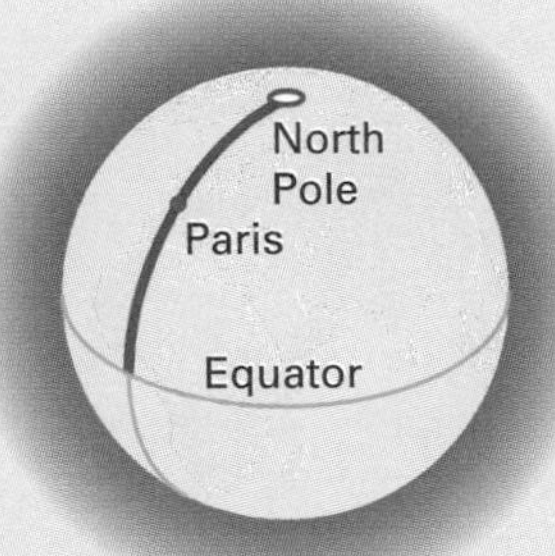
North
Pole
Paris
Equator

Prefixes

Name	Symbol	Meaning	Numerical value
mega-	M	one million	1 000 000
kilo-	k	one thousand	1000
hecto-	h	one hundred	100
deca-	da	ten	10
deci-	d	one-tenth	0.1
centi-	c	one-hundredth	0.01
milli-	m	one-thousandth	0.001
micro-	µ	one-millionth	0.000 001

How to Write About Measurements

1. Each metric unit has an international symbol. Don't make up your own abbreviations or put periods after the symbols as if they were abbreviations.

   Example: 20 m^2, not 20 sq. m.

2. Symbols stay the same whether a unit is plural or singular.

   Example: 8 g, not 8 gs

3. If you spell out a number, spell out the unit as well, rather than using its symbol.

   Example: seven kilometres, not seven km

4. When no number is involved, spell out the unit rather than using its symbol.

   Example: How many kilograms do you weigh?

5. When writing numbers of a quantity less than one, place a zero before the decimal point.

   Example: 0.78 m^2, not .78 m^2

6. If a number has more than four digits, use a space to separate groups of three digits. Commas should not be used because in some languages commas represent decimal points.

   Example: 39 344 km, not 39,344 km

Commonly Used Units of Measurement

Length

To measure length, use metres (m).

Most common length units	Symbol	Used for:
kilometres	km	roads, ocean depth, bike races
metres	m	fabric, carpeting, wire
centimetres	cm	paper, TV screens, rainfall
millimetres	mm	nails, jewels, rope thickness

Area

To measure area, use square metres (m^2).

Most common area units	Symbol	Used for:
square kilometres	km^2	cities, lakes, forests
square hectometres/hectares	hm^2/ha	farms, parks, hockey rinks
square metres	m^2	floors, gardens, offices
square centimetres	cm^2	footprints, cards, leaves

Volume

To measure volume, use litres (L).

Most common volume units	Symbol	Used for:
kilolitres	kL	reservoirs, gasoline in tankers
litres	L	paint, ice cream, milk
millilitres	mL	toothpaste, juice, cologne

Weight

To measure mass (weight), use grams (g).

Most common mass units	Symbol	Used for:
tonnes	t	cars, ships, sand
kilograms	kg	flour, people, fruit
grams	g	butter, cheese, fish
milligrams	mg	vitamins, minerals, medicines

Glossary

A

acronym A word made from the first letters of a series of words, as in *radar* (radio detecting and ranging) or *UNICEF* (United Nations International Children's Emergency Fund).

action verb A word that expresses physical or mental action.

ad libbing See *improvise.*

adjective A word that describes or modifies a noun or pronoun.

adverb A word that describes or modifies a verb, adjective, or other adverb.

agreement When words match each other in number, person, and case.

alliteration The repetition of sounds at the beginnings of words, as in *wind whispering in the weeds.*

almanac A book that contains lists, charts, and tables of information on hundreds of topics.

anecdote A short retelling of a funny or interesting incident.

angle See *slant.*

animation A series of pictures shown so quickly that the images seem to move.

antiphonal A reading shared between two voices that answer each other responsively.

article The adjectives *a, an,* and *the,* used to introduce nouns.

autobiography A true story written by a person about his or her own life.

B

ballad A poem or song that tells a story and follows a traditional form.

bias An opinion that sways your understanding of certain events or people.

biography A true story written by an author about the life of another person.

blackout To darken a film or video scene to black.

body The middle of an essay, article, or letter, in which you explain the points you want to make.

brainstorm To search for ideas by writing down every word that comes to your mind.

buzz group Three to five people who brainstorm as a group.

C

call number A number used by a library to classify a non-fiction book and to organize books on the shelves.

camera angle The position from which a camera takes pictures: from above, at eye level, or from below.

case The grammatical feature of nouns and pronouns showing how they are used in a sentence.

catalogue A library's listing of the subject, author, and title for each book in the library.

CD-ROM An acronym for *compact disk read-only memory;* a disk that holds information that a computer can read but cannot change.

characterization A writer's description of a character.

characters The people whose actions create a story.

choral reading A group reading of a poem.

classification The grouping of items into categories.

clause A group of words containing a subject and a verb and forming part of a compound or complex sentence.

climax The dramatic turning point in a story.

cluster See *webbing*.

coherence A clear, logical flow in writing, with smooth transitions from sentence to sentence and paragraph to paragraph.

collage An arrangement of materials and objects on a surface.

complex sentence A sentence made up of one independent clause and one or more subordinate clauses.

compound sentence A sentence made up of two or more independent clauses joined by a co-ordinating conjunction.

compound-complex sentence A sentence made up of two or more independent clauses and one or more subordinate clauses.

conclusion The end of an essay or article, in which you summarize your ideas and leave your readers with something to think about.

conferencing Discussing a draft with other people and looking for ways to improve it.

conflict The problem in a story that the characters have to work out, making up the main part of the story's plot.

conjunction A word used to connect words or groups of words in a sentence.

connotation The attitudes, feelings, and opinions suggested by a word, apart from its dictionary definition.

contraction The shortened form of two words, with an apostrophe replacing what was left out.

copyright date The date following the symbol © on a written work, usually signifying when the writer completed the work and achieved the legal ownership of it.

critical response Reacting to something you see or hear with comments about its quality and effectiveness.

critique A review or commentary of an artistic work that discusses its strengths and weaknesses.

D

debate Presentation of opposite sides of an issue by two people or teams before an audience or judge.

descriptive essay A piece of writing in which you use your senses, memory, and imagination to bring an experience to life.

Dewey decimal system A system of organizing library books into ten major categories and many subcategories, developed by Melvil Dewey (1851–1931).

dialogue A quoted conversation between two or more people.

dialogue journal A place for having a written conversation with a friend about opinions, thoughts, and feelings.

dissolve To make two film or video scenes blend for a split second as one fades out and the other fades in.

documentary A television show or film that presents and analyses events, people, or issues in a factual way.

draft The stage of the writing process in which you turn ideas and plans into sentences and paragraphs.

E

edit A part of the writing process in which you check for wording, punctuation, or organization that is incorrect or confusing. *Or*, to arrange film or video shots and scenes, during or after shooting, in order to create a desired effect.

editor Someone who helps you revise your draft by reading it and looking for errors and unclear writing.

either/or fallacy A claim that there are only two options when there are actually more.

essay A written paper on a single topic that includes an introduction, body, and conclusion.

evidence Facts used in a debate or in persuasive writing to support an argument.

F

fade in To make a film or video image slowly appear from a black screen.

fade out To slowly darken a film or video image until it disappears.

faulty cause and effect When someone claims that one event is caused by another event without being able to prove it.

feature article An essay that informs and entertains readers, usually published in newspapers and magazines.

figurative language Writing that contains words or phrases, called figures of speech, that are not literally true but make you see something in a new way.

flash-back The insertion of an earlier event into the time order of a story.

foreshadowing Creating suspense by hinting at things to come.

form A type of written work, such as poetry, novels, or essays.

format A plan for organizing words and/or images on a page.

frame One photograph on a reel of film.

free verse A poetic form that does not have a set pattern of rhyme or metre.

freewrite To search for or explore ideas by setting your mind free and writing about topics as they come to mind, without worrying about correctness.

G

gender The grammatical division of nouns and pronouns into masculine, feminine, and neuter.

genre A category of literature, such as mystery, romance, or science fiction.

H

haiku An unrhymed poem of Japanese origin, arranged in three lines: the first has five syllables, the second has seven syllables, and the third has five syllables. Haiku often describe a single sound or sight and show a mood or impression inspired by nature.

I

illustration Drawings or photographs that accompany and add to a piece of writing.

imagery Vivid descriptions or figures of speech used to create mental pictures or to appeal to the senses.

improvise To create a performance without having planned ahead.

independent clause A group of words that can stand alone as a simple sentence.

index An alphabetical listing of contents (such as names, places, and topics) in a book.

infinitive A verb form (*to* + basic form of verb) used as a noun, adjective, or adverb, such as *to give*.

informative essay A short report that gives facts and explains ideas about a topic.

interjection A word used to get attention or express strong feeling; can be treated as an entire sentence.

interview To talk with someone in order to learn something from him or her, while taking notes or recording the conversation so you can refer back to it.

introduction The beginning of an essay or article, where you first present the main idea and interest your readers.

J

jigsaw A discussion among three to five people who share with each other what they have learned separately.

journal A place for writing your opinions, thoughts, and feelings.

K

KWL plan A reading strategy in which you consider what you know about a topic, what you want to know, and what you learn after reading about it.

L

lead The opening sentence or sentences you write to grab a reader's attention.

learning log A place to record information you're learning about a particular topic.

legend A traditional story about a heroic person or event. *Or,* an explanation of the symbols appearing on a map.

Library of Congress system A system of organizing library books according to twenty main categories and many subcategories, set up by the U.S. Library of Congress.

literary circle A discussion among three to eight people with the goal of critically responding to literature.

logic Reasoning that makes sense.

looping Looking for an angle on a topic by freewriting on index cards, choosing the most interesting phrases, and then freewriting about those phrases.

M

map scale A rule on a map that shows how distances on the map relate to actual distances.

mechanics Spelling, capitalization, and punctuation.

metaphor A figure of speech that speaks of one thing as if it were another thing in order to show a connection between the two, as in *The wind is a dancer.*

metre The pattern of stressed and unstressed syllables in a poem.

microfiche A sheet of film used in libraries that contains miniature photographs of printed information.

microfilm A roll of film used in libraries that contains miniature photographs of printed information.

monologue A speech by one person.

myth A traditional story that explains natural happenings (such as the sun disappearing at night) or tells of heroes or superhuman beings.

N

narrative A fiction or non-fiction story that has a beginning, a middle, and an end.

narrator Someone who tells a story.

noun A word or words that name a person, place, thing, or idea.

O

on-line Hooked up to a computer data base and able to share information with it.

onomatopoeia A figure of speech in which a word sounds like what it means, such as *buzz, clank*, and *splash*.

overgeneralization A claim that goes beyond what the evidence supports.

P

pan To move a film or video camera horizontally to follow an action or show a wide view of a scene.

panel discussion A group of people invited to speak about their ideas on a certain subject and to respond to one another's comments.

paraphrase To explain someone else's ideas in your own words.

peer conferencing Discussing a draft with other students and looking for ways to improve it.

periodical A printed work that is published at regular intervals, such as a magazine or newspaper.

personal narrative A true story written about something that happened to the narrator.

personal response Reacting to something you see or hear by expressing your feelings and thoughts about it.

personification A figure of speech in which human qualities are given to animals or objects, as in *Flowers danced about the yard.*

photo essay A series of photographic images, sometimes including words, put together to communicate an idea.

phrase A group of words that does not contain both a subject and a verb.

pitch The highness or lowness of a sound.

plagiarize To use someone else's words or ideas as if they were your own.

plot The series of actions that makes up a story.

poetic device A tool, such as alliteration or imagery, used in poetry to appeal to the senses.

point of view The position of a story's narrator; how much the narrator knows about the characters' thoughts and the story's outcome. Also called *voice*. In film and video, abbreviated *POV*; the narrator is the camera.

political map A map that shows boundaries between political areas such as towns, provinces, and countries.

predicate A verb, or a group of words including a verb, that tells something about the subject of a sentence.

predraft The stage of the writing process in which you search for ideas and plan your writing.

prefix A word part added to the beginning of a root or word to change its meaning.

preposition A word that relates a noun or pronoun to another word in the sentence.

prepositional phrase A phrase that begins with a preposition and ends with a noun or pronoun that is the object of the preposition.

preview To glance through something you're about to read so you can prepare to think about the material.

pronoun A word that takes the place of a noun.

proofread A stage of the writing process in which you check for errors in grammar, usage, and mechanics.

propaganda Manipulative communication that tries to influence what people think.

publish The final stage of the writing process, when you present your final draft to others.

publisher A person or company that produces a book, periodical, or other form of communication.

purpose What you hope to accomplish when you begin a task.

Q

quotation The direct use of someone else's words, with credit given to that person.

R

rap A kind of talk-singing that began in West Africa and the Caribbean and that uses many poetic devices.

Readers' Theatre A presentation of a script or text by a group of people who use only their voices to create dramatic effects.

redundant To needlessly use several words or phrases that mean the same thing, as in *a long and lengthy speech*.

reference section The area of a library that holds collections of factual sources like encyclopedias, almanacs, and dictionaries.

refrain A phrase or verse repeated throughout a poem or song, often at the end of each stanza.

research Careful study of a topic, which involves reading various sources and taking notes.

resolution How the problems or conflicts in a story are worked out in the end.

response journal A place for writing your opinions, thoughts, and feelings about what you read or experience.

revise The stage of the writing process in which you look critically at what you have written and make improvements.

revising checklist A list of problems to look for when revising your writing.

rhetorical question A question you ask without expecting an answer.

rhyme Matching word sounds; often used in poetry.

rhyme scheme A pattern formed by the rhymes at the ends of certain lines in a poem.

rhythm The pattern of beats or stresses in spoken or written language.

root The word part that carries the main meaning of a word; also called the *base*.

round table A discussion among five to eight people with the goal of reaching an agreement.

run-on sentence Two or more sentences punctuated as if they were one sentence.

S

scan To glance through written material in an effort to find something.

score To write performance directions for a poem to prepare it for a choral reading.

script A story made up of dialogue and stage directions, written to be acted out.

sculpture A work of art that has three dimensions: height, width, and depth.

sensory language Wording that brings to mind sights, sounds, smells, feelings, and tastes.

sentence A group of words that expresses a complete thought.

sentence fragment Part of a sentence punctuated as if it were an entire sentence.

sequential A choral reading in which three or more voices take turns reading.

setting Where and when the action takes place in a story.

sfx See *special effects*.

shooting script The complete text used to create a film or video, containing the dialogue and a description of the action and props.

simile A figure of speech in which seemingly unlike things are compared using the word *like* or *as*, as in *He's as light as a feather.*

skim To glance through written material for a general idea of the contents.

slant The opinion, perspective, or bias that affects how information is presented or what aspects of a story are emphasized.

sonnet A fourteen-line poem that follows a set rhyme scheme and metre.

sound effects Recorded or made-up sounds that add to a performance.

spatial order Organizing a description according to where objects are located in relation to others.

special effects Sounds or images that are added to film or video scenes; abbreviated *sfx*.

specialized map A map that shows certain details about an area, such as rainfall, population, or natural resources.

sq3r plan A reading strategy in which you survey what you are about to read, ask

yourself questions about it, read it to answer the questions, rephrase the answers in your own words, and review the main headings.

stanza A group of lines in a poem that stand together, separated from other stanzas by a blank line.

storyboard An outline of a story or advertisement to be filmed, usually containing descriptions, dialogue, and illustrations for each major shot.

subject The word or words, always including a noun or pronoun, that name who or what a sentence is about.

suffix A word part added to the end of a root or word to change its meaning.

summarize To restate in a few words or sentences the main points of a longer work.

symbol Something that stands for a complicated or abstract idea.

symbolism Using an object in your writing to represent an idea or feeling.

T

tempo The speed or pace of the beat.

tense The feature of a verb that shows time.

theme The message or point of a piece of writing.

thumbnail A small sketch you draw to show what a final product might look like.

tilt To move a film or video camera vertically in order to follow an action or to show an unusual point of view.

time order Organizing the events in a story in the order in which they happened.

tone The attitude you communicate when you speak or write.

topic sentence The sentence in a paragraph that states the main idea of the paragraph.

track To follow a moving object while you film it with a film or video camera.

transition A change; transition words and sentences prepare readers for changes in topic so they don't get lost or confused.

U

unity A quality of writing in which all the sentences and paragraphs support one main idea.

V

verb A word that expresses action or a state of being.

viewpoint See *bias*.

voice-over Talking that comes from someone other than the people shown in a film or video scene; abbreviated *v/o*.

W

webbing Searching for ideas or organizing a topic by writing down a word and surrounding it with related words. Each related word is then surrounded with words related to it, and the process continues.

writing process A series of stages for creating a written work, from thinking about it to showing the final product to others.

Z

zoom To adjust the lens on a camera in order to bring the picture closer or move it back.

Index

D

Acknowledgments

Grateful acknowledgment is given to authors, publishers, and agents for permission to reprint the following copyrighted material. Every effort has been made to determine copyright owners. In the case of any omissions, the publisher will be pleased to make suitable acknowledgments in future editions.

41 From *Do Whales Jump at Night?* edited by Florence McNeil. Copyright © 1990 by Douglas & McIntyre Ltd. Reprinted by permission of the author.

43 From *The Sidewalk Racer and Other Poems of Sports and Motion* by Lillian Morrison. Copyright © 1965, 1967, 1968, 1977 by Lillian Morrison. Reprinted by permission of Marian Reiner for the author.

138 Appeared in *Sixteen: Short Stories by Outstanding Writers for Young Adults* edited by Donald R. Gallo. Copyright © 1984 by Donald R. Gallo. Published by Delacorte Press.

145 Appeared in *The Moon Is Like a Silver Sickle: A Celebration of Poetry by Russian Children* collected and translated by Miriam Morton. Copyright © 1972 by Miriam Morton. Published by Simon & Schuster. Reprinted by permission of Miriam Morton's estate.

145 From *Selected Poems* by Langston Hughes. Copyright 1926 by Alfred A. Knopf, Inc. and renewed 1954 by Langston Hughes. Reprinted by permission of the publisher.

148 From *See My Lovely Poison Ivy* by Lilian Moore. Copyright © 1975 by Lilian Moore. Published by Atheneum.

149 Permission owned by the estate of John Ciardi and Rutgers University Press.

149 From *The Poetry of Robert Frost* edited by Edward Connery Lathem. Copyright © 1969 by Henry Holt and Company, Inc. Reprinted by permission of Henry Holt and Company, Inc.

150 From *The Children's Bells* edited by Eleanor Farjeon. Published by Oxford University Press.

150 From *Do Whales Jump at Night?* edited by Florence McNeil. Copyright © 1990 by Douglas & McIntyre Ltd. Reprinted by permission of the author.

151 From *The Wandering Moon and Other Poems* by James Reeves. Copyright © James Reeves. Reprinted by permission of the James Reeves Estate.

151 From *The Collected Poems of F. R. Scott* by F. R. Scott. Used by permission of the Canadian publishers McClelland & Stewart, Toronto.

152 From *Elephants, Mothers, and Others* by John Newlove. Copyright © 1963 by John Newlove. Reprinted by permission of the author.

152 Appeared in *Haïku* edited by Dorothy Howard and André Dubaime. Copyright © 1985 by Les éditions Asticou enrg. Reprinted by permission of the author.

153 From *Collected Poems of Edna St. Vincent Millay.* Copyright © 1917,1945 by Edna St. Vincent Millay. Published by HarperCollins.

178 Recorded on *Soul II Soul, Vol. II, 1990: A New Decade.* Released by Jazzie B. Music/Virgin Music, Inc./Soul II Soul Mad Music, Inc. (ASCAP). Copyright © 1990 10 Records Ltd.

253–254 From *Life Nature Library: The Insects* by Peter Farb and the Editors of Time-Life Books. Copyright © 1962 by Time-Life Books Inc.

328 From *Gage Canadian Dictionary.* Copyright © 1983 Gage Publishing Limited.

330 From *Young Canada Thesaurus.* Copyright © 1988. Used by permission of Nelson Canada, A Division of Thomson Canada Limited.

Art Credits

189 National Gallery of Canada, Ottawa; **190** Courtesy Dany Keller Galerie München; **192** Paris, Fribourg Collection, Art Resource, NY; **193** Rosenwald Collection, © 1993 National Gallery of Art, Washington, D.C.; **195** © 1993 The Museum of Modern Art, New York; **196** © Roy Henry Vickers, 1979; **198** © 1992 Francisco Rios; **200** Courtesy of Edward Thorp Gallery; **202** © 1993 Andy Warhol Foundation, Inc.; **208** © 1992 Lisa Taft (all); **209** "(Nothing but) Flowers" by Talking Heads; produced by M & Co., directed by Tibor Kalman, designed by Tibor Kalman and Emily Oberman(tr) ; **211** Cinema Memories; **212** George Eastman House; **213** Movie Still Archives; **214** Walt Disney Productions; **219** NASA; **220** © Much Music(br) ; The MTV: MUSIC TELEVISION logo is a registered trademark of MTV Networks, a division of Viacom International Inc. © 1993 MTV Networks. All Rights Reserved(bl). All photographs of models taken by Tracy Wheeler.